ACROSS THE GOLDEN GATE

CALIFORNIA'S NORTH COAST,
WINE COUNTRY, AND REDWOODS

Alan Magary & Kerstin Fraser Magary

Harper Colophon Books
Harper & Row, Publishers   New York
Hagerstown • Cambridge • Philadelphia • San Francisco
London • Mexico City • São Paulo • Sydney

To the
Frasers and Magarys,
Forsbergs and Olssons,
who arrived
by whaling ship
and steam train
and made us natives
of California

ACROSS THE GOLDEN GATE: *California's North Coast, Wine Country, and Redwoods.*
Copyright © 1980 by Alan Magary and Kerstin Fraser Magary. All rights re-
served. Printed in the United States of America. No part of this book may be
used or reproduced in any manner whatsoever without written permission
except in the case of brief quotations embodied in critical articles and reviews. For information address Harper & Row, Publishers, Inc., 10 East 53rd
Street, New York, N.Y. 10022. Published simultaneously in Canada by Fitz-
henry & Whiteside Limited, Toronto.

FIRST EDITION

Designer: Trish Parcell

Maps: Bernhard H. Wagner

Library of Congress Cataloging in Publication Data

Magary, Alan 1944–
    Across the Golden Gate; California's north coast, wine country, and red-
woods.
    (Harper colophon books; CN 821)
    1. California—Description and travel—1951-
—Guide-books. 2. Wine and wine making—California.
I. Magary, Kerstin Fraser, joint author. II. Title.
F859.3.M33 1980   917.94'10453   78-2149
ISBN 0-06-090821-1 (pbk.)

80 81 82 83 84 10 9 8 7 6 5 4 3 2 1

Contents

To Begin: Notes to the Reader   vii
    CHAPTER ORGANIZATION   vii
    SIGHTSEEING RATING SYSTEM   viii
    PRICES   ix
    PRIMARY SOURCE OF TRAVEL INFORMATION   ix
    MAPS   ix
    OTHER BOOKS   ix
    EVENTS   x

To Commence the Journey: The Golden Gate Bridge   xiii

PART I: WINE COUNTRY   1

Chapter 1: California Wine: An Introduction   5
    YESTERDAY AND TODAY   6
    FROM GRAPES TO WINE   12

Chapter 2: Reading a Bottle of California Wine   31
    WHAT'S IN THE BOTTLE?   33
    WHERE DOES THE WINE COME FROM?   45
    WHO MADE THE WINE?   54
    WHEN WAS THE WINE MADE?   65
    DO PRESTIGE DESIGNATIONS MEAN ANYTHING?   68
    WHAT ELSE DOES THE BOTTLE SAY?   73
    DOES PRICE MEAN QUALITY?   78
    LABEL-READING TEST   87

Chapter 3: Tasting California Wine   91
    BASIC TASTING CRITERIA AND QUALITIES   92
    TASTING CALIFORNIA VARIETALS   95
    GOING WINE TOURING   103

iv • CONTENTS

Chapter 4: Napa Valley   106
   HIGHLIGHTS   106
   WHAT TO SEE AND DO   112
      WINERIES   112
      OTHER ATTRACTIONS   121
   PRACTICAL INFORMATION   127

Chapter 5: Sonoma and Mendocino   129
   HIGHLIGHTS   129
   WHAT TO SEE AND DO   133
      WINERIES   134
      OTHER ATTRACTIONS   143
   PRACTICAL INFORMATION   163

SOURCES OF INFORMATION—WINE COUNTRY   164

PART II: COAST: MARIN, SONOMA, MENDOCINO   171

Chapter 6: Marin County   177
   HIGHLIGHTS   177
   WHAT TO SEE AND DO   178
   PRACTICAL INFORMATION   204

Chapter 7: Sonoma Coast   208
   HIGHLIGHTS   208
   WHAT TO SEE AND DO   208
   PRACTICAL INFORMATION   215

Chapter 8: Mendocino Coast   216
   HIGHLIGHTS   216
   WHAT TO SEE AND DO   218
   PRACTICAL INFORMATION   228

SOURCES OF INFORMATION—COAST   229

PART III: REDWOOD COUNTRY   231

Chapter 9: Southern Redwoods   239
   HIGHLIGHTS   239
   WHAT TO SEE AND DO   240
   PRACTICAL INFORMATION   245

Chapter 10: Eureka Area   247
   HIGHLIGHTS   247

WHAT TO SEE AND DO   247
PRACTICAL INFORMATION   259

Chapter 11: Northern Redwoods   261
HIGHLIGHTS   261
WHAT TO SEE AND DO   261
PRACTICAL INFORMATION   274

SOURCES OF INFORMATION—REDWOOD COUNTRY   275

PART IV: WHERE TO STAY AND EAT   277

PRICE CATEGORIES   280
CREDIT CARDS   282
RESERVATIONS   282
FINDING A PLACE TO STAY OR EAT   283

CALISTOGA/NORTHERN NAPA VALLEY   284
CLEAR LAKE/LAKE COUNTY RESORT AREA   286
CRESCENT CITY/NORTHERN REDWOODS   286
EUREKA/CENTRAL REDWOOD COUNTRY   287
FORT BRAGG/NORTHERN MENDOCINO COAST   289
GARBERVILLE/SOUTHERN REDWOODS   290
GUALALA/SOUTHERN MENDOCINO COAST   292
GUERNEVILLE/LOWER RUSSIAN RIVER   293
HEALDSBURG/UPPER RUSSIAN RIVER   295
LAKE BERRYESSA/NAPA HIGHLANDS   297
MARIN COAST   297
MENDOCINO/CENTRAL MENDOCINO COAST   299
MILL VALLEY/MT. TAMALPAIS   302
NAPA   303
PETALUMA/COTATI VALLEY   305
ST. HELENA/CENTRAL NAPA VALLEY   306
SAN RAFAEL/NORTHERN MARIN   307
SANTA ROSA   309
SAUSALITO/BAYSIDE MARIN   310
SEBASTOPOL/APPLE COUNTRY   313
SONOMA/SONOMA VALLEY   314
SONOMA COAST   317
UKIAH/INLAND MENDOCINO COUNTY   319
YOUNTVILLE/SOUTHERN NAPA VALLEY   320

Index   323

Maps

The Redwood Empire—Across the Golden Gate   xv
Wine Country: Napa, Sonoma, and Mendocino   xvi
Marin and Southern Sonoma Coast   xvii
Northern Sonoma and Southern Mendocino Coast   xviii
Central and Northern Mendocino Coast   xix
Redwood Country: Humboldt and Del Norte   xx

TO BEGIN:

Notes
to the Reader

This book is a travel guide to the counties across the Golden Gate from San Francisco, an area aptly called the Redwood Empire by tourism authorities. In the first three parts we cover:

- the essential California Wine Country—Napa and Sonoma—including an introduction to wine and California wine;
- the long, sometimes lonely, sometimes lost, but always scenic coast; and
- the Redwood Country, where stand the tallest trees in the world.

Across the Golden Gate the traveler can't miss something of interest, of wonder, or of drama.

Although this is primarily a sightseeing guide, Part IV is as helpful and wide a listing of accommodations and restaurants as our time and resources allowed us to put together with confidence.

CHAPTER ORGANIZATION

Each chapter, except for the introduction to California wine, covers a county or part of a county. Counties are, somehow, quite important in California for keeping things organized, and we don't attempt to re-arrange the system. But parts of the same county may be separated (inland Sonoma in Chapter 5, Sonoma coast in Chapter 7), and parts of some counties are sketchily covered (inland Mendocino); Lake County is nearly ignored.

Most chapters follow this pattern:

- an introduction;
- "Highlights," a brief list of principal attractions, with page numbers (extending the main table of contents);
- "What to See and Do," touring information organized linearly (mostly south to north), as along or off a main road; and
- "Practical Information," a tail-end section covering transportation and giving signposts to the hotel and restaurant listings in Part IV.

"Sources of Information" follows each part.

SIGHTSEEING RATING SYSTEM

Like the Michelin green guides, we apply one, two, or three stars to attractions—or omit them—so that the reader has some way to judge how worthwhile one place is in relation to another:

*** "worth a journey" or "highly recommended";
** "worth a detour" or "recommended";
* "interesting";
no star interesting but perhaps only to read about as you travel on (such things add texture) or to visit if you're a specialist or California resident with time to spare.

A relativity is involved in this system: the significance of the number of stars depends on where you are. To take an example outside this book, if you're planning a trip to California from New York or Knoxville or Phoenix, **Yosemite National Park***** means that this large area is worth including in a trip of hundreds or thousands of miles. Once you're in the park, **Yosemite Valley***** means that's among the most important areas smaller than the entire park. And when you're in Yosemite Valley, **Yosemite Fall Trail***** means that is one of the most worthwhile things within the valley. Quite obviously, one would not rush across the continent just to walk on this trail, though the visitor could do a lot worse. It is assumed that even a one-day, one-stop tourist will take in a number of sights, at least casually.

PRICES

Inflation makes authors of travel guidebooks shy away from quoting prices. We say "small admission fee" or something similar if admission to a state park or other attraction is (at this writing) less than about $2 per adult, $1.50 or less per child. The introduction to Part IV describes the four-level price-category system ($:budget, $:intermediate, $:expensive, $:luxury) that we devised for indicating relative costliness of hotels and restaurants.

PRIMARY SOURCE OF TRAVEL INFORMATION

The first place to write to or go to for information is the region's visitors' bureau, the Redwood Empire Association, whose office (open Mon.-Fri. 9–5) is in the Qantas Building on the north side of San Francisco's Union Square (360 Post St., Suite 201, San Francisco 94108, 415/421-6554). The 40-page annual visitors' guide is fact-packed, though listings seem confined to REA members and no opinions are expressed.

MAPS

The traveler should get detailed road maps to avoid too much freeway travel, which involves driving but seldom traveling, and to find many of the places we mention. The American Automobile Association has these maps for members: *California; San Francisco; North Bay Counties; Marin; Sonoma and Napa; Mendocino and Lake; Northwestern California.*

OTHER BOOKS

Readers with special interests should have specialized travel guidebooks. We list many in the "Sources of Information" in Parts I and III. We also recommend these:

General: Hart, James D. *A Companion to California.* New York: Oxford University Press, 1979. A–Z listings, from art to zoos.

Place-names: Gudde, Erwin G. *California Place Names*. 3rd ed. Berkeley: University of California Press, 1968. The authority. Place-name books always have some good anecdotes.

Local history: Hoover, M. B., et al., *Historic Spots in California*. Revised by W. N. Abeloe. 3rd ed. Stanford: Stanford University Press, 1966. Can't be beat for sheer detail. No levity.

Architecture: Gebhard, David, et al. *A Guide to the Architecture in San Francisco and Northern California*. Rev. ed. Santa Barbara: Peregrine Smith, 1976. Tall, fat guide with pictures and maps. Standard.

Golden Gate Bridge: Cassady, Stephen, et al. *Spanning the Gate*. Mill Valley: Baron Wolman/Squarebooks, 1979. Dramatic 1930s photos. Dillon, Richard, et al. *High Steel: Building the Bridges Across San Francisco Bay*. Millbrae: Celestial Arts, 1979. Includes the work of the official photographers, the Moulin brothers.

Coast: Sunset editors. *Discovering the California Coast*. 2nd ed. Menlo Park: Lane, 1978. The usual superb Sunset pictorial.

Nature near The City: Hart, John. *San Francisco's Wilderness Next Door*. San Rafael: Presidio Press, 1979.

Natural history: Bakker, Elna. *An Island Called California: An Ecological Introduction to Its Natural Communities*. Berkeley: University of California Press, 1972. Quiet, well-written, and authoritative.

Tree identification: Watts, Tom. *Pacific Coast Tree Finder*. Berkeley: Nature Study Guild (Box 972), 1973. Because few trees have labels.

Geology: Alt, David D., and Hyndman, Donald W. *Roadside Geology of Northern California*. Missoula, Mont.: Mountain Press Publishing Co., 1975. Helps understand where California came from and where it might be going.

Hiking, walking, etc.: Whitnah, Dorothy L. *An Outdoor Guide to the San Francisco Bay Area*. Rev. ed. Berkeley: Wilderness Press, 1978. Almost 180 pages devoted to Marin, Sonoma, Napa.

Fishing: Hayden, Mike. *Exploring the North Coast*. San Francisco: Chronicle Books, 1976. General guide, good on fishing spots.

EVENTS

It's difficult to travel by calendars of events, but here's a list of some events you might find yourself in the middle of; details from the Redwood Empire Association and local chambers of commerce.

January: to March, steelhead fishing (Eel River); until mid-March, graywhale watching (Point Reyes, Sonoma coast bluffs, Mendocino Headlands, Patrick's Point, and other prominences).

February: Cloverdale Citrus Fair and Parade; World Championship Crab Races and Crab Feed (Crescent City).

March: Spring Blossom Tour and Festival (Healdsburg); Daffodil Show (Fortuna).

April: Bodega Bay Fisherman's Festival; Apple Blossom Festival (Sebastopol); Rhododendron Show, Parade, and Festival (Eureka); Anderson Valley Wildflower Show (Boonville); Antiques Show and Sale (Sausalito); into May, Mendocino Coast Rhododendron Show (Mendocino Coast Botanical Garden, Fort Bragg).

May: Luther Burbank Rose Festival (Santa Rosa); Ram Sale and Sheep Dog Trials (Cloverdale); Russian River Wine Festival (Healdsburg); Spring Art Fair (Mendocino).

June: West Marin Livestock Show and Parade (Point Reyes Station); Dipsea Race (Mill Valley to Stinson Beach); Sonoma-Marin Fair (Petaluma); Ox Roast on the Plaza (Sonoma); Sonoma Valley Art Fair (Sonoma); Redwood Acres Fair and Rodeo (Eureka); Pony Express Days and Rodeo (McKinleyville); Klamath Salmon Festival (Klamath Townsite).

July: Sonoma County Fair, Expo, and Horse Races (Santa Rosa); Napa County Fair (Calistoga); music, dance, drama (Mondavi Winery, Oakville Krug Winery, St. Helena; Geyser Peak Winery and Souverain Winery, Geyserville; and Sonoma Vineyards, Windsor); into October, Dahlia Show (Mendocino Botanical Gardens); Humboldt County Fair (Ferndale); rodeos (Fortuna, Orick).

August: Marin County Fair (San Rafael); Old Adobe Days (Petaluma); Statewide Outdoor Art Show (Santa Rosa); Summer Art Fair (Mendocino); Redwood Empire Fair (Ukiah); Del Norte County Fair (Crescent City); King Salmon Run (Klamath and Smith rivers).

September: Sausalito Art Festival; Fall Arts Festival (Mill Valley); Scottish Gathering and Caledonian Games (Santa Rosa); Vintage Festival (Sonoma); Anheuser-Busch Golf Classic (Silverado Country Club, Napa); Renaissance Pleasure Faire (Novato); Russian River Jazz Festival (Guerneville); Pageant of Fire Mountain (Guerneville); Paul Bunyan Days (Fort Bragg); Mendocino County Fair and Apple Show (Boonville).

October: Grape Festival (San Rafael); Harvest Fair (Santa Rosa); Western Regional Folk Festival (Marin Headlands); World's Wrist Wrestling Championship (Petaluma); Humboldt Redwoods Marathon (Avenue of the Giants); Fall Colors Winery Tour (Geyserville).

November: Thanksgiving Art Fair (Mendocino); Hollyberry Fair (Souverain Winery, Geyserville); Festival of Trees (San Rafael).

December: Illuminated Manuscripts Exhibit (Silverado Museum, St. Helena).

TO COMMENCE THE JOURNEY:
The Golden Gate Bridge

The narrow passage from the sea into the great blue bay is a fine creation of nature, but man has made it a work of art by putting the Golden Gate Bridge there. Bridge and setting are the picture-postcard symbol of San Francisco around the world, and symbolize as well the exhilaration that awaits the traveler to Northern California.

The Golden Gate Bridge would be beautiful anywhere, but its actual location is splendid. Two coastal peninsulas—one high, rugged, and green, the other a white Mediterranean city on low rolling hills—reach toward each other, missing by only a mile. In the gap is water, dangerous whitecapped water. On one side of the peninsulas the vast Pacific doesn't end until it beats on the shores of Hawaii, China, Australia. On the landside is one of the world's great natural harbors, a protected 60-mile-long bay of blue or green or gray, depending on the season and the fogs that roll through the gap.

In 1846 John Charles Frémont, the Pathfinder, named the strait Chrysopylae—"golden gate"—because he fancied a resemblance to a place he had never seen, Chrysoceras, or Golden Horn, the harbor of Constantinople. In 1849 the Golden Gate (as a cartographer after Frémont wisely put on his map) was the dramatic gateway to riches for the Argonauts, who came from New York and New England, from England and France, from Chile and China, bringing the world to California.

Railroad tracks crossed the Sierra Nevada almost seven decades before a bridge could be suspended across the Golden Gate. In the 1930s engineers under the direction of Joseph B. Strauss spun steel strands over the fast water. They put foundations 110 feet below the surface, raised the twin towers 746 feet above the water, and suspended more than a mile of roadway 20 stories above the tide, making it flexible enough to sway 27 *feet* in a high wind. Then they painted it with 10,000 gallons of a rust-preventive shade called international orange, which is truly gold to all those with eyes to see. As noble a symbol as a city could have, the bridge opened May 27, 1937, and became San Francisco's gateway to the counties north to Oregon—the Redwood Empire—and their grand approach to The City.

Now, across the Golden Gate.

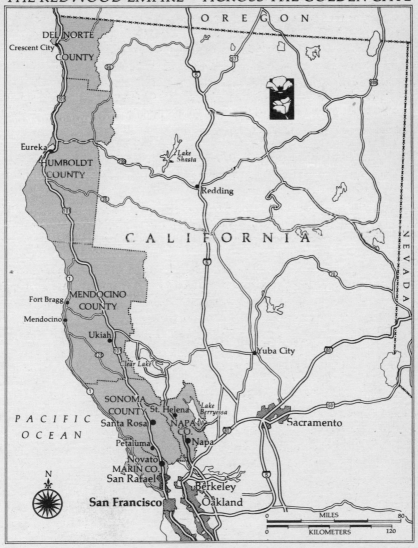

WINE COUNTRY: NAPA, SONOMA, AND MENDOCINO

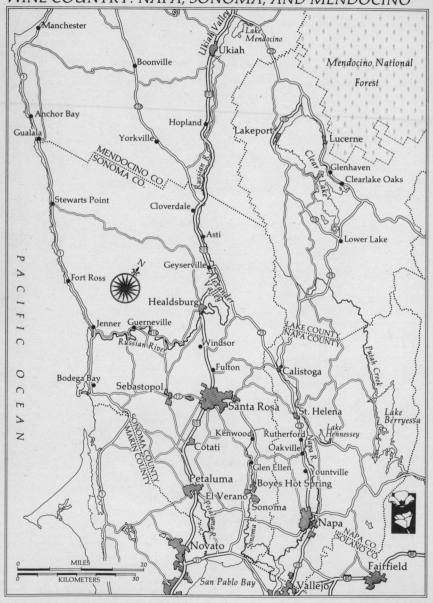

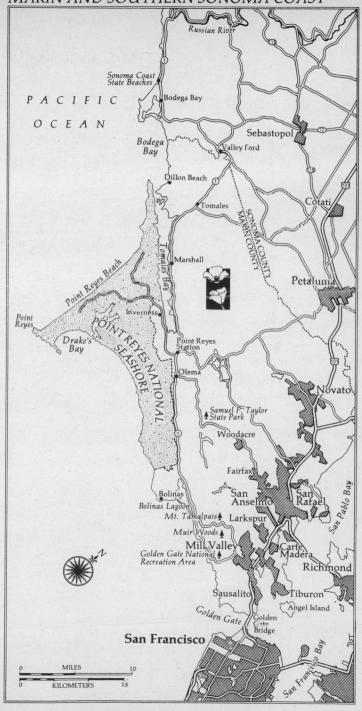

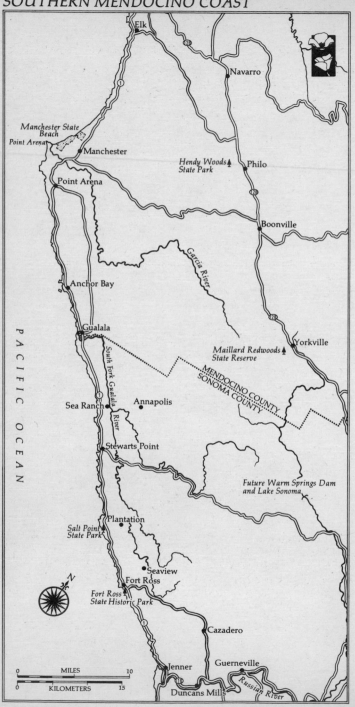

Elk

Navarro

Manchester State
Beach
Point Arena
Manchester

Hendy Woods
State Park
Philo

Point Arena

Boonville

Garcia River

Anchor Bay

Gualala

Yorkville

South Fork Gualala River

Maillard Redwoods
State Reserve

MENDOCINO COUNTY
SONOMA COUNTY

P A C I F I C   O C E A N

Sea Ranch
Annapolis

Stewarts Point

Future Warm Springs Dam
and Lake Sonoma

Plantation

Salt Point
State Park

Seaview
Fort Ross

N

Fort Ross
State Historic Park

Cazadero

Guerneville

Jenner

Russian River

Duncans Mills

MILES   10
0

KILOMETERS   15
0

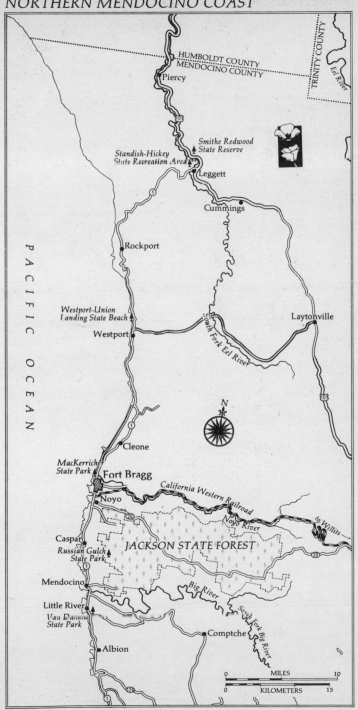

TRINITY COUNTY

Eel River

HUMBOLDT COUNTY
MENDOCINO COUNTY

Piercy

Smithe Redwood
State Reserve

Standish-Hickey
State Recreation Area

Leggett

Cummings

Rockport

Westport-Union
Landing State Beach

South Fork Eel River

Laytonville

Westport

P A C I F I C   O C E A N

N

Cleone

MacKerricher
State Park

Fort Bragg

California Western Railroad

Noyo

Noyo River

to Willits

Caspar

Russian Gulch
State Park

JACKSON STATE FOREST

Mendocino

Big River

Little River

Van Damme
State Park

South Fork Big River

Comptche

Albion

MILES
0   10

KILOMETERS
0   15

REDWOOD COUNTRY:
HUMBOLDT AND DEL NORTE

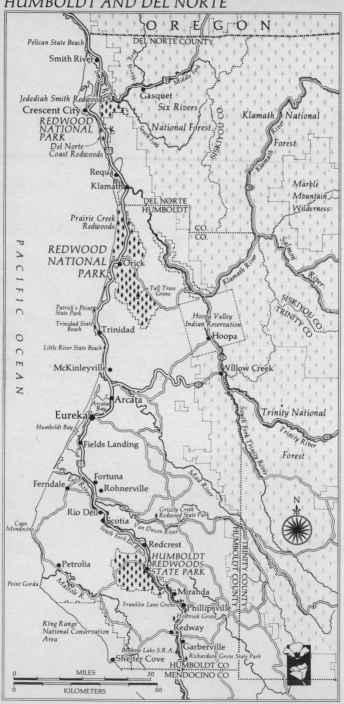

Part I

WINE
COUNTRY

Robert Pecota
1979
Gamay Beaujolais
Napa Valley

Grown, Whole Cluster Fermented and Bottled by
Robert Pecota Winery, Calistoga California
Bonded Winery #4845 Alcohol 12% by Volume

One of wine's delights is the countryside in which it is produced. A visit to California's Wine Country, particularly to the premium winegrowing areas north of San Francisco, makes a pleasant excursion, even a mild spree, which is, if you like, highly educational as well.

Grapes and wine are a big industry in the state, with a value once set at $6 billion. Grapes are California's most valuable crop (and that crop makes up 90 percent of the nation's grape harvest), worth more than $1 billion in 1979. While many grapes are marketed as table grapes or dried to become raisins, the largest portion goes into wineries for crushing to make wine, grape juice, brandy, and other products. The state's more than 410 wineries produce all the brandy and about 82 percent of all wine made in the U.S.—or about 70 percent of all wine (foreign and domestic) that Americans drink. Furthermore, the wineries themselves are visited by four million tourists each year; the Napa Valley alone gets two million.

That's quantity. There's the quality factor, too. California wine is—there is no longer any doubt—among the best in the world: premium wines from Napa have defeated the best Bordeaux in tastings by French judges, and California jugs contain *vin ordinaire* far superior to that of France.

Part I is two things: an introduction to wine in general and, in its details and examples, California wine in particular (Chapters 1, 2, and 3); and a tour guide to the North Coast winegrowing districts, including general points of interest (Chapter 4, Napa; Chapter 5, Sonoma and to a lesser extent Mendocino).

Companion volumes to *Across the Golden Gate* cover other wine-growing areas (though not in as great detail). But despite the huge production of wine in the San Joaquin Valley to the south, even despite the recent great gains in quality and prestige made by Central Coast wineries, the North Coast wine valleys are the essential California Wine Country.

The reader who glances at the introductory chapters will immediately see that we have not avoided some of the technical aspects of wine. We have not tried, like wine snobs, to mystify wine, make it more difficult than it is, or declare it a field forbidden to amateurs. Far from it: we have tried to simplify the subject, demolish snobbish barriers, give frank consumer-oriented advice (especially Chapter 2, "Reading a Bottle of California Wine," which will teach drinkers of other wine to be skeptical as well), and in general help any willing reader gain a good appreciation for the brilliant, luscious liquid in that beautiful, fragile glass.

But appreciation of a subject requires some effort to master details that are often technical—in the case of wine, details on agriculture, chemistry, industrial technology, marketing, and finance. We have tried always to be interesting, but your attention in the middle of long sentences will be rewarded. After all, you can be innocently awed by, say, Yosemite Valley, but your impression will be greater and longer-lasting if you learn something about the origins of volcanic rock and the equally dramatic action of glaciers and erosion. Your visit to the Grand Canyon then becomes a more rewarding experience, and soon you are looking at road cuts with an appreciating eye. So it is with wine, a beverage whose qualities are enhanced by the wine drinker's understanding.

CHAPTER 1:

California Wine: An Introduction

California has four principal wine-producing regions, each divided into several districts:*

• **North Coast:** Five districts: Mendocino County; Lake County; Sonoma and Marin counties; Napa County; Solano County. This mostly cool region, with 62,000 acres of wine grapes (half again the acreage of the premium winegrowing districts of Bordeaux), sends out much of its good wine in bulk for blending with lesser-quality (bland or neutral, low-colored, less acidic) Central Valley wine, but also produces and bottles some of the state's best fine wines. Among the big wineries here, or labels associated with the area, are Italian Swiss Colony (Sonoma County) and Inglenook and the Christian Brothers (both Napa Valley). Among the well-known medium-size wineries are Sebastiani, Souverain, Sonoma Vineyards, Simi, Korbel (all Sonoma), Charles Krug, Louis M. Martini, Beringer, Robert Mondavi, Beaulieu, and Sterling (all Napa). The wineries getting the most attention from wine collectors are the smallest ones, often called "boutiques."

• **Central Coast:** Three districts: northern section (including Livermore and Santa Clara valleys); central section (including Monterey and San Benito counties; and southern section (including newly developed vineyards in San Luis Obispo and Santa Barbara counties). This area has 52,000 acres of wine grapes in temperate coastal valleys.

---

* In point of fact, the federal and state agriculture departments in 1979 dropped the idea of wine regions when they expanded the number of districts from eleven to sixteen. Wine writers are, however, incorrigible, so we have regrouped the new districts under the old regional names.

The best-known wineries in this area include the giant Almadén, Paul Masson, and Taylor California Cellars and medium-size San Martín, Monterey Vineyard, Wente Brothers, Concannon, and Mirassou. Many wines with Central Coast place-names are expensive—and worth it.

• **Central Valley:** Six districts: Sacramento Valley area; Sierra Foothills; Lodi area; Modesto area; central San Joaquin Valley; southern San Joaquin Valley. With an unbelievable 193,000 acres of wine grapes alone (table and raisin varieties are also grown and crushed for wine), the hot, heavily irrigated Valley grows about 88 percent of the grapes that are crushed and two-thirds of all bottled—mostly jugged—California wine. You've heard of the biggest one, E. and J. Gallo, whose four plants around Modesto store 250 million gallons in huge outdoor, temperature-controlled tanks (compare this with the Napa Valley's prestigious Heitz Cellars, which holds only 175,000 gallons of the best). You may not recognize the names of the other big ones—Guild, Vie-Del (grape brandy only), M. LaMont, Sierra, JFJ Bronco, Franzia, California Growers, Giumarra—but they make standard Chablis, Burgundy, and other wine for sale under their own labels or in bulk to others for blending and bottling. Few small wineries are found on the Valley floor, but a couple have started in the Sierra foothills above Lodi.

• **Southern California:** California's principal winegrowing region until the 1880s, Southern California (with two districts) now grows less than two percent of grapes crushed, in vineyards around Cucamonga and Temecula.

The Central Valley and Southern California, with their high summertime temperatures, grow table and raisin grapes as well as wine grapes, the latter mostly for sweet and jug wines. The coastal areas, scattered from Santa Maria north to Ukiah, with a cooler summer climate and an enormous range of "microclimates," produce only about 13 percent of the wine—but that is more likely to be "poetry in a bottle," as Robert Louis Stevenson wrote of Napa Valley wine.

YESTERDAY AND TODAY

Though modern winemaking in California dates only from the end of Prohibition in 1933, and started booming only in the 1960s, wine has been made here from the beginning of European settlement—1782 being the best guess as to the first California vintage. The Franciscan fathers set out vines that had been grown from the seeds of European grapes, vines that produced a black grape adequate for a rough wine for sacramental and other purposes. (Even today the Mission grape is grown on 6,400 acres.) Grapes were planted at most of the 21 missions; Captain George Vancouver in 1790 observed "vines, figs, and fruit trees of various sorts" flourishing "in great perfection." Even the Russians, established at Fort Ross in 1812, grew Black Sea grapes for wine, though they probably found the beverage a poor substitute for vodka.

Mission San Gabriel near Los Angeles had the largest winery (three presses), and it was nearby in 1824 that an American, Joseph Chapman, planted 4,000 vines in California's first commercial vineyard. A few years later Jean Louis Vignes, of a Bordeaux winemaking family, started a commercial vineyard about where Union Station is in downtown L.A. In time he transplanted cuttings of classic French varieties and by the 1840s was making both brandy and the finest California wine, 40,000 gallons at a time. Wine soon became L.A.'s most important business.

In the north, General Mariano Vallejo took over and developed the mission's vineyard near Sonoma Plaza in 1836, and the Napa Valley's first settler, George Yount, planted cuttings near present-day Yountville in 1843.

Enter Colonel Haraszthy

By 1850 California wineries were producing 58,000 gallons per year, mostly from the Mission grape and other lesser varieties. The enormous tide of gold-seekers no doubt swelled the demand for anything alcoholic, but luckily there was interest in producing distinctive California wine as well. The legislature in 1859 boosted the industry by exempting vineyards from taxes. In the 1860s, an egoistic Hungarian, Ágoston Haraszthy (pronounced ha-RAS-tee), did so much to promote the making of fine wine that he has been called, deservedly or not, the Father of California Wine.

"Colonel" or "Count" Haraszthy came to California by way of Wisconsin, where he founded Sauk City and introduced the hops from which grew that state's beer industry; to San Francisco by way of San Diego, where he was mayor and sheriff; and to the Sonoma Valley by way of the San Francisco mint, where he was the assayer and head of melting and refining until suspected of converting government gold into California landholdings. In 1857 Haraszthy established the Buena Vista vineyard and winery (now a state historic landmark), became a state viticultural commissioner, and in 1861 traveled, at the governor's behest, through France, Germany, Italy, and other countries collecting rootstock and one or two hundred thousand cuttings of some 300 grape varieties (a trip for which he was never reimbursed). In the process of selling and distributing the cuttings, some vine identifications were lost, which may account for the dubious origin of such varieties as Green Hungarian. Meteorically, Haraszthy wrote the first bible of the California wine industry, experimented with many grape-growing (viticultural) and winemaking (vinicultural) methods, introduced redwood casks, began cultivating hillside vineyards, and helped found the California Wine Growers' Association. But then he sold control of Buena Vista's 400 acres to financier William C. Ralston, had a falling out, emigrated to Nicaragua, and disappeared into a crocodile's jaws in 1869. His two sons married into General Vallejo's family; one, Arpad, made the state's first Champagne.

Haraszthy's role in research and development was taken over in the 1870s by Eugene W. Hilgard of the University of California. Among other things, Hilgard discovered that the now common cool-fermentation technique would produce very clean, fresh, fruity wines. Out of his activities grew the Department of Viticulture and Enology at the Davis campus of the University of California. That department developed the standard 20-point wine-judging system and bred such popular hybrids as Emerald Riesling and Ruby Cabernet.

Although passing through the usual agricultural cycle of boom and bust, the California wine industry kept growing, with a vintage of 4.2 million gallons in 1869, 28 million gallons in 1900, 58 million gallons in 1911. Progress was slowed in the latter part of the century when the dread phylloxera, an unpleasant-looking green root louse, hit California after a decade of vineyard-by-vineyard devastation throughout Europe. The phylloxera attack had some ironies. The louse is a native American and was accidentally exported to Europe. While the native American "foxy" grape species, Vitis labrusca, is immune to phylloxera, the higher-quality species common to Europe and planted in California, Vitis vinifera, is not. Europe and California were able to defeat the pest, at great expense, by grafting vinifera cuttings on labrusca and other American rootstock, thus giving Bordeaux, Moselle, and Napa

Valley vines solid New York and Missouri roots. Interestingly, most grapes in Monterey and newer grape areas to the south were not afflicted with phylloxera.and are growing on natural *vinifera* rootstock.

Bust and Boom

What nearly killed the wine industry in America was man-made: a moralistic law aimed at John Barleycorn rather than Bacchus. In the 14 dry years of Prohibition, 1920–33, thousands of acres of wine grapes were uprooted and replaced with fruit trees or table- or raisin-grape varieties. Some vineyards kept going by selling grapes to families, who were each allowed to make 200 gallons a year; this unfortunately favored varieties that shipped well over those that made good wine. Hundreds of wineries (there were 700) closed and dozens mysteriously burned, but a few survived by producing sweet altar wine, others by turning out "medicine" or bootlegging their products.

With Repeal in 1933, the California wine industry had to begin again, and recovery was slow. Remaining vineyards had mediocre grapes; winemaking tradition had been lost as families (mostly Italian-American) went into other businesses. The principal products for the next quarter of a century were not fine wines but inferior table wine produced from raisin and table grapes or low-grade wine grapes, brandy, and sweet, high-alcohol Sherry, Port, Tokay, and Muscatel. In 1948 the fortified wines outsold table wines four to one. Demand for premium varietals (wines named for the grape variety) was for decades so low that the only vintage-dated California Cabernet Sauvignon (similar to the red wines of Bordeaux chateaux) was produced by just four wineries in the Napa Valley: Beaulieu, Inglenook, Charles Krug, and Louis M. Martini.

What follows bust, however, is boom, and the boom began in the 1960s with an unaccountable craze for fizzy pink Cold Duck and flavored "pop" wines like Ripple and Boone's Farm. The consequence was a renewed interest in table wine. Thanks to technological advances such as slow, cool fermentation, ordinary jug wine—especially white—suddenly was more palatable to more people. Table wine overtook dessert wine on the sales charts in 1967, outsold it almost six to one in 1979, and may soon account for 90 percent of consumption. Nationally, per capita consumption jumped from less than a gallon in 1965 to nearly two gallons in 1978; Californians consume twice the average amount. While two gallons is modest by European standards—the

French and Italians swallow 25 gallons per person—it doubled the size of an industry in a nation of 220 million, and most authorities predict per capita consumption will triple by the year 2000.

California wine, once associated with Skid Row winos, became the subject of conversation in corporate boardrooms. Although profits aren't all that good in such a capital-intensive industry, big corporations snapped up raw land (it costs $10,000 to $12,000 to buy an acre and put in vines in the Napa Valley), vineyards, wineries. United Vintners, a co-op which owned Italian Swiss Colony, bought Inglenook, then was itself consumed by Heublein—which picked up Beaulieu for extra prestige. Pillsbury purchased Souverain, Nestlé bought Beringer Brothers. The Beatrice Foods conglomerate glommed on to Brookside and its chain of roadside tasting rooms. Taking a chance with their wholesome image, Coca-Cola Bottling Company of New York bought the Franzia jug winery while Coca-Cola of Atlanta plucked Monterey Vineyard and Sterling along with New York's big Taylor Wine Company, which has now invaded the California industry. Schlitz beer bought Nervo and Geyser Peak, Rainier beer put money into Robert Mondavi, and Schieffelin liquor importers picked up Simi. Seagram's Paul Masson and National Distillers' Almadén both expanded. In a twist, Moët and Chandon of Épernay, France, makers of Dom Perignon Champagne and Hennessy Cognac, gave signal recognition to California wine by setting up a new sparkling wine operation in the Napa Valley.

In the wake of the corporations, tax-shelter partnerships rushed in, and airline pilots, psychiatrists, lawyers, corporation executives, millionaire socialites, movie directors and TV stars, even engineers and photographers, discovered the pleasures and pains of operating miniature boutique wineries or a few acres of vines.

The boom had a desirable effect on the quality of wine. Vineyard owners planted thousands of acres in premium varieties. The North Coast doubled its grape acreage from 1970 to 1978. They also searched for new land, opening up much of northern Sonoma (Alexander Valley), Monterey's Salinas Valley (where acreage increased eightfold in eight years), and—few had thought of it before—river valleys in San Luis Obispo and Santa Barbara counties. Dedicated amateurs and a crop of bright enologists from the Davis and Fresno winemaking schools applied the lessons of modern technology (long cool fermentation, membrane filtration, centrifugation), advances in research (grapes should be picked when the sugar-acid balance is just so), and solid European tradition (aging in French oak from the Nevers and Limousin forests) and created premium wines that stunned critics. Best, jug wines—especially whites—became better and better.

It was dazzling. Wine-grape acreage doubled in only five years; the number of bonded wineries increased every week (there are now 410 or so). One estimate is that about $750 million was invested in new vineyards and another $250 million in wineries in the late 1960s and early 1970s alone.

Mid-1970s: Shakeout

The boom faltered in the 1973–74 recession. The price of Cabernet Sauvignon grapes from the Napa Valley, for instance, which sold for only $170 a ton in 1962, soared to $810 in 1973—then plummeted to $325 two years later. Soon there was a glut of good red grapes when the public wanted white wine. Corporations realized that it takes new vines three or four years to produce the first crop—and that good wine must be aged for two or more years in barrels that cost $300 or more apiece. Looking at the bottom line, Nestlé and Pillsbury both shucked their wine operations, some absentee investors pulled their money out, and some growers even ripped out young vines for more profitable produce.

The industry tripped, then recovered. The public still wanted more and more wine. One side effect of the price drop and oversupply of some varietals was that some wineries started bottling Cabernet and other premium grapes in half-gallon jugs; customers liked that. The overplanting in the early 1970s became a plus in 1976 and 1977 when the California drought decreased production. Sales kept increasing and grape prices crept up again (Cabernet grapes from Napa were selling for 522 inflated dollars a ton in 1979—but white Chardonnay grapes had shot up to $907 per ton).

Wine people these days are pretty happy. Their market is approaching $4 billion a year and growing at a steady eight percent a year. Per capita consumption is increasing and may surpass hard liquor for the first time in history, though wine is a couple of dozen gallons behind beer and soda pop.

Along with steady increase in interest in fine table wine and startling falloff in sales of aperitif and dessert wines (only half as much is produced as in 1949), there are other trends that the industry is coping with or encouraging. The biggest is that consumers have switched to white wine from red, which once accounted for 60 to 70 percent of table-wine sales but now comprises only 30 percent; Chablis became a party drink, an aperitif, and a substitute for a cocktail as kids grew up and graduated from Annie Green Springs.

Other wrinkles: faintly pink "white" wine made from black grapes, a consequence of the surplus of red-wine grapes; *nouveau* or *primeur* wines, which are quickly made, bottled, and sent to market, like France's Beaujolais; an 80-proof vodka made from grape juice; a single drink of wine packaged neatly with its own plastic glass; jug wine in plastic-lined square boxes; bulk-produced varietals in frosted-glass bottles with Art Nouveau labels; and a consumer demand for a light (soft) wine with less alcohol (7 percent and up vs. the standard for premium wines of 10 to 14 percent).

The industry is not only full-bodied and vigorous but mature as well. Defensive comparisons with the finest French wines were commonplace until a famous blind tasting in Paris in our bicentennial year: two 1973 Napa Valley varietals, a Chardonnay from Chateau Montelena and a Cabernet Sauvignon from Stag's Leap Wine Cellars, outpointed their French counterparts. Indeed, since then California wines have become so chic in certain French circles that a critic in *Le Figaro* has condemned both American *"vins de cowboys"* and Parisian *"snobisme."*

Many wine buffs now say that comparisons are fallacious anyway. As with the English language spoken in America, England, Australia, and elsewhere, there are as many varieties of wine as there are places growing them. It is, in the end, a matter of taste, not measurement according to a universal rule.

FROM GRAPES TO WINE

We've been using the word *wine* somewhat loosely until now. "A bottle of wine" is no more adequate a description than "a book" or "a rock." Coming under the label *wine* are such things as apple wine, dandelion wine, and even blueberry "Champagne," but we won't consider those here. Instead, we'll define wine as the fermented juice of grapes. Beyond that, wine can be categorized from two to eight different ways. We think these are the three basic types: table wine, sparkling wine, and cocktail wine. The third has several subdivisions, and the second is a simple category. Table wine, however, has classifications and subdivisions that overlap and confuse. You don't have to explore the world of wine very long to realize that there are probably as many subdivisions as there are vineyards and winemakers, for each wine can be regarded as unique. "Reading a Bottle of California Wine" (Chapter 2) will give further details, but here, so that you can follow the description of how wine is made, are the wine categories in brief.

Table Wine

Table wine, also called dinner wine, accounts for 80 percent (rapidly heading toward 90 percent) of wine consumption in the U.S., and it's the category that is the most fun to talk about. (If you're in a London club, though, the talk is about Port.)

Table wine can be divided into (a) varietals, generics, and proprietary-named wines; (b) red, rosé, and white; or (c) all of the foregoing.

A **varietal** is named for the grape variety from which it is made, in whole or in part, such as Cabernet Sauvignon (red), Chardonnay (white), and Grenache Rosé. While in Europe the name of the wine-making locality largely defines the kind of wine produced, in California the name of the variety is the key. Most varietals are so-called premium wines.

A **generic** is a blend of various reds or various whites that is given a name appropriated from Europe: Burgundy, Chablis, Rhine Wine, Sauterne, Chianti, occasionally Claret and Moselle. Generics are bottled in jugs and low-priced fifths and placed on liquor store and supermarket shelves, so they dominate the market. Generics are controversial, as "Reading a Bottle of California Wine" will explain. Hardly anyone knows just what's in the bottle labeled "Burgundy." At the moment, the consumer doesn't want to know: he asks for "Burgundy" and he gets it.

The third kind, the **proprietary** or **trademark-named wine,** is a smaller category but it may be growing. Paul Masson's "Baroque" is a proprietary name.

Beyond these differences, table wines vary tremendously in such features as alcohol, dryness, fruitiness, aroma, and color, as will be explained. A murmuration (a group larger than a coterie) of wine critics is employed to describe in excruciating detail differences among fine table wines.

Sparkling Wine

Sparkling wine, which is naturally effervescent, accounts for about six percent of U.S. consumption (increasing a bit). These wines can be white, pink, or red, and can be anything from sweet (*doux* and *demi-sec*) to dry enough to parch your tongue (*brut* and *natur*). This category includes, obviously, Champagne, Sparkling Burgundy, Pink Champagne, Sparkling Muscat, and Cold Duck. Alcohol content is the same as that of premium table wines—but the bubbles intensify that 10 to 14 percent. "Champagne" is, by the way, another generic name appropriated from France.

Cocktail Wine

The third category, the consumption of which is steadily declining, is a mixed group to which we've given our own label. Cocktail wines can be served as appetizers (aperitifs), as postmeal (dessert) drinks, and as party or anytime beverages. As opposed to table and sparkling wine, they are rarely drunk with main dishes at dinner. Further, cocktail wines are either fortified—made more alcoholic—by the addition of wine spirits (brandy), flavored with herbs or various extracts, or given a mild amount of carbonation. In this category are the traditional **aperitif wines** like Dry Sherry and Vermouth and **dessert wines** like Cream Sherry, Port, and Muscatel, which all have an alcohol content above 17 percent. Also in this category are the so-called **special natural wines,** which include artificially carbonated red or white wines and the past-fad "pop" wines that are made with special flavors; alcohol content is 10 to 14 percent. **Vermouth,** which is flavored with herbs (a secret mixture), is often put in a special category because of its importance as a mixer. **Brandy,** distilled from grape wine, is regarded as a product of the grape and wine industry but is basically liquor, not wine.

The changing of grape juice into all the various kinds of wine has at its heart the very natural process of fermentation. But man now guides the entire process, from the growing of the grapes through the fermentation, and after that takes it over altogether—though one cannot say that the product is manufactured. Nature doesn't make wine, say wise winemakers; nature makes vinegar. Or as the trade magazine *Wines and Vines* puts it, "Wine is a subtle composition influenced by every person attending its progress, including the truck driver who lets a load [of grapes] sit for three hours in the sun."

Indeed, as can be seen from the following description of how one puts the fruit of the vine into bottles, there are so many variables and methods that it is surprising that even two bottles of the same varietal, from the same vintage, and from the same viticultural area taste the same; very often they do not.

From the Vineyard . . .

It does start in the vineyard. While scientists have managed to isolate at least 70 different compounds that make up about 98 percent of wine, Alexis Lichine observes that mixing these together in the right proportions does not create wine. You must have grapes grown in soil in the sun.

Of the 8,000 known grape varieties, only 5,000 are named, less than 100 are important in California and Europe, a dozen are premium, and as few as four—Cabernet Sauvignon, Pinot Noir, Chardonnay, and White Riesling—are regarded as "noble."

In California's 16,000 vineyards (which are under 9,500 managements), grapes are categorized according to their principal end use: wine, raisin, or table.

Wine grapes: Of the state's 645,000 acres of vineyards (that's more than a thousand square miles), just over half are planted with wine-grape varieties. Two-thirds of that acreage is planted in some 45 "black" varieties, a share that is decreasing because of the popularity of white wine, and one-third is planted in about 32 "white" varieties, a share increasing with every new planting and grafting over. Not all of these 77 varieties are important, for seven black varieties (in order of importance: Zinfandel, Carignane, Cabernet Sauvignon, Barbera, Ruby Cabernet, Grenache, and Petite Sirah) and three white varieties (French Colombard, Chenin Blanc, and Chardonnay) account for two-thirds of the acreage. Crushing statistics are different, incidentally, because some varieties produce far more per acre, and the premium varieties are undercropped in the best vineyards.

Raisin grapes: The six varieties classified as raisin grapes are grown on more than 250,000 acres, or 40 percent of the total under vines. Two raisin varieties—Thompson Seedless (grown on 36 percent of all grape acreage in California) and Muscat of Alexandria—are called "three-way grapes" because they can be picked early for sale as table

As the French have known for centuries, the poorest-looking vines in the rough-est-looking soil can produce the best wine. But pretty vineyards produce pretty wine, too. (Wine Institute)

grapes or for drying to make raisins, or picked later for crushing at wineries. (More below on the controversial role of Thompson Seedless, which has been dubbed "Fresno Chardonnay.") Between 32 and 36 percent of raisin varieties is crushed.

Table grapes: The other 10 percent of the state's vineyard land grows some 25 varieties either destined for being eaten off the stems (50 percent) or crushed at wineries (the other half). The Flame Tokay is a table grape that is widely used to make dessert wine and brandy.

Despite the distinction made between black and white wine-grape varieties, grape skins may be white, yellow, gold, green, pink, red, brown, purple, blue, or nearly black, and at harvest time may be speckled darkly or splashed with orange. The fruit or pulp is nearly always pale green or yellow. White wines often are made from black grapes if the skins are separated before fermentation of the juice. Gray Riesling, Flora, and Gewürztraminer have purple or red-brown skins but make white wine, and the purple Pinot Noir grape makes a principal base wine for Champagne.

Grapes can be grown in many places in the world but flourish best in temperate regions. Over the millennia winemakers have learned to match grape to land and climate as well as to the desired beverage. "Vines love an open hill" was Virgil's advice to Roman growers, and a professor at Davis would echo it. The Romans didn't make what we would regard as palatable wine, but they managed to plant vineyards in all the best places in Italy, Germany, and France (Bordeaux was producing wine in the first century B.C.). Europe makes three-quarters of the world's wine; the U.S., Argentina, Chile, Algeria, South Africa, and Australia—all temperate countries—make nearly all the rest.

California has an ideal climate, differing from Europe in rarely having summer or harvest-time rain. The temperature over the length of the growing season, combined with a winter cold enough to make the vines dormant but not dead, suits grapes admirably, and the depth and texture of the soil are satisfactory. The several grapes used for jug wine, for neutral wines used in distilling brandy, and for sweet dessert wines achieve the highest yield and quality in the irrigated deep soils and hot summers of the Central Valley, and that's where nearly 90 percent of the grape crush originates. The several premium varieties used for dry table wines develop their best quality in the nonirrigated, shallower, more gravelly, less fertile soils and cooler climate of the North and Central Coast valleys and hillsides; the coastal fog that obscures the sun on summer mornings and holds the temperature down (and upsets tourists) seems to be the critical element. A little adversity, it is said, breeds wines of character. These geographical differences show up in the yields: eight to twelve tons per acre in the Central Valley, three tons per acre in the Napa Valley.

A long time before anything goes into a bottle, cuttings from parent vines are grown in nurseries for a year, then put into vineyards on pestfree rootstock, with between 350 and 600 vines per acre. Cultivation is mechanized, supervision constant and careful. For the next four years, before the first full crop, pruning and training the vines on stakes or trellis wires (the latter for mechanical harvesting) are the major tasks for vineyard workers. Up to 95 percent of the shoots are pruned in order to concentrate the sugar and varietal flavor in the remaining grapes.

Because good pruning and other viticultural techniques can produce better grapes, many winemakers prefer to be their own vineyardists. However, because vineyards represent a sizable investment for small wineries, or out of the belief that it's best to concentrate on making wine, many small winemakers contract for grapes with independent growers—in whose vineyards they may still spend much time overseeing operations, with daily checks just before harvest.

The life of vineyard owners is not without the usual worries of farming. Depending on the grape variety and the location of the vineyard, they might worry about nematodes, Pierce's disease, powdery mildew (oidium), leaf-roll virus, fanleaf virus, Phomopsis cane, Eutypa die-back, or dead-arm fungus, which all sound awful; a new one is called grapevine measles. They might worry about such colorfully named pests as omnivorous and sharpshooter leafhoppers and western grape-leaf skeletonizers, along with thrips and spider mites, linnets and starlings. Growers hate Bermuda grass and bindweed (morning glory!). If it rains at the wrong time they worry about root, crown, collar, or bunch rot. If it doesn't rain—and it didn't in 1976 and 1977—they worry that the crop will be too small. (Some of the drought wines were actually well received, for not only did the roots go deep into interesting soils but berry size was smaller, concentrating flavor.)

Winegrowers have other weather worries: late frosts in the spring, heat and shock and sunburn in the summer, and early rains during harvest. Dire problems are bloom shatter, bud failure, poor setting, spindle shoot, small berries, hard berries, shot berries, berry cracking, late maturity. If it's not lack of vigor, it's excessive vigor. Distant forest fires cause a smoke cover; nearby highways generate smog. The government bans a favored pesticide; the water district raises pumping costs (it takes, according to one calculation, 500 gallons of water to produce a gallon of wine).

Sometimes they worry about all the grapes maturing at the same time and overloading pressing and fermentation facilities. They fret about growing too many red grapes. They worry that overproduction will send prices down. They worry about unionization of pickers and harvest-time strikes. And they recall what twice-bankrupt Georges de Latour, founder of Beaulieu Vineyards, had to say: of the three ways to go bankrupt, horse racing is the most exciting, keeping a famous mistress the most romantic, and farming the most certain.

Nevertheless, they keep at it, whether they are third-generation farmers or millionaire socialites who find the Napa Valley a nifty summertime address.

When properly ripe, the grapes must be rapidly picked and moved to the wineries. Different varieties ripen at different times. In the North Coast counties Chardonnay, Gewürztraminer, Gray Riesling, and Pinot Noir mature early (late August to mid-September); Sauvignon Blanc, Sémillon, Sylvaner, White Riesling, Chenin Blanc, French Colombard, Zinfandel, Petite Sirah, and Merlot ripen midseason (mid-September to mid-October); and Carignane, Cabernet Sauvignon, and Gamay ripen late (mid-October to early November). As in Bordeaux

Seventy-five percent of the California grape crop is harvested by hand . . .

. . . but mechanical harvesting and field crushing (right) are widely used. A gondola-load of grapes is tipped into a crusher. (Wine Institute)

Fermentation (here, of black grapes for red or rosé wine) can be hot and violent and is monitored for temperature, acidity, alcohol, and sugar levels. (Wine Institute)

it's nip and tuck to see if the Cabernet can be picked before it rains.

In determining ripeness, growers seek a balance between sugar accumulation (by some magic of nature, most of the grape sugar is transferred from the leaves into the grapes near harvest time) and amount of acidity. Table-wine grapes at harvest must have enough sugar (by weight, 22 percent or better for red wine, 20 to 21 percent for white) to convert to the desired 11 to 13 percent alcohol during fermentation. At the same time they need acidity so the wine doesn't taste flat. Sugar is automatic in the Central Valley, acidity in the cooler coastal areas, but there is in both places a point when the optimal balance is reached.

Handpicking was formerly the rule, but many large vineyards and some small ones now use mechanical pickers, which ideally shake off the ripe grapes without breaking them or damaging the vine, and a field crusher (from vine to juice in two minutes) so that the grape juice is fresh and unoxidized. Evening or early morning picking is preferred.

... to the Winery ...

If not crushed in the field, the grapes are taken to the winery in boxes or gondolas as quickly as possible. The first operation is to remove the stems, either in a stemmer or a crusher-stemmer. One widely used crusher-stemmer is the Italian-developed Garolla, a mechanism with a large, coarsely perforated horizontal roller inside of which paddles revolve. The paddles separate the stems, break the grape skins open without breaking the seeds (which would make a wine bitter), and crush the grape pulp. Stems are spewed out one end; they can be used in the vineyard as mulch.

During initial crushing, sulfur dioxide is usually metered into the mass of crushed grapes—called "must"—in order to kill off wild yeasts and other undesirable organisms. SO_2 is only one of the things put into wine at some point before it is bottled, but most of these additions are absent by the time the wine is drunk.

Regardless of what the final product will be—table, sparkling, or cocktail wine—the next step is to ferment the grape juice, either with the skins and seeds to produce basic red and rosé wine or without the solid matter to produce basic white wine. For reds and rosés the sequence is fermentation, then pressing; for white wines the sequence is pressing, then fermentation. Differing fermentation and cellar treatment create the different wine types; Port, for example, is made from basic red wine, as will be explained below.

Freshly crushed grapes anywhere in the world will ferment into an alcoholic drink because wild yeasts on the grape skins—in the light waxy coating called the bloom—will cause the conversion of the grape sugar (dextrose and levulose) into roughly equivalent amounts of ethyl alcohol (ethanol) and gaseous carbon dioxide, with several by-products and a lot of heat. This is grossly simplified; enologists describe the process with a lot more words and make it sound as if something might explode.

To make **red** or **rosé wine,** the must, consisting of juice, skins, and seeds, goes from the crusher-stemmer directly into the fermenting container, either the traditional open wooden or concrete vat or the more modern refrigerated tank of lined steel or concrete. While many Old World winemakers rely on the complex wild yeasts to begin the fermentation, modern wineries use pure, cultured, single-strain yeasts to start the fermentation rapidly (before spoilage) and make it continue uniformly.

During the several days of natural turmoil inside the vat, nearly all of the sugar is converted (for most red wine is dry), the expected amount of alcohol is created, and the CO_2 gas escapes. And since the skins and seeds have been fermenting with the juice, the wine picks up tannin (the "pucker" element) from the skins and seeds, and color elements from the skins once alcohol has acted on them.

For rosés, the juice and skins ferment together only long enough (18 to 36 hours) for the wine to turn pink and pick up just a little tannin, then the wine is drawn off to finish fermenting alone. Lighter red wines that mature more quickly than others and can be bottled and drunk sooner are made by drawing off the juice after only three to four days. In all cases, the temperature of the fermenting wine is kept below 85°F.—sometimes well below—to keep the heat from stopping the fermentation by killing the yeast.

This period in making a wine usually requires the closest supervision; in some wineries the winemaker may even sleep close by to monitor the progress. One necessary operation is to keep the grape solids from rising and forming a fermentation-stopping cap. Winemakers either punch the crust with poles to break it up or pump juice from the bottom of the vat over it.

White wine, in contrast, is the pale color of the pulp, is less astringent (tannic) because the juice ferments alone, and in many cases is sweeter than red wine because fermentation is deliberately stopped.

After the grapes (either black or white varieties) are crushed and destemmed, the must goes immediately into a press. Presses in most California wineries these days are one of two types, the Willmes bag (or bladder) press, or the continuous (or screw) press. The Willmes consists of a slotted horizontal cylinder with a rubber bladder along the axis. The grapes are dumped in and the cylinder rotated; the bladder gradually inflates and forces the mostly clear juice through the slots. Inside the slotted screwpress cylinder is a screw whose blades (like a meat grinder's) are relatively wide apart at one end and close together at the other. After the grapes are dumped in, the screw rotates and moves the grapes along while continuously exerting more pressure to expel the juice. With either press, the "free-run" juice that flows either by gravity or a very light pressing (60 to 70 percent of the total) is kept separate from the "press-run" juice; these are fermented separately but may be blended later.

Today's fermenting vats for white wine are usually big closed stainless-steel tanks with elaborate cooling systems, for it has been found that controlled cold fermentation (55° F. or less), which proceeds quite slowly, produces wines with greater varietal flavor and good acidity.

In making both red and white wine, fermentation can either proceed to its natural conclusion—all the sugar becomes alcohol, which kills the yeast—or stopped so that some sweetness is retained. The winemaker can stop the fermentation either by adding another dollop of sulfur dioxide or a dose of wine spirits (brandy), or by instantaneous heating and then cooling. The latter is, of course, pasteurization; Louis Pasteur actually developed the bacteria-killing process for wine and beer, not milk. The use of sulfur dioxide is common, but too much can impart a sulfuric taste.

For the various aperitif and dessert wines fermentation is largely the same. The grapes are often of different varieties, but the distinctive treatment during fermentation is in the addition of neutral wine spirits (grape brandy) to stop fermentation, boost the alcohol content, and perhaps guard some of the unresolved sugar.

... and into the Cellars

The processes after fermentation depend more than anything else on what the final product is to be. No wine is ready for drinking after fermentation: most of it looks dirty, smells terrible, and tastes raw. It must be, to varying degrees, stored, racked, fined, filtered, aged, and perhaps blended. Champagne must undergo a second fermentation in the bottle. Port must be blended. Sherry must be given its oxidized flavor. Vermouth and the special natural wines must be flavored.

Clarifying and Aging. In the case of table wines, the wine is first allowed to sit quietly in barrels and other containers while the grape solids in suspension settle gradually to the bottom or sides and the last, diminished fermentation is finished (a water seal allows CO_2 to escape without letting air in). Then clarified wine is drawn off from the sediment (lees) by racking, or transferring from barrel to barrel. Since wine is lost by evaporation (ullage), the barrels have to be kept filled to the brim (topped) to decrease contact with the air.

While the wine is clarifying it is also aging. Aging is the gradual development of mellowness and character. It has, actually, two phases: maturing or bulk aging (jug and fine wines) and bottle aging (fine wines only). Wine aging involves some still-mysterious chemical changes that create the subtle differences in flavor and aroma among good wines. One aspect of aging is oxidation: the wine oxidizes slightly and desirably by breathing through the wood of casks (which also means loss in quantity of wine because of evaporation). Another aspect is the combining or "marrying" of the grape variety's or blending wine's elements, which include tartaric, malic, citric, and other acids, residual sugars, four or more alcohols, several aromatic esters, seven or more minerals, proteins, vitamins, coloring agents, and some other unidentified flavoring and aroma constituents, along with some of the flavor of the wood. At the very least, maturing means softening the harsh or "green" flavors resulting from tannin and yeast.

The traditional cooperage is 58-gallon barrels made of oak; French oak from the Limousin and Nevers forest is much in demand at boutique wineries, but American oak (of several species) and Yugoslavian oak, both of which taste different from French oak, are also widely used. Some wineries have huge redwood tanks, but the modern bulk wineries mostly use stainless-steel tanks and specially lined concrete vats.

One of the latest technological developments allows aging-in-wood outside wood barrels—with the addition of oak in granular form or even of oak-flavored blending wine. Either, it is said, can impart oak flavor under more controlled conditions and eliminate the need to keep buying fresh barrels. Not all wines, however, gain anything by contact with oak.

More Clarifying and Blending. After maturing and clarifying, the principal cellar operations are further clarifying and blending. Though enologists believe that a slight cloudiness does wine no harm, American wine drinkers demand a brilliant product. Centrifuges accelerate the settling of solids; coarse or fine filters can be used; fining agents (egg white, gelatin, casein, bentonite) can be put in to precipitate hazes and colloids; cold stabilization is widely used to crystallize the potassium bitartrate before it is filtered out. (Tartrate—or tartaric crystals—often found at the bottom of overly chilled bottles of white wine, resembles glass shards but is quite safe to swallow.) Many small wineries handle the wines as little as possible, saying that too much mechanical and chemical processing knocks the character out of wine. As a result, a few boutique wines may have, for example, a touch of cloudiness. Bulk wineries, however, couldn't operate without modern processes.

The major operation at this stage is blending. Blending can be considered as either the winemaker's true art or his most commercial. There are several reasons for blending:

• To make a varietal wine palatable, or drinkable earlier. Cabernet Sauvignon alone may be undrinkable for years, until the high tannin content and other strong elements have mellowed by long bottle-aging. Few wineries or wine buffs can afford to keep much wine in storage for a half-dozen to 20 years or more. So winemakers use Merlot and other varieties to modify the strength and add softness and fruitiness without destroying the Cabernet quality. That would seem to be a permissible reason for blending.

• To make a varietal wine that is uniform from year to year. While uniformity throughout the industry is not desirable, uniformity in each of one winery's various products can be defended since it allows the uncertain consumer to select a wine with confidence. The Christian Brothers, tenth largest winery in the U.S., have had such a policy of producing uniform wines from year to year. Here is an example, as described by wine critics Hugh Johnson and Bob Thompson, of how the winery used fractional blending to produce 12,000 bottles of a varietal blend called Gamay Noir (the recommended name for what has been called Napa Gamay). The winery staff first gathered half-bottle samples of different but appropriate varietals from different vintages and vineyards. Once, 120 different samples of Cabernet Sauvignon were gathered, but 20 is more typical in such blending. Under the head winemaker (for decades, the famous Brother Timothy), the samples were tasted and some eliminated. Then a few trial blends were produced using a rigid ratio of one cubic centimeter for each 100 gallons of that wine on hand in barrels. (One trial blend may be enough. If not, the best trial blend becomes the starting point for another round.) The final recipe used various lots of Napa Gamay, Grand Noir, and Pinot Noir in these proportions: 2,000:2,000:2,000:2,000:1,100:520:2,000. (There, now you can do it in your kitchen.)

• To produce a good drinkable everyday wine at a reasonable price. This is, of course, the goal of giant wineries. Medium size and small wineries like to produce some *vin ordinaire* of distinction if only because no one can tolerate too rich a wine every day. Los Angeles wine columnist Nat Chroman described how Sonoma Vineyards' winemaker, Rod Strong, produced "super," clean, but inexpensive White Table Wine (which other wineries would dub Chablis) using 60 percent Thompson Seedless, 25 percent French Colombard—both of which have little or no varietal flavor—and 15 percent Chardonnay. The Thompson was fermented slowly over two weeks at 55° F. in small containers and treated well in other cellar operations. French Colombard was blended in to add the acidity that Thompson lacks and temper the fruitiness that Thompson has to excess. Then the Chardonnay was blended in to add some subtle, fine-varietal flavoring. The price in mid-1979 was $3.69 per magnum ($1.85 per fifth). The Red Table Wine was made with 25 percent Cabernet Sauvignon, 35 percent Ruby Cabernet, 20 percent Pinot Noir, and 20 percent Zinfandel, all grown by Sonoma Vineyards.

• To exploit the market for high-priced varietals. This is, of course, the unscrupulous aspect of blending. While the Christian Brothers and Sonoma Vineyards may make public their blending operations, no winery is going to boast of blending the least possible amount of flavorful, expensive Napa Valley Chardonnay with the greatest possible amount of a cheap "stretcher" wine like Thompson Seedless from the Central Valley—and then marketing it as vintage-dated Napa Valley Chardonnay for $9 a bottle. At the moment, federal regulations allow such a 51:49 blend to be so labeled, without any hint that it is not 100 percent Chardonnay.

On the whole, blending is an eminently defensible practice, and the major part of California wine marketed, both the finest premium wines and the gallon-jug wines, is blended.

Incidentally, winemakers sometimes use what's called a vineyard blend—different varieties from the same vineyard. It is not infrequent that an old vineyard has many vines that can't be identified—ampelography (grape identification) is a high art—and, therefore, it can't be said for certain that all the grapes harvested are of one variety or another. Hop Kiln calls one such vineyard blend "Marty Griffin's Big Red." Another kind of blend is made by mixing grapes during the crush. Both are less predictable than blending finished wine.

Other Finishing Operations. As part of blending operations, winemakers are permitted to add some things that didn't come through the door with the original grapes. The principal grape acid, tartaric, may not be present in sufficient quantity in ripe grapes, even in premium varietals grown in recommended climates, so the acid alone may be added. Also legal is the addition of unfermented grape juice or concentrate, either of which has a good amount of grape sugar, to sweeten wine after it is made. Adding straight sugar (chaptalization, common in Europe) is not legal in California, but adding concentrate is, and the trade in it is brisk. We think the use of these ingredients is problematic, and makes wine seem a manufactured product. Needless to say, wine labels do not state that tartaric acid or grape-juice concentrate has been added, and the new ingredient-labeling regulations do not require them to.

During all cellaring operations the wine must be kept cool, about 55° F. Since natural coolness is found underground, where it is free, the oldest California wineries have either real cellars or hillside caves (often dug by Chinese coolies in the last century); newer wineries have refrigerated surface buildings or tank farms.

When the wine is "ripe," or properly matured in bulk, it is promptly bottled, for further cask aging might ruin it. Red wine, especially, is usually filtered one more time before bottling. The bottling operation must be done carefully to avoid overaeration or infection by spoilage bacteria. Some wineries even fill from the bottom of a bottle in a blanket of inert gas. Some bottling lines, by the way, are located beneath the aging rooms so that gravity brings the wine to the bottle.

Before marketing the wine, many small wineries often put the unlabeled bottles of fine wine on their sides in bins for what may be a couple of years of aging. Bottle aging, whether done by the winery or the wine buyer, cannot be indefinite. Some wines must be drunk very quickly after bottling; others may not be ready for several years, and bottles should be periodically recorked. At some point any wine will die, maybe even turn into vinegar, as buffs who have paid hundreds of dollars for cobwebbed nineteenth-century chateau wines occasionally find out. Bulk wines, on the other hand, are usually of lesser quality and have been processed to such a degree that bottle aging could be injurious.

The final steps are labeling, boxing, and shipping—and drinking.

Making Champagne and Cocktail Wines

Although non-table wines may undergo some special treatment before fermentation, they generally acquire their distinctive character—become their "type"—in treatment after fermentation has begun.

For example, two sweet white dessert wines of extremely low status,* **Angelica** and **White Port,** are created after fermentation is stopped early by the addition of wine spirits (brandy); they then go through fining, hot and cold stabilization, refrigeration, and get another bit of sulfur dioxide before being bottled in pocket-size bottles with easily removable screw caps.

The common sweet red dessert wine **Port** or **Ruby Port** must gain as much heavy red coloring as possible before fermentation is halted with brandy, but can be artfully blended later; it goes through the usual finishing operations and is put on the market quickly. Another round of heating and cooling red Port can produce an "aged" **Tawny Port.**

---

*Interestingly, the prestigious Napa Valley champagnery, Domaine Chandon, produces Angelica, under the name Panache, an indication this unique California wine may be having a revival.

California **Sherry** is produced from a white base wine to which brandy has been added; the shermat, as the base blend is called, is then carefully oxidized to its distinctive color and nutty flavor by one of three processes: heating ("baking," but at low temperature), aging for a long time in air, or growing flor yeast on the surface aerobically (in air).

We're not going into much detail here because California's aperitif and dessert wines are not highly regarded and are declining in popularity. We will, however, explain how the principal sparkling wine, Champagne, is made, because California's bubbly has a good reputation even if the French think the name has been stolen.

Champagne begins as select white table wine, usually dry and most often a blend, in which a neutral or vinous-fruity quality is preferred over any varietal flavor. The best grapes for California Champagne are Chardonnay and Pinot Noir; the latter is a black grape but only the light-colored pulp and juice are fermented.

After the usual racking, clarification, stabilization, and fining, the *cuvée*, as the blend is called (most sparkling winemaking terms are French), is ready for a second fermentation in a closed container. The carbon dioxide, instead of escaping, thus stays in the wine.

In the classic *méthode champenoise*, more yeast, sugar, and perhaps yeast food are mixed with the base wine in a vat, then the mixture is put in the traditional thick bottles with dimpled bottom and the cork is wired to the neck. The secondary fermentation or *tirage* may take several weeks at cool cellar temperatures, but the bottles are usually left undisturbed for a year, if not three or four, while the yeast dies and settles and the Champagne develops flavor and bottle bouquet.

After aging comes the tedious, labor-intensive process of riddling (*remuage*) and disgorgement. The bottles, which had been on their sides, are placed upside down in special racks and given a quarter-twist daily until the yeasty sediment accumulates in the neck. Then the neck and contents are frozen in a brine solution, the cork is removed, and the sediment is forced out by the carbon dioxide pressure, which is four times that of the atmosphere (4 atmospheres, or 60 pounds per square inch of bottle area).

Before the bottle is reclosed, a *dosage* is added. Depending on how much sweetness is desired (the least, *natural,* has practically no sweetness but *doux* may be 10 percent sugar), the dosage contains syrup of cane sugar, aged white table wine, and perhaps 10 percent brandy, all to replace the lost amount of Champagne. The sugar in the dosage does not ferment because the levels of CO_2 and alcohol are too high for any yeast that might survive. The bottles are recorked and wired, stored briefly, then labeled and shipped. Champagne made this way is labeled "Fermented in This Bottle."

Two alternative methods are used. In the transfer process the bottled Champagne is transferred into a vat under counterpressure, mixed, filtered to remove the sediment, then rebottled. While this results in a uniform product (no bottle-to-bottle differences), the Champagne can suffer some oxidation in the process. Champagne made this way can be labeled "Fermented in the Bottle." In the bulk, or Charmat, process the Champagne undergoes its entire second fermentation in a large container before being put into individual bottles. Lacking bottle aging, such Champagne is only adequate but is certainly less expensive. It must be labeled as being made by the Charmat bulk process.

Wine can be artificially carbonated on the bottling line, but the result cannot be labeled Champagne; the bubbles last only as long as those in soda pop do, and such gassed wine has never been popular.

The Result: Infinite Variety

Thus wine is made. From dozens of grape varieties grown in places with varying growing conditions, different kinds of wine are produced. Even the person who has never drunk wine can conclude that grape growing and winemaking are subject to so many whims of nature and different decisions by winemakers that it is not surprising that a mind-boggling number of distinctive wines are made in California and around the world.

Particularly with table wines, the decisions made in the vineyard (what yield per acre to allow by pruning and when to begin picking are two of the most important) and in the winery (the kind of yeast, the temperature and duration of fermentation, the kind of fermentation and maturing containers, and the degree of blending are critical) are so numerous that the word *style* must be used to differentiate among bottlings of the same varietal even from the same area and same vintage. For example, some Zinfandels are purposely made "big"—very tannic, with concentrated varietal flavor, full body and alcohol content, deep color—so they can be aged for a long time. This winemaking style really aims at producing the chateau wines of California, wine for drinking in the next century. (California's ability to consistently produce wines that gain with decades of cellar age is so far unproved.) On the other hand, some Zinfandels are made light, fresh, fruity—ready to drink soon like the Beaujolais wines that are rushed from vineyard in September to market in November. There are many styles in between for Zinfandel, Cabernet Sauvignon, Chardonnay, and a few other varieties.

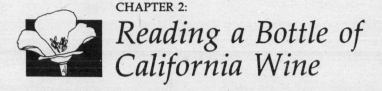

CHAPTER 2:

Reading a Bottle of California Wine

California wines represent one of the countertrends to increasing uniformity, standardization, monolithism, monopoly, and monotony in American life. The consumer walking into a liquor store will not find only two different-colored Gallo wines; on the contrary, he will find that today's marketplace displays a dazzling—yes, confusing—variety of wine. This makes wine an appealing beverage and fascinating subject of conversation, but it's easy to be intimidated.

Initially, the greatest confusion arises when you start reading the labels in an effort to find more than an everyday wine, perhaps to take to someone's house. Before you choose you had better be aware that wine-label language is an elaborate, officially sanctioned code: some words that seem to have simple definitions schoolkids would agree on actually have other meanings; some phrases have no meaning; language that appears to say something complex to the connoisseur actually may mean something very simple; some language merely wears theatrical costume (or disguise); some language you recognize as quite blunt—but you don't know what it means because you're not a wine expert. What isn't written in code may be absent altogether, and that includes vital facts about what's in the bottle.

This long chapter is an explanation of the meaning behind a lot of the legal, technical, and commercial mumbo jumbo on wine labels and in wine advertising, and is a guide to reading between the lines. This is not meant to intimidate you more. The knowledgeable consumer can't be intimidated.

California and federal law both appear to be strict (California more so) about what goes into a bottle and what is said on the labels and in ads (which must conform to the same regulations as labels). Ideally, the regulations should protect both the consumer and wine industry from being victims of the latter's marketing excesses and internal needs. There are a lot of regulations, though not as many as in Europe. French wine law is minutely detailed, if not rigorously enforced. In Germany each bottling of *Qualitätswein* (fine wine) must have a special *Prüfungsnumber*, or test-bottle number, on the label. The American wine law is tightening up. The most recent regulations, the first major revisions since 1936, were adopted by the Treasury Department's Bureau of Alcohol, Tobacco, and Firearms in 1978–79 and will all be mandatory by 1983. As too often has been the case, the industry and the regulators compromised in ways that are blatantly anticonsumer, and the regulations are being tested in court by the Massachusetts attorney general and by a group of Californians, who won the first round in federal district court in 1980.

Two Concannon labels separated by decades of time and regulations.

Nevertheless, the American buying his own country's wines is in many ways more apt to become informed by the careful reading of labels. French wine labels are so sparsely written that they don't even identify the color of the wine. The French wine drinker must learn that "Meursault-Perrières" identifies a flavorful dry white wine made from Chardonnay grapes grown in the 42-acre Perrières vineyard in the commune of Meursault in the Côte de Beaune district of Burgundy: under French law that *appellation contrôlée* (controlled name) can *only* go on a bottle containing exactly that wine and no other. Remembering past wine scandals, such as Bordeaux's "Winegate" in 1974, which brought down a famous shipper for mislabeling a wine from another district, the Frenchman has to trust the government to keep winegrowers in line. American wine labels are, by contrast, positively cluttered with information—but the consumer shouldn't think that the government is virtually guaranteeing an honest product.

After interpreting the information on the brand label, neck label, back label, bottle, and even the closure in accordance with some of the general principles described here, you should be able to answer two questions: Is this wine what the winery wants me to believe it is? Is this the wine I want at a reasonable price?

WHAT'S IN THE BOTTLE?

That French wine drinker, unless he was familiar with the varietally labeled wines of Alsace, would probably be confused after a few minutes of reading labels in a California wineshop. How, he might ask, is it possible that one winery can make a dozen different kinds of wine? What are all these grape names doing on the labels? And—*sacré bleu!*—what is this American wine labeled "Burgundy"?

On a California wine label, two names are usually in the largest type: the brand name, which is most often that of the winery, and the name of the wine itself, which is either a class name (such as Sherry) or a generic, varietal, or proprietary name.

Generic Wines

Generic names are mostly of some geographical significance and theoretically denote wine that is like that of the geographical area named. Generic names, their origins, and qualities of the American versions are:

• **Chablis.** French district in northern Burgundy that exclusively produces dry white wines. "Chablis" is the basic American white wine: rarely as dry, rarely as tart, as the French, tending to be light (not too alcoholic) and maybe fruity.

• **Moselle** and **Rhine.** The two German rivers along which most German wine, which is mostly white, is grown. American generics with these names are apt to be drier and more tart than "Chablis."

• **Sauterne.** Sauternes is the name of both a village and district in the Bordeaux region that specialize in sweet white wine. American Sauterne is less sweet and may even be dry—but may be more mellow than "Chablis," which is largely displacing it in supermarkets and liquor stores.

• **Burgundy.** French wine region that produces both red and white wines. The basic American red wine: dry (but not too dry) with a little "pucker," enough alcohol for excitement, and none of the subtlety of the genuine article.

• **Chianti.** An Italian wine region. American Chianti is usually red, usually sweeter, more alcoholic—bigger bodied—than "Burgundy."

• **Claret.** Not a geographical name but the traditional British term for red Bordeaux wine. Disappearing as a generic in the U.S.

• **Vino Rosso.** Another Italian term, less frequently used, signifying a robust sweetish red.

• **Rosé.** Universally used to denote pink table wine.

• **Champagne.** The French wine region of Champagne doesn't make much more than the only sparkling wine in France entitled to be called Champagne. The French have probably fought harder to protect this name than any other, but to no avail in the U.S. American law at least restricts the name to wine that is naturally sparkling from a secondary fermentation, not given a dose of carbon dioxide on the bottling line.

• **Port.** From Oporto, the Port-marketing town of Portugal. In the U.S., a heavy red dessert wine with extra alcohol.

• **Sherry.** From Jerez de la Frontera, town south of Seville, around which are the vineyards growing the grapes that make the distinctive Spanish wine. American Sherry is brown, dry (aperitif) or sweet (dessert), and more alcoholic than table wine.

The use of generic names is controversial. The U.S., Australia, and Russia are the only major winegrowing countries that haven't signed a treaty with France banning the use of "Champagne," "Burgundy," etc., for native wines or agreed with Italy, Spain, and Portugal to recognize the uniqueness of their national products. While other countries bend the law (Canada makes "Champers," Spain has a "Xampan," England "Baby Cham"—the last a low-alcohol apple and pear wine!), the U.S. wine industry unabashedly relies on generic names to sell the overwhelming majority of wine (jugs are apt to have these names on them), and in turn many American wine drinkers keep asking for "Chablis" when they are only thinking of white wine for everyday use.

The wine industry argues that it was French, German, Italian, and other immigrants who started winemaking in the U.S. and brought their place-names with them. While admitting that "White Table Wine" could probably be successfully substituted for "Chablis," the industry wonders what substitutes there are for "Sherry" and "Port." France's Moët and Chandon refuses to call its new Napa Valley sparkling wine "Champagne." "Chandon Napa Valley Brut" and "Chandon Napa Valley Blanc de Noirs" are the two full names. (But the winery nevertheless takes advantage of inevitable associations in its advertisements aimed at visitors: "Entire *méthode champenoise* shown . . . Champagne museum . . . ")

The only legal concessions the U.S. has made to affronted Europeans are, first, preventing "Bordeaux," "Médoc," "Beaujolais," "Liebfraumilch," and other names from assuming generic status too, and, second, requiring wines with any permitted generic name of geographical origin to show the true origin. "Ohio Chablis" and "California Sherry," for example, may keep the French and Spanish from being misled but not, however, from laughing.

All this ignores the big problem with "Burgundy" and such: you don't know what's in the bottle. U.S. law doesn't require Burgundy made in Fresno to taste anything like the red wine made in any of the five districts in Bourgogne. The Wine Institute, a trade organization in San Francisco with 324 winery members, can only suggest certain recipes: in Burgundy, Carignane grapes for the color, Zinfandel for the fruit, Petite Sirah for the acid and tannin. If that mixture tasted anything like genuine red Burgundy, which is made nearly exclusively from Pinot Noir grapes, it would be a surprise.

California recipes vary in any event. Sebastiani (Sonoma Valley) happens to use the Wine Institute recipe for Burgundy. J. Lohr (Santa Clara Valley) has blended Zinfandel (43 percent), Pinot Noir (22),

Gamay (20), and Cabernet Sauvignon (16). In the Napa Valley, Beaulieu has used Gamay and Mondeuse, while Franciscan has made it with Charbono and Petite Sirah. The Central Valley's Del Rey has put Grenache and Carignane together.

For readers who care more about what "Chablis" might be, the French version contains Chardonnay grapes exclusively, but the American versions are more likely blends of French Colombard and Chenin Blanc with several percent of such varieties as Sauvignon Vert, White Riesling, Semillon, Golden Chasselas, Emerald Riesling, Sylvaner, and—surprise!—Chardonnay.

Because of the varying recipes, critics don't compare generics but judge each on its own merits. Most criticize the use of the names as meaningless. English wine expert Hugh Johnson says that some big wineries admit bottling "Chablis" and "Rhine Wine" from the same million-gallon tank. American critic Bob Thompson wants consumers to demand Stony Ridge's "Our Daily Red" and other honestly named blends if they want *vin ordinaire*. We agree.

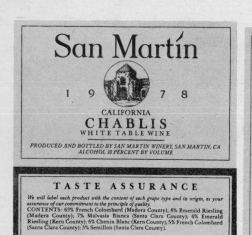

San Martín

1 9 7 8

CALIFORNIA
CHABLIS
WHITE TABLE WINE

PRODUCED AND BOTTLED BY SAN MARTIN WINERY, SAN MARTIN, CA
ALCOHOL 10 PERCENT BY VOLUME

TASTE ASSURANCE

We will label each product with the content of each grape type and its origin, as your assurance of our commitment to the principle of quality.
CONTENTS: 63% French Colombard (Madera County); 8% Emerald Riesling (Madera County); 7% Malvasia Bianca (Santa Clara County); 6% Emerald Riesling (Kern County); 6% Chenin Blanc (Kern County); 5% French Colombard (Santa Clara County); 5% Semillon (Santa Clara County).

The San Martin
COMMITMENT

Specific kinds of grapes grow best in different places because of climate, soil composition, and moisture. The French, for instance, have known for two centuries that Cabernet Sauvignon is the master grape of Bordeaux, that Pinot Noir flourishes in Burgundy, that Chenin Blanc thrives in the Loire Valley.

Our varietal grapes are all from specific regions in California. We feel that they make worthy wines because their tastes represent the character of their geography; a meeting of the correct grape with its most positive place for natural growth.

It will be our policy to label each bottle with:
—the varietal grapes in each wine.
—the percentage of varietal grape in each wine.
—the geographic origin of each varietal grape.

We believe that fine wines require grapes of specific origin. Our commitment to quality is based on this principle.

Proprietary Wines

Sensitive wineries have ceased using generic names, substituting proprietary names for basic wines and applying them to distinctive blends and specialties as well. It's amusing to categorize these names:

• **Plain-Jane names:** Robert Mondavi's Red Table Wine, Louis M. Martini's Mountain Red Wine (subtitled, however, Light Burgundy).

• **Playing-it-safe generic names:** Gallo's Hearty Burgundy, Chablis Blanc, and Rhine Garten; Paul Masson's Rhine Castle.

• **Noms étrangers:** Emilio Guglielmo's Blanc Sec ("white dry"), Cribari's Vino Bianco da Pranzo ("mello [sic] white table wine").

• **Noms étrangers, et uniques et exotiques aussi:** Charles Krug/ CK Mondavi's Fortissimo (like a southern Italian mellow red) and Bravissimo (like Sicilian Moscato di Siracusa mellow white), Beringer's Bärenblut ("bear's blood," blend of Pinot Noir and Grignolino) and Traubengold ("gold of the grape," blend including White Riesling).

• **Descriptive names:** Masson's Emerald Dry (from Emerald Riesling, a hybrid), Jacaré/United Vintners' Crystal Blanc (white wine in a frosted bottle).

• **Evocative names:** J. Lohr's Jade (blend of White Riesling, Sylvaner, and Gewürztraminer), Edmeades' Opal (white Pinot Noir) and Queen Anne's Lace (a white blend), Hop Kiln's One Thousand Flowers (white blend), Masson's Rubion and Baroque (both red, the latter a richer wine), and various makers' Oeil de Perdrix ("eye of the partridge," for white wine made from Pinot Noir or Zinfandel).

• **Brand-name adaptations:** Concannon's Chateau Concannon (Light Sémillon), Beaulieu Vineyards' Beau Tour, Beau Velours, Beaumont, Beaufort, Beauclair, etc., followed by a varietal name, and Beau Rosé.

• **Geographical names:** Monterey Vineyards' Del Mar Ranch (dry white wine), Christian Brothers' Chateau LaSalle (Muscat Canelli), Dry Creek's Idlewood White Wine.

• **Funny names:** Llords and Elwood's Dry Wit Sherry and Ancient Proverb Port, Windsor Vineyards' Adequate Red, Adequate White, and Adequate Pink, Edmeades' Whale Wine (a Muscat from near the Mendocino coast).

• **Unintentionally funny names:** Wine and the People's Berkeley Red.

• **Obnoxious names:**   Sonoma Vineyards' The Red Table Wine, etc.

Again, there is no law compelling wineries to say anything about what is behind the name, though many labels do explain things. Proprietary-named wines are even less comparable than generics, but add usefully to the wonderful chaos of choice.

Varietal Wines

It should be evident that, in seeking a fine wine to take to someone's house, neither a generic nor proprietary-named wine will necessarily impress anyone with your good taste. On that occasion, you should get a varietal wine; that is, one named for the only or the principal grape variety used, such as Cabernet Sauvignon and White Riesling. The variety used is a basic indicator of quality, though it must be linked to the region where it is grown (appellation of origin), for not all varieties do as well at every location that can grow grapes. We'll link the two in "Where Does the Wine Come From?," p. 45.

The interested wine drinker shouldn't feel intimidated by varietal labeling. There aren't that many names to master, and a little conscientious tasting of good varietals will give definition to the names.

First, then, which are the good varietals? They are the ones that are most successful where they are grown, which is in California, not Europe. Two of Europe's "noble" varieties do extremely well in California: **Cabernet Sauvignon** (red) and **Chardonnay** (white; Hugh Johnson thinks this is "the wine grape" for the state). To these may be added California's unique grape, **Zinfandel** (red), **Sauvignon Blanc/ Fumé Blanc** (white), and **Grenache** (only for rosé wine, not red). In a second tier one may put the other two noble varieties, **Pinot Noir** (red) and **White Riesling,** along with two that are coming on strong, **Gewürztraminer** (white) and **Merlot** (red). **Chenin Blanc** (white) and **Petite Sirah** (red) may or may not belong in the top 10. Some will say that Pinot Noir is misplaced here because it just can't meet the standard of French Burgundy and that White Riesling is still only an echo of the best German Riesling; but both can produce extremely satisfying wine in the right area.

There are more varietals than these. To indicate how far you should try to stretch your memory at first, here are red and white *vinifera* varietals in order of frequency of production at all American wineries, as listed by *Wines and Vines* in 1979:

Red, Rosé, and "Blanc de——" Varietals	White Varietals
Cabernet Sauvignon (221)	Chardonnay (194)
Zinfandel (173)	White Riesling (145)
Pinot Noir (149)	Chenin Blanc (103)
Petite Sirah (69)	Sauvignon Blanc/Fumé Blanc (94)
Gamay Beaujolais (50)	Gewürztraminer (86)
Merlot (49)	French Colombard (43)
Barbera (35)	Sémillon (21)
Napa Gamay (34)	Pinot Blanc (20)
Ruby Cabernet (30)	Gray Riesling (19)
Grenache (29)	Muscat (Moscato) Canelli (18)
Carignane (12)	Green Hungarian (13)

For the record, red varietals produced in 1978 and 1979 by fewer than a dozen wineries (but often by large ones) are Charbono, Pinot Gris, Pinot St. George, Mission, Grignolino, Carnelian, Early Burgundy, Souzao, Pinot Meunier, and Cabernet Franc; produced by only one winery are Alicante-Bouschet, Aleatico, Dido Noir, Malbec, Mission del Sol, Nebbiolo, and Royalty.

White varietals produced that year by fewer than a dozen wineries are Muscat of Alexandria, Sylvaner, Malvasia Bianca, Emerald Riesling, Light (Dry) Muscat, Golden Chasselas, Aligote, Flora, Gold, Muscat Ottonel, Sauvignon Vert, Traminer; produced by only one winery are Burger, Early Muscat, Folle Blanche, Italian Riesling, Kleinburger, Moscato d'Or, Muller-Thurgau, Muscadelle de Bordelais, Pedro Jimenez, Rkatsiteli, St. Émilion, Saperavi, Sereksia, Thompson Seedless, and Vertdoux Blanc.

Chapter 3, "Tasting California Wine," describes the sensory characteristics of 31 *vinifera* varietals.

This listing ignores the native American (*labrusca*) grape varieties; the most popular are Concord, produced by 47 wineries, and Catawba (42). Similarly left off are the French-American hybrids; most popular are Seyval Blanc (48), De Chaunac (36), Baco Noir (34), and Aurora (34).

With the exception of one or two areas, the eastern climate is too cold for *vinifera* grapes such as Cabernet and Chardonnay; nearly all the *vinifera* wine bottled by eastern wineries is produced in California and shipped back East in bulk or as wine concentrate. By contrast, none of the wine made back East from *labrusca* and French-American hybrids finds its way to California for bottling.

Alternate Varietal Names

The general origin of *vinifera* varieties grown in California is Europe, but the genealogy is occasionally confused, clones and variants are many, and the science of grape identification is difficult. One result is that the same grape may have two or more names. Chardonnay is called Pinot Chardonnay, even though it is not in the Pinot family, as well as Weisser Klevner, Beaunois, Melon Blanc, Pinot Blanc, and White Pinot. White Riesling is also named Johannisberg Riesling, in honor of the German estate that excels in producing it. Some wines labeled simply "Riesling" are actually made from the Sylvaner grape, whose other name is Franken Riesling.

Two grapes became incorrectly identified and took on American names in the last century: Gray Riesling, which is not a Riesling but may be France's Chauché Gris, and Petite Sirah, which is not the Rhone's Syrah but may be that region's Durif. Zinfandel is likewise of uncertain origin but is apparently the same as Italy's Primitivo di Gioia.

Some names have been transferred, adopted, or changed in more recent times. Robert Mondavi renamed his wine made from Sauvignon Blanc grapes "Fumé Blanc" ("white smoke") after the Loire Valley's Pouilly-Fumé wine. Other California wineries adopted his name or reversed it to Blanc Fumé.

The most dizzying confusion has been about which grape makes the famous French Beaujolais wine. In the last century Paul Masson took what he thought was the Beaujolais area's Gamay Beaujolais grape and made Gamay Beaujolais wine. Meanwhile, Napa and Sonoma vineyard owners started planting what they thought was a different Gamay grape, which became known as Napa Gamay; that wine didn't sell for as much as Masson's Gamay Beaujolais. Only a few years ago a Davis viticulture professor and plant geneticist, Harold P. Olmo, discovered that the principal grape of the Beaujolais district is Gamay Noir, that the "Gamay Beaujolais" grape Masson and many others planted in California is really one of the couple of hundred clones or variants of Pinot Noir, and that the "Napa Gamay" is actually the Gamay Noir. Theoretically, the "Gamay Beaujolais" wines should probably be renamed "Pinot Noir," but the main outcome of Olmo's findings has been that some makers of "Napa Gamay" renamed their product—not "Gamay Noir" but "Gamay Beaujolais"! Good luck in determining which one you just bought.

The same Dr. Olmo should be mentioned here as the Luther Burbank of the grape for having developed several highly successful new varieties: Ruby Cabernet (a cross of Cabernet Sauvignon and Carignane), Emerald Riesling (White Riesling x Muscadelle), Flora (Gewürztraminer x Sémillon), Carnelian (Cabernet x Grenache x Carignane), Centurion, Royalty, and Rubired. These hybrids were bred for specific characteristics, such as high acidity, high color, and productiveness, which enable them to be grown successfully in hotter parts of California. Ruby Cabernet (planted on more than 18,000 acres) and Emerald Riesling (almost 3,000 acres) have produced the most drinkable varietals.

The duplication of varietal names is mostly due to the ease with which the *vinifera* grape species multiplied around the world. (Dr. Olmo tracked down the original, or basic, *vinifera* vine to vineyards near the border of Iran and Afghanistan.) It is unfortunate that there is potential for confusing the consumer. "Riesling" sounds as if it could be the same as "White Riesling," since both are equally white, but the first is a generic that should be priced at least 20 percent lower than the second, which is a more noble varietal. And "Gamay Beaujolais"—we throw up our hands at that one.

The other problem is that consumers might come to think that any varietal is better than any generic or proprietary-named wine. Many critics protest the bottling of Carignane, French Colombard, and Green Hungarian because those lack the distinctive flavors of the better varieties. Varietal naming perhaps reached the pinnacle of foolishness with Central Valley Vineyards' marketing, at $3 a bottle, of vintage-dated 1978 Thompson Seedless, the ultimate no-flavored varietal. (Santa Clara Valley's Thomas Kruse bottled Thompson, too—for $4 a bottle under the name Chutzpah!) But we hasten to say that the honest use of varietal names is far preferable to the use of geographical generic ones which are plain misleading.

California pioneered the use of varietal names for wines. Wine authority Leon D. Adams believes that use of the names helped differentiate the prices of high-quality grapes from any-quality grapes, thus encouraging vineyard owners to switch from such varieties as the Mission grape and Alicante-Bouschet (a popular Prohibition-era grape that was thick-skinned enough for easy shipment from California to the East, and red-skinned enough to produce two batches of rotgut red from the same skins) to the more profitable Cabernet and other premium grapes. Varietal names more than anything else have helped the California wine industry recover from Prohibition, mature quickly, and develop its potential for producing the finest wines.

Varietal Labeling Regulations

The federal government only dimly recognized the importance of varietal names in the 1930s when it approved their use—but established the minimum quantity that must be used at only 51 percent. That may have been adequate when only a handful of first-class California wineries were turning out premium wines. But in the boom during the late 1960s and early 1970s it became obvious that some rascally new wineries wouldn't think twice about using 51 percent Chardonnay and 49 percent Thompson Seedless, the former selling for five times the latter at harvest time. Worse, because of a loophole in the regulations, place-named varietals (for example, "Napa Valley Cabernet Sauvignon") could contain as little as 26 percent varietal wine from that place, the remaining 74 percent consisting of 25 percent Cabernet from a less-expensive region and 49 percent some plain red wine from anywhere.

To discourage hucksters and close the loophole, the Bureau of Alcohol, Tobacco, and Firearms in August 1978 increased the minimum percentage from 51 to 75 percent—or 85 percent if the label also carries the name of a designated "viticultural area" (see p. 49). The exception to the rule is varietals made from native American *labrusca* grapes, like the Concord, which are regarded as too powerful to be drinkable at 75 percent. The BATF will also allow the names of two or three varieties (for example, "Cabernet Sauvignon-Merlot") if the percentages are listed and add up to 100. Finally, a varietal name can be used only with an appellation of origin (see p. 48) in the same size type. Unhappily for consumers, the BATF decided that wineries needed more than four years to implement the new regulation, which won't be mandatory until 1983.

Raising the floor level has caused controversy. The BATF said it was increasing the level because 51 percent was too low for most varieties and permitted so much blending that the finished product often bore little or no resemblance to the grape variety used to designate the wine.

If that is the case, why didn't the BATF set the minimum at 100 percent or establish minimums for individual varieties? Under pressure from the industry, the bureau used a one-sided rationale: Because 100 percent of *some* varieties, even if grown under the best soil and climate conditions, does not make a palatable wine, blending is practically required.

This liberal view is very much based on the defensible idea that the winegrower knows best. French wine law, for example, has largely endorsed traditional practices: the growing of these grapes exactly in this place, the use of these particular grapes in blending a wine entitled to that appellation, and so forth. As a result, chateaux in Bordeaux use different percentages in blending distinctive red Bordeaux wine. One fine Médoc wine is 65 percent Cabernet Sauvignon, yet, nearby, Chateau Latour uses 90 percent Cabernet and Chateau Mouton-Rothschild even more, the greatest amount in the district. Enologists at the University of California at Davis say that Cabernet can retain its character if blended with 25 percent or even 35 percent of another wine, such as Merlot (another Bordeaux variety), which is usually added to soften the Cabernet and make it drinkable younger.

That is the argument for Cabernet. But Cabernet is very strongly flavored and highly tannic. Pinot Noir and Chardonnay (the two grapes used in red and white Burgundies) are more delicately flavored, and many connoisseurs protest any blending whatsoever if the wine is to have those varietal names—and be sold for high prices.

With all the subtlety of a cheap Muscatel, the BATF simply hiked the minimum from 51 to 75 percent.

Unfortunately, the wine industry's opposition to the 75-percent minimum wasn't entirely based on how fine the winemakers' taste buds are. In big corporations, the account books, marketing strategy, and stock value are influential factors in determining what kind of wine is made. The chairman of United Vintners (mostly owned by Heublein) argued during the BATF hearings that it would cost a quarter of a million dollars to raise the varietal percentage in just Italian Swiss Colony Cabernet Sauvignon and the Pinot Noir. (The Cabernet at the time was made with 60 percent Cabernet Sauvignon, 33 percent Ruby Cabernet, and 7 percent Petite Sirah.) Another blatantly commercial argument was that there wasn't enough of some varieties planted in premium grape-growing areas to produce higher-percentage wines without driving up the price of finished wine. A third, disingenuous argument was along the lines of "when I kiss my wife, I'm not interested in what the lipstick is made of, I'm interested in the kiss."

What Else Is Blended?

But assume for a moment that the BATF's 75-percent minimum is valid. The question then arises, What is the other 25 percent? Could it be a cheap, ordinary wine—a filler or stretcher wine—whose merit is not quality but quantity—made from a widely grown, high-producing, low-priced variety? Could it be that the winemaker has even used neutral white Thompson Seedless to blend his *red* varietal wine? Perhaps, because undisclosed blending is now, and even after 1983 will be, permitted by law. You won't actually know whether a varietal is 75 percent, 100 percent, or something in between, or what the blending wine is unless the winery decides to tell you.

The BATF wanted to require that the actual percentage be printed in the same size type, but the industry lined up its tame critics to argue that this would mislead consumers into thinking a higher percentage automatically meant a better wine. The BATF dropped that idea. And any suggestion of forcing wineries to disclose the blending wine was shot down by the industry's protest that it would require the registration of too many different labels in most of the 50 states.

The unstated argument against percentage labeling and disclosure of blending wines is that some varietal names have such great market appeal that any mention of the names of minor varieties (French Colombard, Carignane) or non-wine-grape varieties (Thompson Seedless) would lead to lower price tags and even customer resistance.

So What?

But assume for a moment that full disclosure becomes mandatory. The question then becomes, So what? Does it matter whether a wine is 100 percent or no percent as long as it tastes good?

Yes, it does matter. It matters in the same way a superb Picasso could be a forgery or that a new Oldsmobile could be powered by a Chevy engine. If a winery is proud of its products, it shouldn't hesitate to say what's in them. If Thompson Seedless added to Chardonnay actually makes a good wine, the winery shouldn't be afraid to say so; the taste of the wine will confirm his good judgment. If the winemaker believes a 75 percent varietal would be unpalatable, let him blend it, call it "Cabernet-Petite Sirah" (as Italian Swiss Colony's recipe might be named), and list the percentages on the label. If he's unwilling to disclose the contents, let him bottle the blend as "Red Table Wine."

The BATF could overcome industry resistance to voluntary disclosure simply by applying *in vino veritas* (truth-in-wine!) regulations to all wines, including foreign ones whose identities are really known only to buffs. Such regulations may be difficult to enforce—but, then, don't we have to trust regulations to prevent someone from packaging sliced-up Mignon Eberhart mystery novels as "Filet Mignon"?

Until disclosure is required, the 1983 regulations basically mean that the government insists that some varietals taste like the grapes they are named for—perhaps.

Mercifully, a very large number of small wineries not only believe in the desirability of many 100-percent varietals but also, in the case of blends, disclose the percentages and speak in their defense. Beaulieu and others sometimes give rounded-off percentages; San Martín and many "miniaturists" with loyal followings make it a policy to list exact percentages. Write on!

WHERE DOES THE WINE COME FROM?

An expert at a blind tasting may sample a dozen wines made of 100 percent of the same grape variety, and of the dozen he may say that every one of them tastes different. That may be the case no matter how the wine is labeled, and one is entitled to wonder what all the fuss about California varietals is about, especially if one is familiar with European wines that rarely carry a varietal name.

The taste depends on where the wine comes from. As Hugh Johnson, in mapping his *World Atlas of Wine*, says, "It is the exact spot of earth which is the governing factor." Europeans have had two millennia to determine which grapes to plant in which spots to produce the best wine—so the place-names "Nuits-Saint-Georges" or "Chateau Margaux" say it all.

The California wine industry, still youthful, is still finding out which spots are best for which grapes. It is conceivable that someday there may be a wine labeled simply "Rutherford," assuming that everyone knows that that central Napa Valley area is best for growing only Cabernet Sauvignon, which is nearly true. (Indeed, in 1980 Beaulieu's radio ads started talking about " . . . Napa Valley Cabernet, which we prefer to call Rutherford Cabernet. . . .")

Until that time, it is critical that both place-name and varietal name appear on the label, because Napa Valley Cabernet and San Joaquin Valley Cabernet (if there were one) would not, in the final determination, both be worth $7 a bottle.

The principle is: Not every winegrowing area can or should make the same wines.

Five Winegrowing Regions

Wine regions in California have been broadly delineated by the University of California at Davis on the basis of "degree-days," a measure of the total of mean daily temperatures above the lowest vine-growing temperature (50° F.) during the April 1–October 31 growing season. As described by professors V. S. Singleton and M. A. Amerine (co-developer of the system with A. J. Winkler):

• **Region I,** which is 2,500 degree-days or less, takes in the coolest sections of the Napa, Sonoma, Salinas, and Santa Maria river valleys (the lower, ocean- or bay-affected areas) and the Santa Cruz Mountains. These sections have a climate resembling the Rhine, Moselle, and Champagne districts. Varieties that do their best in Region I climate: Cabernet Sauvignon, Chenin Blanc, Napa Gamay, Gamay Beaujolais, Gewürztraminer, Pinot Blanc, Pinot Noir, White Riesling, and Zinfandel.

• **Region II,** still cool (2,501-3,000 degree-days), describes the central Napa Valley as well as the Sonoma Valley, Santa Clara Valley, and central Salinas Valley. These areas are similar to Bordeaux and the Piedmont in Italy in grape-growing capability. Varieties that do well in Region II: Cabernet Sauvignon, Chardonnay, Napa Gamay, Gamay Beaujolais, Grenache, Petite Sirah, Sauvignon Blanc, Sémillon, and White Riesling.

• **Region III,** which is moderately cool (3,001-3,500 degree-days), takes in the northern Napa Valley, some parts of the Salinas Valley, and the Livermore and Temecula areas, all similar to the Tuscany (Chianti) wine region. Good wine grapes for Region III: Barbera, French Colombard, Ruby Cabernet, Sauvignon Blanc, Sémillon.

• **Region IV,** characterized as warm (3,501-4,000 degree-days), describes Mendocino's Ukiah Valley, the relatively cool Davis and Lodi areas of the Central Valley, and Cucamonga; the climate resembles that of Greece and central Spain. Varieties that produce the best Region IV wine: Barbera, French Colombard, and Ruby Cabernet.

• **Region V,** the warmest grape-growing area (4,001 or more degree-days), takes in the rest of the Central Valley, which has a climate like Algeria and southern Spain. The hot Valley is superb for raisin and table grapes and—well, there's more to be said below on this point.

The cooler (that is, coastal) areas are better for white varieties and slow-ripening red varieties, while the warmer areas are in general good for reds only. The hotter the area, the less acidic (that is, flatter), the sweeter and more alcoholic, the less aromatic and less varietally flavored, and sometimes, the less colored the wine that can be produced.

The Central Valley should restrict itself to growing the grapes it is best suited for. These include table, raisin, and wine varieties that go into aperitif and dessert wines, whose merits are usually sweetness and alcohol content, not the subtle flavor and acidity (tartness) that characterize varietal table wines. Though temperature-controlled fermentation has made hot-area white wines more palatable (most of California's Chenin Blanc, Emerald Riesling, and Sémillon is grown in the Central Valley), the Valley grows and crushes sizable amounts of premium varieties that are not suited to hot regions: Cabernet Sauvignon (18.4 percent of the state crush in 1979), White Riesling (7 percent), Pinot Blanc (6.3 percent), and Chardonnay (3.4 percent). Though these varieties don't fetch much money for Valley vineyard owners, they were grown and used in some way—for their name value, we guess. To be fair to the wine industry, we should also observe that those Valley wineries that market varietal wines—like Gallo—are heavy buyers of coastal grapes. Unfortunately, statistics imply that grapes of lesser quality are used as well in those varietals.

That is the broad delineation system for matching wine quality and winegrowing area. But there are subregions (or districts), and subdistricts (or microclimates) with slightly different temperature conditions or different soil, rainfall, fog, humidity, wind, exposure, elevation, and other conditions that also determine the character of the grapes that go into the fermentation vats. These are the most exact spots that the wine drinker should be interested in.

Thus, in common with European wines, the best California wines tend to have the most specific place-names on their labels, to the point in the mid-1970s that vineyard names began coming into common and, it is to be hoped, meaningful use.

There was some anarchy in the regional appellation system until 1978 when the Bureau of Alcohol, Tobacco, and Firearms established geographical labeling requirements (effective in 1983). Indeed, the last round of wine-law revisions came about during an attempt to define the California "North Coast," a designation deemed worthy of a higher price for table wines.

A Rough Appellation System

While the BATF declined to establish a rigid hierarchy of appellations, the place-name regulations do comprise a system that will eventually bear comparison to the French Appellation d'Origine Contrôlée (AOC) system.

Beginning with the grossest area and moving to the smaller, progressively more marketable areas:

"American," formerly "domestic," can go on wines 75 percent of whose grapes are grown in the U.S. and fully finished in this country. In this case, however, "finished" excludes such cellar processes as filtering, fining, pasteurizing, and refrigeration (as long as these don't change the composition of the wine) and blending (as long as it doesn't change the class or type of the wine). In other words, it's possible that an "American" wine could be 25 percent foreign wine, brought over in tankers.

The names of **two or three states** that are contiguous can be used on wines completely grown in those states (percentages must be listed) and finished in one of them, though "finished" has the same definition as above. This provision is mostly for the benefit of winegrowers in the Northwest, around Lake Erie, and elsewhere outside California.

The name of a **state** can be put on the label as place of origin if 75 percent of the grapes were grown there and the wine completely finished (for real, this time) in that state or an adjacent state. However, because relevant state laws must also be followed, "California" can go only on wine completely produced within California. The BATF relaxed its former 100 percent rule for state appellations because, it said, modern transportation and the advent of field crushing of grapes meant that wine grown, crushed, and fermented in one state doesn't change essential character by being bottled in a state close by. There is room for argument on this point. Many fine wines are not good travelers, which is one reason many aficionados dislike comparisons between California and French wines.

The names of **two or three counties** in the same state can be used on wines if all the grapes were grown in those counties; percentages must be listed. The wine presumably can be finished anywhere in the same state. This rule benefits California wineries that often blend wine from adjoining counties. Mendocino-Lake, Sonoma-Napa, Santa Clara-Monterey, and San Luis Obispo-Santa Barbara are likely label pairs.

The name of a **region** or multicounty area within a state was not directly addressed by the BATF. "California North Coast" or "North Coast Counties" and such may gain definition simply as large viticultural areas. This particular name is quite valuable on a label but it has never been defined. While the authors and many others believe the term should refer only to those counties on or near the coast north of San Francisco (Napa, Sonoma, Mendocino, Lake), the trade and the government have allowed the term to be used for any wine deriving from the entire coastal area north of Santa Barbara and San Luis Obispo—which defines three-quarters of the coast as "north." One of the first large viticultural area appellations requested was for Napa, Sonoma, Mendocino, and Lake counties plus Marin and Solano, but the BATF turned it down because the petitioners didn't say what was magic about these six counties. A second petition, from another group, asked for Napa, Sonoma, and Mendocino only to be designated North Coast, and the BATF is looking at it. Despite lack of legal definition of the term, Souverain rushed the official-sounding "Appellation North Coast" onto its 1978 vintage wines. Other regions that may also need definition: Central Coast (which should be Santa Clara south to Santa Barbara), Lodi Area, Sierra Foothills, San Joaquin Valley.

The name of a **county** (full name, including "County," in the same size type as the wine name) can be used if 75 percent of the grapes were grown in that county and the wine fully finished within the state. The BATF wanted to make sure that "Sonoma," for example, was not construed by the unwary buyer to mean "Sonoma Valley." Buyers of California wine will, from 1983 on, find the names of California counties more common on wine labels as winemakers endeavor to put the most specific place-names on their wine.

The name of a **viticultural** area, like "Napa Valley," may be the appellation of origin only if 85 percent of the grapes were grown in that area and the wine fully finished within the state. This represents a significant improvement in wine-labeling requirements because the BATF, for the first time, will be establishing the boundaries and names of these viticultural areas, upon nomination by interested parties. Presently used viticultural-area names include the Napa Valley; Dry Creek and Alexander Valley in Sonoma County; Livermore Valley in Alameda County; Shenandoah Valley in Amador County in the Sierra foothills; Lodi in San Joaquin County; Hecker Pass in Santa Clara County. These will be defined, based on evidence of distinguishing geographical features such as climate, soil, and elevation. The BATF announced that no vineyards would be grandfathered into a designated viticultural area just because they are presently regarded as being in that area.

The old rules for these valuable viticultural area names had, first, established only a 75-percent minimum (95 percent for vintage-dated wine) and, second, relied upon the general requirement that all label statements be truthful and not misleading. (The bureau reviews all labels before bottles are released.) The higher percentage and more restrictive map lines are necessary, said the bureau, to hold wine from prestigious areas to a higher standard and to protect smaller winegrowing areas. The rule changes also close the loophole that allows, until 1983, a wine containing as little as 26 percent of a varietal wine from a particular area to carry the name of that area on the label. However, in dropping the 95-percent geographical requirement for vintage-dated wine, the bureau actually lowered the standard, thus allowing the undisclosed blending of cheaper wine from a less prestigious area into what should be wines that wear their good character around their necks.

The result of this proposed designation of viticultural areas will be that winegrowers, to protect the marketability of their place-names, will nominate the smallest possible areas for the most attractive place-names. The 100 growers who sponsored the first petition, for designating the Napa Valley, drew the line around the 23,500 acres of vineyards in the Napa River watershed—leaving out 1,000 acres of mountain vineyards whose owners thought they were in the valley. The next petitions asked for designations for Sonoma Valley, Santa Cruz Mountains (all the area above 400 feet), the Pinnacles (Monterey County), Santa Maria Valley (Santa Barbara County), and, as an example of a viticultural area inside a larger one, Los Carneros, the cool, foggy area between the town of Napa and the shore of San Francisco Bay. (Outside California, Augusta, Mo., and Umpqua Valley, Oreg., also put in for designation.) If the BATF approves Los Carneros, which may be the chosen spot for the most sensitive of European varieties, wineries in other small areas, such as the Cabernet-rich Rutherford area or the Mayacmas Mountains on the western edge of the valley, may petition for designation on the grounds that the grapes grown are considerably more distinctive than "Napa Valley" grapes. Look for labels on higher-priced wines to become more specific.

Producer or brand **names of geographical significance**—"Sonoma Vineyards," "The Monterey Vineyard," "Dry Creek Vineyard," and a dozen others—posed a problem for the wine regulators, who were justifiably concerned that consumers might automatically believe the wine was grown in that area by that winery.

Initially, the bureau wanted all such names, including any with "vineyards" in them, to be qualified with a "TM" (trademark) or "R" (registered) symbol or the word "brand." The new rule, effective in 1983, is that these names can't be used unless the bottling winery is in that area and the wine meets the appellation of origin requirements. If the wine doesn't originate there, the brand name must have the word *brand* after it in the same size type and the label must carry the actual appellation of origin: "Napa Vineyards Brand San Joaquin Valley Pinot Noir," to take a fictitious example. Furthermore, the bureau may require a specific geographical disclaimer to be prominently displayed.

This regulation will, we think, protect the integrity of viticultural area names. The wine industry says it will be a hardship for wineries (such as Dry Creek Vineyard) that long ago located in—indeed, pioneered—small winegrowing areas that might be officially designated, discouraging them from producing wines of a larger or different appellation. And it could lead to a few bizarre labels if some wineries continue current blending practices. For example, Sonoma County's Geyser Peak Winery bottled a 1977 Cabernet Rosé from grapes grown next door in Lake County and far to the south in Santa Barbara. This is obviously the sort of wine that should be labeled simply "California."

"Estate Bottled" will, under the new rules, have a certain definition for the first time. Historically, "Estate Bottled" was simply the English version of "Mis en Bouteilles au Chateau," which tickles snobs silly. Some winemakers were stretching the term beyond reason, and the

BATF at first proposed an outright ban. The wine industry hurled grapes of wrath, however, because the prestigious term has great marketability for fine wines.

Beginning in 1983, "Estate Bottled" can be used only on wine carrying an approved viticultural area appellation, only if the bottling winery (including a cooperative winery) is located in that area, and only if it grew all of the grapes on land it (or a co-op's members) owned or controlled, with the legal right to perform all viticultural operations, within that viticultural area. The practical effect of this new definition will be that some wineries will try to strictly formalize their traditional control over an outside vineyard and the owner's viticultural practices. Winemakers who ferment in one place and bottle in another will apparently be prevented from using the term. "Estate Bottled" will tend to be on wines from the most specific areas. In connection with this, look for more back-label information describing the location and attributes of vineyard/winery.

The name of the **vineyard** where the grapes were grown, which would be equivalent to the name of a chateau in Bordeaux, a domaine in Burgundy, or an estate on the Rhine, would be the most specific appellation of origin possible. The BATF proposed demarcating vineyards and establishing a 95-percent minimum, but abandoned the effort.

Following the lead of Heitz Cellars' 1966 Napa Valley "Martha's Vineyard" Cabernet Sauvignon (Martha being the name of the wife of the vineyard's owner), a number of boutique wineries in the 1970s began specifying the vineyards where the grapes were grown, for both pride and marketing reasons. Boutiques can do it easily because their fermenting vats and cooperage for aging are small. Chateau St. Jean (Sonoma Valley), for example, one year made and labeled White Riesling from seven different vineyards and Chardonnay from five; all the different batches were purchased from independent growers in the neighborhood.

The justification for vineyard name-dropping is that more and more microclimates within winegrowing areas are being identified, and many appear to grow wines that are better than the standard for the area—or, at least, more individualized. Wine critic Philip Reich tasted a Heitz wine from Martha's Vineyard, a eucalyptus-lined field near Oakville, and perceived that it had a "unique minty-eucalyptus scent." He wrote that he caught a whiff of "Rutherford dust"—an allspice-like flavor—in a wine grown across from the Beaulieu winery in Rutherford.

It's possible such sensory differences are in the eye or reference book of the beholder, but there's no doubt about the marketability of vineyard-named wines. Giant Almadén, fourth largest American winery, started doing it for higher-priced fifth-size wines from its 3,900-acre Paicines Vineyard in San Benito County—26,000 gallons at a time. Paul Masson, the twelfth largest, has a special "Pinnacles Selection" line of varietals for wines grown in a huge Salinas Valley vineyard. Some wineries show more discretion: one year Dry Creek bought Cabernet from six different vineyards but bottled only two with vineyard names, blending the remainder because it wasn't outstanding enough.

It's likely the BATF will have to step in and regulate vineyard naming because there's no present requirement that the winery naming the vineyard has to be close by or even within the viticultural area, yet the name of a vineyard—*any* vineyard—conjures up ideas of "estate bottling." In Burgundy and elsewhere only the very best wines deserve such specific appellations.

From merely "American" all the way to the name of some tiny hillside plot, the wine industry has available a framework to contrive an elaborate appellation of origin system that will probably make a detailed California wine atlas (there isn't one yet) future required reading. The unfortunate thing is that place-naming a wine may dignify some unworthy wines, and the proliferation of names will unnecessarily confuse many consumers.

Appellations and Quality

But, you ask, isn't it the same in Europe? Not completely, for the French AOC is partially a quality-control system. Essentially, the more specific the place-name used on the label, the more restrictive the regulations that define exact areas for vineyards, permissible grape varieties, viticultural practices such as pruning and fertilizing, vinicultural practices, and distilling. Most important, the amount of permissible harvest is regulated. For example, for "Sauternes" to be on the label, winegrowers can produce only 267 gallons per acre, while "Graves" (district) winegrowers are allowed to produce 428 gallons per acre and "Bordeaux" (region) 535 gallons. Any excess of the yield from small appellations was formerly allowed to "cascade" to the next best appellation, but this practice has been reformed since it defeated the purpose of controlling production—maintaining quality.

By contrast, American vineyardists are free to force the greatest yield from any acreage, which means a good regional appellation is allowable on a mediocre wine made from a bumper crop. Reputable wineries, of course, won't buy unsatisfactory grapes—at least not at high prices and not for the best wine.

WHO MADE THE WINE?

On premium wines the largest or second largest type on the label features the brand name, and that is almost always the same name as the winemaker, whose name is officially listed at the bottom of the label. Occasionally, there are secondary (second label) brand names.

The Bottom Line

The statement at the bottom of the label must be carefully examined if you want to know whether or not the winery named actually made the wine and where they did it:

• **"Bottled by,"** with somebody's name and post-office address of the principal place of business, is the minimum requirement. It is rarely seen alone; by itself, bottling isn't a function worth advertising. Until 1983 it's okay to list the address of the business headquarters, which may be in San Francisco (and often is for bulk wineries); starting then, the actual place of bottling must be named, and bottling cellars are already moving to places with better names.

• **"Produced and Bottled by"** is allowed if the bottler made 75 percent or more of the wine by fermenting the grape must and clarifying the wine, or by transforming the wine into a sparkling or flavored wine. Someone else could have made the other 25 percent (that amount may be blending wine), but it's still the phrase to look for on the best wines.

• **"Grown, Produced, and Bottled by"** is allowed if the bottler grew 75 percent of the grapes and produced 75 percent of the wine. The tag is rarely seen.

• **"Made and Bottled by"** is theoretically allowed if the bottler produced none—absolutely none—of the wine. In practice, the line isn't okayed by the BATF unless the winery produced at least 10 percent. This doesn't exactly meet the everyday definition of *made*. We think it defrauds the consumer. And who produced the other 90 percent? The label doesn't have to tell you. The phrase appears on jugs, mostly, but on occasional fifth-size varietals from small wineries as well.

Otherwise, if the bottler did anything other than "producing" or "making" between 10 and 100 percent, he is permitted to use other supposedly truthful, unmisleading terms:

• **"Blended and Bottled by"** seems straightforward enough.

• **"Prepared and Bottled by"** has a significance that escapes us.

• **"Cellared and Bottled by"** implies the named party aged it— but it could mean a couple of tankloads were trucked on Wednesday from Fresno, kept overnight in cellars in the Napa Valley, and bottled there on Thursday. When Coca-Cola decided to invade the jug-wine market, it set up San Francisco offices under the name of a big East Coast winery it owns, Taylor, but used the blending and finishing facilities of the Salinas Valley winery Coke also owns, Monterey Vineyard, and the bottling facilities of the Central Valley winery Coca-Cola Bottling of New York owns, Franzia—with the result that "Taylor California Cellars" wines are "Cellared and Bottled by Taylor California Cellars, San Francisco."

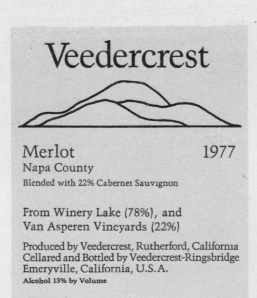

Veedercrest

Merlot   1977
Napa County
Blended with 22% Cabernet Sauvignon

From Winery Lake (78%), and
Van Asperen Vineyards (22%)

Produced by Veedercrest, Rutherford, California
Cellared and Bottled by Veedercrest-Ringsbridge
Emeryville, California, U.S.A.
Alcohol 13% by Volume

• **"Vinted and Bottled by"** was apparently pioneered by Italian Swiss Colony/United Vintners but is widely used now that the BATF has endorsed it. That's unfortunate for the English language and American consumers, for only one dictionary, the notoriously permissive *Webster's Third New International* unabridged, recognizes this as a verb (a back-formation from *vintner*, the common meaning of which is "wine seller"!). "Vinted" has something to do with wine—only that much is certain. Until the next generation of dictionaries comes along, the unprintable BATF allows wineries to use a nearly fictitious word to imply that they produced the wine. Odds are that the "Vinted and Bottled by" winery did little more than bottle it, but they want the consumer to believe a "little old winemaker, me" made it by himself. Just look at the bottom line of the new line of Gallo varietals: "Ernest and Julio Gallo vinted and cellared this wine and bottled it in Modesto, Calif."

For the most part, we'll give jug-wine makers the benefit of the doubt and assume from any phrases lacking the word *produced* that they selected bulk wine made by someone else, blended it artfully, bottled it, and placed it on the market at a price representing good value. There's nothing inherently wrong with this. The giant wineries do it all the time. So do liquor stores, restaurants, and department stores. So do some boutique wineries; Joe Heitz, for example, buys varietals from Napa Valley neighbors, blends, and labels the product **"Perfected and Bottled by**," which is not deceptive. Why can't they uniformly tell the truth about the wine's origin? The BATF wanted to restrict some of this crazy terminology but ended up endorsing "vinted." Our government in action.

Who Really Made It?

The legal but fallacious distinctions among "produced," "made," "vinted," and such may help to explain what was done to the wine but still don't point directly at who did it, for the identity of the party named is sometimes impossible to pin down. Try this line on a bottle of Champagne: "Vinted and Bottled by Jacques Bonet & Cie., San Francisco, Calif." Who's Jacques Bonet? Neither he nor his *compagnie des vins* is in the San Francisco phone book (and we doubt they're in the Reims or Épernay directories, either); Bonet is not in the *Wines and Vines* annual trade directory. We were led by chance to the door of United Vintners, the nation's second largest winery (eight plants, 110 million gallons storage) and bottler of wines under some 14 different brand names—none UV-identified on the label—and now masquerading as a French bubbly maker. We assume that UV's marketing wizards decided that one segment of the market, one collection of demographic digits or noughts, needed further exploitation: the unsophisticated Americans who buy "Champagne" at Safeway. (Besides "Vinted" and the "Jacques Bonet" nonentity, the other tipoff that this is not Veuve Cliquot is the San Francisco address. That wonderful city has numerous headquarters and, in the case of consumer-marketing folks, many hindquarters, but no operating wineries.)

At least one of the wine giants wears the emperor's new clothes. E. and J. Gallo, the largest winery in creation, is so large that it ferments 100 million gallons at a time and stores a quarter of a *billion* gallons, and packs 250,000 cases a day with bottles made by its own glass plant. Gallo bottles and sells about 33 percent of California wine. Not unexpectedly, Gallo has wanted to avoid looking like a monopoly, especially when the United Farm Workers were shouting "Boycott Gallo" in the late sixties and early seventies. So it has hidden behind "Carlo Rossi/ Red Mountain," "Paisano," "Thunderbird," "Ripple," "André Champagne," and other brand names, made by various Modesto, California, companies. The secret decoding device. Gallo is the only winery with a Modesto address.

This begins to betray the fact that, despite the hundreds of tiny wineries, the wine industry is oligopolistic: the 20 largest wineries in California produce 91 percent of the wine. Some of the biggest companies, such as Vie-Del and Sierra, mainly sell in bulk to others; other big ones disguise some of their products.

This is a good place to name the names. California wineries can be divided into three size-categories: giant, the ones with storage capacity of more than 10 million gallons (up to Gallo-size); medium, those that can store 400,000 to 10 million gallons; and small, those that store less than 400,000 gallons.

Giant Wineries and Their Brand Names

The giants may produce varietals in fifth-size (750-milliliter) bottles, but their sales volume is really in half-gallon-size (actually 1.5-liter) and gallon-size (3- or 4-liter) jugs. They distribute across the country (rarely overseas—a minute portion of American wine is exported for regular sale). They advertise heavily (Gallo spent more than $19 million in 1977). They pay less for greater amounts of grapes.

Most of the grapes are grown in the Central Valley but substantial amounts come from the coastal districts (indeed, Gallo is the biggest single buyer of Napa Valley grapes). Most of their wine is labeled, simply, "California," the best indication a consumer has that it is essentially a Central Valley wine; wine with any other name could be priced higher, at least within the state.

Regardless of origin, the wine made by the giants is, these days, quite palatable; their "Burgundy" and "Chablis" and other generic table wine in jugs is frequently very good value as everyday wine. But their varietals, even with good appellations and dates of vintage, are usually mediocre, simply because wine that is made in million-gallon tanks just cannot achieve the best. Economy of scale and the demands of marketing across the country necessitate a lot of uniform, predictable wine, not a small amount of nectar.

The giants whose names you may or may not find on labels, along with their headquarters and brand names, are in order of storage capacity:

Gallo, Modesto	Gallo, The Wine Cellars of Ernest and Julio Gallo, Paisano, Carlo Rossi, Madria-Madria, Ripple, Thunderbird, Boone's Farm, André Champagne
United Vintners, San Francisco	Italian Swiss Colony, Colony, Jacaré, Inglenook, Petri, Annie Green Springs, T. J. Swann, Jacques Bonet Champagne, Esprit
Guild, San Francisco (which owns Cresta Blanca)	Cresta Blanca, Winemasters, Cribari, Roma, Tavola
Almadén, San Jose	Almadén, Charles Le Franc, Le Domaine Champagne
M. LaMont, DiGiórgio	M. LaMont, Mountain Gold, Mountain Peak, Gold Peak
Taylor, San Francisco	Taylor California Cellars
JFJ Bronco, Ceres	JFJ, Bronco, CC Vineyard

Christian Brothers, Napa (Mont La Salle Vineyards)	Christian Brothers, Mont La Salle
Franzia, Ripon	Franzia
Paul Masson, Saratoga	Paul Masson
A. Perelli-Minetti, Delano (which owns California Wine Assn., Burlingame)	Fino Eleven Cellars, Pirelli-Minetti, Vino Fino, L&J, Guasti, Ambassador, Calwa, Greystone
California Growers, San Francisco	Growers, L. LeBlanc, Bounty, Setrakian
Delicato, Manteca	Delicato
Giumarra, Bakersfield	Giumarra Family, Giumarra Classic, Breckenridge Cellars, Ridgecrest

These wineries and those that make bulk wine for sale to other bottlers can store some three-quarters of a billion gallons of wine; they produce well over three-fourths of all types of California wine and a like percentage of American brandy.*

Medium-Size Wineries and Their Brand Names

The ranks of the medium-size wineries contain many names you are accustomed to seeing on bottles that apparently contain some of the best premium wine. Almost all are large enough to distribute nationally, at least to those states with substantial urban wine-drinking populations and less restrictive liquor laws. They advertise more selectively.

Most of these wineries produce both premium wine in fifths and good-quality generic and varietal wine in jugs; a few also make aperitif and dessert wines, sparkling wines, special natural wines, and other products. The jug wine may be labeled simply "California" because it may contain wine made in the Central Valley, but a lot of jugs often have smaller appellations of origin; "North Coast" is prized. With jugs, these wineries compete with the giants, though their prices are

---

*A veteran wine industry consultant, Louis R. Gomberg, in 1979 guessed that, nationwide, the top ten wine firms in terms of sales (rather than storage) were Gallo, United Vintners, Masson/Christian Brothers, Almadén, Mogen David/Franzia/Tribuno, Taylor/Great Western, Canandaigua, Guild, Monarch, and—surprisingly—Sebastiani.

usually higher. Possibly because the jug generics earn money, many of the medium-size wineries produce premium wine in small lots, and thus compete favorably with the small and boutique wineries in judgings.

Here, in alphabetical order, are the medium-size wineries of California that bottle their own wine, mostly under their own names (secondary brand names are shown in parentheses):

Barengo (Kirkwood, Dudenhoefer)
Beaulieu Vineyards (B.V.)
Beringer (Los Hermanos)
Bisceglia (Paradise, Canterbury, Old Rose, La Croix)
Brookside (Assumption Abbey, Vache, Vin de Biane Fres)
Buena Vista (Haraszthy Cellars)
Cambiaso
Concannon
Cucamonga Vineyard (California Bonded Winery No. 1, Cuvée d'Or)
Del Rey
Domaine Chandon (Chandon, Fred's Friends)
East-Side (Royal Host, Gold Bell, Conti Royale)
Fetzer (Bel Arbres)
Filipi (Chateau Filipi, Joseph Filipi, Old Rancho, Pride of California)
Foppiano
Franciscan
Geyser Peak (Summit)
Gibson
Emilio Guglielmo (Emile's, Cavalcade, Mt. Madonna)
Korbel

Charles Krug (CK Mondavi, Mondavi Vineyards)
Lodi Vintners (Bon Core, Chateau Vin, Cucamonga Village)
Louis M. Martini
Martini & Prati (Fountain Grove, M & P)
Mirassou
Robert Mondavi (Oakville Vineyards)
Novitiate
Papagni (Rancho Yerba Buena)
Parducci
Pedrizetti
J. Pedroncelli
Rutherford Hill
San Antonio
San Martín
Sebastiani
Seghesio
Simi
Sonoma Vineyards (Windsor Vineyards, Tiburon Vintners)
Souverain
Sterling
Turgeon and Lohr (J. Lohr)
Villa Armando
Weibel
Wente Bros.

Small Wineries and Their Brand Names

The small and boutique wineries, with storage capacities of less (and considerably less) than 400,000 gallons, include many whose names are barely known to wine consumers outside California because their distribution may be limited to mailing-list customers. Most do very little advertising even in California. Most produce only three or four varietals. Some produce generic table wines but rarely put it in jugs. Some specialize in sparkling wines (Hanns Kornell, Schramsberg). One produces only Port (Ficklin, said by some experts to be the only American Port worthy of bearing the name).

While it is not true that only small wineries produce the best premium varietals, it is an undeniable fact that the best wine of an area can only be made in small, carefully superintended lots from grapes that were nurtured at the best vineyards and picked—even selected—at exactly the right time. Big wineries don't lack the expertise or ability to do this; they don't do it because their costs would be too high per bottle. But a tiny winery that is run almost as a hobby-loss by a couple of dedicated wine fanciers can turn the trick vintage after vintage. It doesn't take genius; it may not take inspiration. It takes handwork and sanitation and the traditional capital- and labor-intensive practices, such as fermentation in small containers, long maturing in small oak cooperage, bottle-fermenting of Champagne, and long bottle-aging. For these reasons, plus the fact that these winemakers pay more for small lots of grapes, boutique wine is far more costly to buy *even if* it is of the same quality as or worse than the same variety produced by a bigger winery—which is by no means uncommon.

Here is a selection, in alphabetical order, of the better-known small and boutique wineries (secondary brand names in parentheses):

Bargetto's Santa Cruz Winery
Beckett Cellars
Bertero Winery
David Bruce Winery
Burgess Cellars (Bell Canyon)
Davis Bynum Winery
Callaway Vineyard & Winery
Carneros Creek Winery
Caymus Vineyards (Liberty School)
Chalone Vineyard (Gavilan Vineyards)
Chappellet Winery
Chateau Montelena (Silverado Cellars)
Chateau St. Jean
Clos du Bois (River Oaks)
Clos du Val (Grand Val)
Conn Creek Vineyard
Cuvaison (Calistoga Vineyard)
Diamond Creek Vineyards
Dry Creek Vineyard
Edmeades (Mendocino Wine Guild)
Ficklin Vineyards
Field Stone Winery
Firestone Vineyard
Fortino Winery
Freemark Abbey Winery
Grand Cru Vineyards

Grand Pacific Vineyard (Alta
  Vista)
Grgich Hills Cellar
Gundlach-Bundschu Winery
Hacienda Wine Cellars
  (Estancia)
Hanns Kornell Champagne
  Cellars
Hanzell Vineyards
Hecker Pass Winery
Heitz Wine Cellars
Hoffman Mountain Ranch
  (HMR)
Hop Kiln Winery (Griffin
  Vineyard, Sweetwater Springs)
Husch Vineyards
Jade Mountain Winery
Johnson's Alexander Valley
  Wines
Kenwood Vineyards
Thomas Kruse Winery
Landmark Vineyards
Llords & Elwood Winery
Lower Lake Winery
Mark West Vineyards
Mayacamas Vineyards
Monterey Peninsula Winery
Mt. Eden Vineyards
Mt. Veeder Winery & Vineyards
Nichelini Vineyards

Pastori Winery
Joseph Phelps Vineyards
  (LeFleuron)
Pope Valley Winery
Martin Ray Vineyards
Raymond Vineyard & Cellar
Ridge Vineyards
Russian River Vineyards
Rutherford Vintners
V. Sattui Winery
Sausal Winery
Schramsberg Vineyard
Shenandoah Vineyards
Sotoyome Winery
Spring Mountain Vineyards
Stag's Leap Vineyard
Stag's Leap Wine Cellars (Hawk
  Crest)
Stonegate Winery
Stony Hill Vineyard
Stony Ridge Winery
Sutter Home Winery
Joseph Swan Vineyards
Trefethen Vineyards
Trentadue Winery
Valley of the Moon Winery
Veedercrest
Villa Mt. Eden Winery
Yverdon Vineyards
ZD Wines

Second Labels

Any winery, whether Gallo-size or garage-size, may produce a wine and want to market it under a brand name other than the company name. Mostly, the reason is to differentiate wines of different price and quality levels.

For boutique wineries that guard their reputations carefully but must make money, so-called second labels are used on premium wines that are not quite good enough to be marketed under the principal brand name. Chateau Montelena, for example, has "Silverado Cellars" as its second label. If you see an unfamiliar brand name and the price seems high, examine the "Bottled by" line to see who made it. You may be wise to buy a wine of similar price made by another winery and sold under its own name.

Another type of second label is for jug wines made by wineries that base their reputation on fifth-size premium wines. C. Mondavi and Sons puts the traditional "Charles Krug" on the fifth-size bottles, "CK Mondavi" on the jugs. In reverse, Almadén, which has always marketed nearly all its wine, both jug generics and fifth-size varietals, under that one name, decided to launch a line of higher-priced wines with labels headed "Charles Le Franc, Founder 1852." (The first releases included 1975 Monterey Cabernet, which was made before the Le Franc line was established; Almadén allows its winemaker to divert the best of stored production to the new line.)

A third use of a second brand name is in conjunction with the primary name. Inglenook has three lines, labeled "Estate Bottled" for Napa Valley varietals, "Vintage" for Napa, Sonoma, and Mendocino blends, and "Navalle" (for a creek on the Inglenook property) for Northern California jug generics; at least occasionally, Inglenook defines all these on the back label. But Beaulieu uses a mixture of names such as "Chateau Beaulieu," "Beauclair," "Beaumont," and "Beau Tour" without explaining either significance or differences; one wine writer suggests the names are used because consumers have difficulty pronouncing "Beaulieu" (BOWL-yuh in radio ads).

Producer Name and Address Regulations

In all cases where the name of the maker is obscured, the BATF's new regulations will, in 1983, force well-hidden winemakers at least to peep out from behind their labels. The actual place of bottling will have to be named, the official registry number of the bonded winery or cellar or bottling house will have to be included in conspicuous type, and the trade or operating name of the winery will have to be identical to the name appearing on the basic permit. Further, the place where *each* of the winemaking operations took place will have to be named.

Beginning in 1983 some lengthy statements of responsibility will appear on some bottom lines, such as "Produced at Fresno, Calif., and Bottled at St. Helena, Calif., by Fancy La Bel Winery, BW-CA-10001." The wine buff will have to become familiar with the real names and the numbers of the BWs (Bonded Wineries), BWCs (Bonded Wine Cellars), and maybe DSPs (Distilled Spirit Permittees), not to mention the PO's abbreviations for CA and other states.

The BATF also virtually prohibited the inclusion in that bottom line of additional place-names that might mislead the consumer. For example, "Vinted and Bottled by Withered Vineyards, Kenmore, SONOMA VALLEY, California" on a wine made someplace else would not be allowed. This misleading practice has not been uncommon. Unfortunately, some obscurely located wineries, in places like Acampo, Ceres, Kerman, Manteca, and Yettem, could *use* an extra place-name: San Joaquin Valley.

In passing, we think it's too bad the BATF isn't cracking down on brand and producer names that do the same thing generic wine names do—trade on someone else's reputation. For instance, a new winery near Soledad, Monterey County, calls one of its new wines "Domaine du Ventana," thus exploiting the prestige of the Burgundy region's word for "estate" (vineyard) and distantly echoing the Napa Valley's Domaine Chandon, which is the legitimately named associate of the French Champagne house of Moët and Chandon. The Frenchified brand name is doubly spurious for misappropriating the Spanish place-name "Ventana" (window) from the Big Sur coast and the expensive resort there. But we might as well complain about the Chateaux Chevalier (French founder of a recently revived Napa Valley winery), Montelena (near Mt. St. Helena), and St. Jean (named for an American Jean, wife of one of the investors in this Sonoma Valley winery) or the Closes du Val and du Bois.

So What?

After all this, one is entitled to ask, So what? Does it really matter who made the wine and where and whether the name and address are misleading?

Yes, because the winemaker should be proud of his product, even everyday wine, and not try to confuse the buyer with various identity tags. Proper identification adds greatly to the interest in drinking wine because of the critical role of the winemaker in the winemaking process: two winemakers, using the same grapes from the same vineyard, might produce the same wine, but only by accident or strenuous effort. Bob Thompson and Hugh Johnson find the truth of this in Burgundy: at the Clos du Vougeot, 50 owners divide a mere 40 acres but "produce an astonishing range of character and quality in wines called Clos de Vougeot."

WHEN WAS THE WINE MADE?

The meanings of "vintage" have been diffused through overuse. What it means simply is the grape harvest. A "vintage year" in the Champagne region and in the Douro Valley means that the sparkling wine and the Port, respectively, were so good that the trade declared the year date could be put on the bottles; vintage years are infrequent. "Vintage wine" strictly means a wine with a vintage date, whether or not the wine is any good.

Vintage Labeling Regulations

Under the BATF's 1978 regulations, effective immediately, the label (or neck ring) can carry the vintage date only if 95 percent of the grapes used for the wine were harvested that year *and* if the wine has an appellation of origin (other than "American"). The old rules said that vintage-dated wine had to be 95 percent harvested that year *within* the named appellation area. The requirements were divorced because, the wine industry said, nonvintage wine had an unfair advantage over vintage wine. The reason for this is in the porous sides of oak and redwood cooperage: wine evaporates at the rate of about two percent a year. To keep the wine from being oxidized too much, winemakers must top off each cask or tank frequently, even weekly. Without that five percent vintage-dating margin, winemakers would have to stock too many small containers of various sizes with wine in each for topping off casks of *each* variety of *each* vintage. The former rule thus encouraged nonvintage wine.

The new regulations weaken standards to the extent that the idea of vintage quality is disconnected from the idea of appellation quality. The separation allows wine marketers to exploit the market value of the two ideas separately if economics dictate, for example, a nonvintage "Napa Valley Chardonnay" and a vintage "California Burgundy."

Furthermore, the new regulations make it necessary, for the 1978, 1979, 1980, 1981, *and* 1982 vintages, for the consumer to mentally juggle several percentages and definitions at the same time—for the varietal labeling rules don't go into effect until 1983. Even then, a "1984 Sonoma Valley Gewürztraminer," 95 percent of which must be from the 1984 California harvest, need be only 85 percent from Sonoma Valley Gewürztraminer grapes, allowing up to 15 percent to be Fresno Thompson Seedless or anything else, as long as two-thirds of *that* was grown in 1984.

This discussion assumes that vintage dating is a good thing, and we think it is on any wine that costs a dollar or so more than everyday wine. The reason is that, despite the Wine Institute's "Every year is a vintage year in California," the weather is sufficiently different from year to year to make vintage dating desirable if not necessary for identifying good wine by the label and thereby *validating the price*. For Napa Valley Cabernets, for example, Hugh Johnson (in his valuable *Pocket Encyclopedia*) charted these variations for just a decade:

1966—Huge and uniformly very good
1967—Weak
1968—Fine, well balanced, for keeping [cellar aging]
1969—Good, not great
1970—Best ever
1971—Average
1972—Uneven; rain; many poor wines
1973—Big and good
1974—Difficult; the best excellent
1975—Good
1976 [drought year]—Small crop but splendid

Vintage dating is also necessary for determining whether fine wine is ready to drink or past its peak. White and rosé wines should rarely age long and, if too old, may be oxidized brown or spoiled. On the other hand, highly tannic reds may need years in the cellar to mellow.

The BATF suggested making all wineries put the date of fill on the label if they wanted a "BATF Seal"—a proposed official category of guaranteed-quality wines—but both the suggestion and the category were dropped. Date of fill would be handy for those who wanted to know how long the winery aged the wine in casks, and a couple of wineries do put both harvest date and bottling date on the label to guide cellarkeepers.

Time of Harvest

One new regulation on age statements has to do less with what year the grapes were harvested than how late in the season they were picked. Although it's a risky business, because rain could ruin the whole crop, vineyardists in the Sauternes, the Rhine, and the Moselle regions traditionally leave the grapes on the vines as long as possible. This has one general effect—grapes tend to grow sweeter—and one possible effect—

the grapes can be attacked by *Botrytis cinerea*, so-called "noble rot." *Botrytis* withers the grapes, causing water to evaporate, sugar, flavor, and other elements to become concentrated, and extra glycerin to develop. (Glycerin in wine makes the "legs" that are seen inside a wineglass when a full-bodied wine is swirled around.) The winemaker fermenting extra-sweet grapes can stop the process and produce an amber-colored, naturally sweet, syrupy-bodied wine with sufficient alcohol content (usually higher than 12 percent) to stabilize it without the addition of brandy. The products include, of course, the sweet white Sauternes wines (Chateau d'Yquem is the most famous and always very expensive) and the sweet white German wines labeled, as progressively sweeter, *Spätlese, Auslese, Beerenauslese,* and *Trockenbeerenauslese.* A variation is *Eiswein,* an expensive wine made from grapes that were frozen in the vineyard before the harvest.

The BATF regulation covers the California versions of these sweet wines, which include an occasional red. While harvest dates can be stated only if the wine is vintage-dated, front-label terms such as "Sec-

FIELD STONE

1978
VINEYARD
PRESSED

This wine was made from botrytised grapes pressed immediately as harvested at 26° Brix in evening coolness by an exclusive mobile press in the FIELD STONE vineyards. This unique process produces a wine with a residual sugar of 6° Brix.

LATE
HARVEST

1978
ESTATE
BOTTLED

FIELD STONE's grapes are grown in ideal soil and microclimate. An exclusive process protects the harvested juice and the wine from oxidation until the moment you uncork the bottle and release the wine's fragrance.

LATE
HARVEST

ALEXANDER VALLEY
JOHANNISBERG RIESLING

Produced and Bottled by Redwood Ranch and Vineyard, Inc.
10075 State Hwy. 128, Healdsburg, CA 95448 • Alcohol 12% by Volume

ond Crop," "Late Picked," "Botrytis Infected," and "Ice Wine"—but no foreign-language terms—can be used if both the sugar content of the grapes at harvest and the residual sugar in the wine are on the front or back label. This kind of technical information may daze even the most dedicated buff. The first California ice wine, made by Edmeades Vineyards (Mendocino County) from the 1977 harvest, was produced from Botrytized grapes whose must-weight sugar content was 33.7° Brix, and the wine had 16 percent residual sugar.* If you don't care about such technicalities, better not pay $35 a bottle for the Edmeades Ice Wine.

This section has, so far, assumed that added years or lateness of harvest mean added quality. That would not be true at all for the so-called "nouveau," "primeur," "nuevo," or "spring" wines. Following the tradition in France's Beaujolais district, some California wineries rush the newly picked grapes through a process called carbonic maceration (whole grape bunches go into the fermenting tanks, and as the carbon dioxide builds up, the skin breaks and releases the juice). They finish and bottle it quickly, sending it to wine shops as early as November. The highly fruity, low-tannin nouveau wine is meant to be drunk chilled and should be consumed within days of release.

The BATF has relaxed its prohibition against most statements about age, as long as they are truthful and specific (to the particular wine in the bottle) and not misleading. But "Old" in a brand name is allowed whether that's the case or not.

DO PRESTIGE DESIGNATIONS MEAN ANYTHING?

You can never know for sure whether a wine is any good until you've tasted it, but the winemaker sometimes tries to assure you beforehand that he's produced something really special.

Prestige designations are part of the marketing game. "Magnum Size Decanter" on a half-gallon green jug is supposed to make you

---

* The Brix or Balling scale is on the hydrometers that vineyardists and winemakers use to determine dissolved sugar content—and, thus, to determine when to pick the grapes, to monitor fermentation and to stop it. Most grapes are 20° to 22° Brix when harvested; multiplying the Brix number by .55 predicts alcohol content if fermentation continues until complete dryness—e.g., 20° multiplied by .55 equals 11 percent alcohol, about average for a dry red wine.

want to prefer that over somebody else's half-gallon green jug, "magnum" and "decanter" summoning up images of dinner with Baron Philippe at Chateau Mouton-Rothschild, or at least a sumptuous repast at a Michelin three-star restaurant. It's a good idea to analyze such prestige designations carefully. "Magnum Size Decanter," besides lacking a hyphen, contains a circular fallacy: decanters are not wine bottles, and if filled on a bottling line, a bottle cannot be its own decanter . . . unless you want to decant twice, which is pretty silly considering jug wine is always well filtered. In short, you would be unwise to expect praise for placing this Magnum Size Decanter on the table.

A number of other terms have such spurious snob appeal. And some terms may be true but mislead you into buying a wine that may be inappropriate. Yet, to be fair to the majority of winemakers, some terms, even those in code, have perfectly simple explanations and are properly used. The reputation of the winery is the best guide to whether a prestige term means anything.

• **"Special Reserve," "Private Reserve,"** and the like. These should refer to grapes and wine specially selected and shepherded through all winemaking processes, then given good cellar aging at the winery. Beaulieu's "Private Reserve" Cabernet Sauvignon has been a hallmark for decades and is suitably high-priced. But "Vintner's Reserve" is virtually a standard slogan on Cambiaso varietals from Sonoma County, while "Reserve" appears on all Barengo (San Joaquin Valley) varietals, even some they didn't produce.

• **"Cask No. 46."** The wine quietly aging in one cask can be different from the same varietal in a similar cask. Inglenook's John Daniel started cask numbering special wines in the 1930s. The label should also state why the wine in Cask No. 46 is special. "Cuvée 362," "Bin No. 116," and similar labels are all variations of "Private Reserve."

• **"Special Selection," "Vintage Selection,"** and the like. These are used in the same way as those above: this way and that way. The Christian Brothers put "Select" on all their Napa Valley varietals; Delicato does them one better by putting "Especially Selected" on their San Joaquin Valley varietals. Good for them.

• **"Bottled Expressly for the Schmoes."** This means that Joseph and Henrietta Schmoe, your hosts, expressed a desire to Windsor Vineyards (or another mail-order operation) to see their name on a label and, what's more, paid for the pleasure. Windsor (Sonoma) Vineyards has made a lot of money doing this. The wine tastes no different.

• **"This vintage produced 7,495 bottles, of which this is No. 7,382."** There's nothing intrinsically better about a numbered bottle; Gallo could number its bottles, to the zillions, if they wanted. Buy a numbered bottle only if the wine is otherwise special, such as Edmeades' unique ice wine. Even then, only the total number of bottles produced, indicating limited quantity and market scarcity, is significant.

• **"Lot 1," "Lot 2,"** etc. As with other terms, these should be explained on the back label. In the case of the David Bruce (Santa Cruz Mountains) 1974 Chardonnay, Lot 1 was not filtered (some winemakers filter or otherwise handle wine as little as possible to avoid overprocessing it), while Lot 2 was filtered; the consumer was told to decant Lot 1 before drinking it.

• **Elevation of vineyard.** There's a notion that hillside vineyards produce wines of greater character, ones worthy of being laid down in the cellar for aging. Hillsides are, of course, higher than valley bottoms and probably cooler, usually have different soils, drain better, and are drier. Hillside wines might, therefore, have different qualities. Elevation, as with any description of the vineyard where the grapes came from, is useful—or, at least, interesting—information. One 1978 blind tasting of Napa hillside and valley floor varietals produced ambivalent results—in fact, the bottomland wines outscored the hillside wines slightly.

• **"Old Vines."** Grapevines usually don't last beyond 50 to 80 years, and may be uprooted well before then because their production falls off. Decreased yield has the effect of concentrating certain grape qualities, such as varietal flavor. A wine labeled "Old Vines," such as the Sonoma Vineyards' 1976 Zinfandel, made from 60-year-old vines in River West Vineyard, is thus not an everyday wine. Wine columnist Hank Rubin termed this one "a monster of a wine that will last practically forever," being a tannic, powerful essence-of-fruit extract.

• **Winery or vineyard founding date.** Simi (Alexander Valley, northern Sonoma County) says on its labels, in its ads, and on its stone winery building, "Since 1876," one of the earlier dates boasted of. Simi leaves out an awful lot of history that belies that date. Wine historian William F. Heintz reported in *Wines and Vines* that the Simi family actually lived on the San Mateo coast until 1881, and didn't construct the historic winery at Healdsburg pictured on the labels until 1890. Even then, one is entitled to question the relevance of any Simi founding date in the last century: by the 1960s the Simi winery was so dormant that there were casks of spoiled wine in the cellar. It went through *three* ownership and management changes in six years, the last in 1976 when it was bought by Schieffelin and Co., New York. Thus, Schieffelin, strictly importers of wine and liquor, overnight acquired an alleged century of Sonoma winemaking experience.

More serious distortions show up elsewhere. Sonoma's Gundlach-Bundschu Winery ("Established 1858") is run by a Bundschu, it is true, but the winery was out of business from 1918 until 1964 and the vineyards weren't replanted until 1968.

Cresta Blanca ("Since 1881"), which uses on its label a replica of the gold medal won at the Paris Exposition of 1889, was indeed founded in 1882 in the Livermore Valley and named for a white cliff there, but the winery petered out under Schenley distillers' ownership in 1965. When Guild bought it in 1971, Cresta Blanca was installed in one corner of the Roma winery in Fresno. Then the name was sent off to adorn the former Mendocino Growers Cooperative Winery in Ukiah, and the labels have Guild's San Francisco address. "Since 1882" our foot.

These examples show why wine historian Heintz after 10 years of research concluded that "much"—60 percent—"of what passes for viticulture and wine history is loose family mythology with little basis in historic fact." Nevertheless, Heintz proposes a general rule that is corrective but extremely liberal: a winery is "as old as the first crush of grapes on the site," regardless of building and ownership changes. That will please young stockbrokers who buy long-abandoned stone wineries in the Napa Valley and put "Since 1880" on their labels.

• **Symbols, emblems, coats of arms, and other illustrations.** The BATF bans any illustrations that might mislead the consumer, particularly any that could imply some different regional appellation than the one stated. But the label on Almadén's Blanc de Blancs Champagne has a coat of arms and "Maison Fondée en 1852." Misleading? Brookside Vineyards of Guasti, near Cucamonga, made a deal in 1956 with the Benedictine monks at the Assumption Abbey to use that name and their coat of arms on its varietals. Misleading? Perhaps—but mostly absurd: Assumption Abbey is in North Dakota.

• **Gold, silver, and bronze medals** awarded at judgings at the L.A. County Fair (the biggest judging), Sonoma Harvest Fair, and elsewhere. Medals are usually awarded on the basis of how close an entry comes to an ideal of that type but sometimes on relative order of merit. More than one gold medal might therefore be awarded in a category. If done properly (no tasting after lunch, for example), judgings are a fair way by which to compare similar wines (same varietal, same vintage). The results can, however, be confusing or meaningless. In 1978 the *San Jose Mercury-News* held a judging at which an inflationary super-medal, platinum, was offered. But the platinum wasn't awarded, and the three different panels (professionals, editors, consumers) each gave a Simi Gewürztraminer a different-colored medal. The next year, with a different judging format and no platinum at stake, some other anomalies were apparent: no gold medals at all, and among the 180 wines entered, only six silver medals. Wine columnist Harvey Steiman knocked the San Jose newspaper for being too stingy, but noted that the L.A. County Fair is criticized for being too generous.

One difficulty in such competitions is that not all wines compete. In fact, there's sometimes a paucity of wines from small but top-name wineries because they don't feel they have anything to gain—but perhaps have something to lose. A second difficulty is that the judges don't all use the same standards, which are vague at best. The San Jose judging, for example, used the common 20-point scoring system (see p. 94). Three of five judges gave one wine perfect scores—but because scores were averaged, the wine received only a bronze medal ("bronze" wines averaged 15.5 points out of 20).

Winning medals indicates some degree of quality. If an ad mentions medal winning, the wine may deserve attention.

• **"Rare Varietal California Wine."** Paul Masson uses this on many varietals because "varietal" has market appeal that is made more piquant by the adjective "rare." But the term is laughable unless the bottle contains Folle Blanche, Rkatsiteli, Kleinburger, Cabernet Franc, Malbec, or some other rarely made varietal. It should be noted that Masson (owned by Seagram, no slouch at marketing) also uses "Rare Premium Wines" as a tag even on California Chablis!

• **"Blanc de Noir," "Blanc de Zinfandel,"** and the like. This means off-white wine made from black-skinned grapes that, right now, glut the market. "Oeil de Perdrix" ("eye of the partridge") is an exotic name for the same thing. "Rosé of Cabernet" and similar names are other indications of a market surplus of black grapes. The wine may taste terrific.

WHAT ELSE DOES THE BOTTLE SAY?

The amount of information that can (or should) be conveyed by a bottle of wine has not yet been exhausted, even if you are.

Wine Definition or Description

American winemakers are to be credited with greatly educating consumers about what wine is and what to do with it. On jug wines and many fifth-size premium wines, the line directly beneath the wine's type name often says something concise like "semidry and fragrant," or more expansive like "light golden in color, with a greenish hue, it is pleasingly tart, but retains a touch of natural sweetness, making it elegantly delicate to the taste"; or it may give a direction about serving it like "mates best with beef . . . serve at cool room temperature."

A lot of this language is helpful but "rich," "full-bodied," and "mellow" have most of the precision of advertising language—which is not much—and are nowhere officially defined. "Dry" is a good example of a term that is used in different ways by label writers and by wine professionals (including the commercial winemaker when he is off-duty). Wineries discovered long ago that Americans ask for and buy "dry" table wine and Champagne that actually is sweetish to a large degree. One label writer, aware of this but trying to describe the wine accurately, will use "semidry" or "mellow" for this slightly sweet wine. But another label writer will accept Americans' desires and give them "dry." Taste Paul Masson's Emerald Dry (proprietary name, made from Emerald Riesling) and see if you think it's dry. You could sure fool us.

Champagne makers have a semiofficial dryness scale: "natur" or "natural" signify the very driest (though there may be a touch of sugar); "brut" is next driest (possibly .5 to 1.5 percent sugar); "sec" or "dry" is third (2.5 to 4.5 percent sugar); "demi-sec" or "semidry" is fourth (perhaps 5 percent sugar); "doux" is fifth (up to 10 percent sugar). No one holds Champagne makers to these terms, however; Korbel's sec is only 1.5 percent sugar, and another Champagne house makes "natural" sweeter than "brut."

It helps at least to know how wine professionals (critics, university enologists, et al.) use some of the descriptives you see on wine labels. Chapter 3, "Tasting California Wine" outlines the basic tasting (looking, smelling, then tasting) criteria and terms, then lists some of the specific descriptives associated with popular varietal wines.

Ingredients and Alcohol Content

The Bureau of Alcohol, Tobacco, and Firearms in 1975 killed a proposal for full listing of ingredients in alcoholic beverages, and the industry opened Champagne. Four years later, under pressure from the Food and Drug Administration and consumer interests, the BATF revived the idea. The industry uncorked the same arguments: costly regulation, label clutter, wine as agricultural product (natural, not manufactured), complaints about "self-appointed consumer advocates" and the FDA's lack of jurisdiction.

The BATF capitulated, of course, and in 1980 said it would issue regulations (effective in 1983) requiring wineries, breweries, and distilleries to disclose a few ingredients—if an interested drinker wrote to an address on the label. The BATF suggested that some wineries would list ingredients on the label if it was to their advantage to do so (for example, "Made from Cabernet Sauvignon grapes and cultured yeast"); others, who put in additives such as sulfur dioxide that remain in the wine, would presumably wait anxiously for people to write in for the ingredients. Even then, the BATF said there need be no disclosure of filtering aids, clarifying agents, or sugars and acids used to correct natural deficiencies.

In other words, the BATF is issuing such a watered-down regulation that they may as well drop the whole idea.

Even the simplest front labels, the ones with the bare-bones listing of wine type, maker, and "bottled by," have one item that doesn't seem interesting or necessary: alcohol content, as a percentage of volume. Wine wouldn't be wine without alcohol but it's not that intoxicating. While brandy and whiskey range from 35 to 50 percent alcohol, California table wine is a mere 7 to 14 percent, with 11 to 12 percent being typical and more desirable in premium wines but 7 to 9 percent "soft" or "light" wine being increasingly popular. Unless the wine is a flavored "pop" wine or a table wine labeled "table wine" or "light wine," the percentage of alcohol must be stated, and, for table wines, must be accurate within 1 percent. Dessert and aperitif wines are all over 17 percent: Sherry is not less than 17 percent, Angelica, Madeira, Muscatel, and Port not less than 18 percent, unless designated "light." These fortified wines are allowed a 1.5-percent tolerance. In the case of table wines, high alcohol content is not always desirable, for it masks subtle flavors and aroma.

The FDA wants to warn pregnant women of the danger of drinking alcohol, which may lead to the Fetal Alcohol Syndrome (FAS), but no regulation has been adopted so far.

Bottle Size, Shape, and Closure

The bottle itself is usually molded with the net contents (by volume) in raised letters on the base. The feds, in metrifying the U.S., have so far been most successful with the wine and spirits industry, and customary measurements like gallons and fifths have been converted to liters and milliliters, though fluid ounces must also be stated. Here are some equivalents:

Liters (fluid ounces)	Closest Customary Measurement (fl. oz.)
4 (135.2)	gallon (128)
3 (101)	⅘ gal., double magnum, jeroboam (102.4)
1.5 (50.7)	⅖ gal., magnum (51.2)
1 (33.8)	quart (32)
.750 or 750 ml. (25.8)	fifth, ⅘ qt. (25.6)
.375 or 375 ml. (12.7)	tenth (12.8)
.187 or 187 ml. (6.3)	split (6.4)

For understandable reasons, the wine and restaurant industries would like you to order larger-size bottles—1.5-liter or magnum-size—with your dinner. Magnums are becoming more popular, while the small half-bottle, the tenth or 375-milliliter bottle, is being steadily knocked off wine lists. Some wine experts welcome dropping the tenth because the wine doesn't keep as well and, as a result of slow turnover, half-bottles of white wine sometimes are too old when opened at a restaurant.

On a dark night in a dark corner of your wine cellar, you can try to guess what kind of wine is in the bottle by the shape. The **Bordeaux bottle** has straight sides, curving but somewhat square shoulders, and a short, slender neck; it is dark green if used for Cabernet Sauvignon,

Zinfandel, and generic Claret wines, lighter green or clear for Sauvignon Blanc (Fumé Blanc), Sémillon, and generic Sauterne wines. The **Burgundy bottle,** which is stocky with sloping shoulders and a long neck, and colored dark green, is used for Pinot Noir, Gamay Beaujolais, and generic Burgundy red wines as well as Chardonnay, Chenin Blanc, and generic Chablis white wines. The **Rhine bottle** (or Hock bottle), which is tall, slender, gently curving, and colored green or brown, is used for Rieslings, Gewürztraminer, and generic Rhine and Moselle white wines. All these are the traditional fifth (750-milliliter) bottle; jugs are often distinctively shaped and randomly green and clear.

Such variety in shape and color may become a thing of the past as the wine industry becomes bigger and more efficient and standardizes everything. The big Owens-Illinois glass company in 1979 introduced an emerald green fifth-size bottle whose shape is halfway between the Burgundy and the Rhine bottles; amber, flint, and two other green bottles will also be produced. Wente Brothers promptly adopted the new "California bottle" for all its wines. The trade magazine *Wines and Vines* predicted that other wineries would follow.

If you want to age a wine, you need not only a straight-sided bottle but one with a cork in it. The mouth may be additionally covered with a lead or plastic capsule, which is to keep rodents from your best vintages. As with bottles with round sides, screw-capped bottles should be drained quickly.

Other Information

Unlike German wine labels, on which nearly everything not required is prohibited, American labels may contain as much information as a printer can squeeze in.

Back-label information often elaborates what is on the front label and goes into grape-growing and winemaking practices. Very common are comments about the grapes used: "This estate-bottled wine was made from Cabernet Sauvignon grapes with a subtle blend of Merlot [which] we find improves the balance of the wine and makes it more drinkable in the earlier years."

Or perhaps the back label discusses vineyard location. Some do this in travelogue terms: "All our wines are made from varietal grapes grown in our own vineyards, which are close-knit in the lee of Mt. St. Helena." Some rhapsodize about conditions: "The Ricetti Vineyards are located high in the Eastern hills above Redwood Valley. Each year the red clay soil, ideal exposure, and excellent cultural practices bring forth a crop of perfect maturity." Some are dry and specific: "Near Black Mountain on Monte Bello Ridge, our main vineyard is 10 miles south of Palo Alto, 15 miles inland from the ocean, and over 2,000 feet in elevation."

For wine buffs, some wineries write labels that describe the whole process: "It is produced entirely from Sauvignon Blanc grapes grown by Joe Rochioli on Fenton Acres Ranch near Healdsburg. Harvested in mid-October at an average sugar content of 22.5° Brix and a total acidity of .82, the grapes were cold fermented to dryness, aged in barrels of American and French origin, and bottled in the Spring of 1975." Others may describe the harvest to the day and time of day, the time it takes to transport the grapes to the winery, the duration of fermentation and the fermenting vessel, malo-lactic fermentation (a secondary fermentation desired for Pinot Noir and other wines when in wood cooperage; bacteria converts malic acid into weaker lactic acid plus carbon dioxide), the name of the winemaker, the kind of equipment. . . .

Gewürztraminer

This is my first attempt at making a sweet "late harvest" style wine, and I am quite pleased with the results. It is produced entirely from Healdsburg area Gewürztraminer grown by Jim Miller. At harvest time on Sept. 14, 1978, the grapes had a mild botrytis infection, an average sugar content of 25.1° Brix (% by wt.), and a total acidity of 0.51% by vol. Part of the juice was given six hours skin contact time prior to pressing. After cold fermentation, the fermentation process was stopped by centrifugation. The wine was briefly aged in French oak and bottled in late January, 1979.

We invite you to enjoy this and our other Dry Creek Vineyard wines, and to visit us at the winery.

Winemaker

DRY CREEK VINEYARD, HEALDSBURG, CALIFORNIA

Tedious detail if you're a novice. But keep reading back labels and you may learn to relate technical information to what your senses tell you as you drink wine.

But the back label is also a repository for more misleading information, despite federal regulations. The BATF had to amend its broad rule in 1978 to require the information to be specific to the wine in the bottle. Previously, some wineries were describing their home vineyards in lavish prose but neglecting to say that the grapes used to make the wine weren't grown there. The BATF also requires that labels not mislead the customer by ambiguity, omission, or implication. We'll wait to see how the agency enforces that one.

DOES PRICE MEAN QUALITY?

The last bit of information put on the bottle is the price tag applied by the retailer. At least in California, wine and other alcoholic beverages are no longer sold under fair-trade agreements, which constituted a legal conspiracy between producers, wholesalers, and retailers to sell products at artificially high prices. Nowadays, in pricing, the fundamental activity of the government has to do with excise, inventory, and sales taxes.

So the price of wine should be governed chiefly by market forces. These include not only the traditional law of supply and demand but the more modern laws written by wine-marketing and advertising people. The authors have a cynical view of what they do. So do they. If they know exactly what the consumer wants, it's because they can make him want it.

In fashioning their products, they exploit some unfathomable and irrational but perfectly understandable human impulses: the desire for something alcoholic to lubricate social relationships, the desire to enjoy what one believes is one of the finer things in life, and the desire to impress other people with a display of money, knowledge, or taste. "Burgundy" satisfies only the first desire, Napa Valley Cabernet Sauvignon satisfies the first and second desires, and Stag's Leap Wine Cellars' 1973 Napa Valley Cabernet nicely satisfies all three.

But fulfilling these desires relates back to supply and demand. Burgundy is put in a billion bottles every year, and is consequently cheap. Napa Valley Cabernet can be bottled from only 15,000 to 20,000 tons per year (less than one percent of California grapes crushed at wineries), so is more costly to buy. And the 1973 Stag's Leap Cabernet was bottled from less than 35 tons that winery bought, and was considerably costlier for the consumer—especially after it outdid reds from famous chateaux in the 1976 Paris tasting.

The trick for the marketing and advertising folks is to get you to pay as much as possible for Burgundy—that's where the sales volume is—*despite* plenteous supply and fairly flexible demand—and to pay even more for Napa Valley Cabernet.

A general rule about the interaction of supply and demand and other market forces can be stated as follows: The price of a bottle of wine is roughly the monetary total of the values of the wine's features as stated on the label. Of course, this rule cannot be uniformly applied to all wines in every marketplace. But it's good enough to explain a lot about the relationship of price and quality of California wines.

One attribute of a wine is the name of the producer. This aspect is imponderable insofar as it involves reputation but can be discussed in terms of the relative size of a winemaking operation. Reputation is too insubstantial to measure, though it can be debated hotly to no end. We'll agree that reputation may be the most important aspect to consider if you desire a risk-free wine-drinking experience. But risk-free wine is unlikely to be the greatest.

Two other aspects we'll also discuss—grape variety and appellation of origin—influence price in measurable ways because of the real cost of the raw product: particular grapes from particular vineyards.

Other features are less easy to analyze in a short space. Vintage date relates to grape prices as well, but market conditions and vintages both change from year to year. The role of bottle age in pricing can't be easily rationalized because it relates not only to annual inventory taxes but also to how quickly a winery wants a return on investment. Other price aspects of the wine that are seen on the label have to do with various prestige designations ("Estate Bottled," vineyard name, bottle numbering, etc.). Unfortunately, it is impossible to tell before you drink a wine whether or not the designation is true and justifies any part of the price.

Only after much experience in buying and drinking wine and keeping up with developments can you confidently link all the elements of price and mentally chart a price-quality scale that will answer that question you always ask as you're standing in a wineshop examining a bottle: Is this wine worth the price? The only true test is to taste it.

Size of Winery and Size of Price

Earlier we put California wineries into three size categories: giant, medium-size, and small or boutique. The reasons for the three categories (which could be five or a dozen) are several, and they point to the strong probability that the premium wines that come closest to fulfilling the promise of the label and the price are nearly always from small wineries and are therefore the most expensive.

Giant wineries have to operate with economy of scale, and to produce enormous quantities of average wine for wholesaling across the country, appealing to the tastes and budgets of the mass market. Small wineries, by contrast, use traditional, labor-intensive methods to make small lots of wine, the higher quality and resulting higher price of which appeals to a select market; indeed, some boutiques sell their entire output at retail on their own doorstep. Only some of the medium-size wineries that are so inclined make both jug generics to compete with the giants and high-quality varietals to compete with the small wineries.

It is easy to shatter this fragile generality. A large winery could use its considerable resources to produce the best premium wines—but it's unlikely they would do it for money, only prestige. At the opposite end, small winery operations are often amateurish and can produce bottles with off-odors, extreme acidity (including volatile acidity—vinegariness), incredible tannin, and so forth—at prices you wouldn't believe. The generality is fine as far as it goes.

A recent proof of high quality at high price and less (but not poor) quality at low price came at the wine judging at the 1979 Orange County Fair. Organizers wanted to do what other fairs don't—which is to include every available California wine in a limited number of categories. For each of nine categories, wines were put in three price ranges: inexpensive (up to $4 for Cabernet, for example), moderate ($4.01 to $8 for Cab), and expensive ($8.01 and up for Cab). That thoughtful categorization alone is significant. So were the results. In blind-tasting the wines in the nine categories, the judges declined to award any gold medals to any of the *inexpensive* Chardonnay, Pinot Noir, French Colombard, Gewürztraminer, or Rosé of Cabernet. Indeed, inexpensive wines got only four gold medals, while moderately priced wines received 16 and expensive wines 12. Giant wineries collected three golds, while medium-size wineries took 13 and small wineries 16. Again, this was a blind tasting, which rules out label snobbery.

So, as you're wandering the aisles of a wineshop, remember to compare Dry Creek Vineyard's Chardonnay with Chappellet's in price and quality, and possibly to Robert Mondavi's, but probably not to Inglenook/United Vintners'. Our listings under "Who Made the Wine?" (p. 58) should help.

Grape Variety and Price Variety

There is no even correlation between price per ton of a grape variety and price per bottle of varietal wine. Yet analysis of grape prices shows what demand is like, and that links firmly to wine prices. To give an idea of the relative cost of grapes, here is a six-level price scale (in descending order) based on prices per ton paid in 1978 for 34 Napa County varieties, which are on average the costliest in California:

- $800 and up: Chardonnay (most expensive grape; for white wine).
- $600 to $800: Gewürztraminer, Pinot Blanc, Cabernet Franc (most expensive red-wine grape), White Riesling.
- $500 to $600: Sauvignon Blanc (Fumé Blanc), Muscat Blanc (Muscat Canelli), Chenin Blanc, Gray Riesling.
- $400 to $500: Cabernet Sauvignon (second most expensive red-wine grape), Merlot, Zinfandel, Charbono (near the average price for the 34 varieties), Napa Gamay, Petite Sirah, Sylvaner, Pinot Noir, Sémillon, Malvasia Bianca.
- $300 to $400: Pinot St. George, Flora, Green Hungarian, French Colombard, Barbera, Ruby Cabernet, Refosco (Mondeuse), Gamay Beaujolais, Early Burgundy, Sauvignon Vert, Burger.
- $300 or less: Palomino, Grenache, Carignane, Grand Noir.

Some of these are not used for table wines (Palomino is used for Sherry). Some are mostly used for making rosés (Napa Gamay, Grenache). A couple are of the distinctive Muscat variety not used for dry table wines (Muscat Blanc, Malvasia Bianca). Some are grown in small quantities for blending and other purposes (Cabernet Franc, Grand Noir, Refosco). Many are mostly used for generics but are occasionally found as varietals (Sauvignon Vert, Charbono, Burger, Flora). And many are used for blending but are also minor-league varietals (French Colombard, Sémillon, Gray Riesling, Green Hungarian, Sylvaner, Gamay Beaujolais, Barbera, Napa Gamay, Ruby Cabernet, Carignane, Pinot St. George).

Looking at only the 22 most often bottled as varietals, the price scale might be of help to the wine-shopper—except that not all varieties picked during any one harvest go on the market at the same time. More attention and additional aging add cost to some of the red varieties that are, while white wine is booming, sold for relatively moderate prices. So here's a rough price gradation that should apply to the output of any one Napa Valley winery if it produced all 22 varietals:

- Most expensive: Chardonnay, Gewürztraminer, Pinot Blanc, White Riesling; Cabernet Sauvignon, Merlot.
- Less expensive: Chenin Blanc, Gray Riesling, Sauvignon Blanc (Fumé Blanc), Sémillon, Sylvaner; Barbera, Napa Gamay, Petite Sirah, Pinot Noir, Zinfandel.
- Inexpensive: French Colombard, Green Hungarian; Carignane, Gamay Beaujolais, Grenache, Ruby Cabernet.

Not every bottle of wine can be priced by this scale. The varietal price gradation, for example, is based on *average* prices. While Napa Chardonnay in 1978 was sold for an average price of a bit more than $800 per ton, wineries actually paid 26 different prices between $200 and $1,400. The boutique winery that paid the $1,400 for each of 16 tons, to make as many as 11,000 bottles, will obviously have to charge more per bottle than the winery that paid only the average price. Special-quality factors can also raise the price of a bottle: late-harvest and well-aged Zinfandels can be expensive. The wineries that try harder with Pinot Noir to match the French Burgundy standard will charge more, even if the result is less superb.

Appellation of Origin and Origin of Price

The price of varietals from Sonoma in 1978 was on the average only 2 percent less than Napa grapes. But, reflecting differences in growing conditions, Sonoma's Gewürztraminer, Sauvignon Blanc, Sylvaner, Green Hungarian, and, interestingly, Barbera (a popular Sebastiani varietal) were considerably more costly than Napa's. But Sonoma's Cabernet, Merlot, Zinfandel, and Pinot Noir were considerably less costly.

Mendocino's grapes were only slightly less costly than Napa's, on the average. But its Gewürztraminer, Sylvaner, Grenache, and Barbera were notably more expensive, and White Riesling, Merlot, Pinot Noir, and Green Hungarian less expensive.

The disparity among grape prices in the vineyard becomes more noticeable away from the North Coast. The northern Central Coast
(Santa Clara Valley, Santa Cruz Mountains, Livermore) produced
only two varieties—Chardonnay and Green Hungarian—more expensive than Napa's. The middle and southern Central Coast (Monterey
to Santa Barbara) grew Sylvaner, Sémillon, and French Colombard
that were more costly. Once away from the coast, all grapes are considerably less expensive.

The following shows the average cost per ton of the 14 most expensive red and white varieties in California winegrowing districts in
1978:

	Average Cost Per Ton	Percentage Less Than Napa
Napa County	$528	—
Mendocino and Lake Counties	525	.5
Sonoma and Marin Counties	518	1.7
Northern Central Coast	508	3.7
Middle and Southern Central Coast	447	15.3
Southern California	341	35.3
Lodi Area	224	57.5
Modesto Area	197	62.6
Central San Joaquin	174	67.0
Southern San Joaquin	162	69.2

The striking differences in price make it obvious why wines with
better appellations of origin should be more expensive. But another
striking thing is the extremely close average prices of the top four wine
districts, which indicates how rapidly vineyards in Mendocino, Sonoma, and the northern Central Coast are gaining on the Napa Valley.

The price differences also show the enormous advantages some wineries can gain by blending expensive coastal wine with as much as possible less-expensive Central Valley wine.

Choosing a Wine

To sum up, as you shop you must keep in mind (1) probable quality differences that are linked to the price differences of giant, medium-size, and small wineries, (2) undoubted price differences among particular varietals, and (3) undoubted price differences among appellations of origin.

These things are indicators, not predictors. We hope you can apply our various price-quality scales, or draw similar ones of your own if market conditions change (some experts see, for example, renewed popularity of red varietals as wine novices follow a "learning curve" up from drinking generic white wine). If there are wines that seem to fly willfully up and down the scales, look for causes in other label statements—vintage date and prestige designations. If those don't appear to explain an anomalous price, put the bottle back on the shelf and continue looking.

You will really have to use all your newly acquired label-reading skills—and the Magary Special Whiz-Bang Deciphering and Decoding Book—to get to the bottom line on the price-quality question. To make your initial selections easier, we have some more advice.

First, consider the expectations of those present when you produce your bottle of wine and place it on the table. Expectations may be non-existent because raviolis are being served and your relatives are chattering busily about kids and lawns and taxes. So you should buy a jug for a low price—plus a dollar, on the assumption that you don't want to poison your kinfolk. If, however, expectations are higher because some of the guests know a little about wine and may want to smack their lips, buy the best possible varietal in the medium-price range from a medium-size winery; it will be safely predictable in quality and won't be wasted on those at the far end of the table. At the other extreme, expectations may be very high because you're dining with four sophisticates who spend their weekends wine-touring. You should definitely buy something from a small winery for the most you can pay or the occasion seems to demand. If it fails, it fails honorably. If it succeeds, so do you.

Assume for now that you're taking a bottle to a friend's house but don't know how high expectations will be and also don't know what food will be served. Don't take Champagne unless it's a celebration. Pick a table wine by process of elimination, aiming for the highest *probable* quality at a price you feel comfortable with. Here's how we, with our biases and rules of four thumbs, would proceed to eliminate:

1. **Eliminate all rosé and "blanc de" wines.** Unless you're going on a picnic or to a patio party, rosés and off-white wines don't cut it.

2. **Eliminate all generically named wines.** The quality just isn't in "Burgundy," "Chablis," and other generic table wines. (Non-table wines with generic names, like Sherry and Port, are not acceptable during the main part of a meal.)

3. **Eliminate sweet wines.** Sweet wines are rarely appropriate with the main course at dinner. Get a dry or semi-dry wine only.

4. **Eliminate wines with proprietary names.** It's not that they're bad, just incomparable. "Red Table Wine," "Rubion," and "Barenblut" are conceivably the same blend but probably not. They are equally anonymous.

5. **Eliminate wines made by the giant companies.** They make too much inoffensive wine, not taking chances by extracting the best wine from nature's best grapes. Wines from big wineries that appear to be made in small lots ("Vintner's Selection," "Cask No. 102") aren't necessarily so made.

6. **Eliminate wines with nonspecific appellations of origin.** With exceptions, "California" and "North Coast" as appellations of origin are too large, indicating either blends of wines grown in the Central Valley or indiscriminate geographical blends.

7. **Eliminate wines only "Made and Bottled by" or similarly labeled.** The consistently best wines are those made by one winemaker from grapes grown under his supervision, and these should be labeled "Produced and Bottled by." Scorn "Vinted and Bottled by" wines.

8. **Eliminate wines from wineries outside the coastal area.** This covers any that have slipped by the elimination of wines from giant wineries and "Made/Vinted and Bottled by" wines. It is one more way to guard against coastal district wines being trucked to the Central Valley for treatment that may make them more uniform and predictable than is desirable for wine at a good dinner table.

9. **Eliminate wines without vintage dates.** Nonvintage wine could be a good blend of wine from two poor years, or wine made to taste exactly the same from year to year. Our rules of elimination certainly aim toward predictable high quality, but it's good to take a chance with vintage. If you don't have a vintage chart, which gives either the consensus or one critic's view of the quality of particular vin-

tages, pick the wine on the basis of how old it is. Eliminate whites that are *more* than three years old unless oak-aged Chardonnay or the like. Eliminate reds that are *less* than two years old, making sure that it's drinkable now, rather than 20 to 30 years from now. "Nouveau" or "spring" wines may be inappropriate at any but an informal dinner.

10. **Eliminate wines not in standard fifth-size (750-milliliter) bottles with straight sides and closed with corks.** Anything else is gimmicky and doesn't deserve to be a vintage-dated varietal with a coastal appellation.

11. **Eliminate wines with dubious prestige designations or misleading or ambiguous back-label statements.** Pay attention to legitimate prestige designations ("Estate Bottled," after 1983, "Private Reserve" if from an old reputable winery). But ignore meaningless designations (bottle numbering, "Rare Varietal Wine") and those that may indicate some special condition or treatment that may make the wine an inappropriate selection as a main dinner wine.

12. **Eliminate wines that are priced too high or too low.** That is, if you have now begun to examine only Sonoma Fumé Blancs, compare prices and get something in the middle range, ignoring low-priced ones as risky bargains and high-priced ones as too good for the people at the far end of the table.

Now you've eliminated all but a few wines in a supermarket and more than half the California wines in a good wineshop. The remaining wines, dry or semidry, are vintaged varietals from coastal wine districts, made by medium-size and small wineries and priced in the middle. That still leaves quite a number. Pick now for preferred color (white is at the moment more popular, but red indicates more sophistication, we think), preferred flavor and characteristics (see "Tasting California Varietals," p. 95), favored appellation of origin (Napa may be safe but Santa Barbara may be more fun to talk about), and, slipperiest factor of all, winery reputation.

You're pretty much alone when you walk into a wineshop. You're equipped with a little knowledge but confronted by ranks, rows, aisles, bins, and boxes of potentially good wines. And you exercise your own judgment, which is based on past wine-drinking, the requirements of the occasion, some geographical prejudices, some common sense and an equal amount of skepticism, advertising, friends' recommendations, miscellaneous critical opinions (if you can remember which is which from the comments on thousands of wines), the wine merchant's recommendations (unless he's trying to push slow-moving bottles), sheer whimsy (the elegance of the label), and, finally, fleeting time. Good hunting.

LABEL-READING TEST

Now that you know as much as we do (or think we do), here are three labels to test your knowledge and skepticism on.

First:

RESERVE

1975
Napa Valley
FUMÉ BLANC
Dry Sauvignon Blanc
ALCOHOL 12% BY VOLUME
PRODUCED AND BOTTLED BY
ROBERT MONDAVI WINERY
OAKVILLE, CALIFORNIA

This is a straightforward label, unpretentious, sparely written. You know that at least 75 percent was crushed, fermented, and finished by Mondavi, that at least 75 percent of the contents comes from Sauvignon Blanc grapes grown in the Napa Valley (on the model of the Loire Valley wine, a crisp, dry wine made from these grapes is called Fumé Blanc), and that at least 95 percent of the wine grapes were harvested in 1975. "Reserve" may not mean anything until you learn of Mondavi's high reputation, after which you may believe Mondavi, after fermenting a particular batch, found it unexpectedly good and gave it more attention than other wines.

Here's another label:

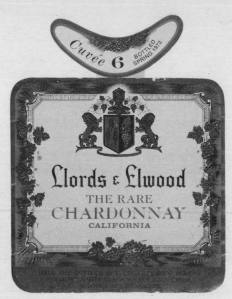

The label (produced in Germany) is printed in black and gilt with a great deal of embossing, including the coat of arms. Note the discreet "R" for registered trademark.

What's wrong with a high price for this impressive-looking wine? Everything, because it's unjustifiably snobbish for what it says and doesn't say. First, there's nothing rare about Chardonnay grapes or wine: it's the third most-crushed white-wine grape in California (almost 32,000 tons in 1979) and second most-produced varietal wine (at least 194 wineries were making it in 1979). "The Rare" is, obviously, a pretentious brand name. "Cuvée 6" initially sounds great—but wait a moment. There's no vintage date, just a bottling date; "Made and Bottled by" indicates that Llords & Elwood produced less than 75 percent, maybe as little as 10 percent, of the wine, using as little as 51 percent Chardonnay grown somewhere in California. Fremont is an industrial city, but Llords & Elwood tries to suggest it is a winegrowing area by slipping in "Santa Clara Valley"—for what that's worth—as part of its address. "Cuvée 6," then, is not some extra-special batch of select Chardonnay but a vat in which bulk wines purchased from outside were blended. A blend can be a superior wine but the label is trying to bully the consumer. "Llords," by the way, was the name of a liquor store in Los Angeles that chain-store owner Mike Elwood bought, but that and the coat of arms suggest kinship with nobility. Can't the winemaker let the wine speak for itself?

Here's the third label:

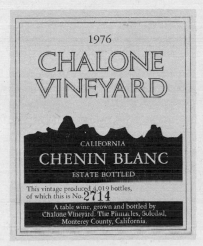

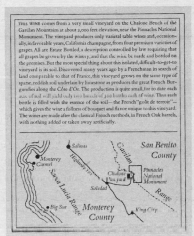

There are some curious things about this label. Despite the back-label description of the vineyard's attributes and a map showing where it is, despite the "Grown and Bottled by" and the spelled-out address (area, town, county, state; other Chalone labels toss in "Mt. Chalone" and all the back labels mention the Gavilan Mountains), despite the "Estate Bottled" designation and the scrupulous definition on the back label— despite all this, the appellation of origin is only "California" and the bottom line doesn't include the essential word *produced*.

Why?

The skeptic may think something is not as it should be, especially since bottle numbering is snobby and the back label, which runs on and on and mentions France five times, stresses Chalone's low production (600 bottles per acre from "a very small vineyard"—50 or 75 acres at that time). Answers may be found elsewhere (most Chalone labels say "California" and "Grown and Bottled by"), but looking at just one label, the consumer may think Chalone grows more ambiguities than grapes. This kind of label can drive you to drink.

There. That's the end of "Reading a Bottle of California Wine," our magic decoder and demystifier.

We'll pick up the theme from the introduction and say that the world of wine is multitudinous, multifarious, and multiform. That's all the better to dazzle the wine drinker, give the wine buff much to talk about . . . and confuse the consumer.

As you wend your way from bin to bottle, aisle to cash register, reading the information on a hundred bottles of wine, remember that piece of advice given by Count Alexey Tolstoy (cousin of the novelist): "Should you read, upon an enclosure with an elephant, a sign saying BUFFALO, believe not your eyes." Of course, there are two ways of interpreting that advice.

CHAPTER 3:

Tasting California Wine

Trying to get acquainted with wine as a sensory experience is like buying your first expensive stereo system: it's easy to be intimidated not only by your own ignorance of the rudiments and the subtleties but by someone else's comprehensive knowledge and easy, articulate opinions. But after visiting a few dealers, you pick up some of the lingo and find that some of the technical aspects aren't that hard to understand. And you learn that there's high fidelity for (1) a fringe of audiophiles who will spend another $400 for .01 percent less total harmonic distortion and (2) everyone else.

Appreciating wine (table wine) is not the exclusive province of frightful snobs. "It's a naïve domestic burgundy without any breeding, but I think you'll be amused by its presumption" is the oft-quoted caption on a James Thurber cartoon. You can appreciate the incredible variety of wine and learn to talk about it if you have an eye, a nose, and a tongue and the willingness to analyze what those senses are telling you. You need not try to develop the parlor-trick ability at a blind tasting to name the wine, the maker, the vintage, the vineyard. (Winemakers sometimes fail to recognize their own creations!)

The first general principle of wine tasting is that it's *your* taste. "Everyone," said Henry Adams, "carries his own inch-rule of taste." If your inch-rule is that you like white wine with steak or red wine with trout, enjoy it. Nevertheless, the lack of universal standards of taste does not mean you should not attempt to discriminate, to try to describe just what it is you like and don't like, and to listen to the opinions of others.

The second general principle of wine tasting is that you must be as expressive as possible. It's often necessary to exaggerate descriptions of flavors and scents in order to distinguish between two or more wines, or otherwise characterize the wine in some way that communicates something to another taster. You don't have to say anything you'd be embarrassed to hear anyone else say, but you should get used to the rich prose of wine criticism if you want to become fully acquainted with the variety of wine. For example, here are four consensus comments from a Vintners Club blind tasting of California Cabernets:

1. "Intense deep color; rich nose, heavy mint, intense; refined, young, elegant, very complex."
2. "Deep purple; full nose, heavy American oak; deep, tannic, oaky, chewy."
3. "Medium light purple; broccoli nose, H₂S [hydrogen sulfide—the rotten-eggs smell of hot springs]; stripped, chemical, slightly acid, off finish."
4. "Light color; weak candy nose; light, simple, anemic, low fruit."

"Chewy"? "Weak candy nose"? "Intense" and "refined"? Bosh, you say—but on the other hand, if these were comments in a wine column in the newspaper, which wine would you select for dinner with your boss? More likely 1 or 2 than 3 or 4. Such exaggerated descriptions are not only valid in making vivid comparisons but, in the end, worthwhile for the consumer.

BASIC TASTING CRITERIA AND QUALITIES

There are methodical ways to approach a glass of wine, taste it, and describe it. Here are the basic criteria and qualities:

Look: A good wine in a clean glass will look brilliant and clear, as appealing to the eye as stained glass. Hold the glass up to the light or against a white tablecloth to see whether "red" is maybe inky and purplish or medium ruby or even amber, or "white" is pale straw or yellow or dark gold or even pale greenish. The quality of the wine is only slightly in the color and clarity—but a look adds to the anticipation.

Smell or **"nose":** A deep, slow sniff and a moment's pause to analyze it may tell you about two things: **aroma,** which is that part of smell coming from the grapes, and **bouquet,** which is that part originating from fermentation and aging (many wines have no bouquet).

The difference between these two qualities may not be noticeable until you've sniffed a well-aged wine that has lost the grapy aroma tending to predominate among young wines. Start by thinking of at least one adjective, then sniff again and think of another. Despite the adjectives in the four Vintners Club descriptions, many tasters don't strive to detect the improbable ("minty cedar nose" or "vegetal, chocolate") but may simply note that a wine is fragrant (or not), fruity (or not), spicy, oaky or woody (from the casks), penetrating, austere, or complex (which means everything—and maybe nothing).

Here are some other nose tags: acetic (vinegary), beery, black currants, corky (spoiled by a bad cork), flinty (like freshly struck gunflint), flowery, foxy (not like a fox but like such native American grapes as the Concord), maderized (white wines can become old, oxidized, flat, musty, and brownish, like Madeira), musty, peppery, smoky, sulfuric (from an excess of sulfur dioxide in the winemaking), yeasty.

"Vinous" or "winy" is a description of the last resort. If no distinctive aroma or bouquet is evident, which is frequently the case with jug wines, the taster may describe it as "closed" or "withdrawn."

You should try hard to use your sense of smell, for it is, according to Professors M. A. Amerine and V. S. Singleton of the University of California at Davis, just as good a sense as a professional's. "There is no reason," they continue, "why the interested wine drinker cannot learn to identify a wide variety of vinous odors if he or she acquires sufficient experience. One cannot identify an odor one has not experienced."

Taste: No fancy snorting or gargling is necessary here: just hold the wine momentarily on your tongue and let it go to different parts of your mouth, including under and in back of your tongue, before swallowing it. First, is it sweet or dry or somewhere in between? Then, is it full-bodied (like milk) or light-bodied (like water) or somewhere in between? Does the alcohol burn your tongue? In the case of reds, how much pucker (astringency, from the tannin in the seeds, stems, and skins) is there? With most reds and more whites, how acidic (tart or crisp—or sour) is it? Sweet or dry, how fruity does it taste? Is varietal flavor apparent? Is it rough (hard, immature, too tannic) or mellow (soft, velvety), or is it well balanced, with the right proportions of sugar, acid, fruit, tannin, and alcohol? Finally, is the finish or aftertaste pleasing too?

There's a whole lexicon of descriptives available to wine tasters, more than just for smell, because, when you taste, you can't help but experience aroma and bouquet once more and include it in the taste. Here are some common tags: bitter, broad, closed (not flavorful), cloying (too sweet), corky (see under "Smell"), earthy, fat (may be complimentary), flabby (not complimentary), grapy, heady (alcohol or carbonation), insipid, long, maderized (see under "Smell"), metallic, oxidized, ripe, round, sharp, thin, watery, woody, yeasty.

That's an outline of what you should have in mind as you taste. Whatever adjectives you decide to use, make sure you believe in them.

The sensory evaluation of wine has been studied with as much scientific precision as the enologists at UC-Davis can muster. Since the 1940s the following 20-point scoring guide developed at Davis has been standard at blind tastings:

- **Appearance:** 0—cloudy, 1—clear, 2—brilliant
- **Color:** 0—distinctly off, 1—slightly off, 2—correct
- **Aroma and bouquet:** 1—vinous, 2—distinct but not varietal, 3 or 4—varietal. Subtract 1 or 2 for off-odors; add 1 for bottle bouquet
- **Vinegariness (acescence):** 0—obvious, 1—slight, 2—none
- **Total acidity (tartness):** 0—distinctly low or high for the type, 1—slightly low or high, 2—normal (well balanced)
- **Sweetness:** 0—too low or high for the type, 1—normal
- **Body (consistency or alcoholicity):** 0—too low or high for the type, 1—normal
- **Flavor:** 0—distinctly abnormal, 1—slightly abnormal or deficient, 2—desirable for the type
- **Astringency and bitterness:** 0—distinctly high, 1—slightly high, 2—normal
- **General quality:** 0—lacking, 1—slight, 2—impressive

The suggested system for interpreting total score is:

- 17–20 points: outstanding quality, fine wines
- 13–16: sound commercial wines
- 9–12: commercial with noticeable defect
- 6–8: common, poor
- 1–5: unsatisfactory

Critics of this system say that, with modern technology, nearly every wine is brilliant in color and hardly a one is vinegary, yet that's automatically 4 points on the score. Meanwhile, at the other end of the scale, with fine wines that are automatically given 15 or 16 points, there aren't enough points left over to adequately quantify differences. Even Amerine and Singleton recognize that the "effective scoring range for most commercial wines falls within a range of no more than 10 points."

What is also imprecise are the standards being used, including what qualities any type of wine should have. That gets back to questions of taste that are satisfied by different wine "styles": some Chardonnays have lots of "chewiness" from the oak cooperage, while others are rich and more fruity than woody.

TASTING CALIFORNIA VARIETALS

While emphasizing that winemakers have different styles of making wine for different tastes, we list here the most typical attributes—including some flower, fruit, and vegetable descriptives—of the 31 most popular California varietals:

Barbera (red): A big, dark grape successfully transplanted from the Italian Piedmont. In cool areas in California it yields a dry, medium- to full-bodied, fruity, richly colored, robust but, when young, very acidic wine, capable of softening with bottle-aging. Barberas from warmer regions are acceptable but softer and more for everyday drinking. Sebastiani and other wineries with Italian family traditions produce fine Barberas.

Cabernet Sauvignon (red): The classic grape of Bordeaux, used in the majority of the great Médoc chateau wines. It is, as well, California's great red grape, producing the finest "big" reds in cool climates, generally in small quantities. Cabernet must be extremely well handled and decently aged. In Bordeaux and California alike, Cabernet's powerful qualities are often softened by blending in Merlot, Malbec, or other varieties—but some California wineries bottle 100-percent Cabernets, which are unheard of in France. Styles differ, but a "typical" Cabernet is deep ruby, full-bodied, dry and astringent, pungently aromatic, fruity and distinctive, reminding tasters variously but fondly of green olives, bell peppers, weeds, black currants, and tea. With age, Cabernet develops an amazing smoothness and great complexity in bouquet and flavor. Even relatively young Cabernet in a jug adds remarkably to everyday meals. This varietal is bottled by more wineries than any other, even by many outside California who purchase bulk wine or grape concentrate. Rosé of Cabernet and Blanc de Cabernet—not to mention Cabernet Champagne, Port, brandy, and vintage-dated jam—are also found these days because of the glut of this good variety.

Carignane (red): A grape from southern France, where it produces a robust, alcoholic table wine of no great distinction, as well as dessert wines. In warmer areas of California, Carignane is wonderfully productive but has drawbacks that make it a poor grape for varietals, so it is most often used in blending generic Burgundy and ordinary rosé. Fetzer, Fortino, Hecker Pass, Thomas Kruse, Parducci, and Trentadue are coastal wineries that have bottled varietal Carignane.

Charbono (red): An Italian grape grown on only 63 acres in Mendocino and Napa. The usual wine is dry, medium-bodied, rough, and without varietal character, but blending and aging can make it acceptable. Inglenook pioneered Charbono as a varietal—accidentally, for they thought the grapes were Barbera until corrected by UC-Davis. Souverain, Fortino, Franciscan, Parducci, and Davis Bynum have also made Charbono.

Chardonnay (white): The classic grape for white Burgundy (epitomized in Chablis, Meursault, and Montrachet) and for Champagne. As with Cabernet, Chardonnay is the most successful grape in California for remarkable—and remarkably expensive—varietals. It does extremely well in cool coastal valleys and produces an unusually "big" white, capable of gaining greater complexity with some aging in oak and in the bottle. As the white varietal most often bottled, Chardonnay differs in style, but a fine Chardonnay is full-bodied, dry, rich and intensely flavored (some hint of apples), fruitily fragrant, with a long, clean finish. It is also used in making California Champagne.

Chenin Blanc (white): The grape of the middle Loire Valley (Anjou and Touraine, epitomized in the Saumur and Vouvray districts), producing both dry and sweet (depending on weather and fermentation method) table and sparkling wines. It is known in Touraine as Pineau de la Loire, which is what the Christian Brothers of Napa also call it, and has been misnamed White Pinot. In California, Chenin Blanc is a versatile grape, doing best in coastal districts; a white grape, it is successful in the Central Valley if fermented cool. Acreage of Chenin Blanc increased more than 900 percent in the 1970s. It is a pleasing varietal and has qualities desirable for blending in generic Chablis and for making inexpensive Champagne. As a varietal it is often made soft and sweet, without much describable character, but is finer if made dry and with concentrated flavor: light, fresh, fruity, slightly tart, even a bit pétillant.

Emerald Riesling (white): A UC-Davis hybrid of White Riesling and Muscadelle, very successful in warm areas in retaining good acidity. Resulting wines are, in fact, tart (maybe too much so), semidry, fruity with some Muscat spiciness, and aromatic with a hint of Muscat's daphne-like floral fragrance. San Martín, Pedrizetti, and Monterey Peninsula are Central Coast wineries that bottle an Emerald Riesling varietal; Paul Masson uses the grape in a proprietary blend called Emerald Dry.

French Colombard (white): A grape of the Cognac district. In California it is very productive and much used in generic Chablis and Rhine wines and inexpensive Champagne. Though it has no distinctive varietal character, it can produce an unpretentious light, semidry, fruity, tart, and clean jug wine.

Gamay Beaujolais (red): If properly labeled, this should be from a Beaujolais district grape that is actually a variant of Pinot Noir and, in California, legally entitled to be labeled as such. Wineries find the name "Gamay Beaujolais" has more commercial appeal, however, and continue to use it on a wine that is good for picnics and barbecues: it's light, probably semidry, tart, fruity, maybe spicy. Drink it soon after you buy it.

Gewürztraminer (white): The grape that produces the notable, unique Alsatian wines, Gewürztraminer (same as Red Traminer) can be highly successful in cooler California areas, producing a semidry (sometimes sweetish), medium-bodied, tart wine with a light, Muscat-spicy aroma and earthy aftertaste. It's rapidly gaining popularity despite its hard-to-pronounce name. Don't give Gewürztraminer any cellar aging.

Gray Riesling (white): A mislabeled grape of uncertain French origin—but definitely not a Riesling. Several North Coast wineries, notably Wente Brothers, produce a pleasing minor varietal that is light, less than dry, fresh, spicy-fruity in flavor but with no distinctive aroma.

Green Hungarian (white): Another grape of unknown origin, but probably not Hungarian. Though not much is available (2,700 tons in 1979), it is used in blending generic white wines and is also bottled as a varietal by a few wineries, including Sonoma neighbors Sebastiani and Buena Vista. At its best, it is light, semidry, and fruity, but without distinctive character. Okay for a quick dinner.

Grenache (rosé): A grape widely planted in France (used in Chateauneuf-du-Pape red, in Tavel rosé, and in Banyuls sweet dessert wine) and in California, where it makes what some say is the best rosé: an orange-pink, generally dry, and fruity wine with a distinctive flowery or estery aroma. Grenache goes into many generic rosés but is put on the front label by Almadén, Beaulieu, Italian Swiss Colony, Sebastiani, and Sonoma Vineyards, among others.

Grignolino (rosé and red): A grape from the Piedmont, where it makes a heady red wine. Grown on 115 acres in California, Grignolino is mostly used in generic rosés but is also bottled as a varietal by Beringer, Emilio Guglielmo, Heitz, and Thomas Kruse. Although UC-Davis says there are several varieties sold as Grignolino, the most distinctive strain produces a pinkish orange, medium-bodied, dry, spicy-fruity wine with a pomegranate aroma and often enough tannin to make it capable of aging to softness.

Malvasia Bianca (white): The Muscat grape that produced the butt of Malmsey in which Shakespeare's Duke of Clarence drowned so famously. Known in France as Malvoisie, also grown in Italy, Spain, and Greece. With a unique orange-blossom fragrance, it makes a wine good with dessert or for sipping chilled. Beringer, Brookside, Kirigin, Monterey Peninsula, Novitiate, San Martín, and Stony Ridge are among the few that make it as a specialty.

Merlot (red): A Bordeaux grape so closely related to the Cabernet Sauvignon (with which it is often blended for desirable softness) that many Pomerol and St. Émilion wines are made predominantly of Merlot, yet compare in taste with the wines of Médoc, which are mostly Cabernet. In California, Merlot was grown on limited acreage for blending with Cabernet until big plantings in 1973–74; now it is coming into its own as a distinguished California varietal, one that is "big" and stands aging. Merlot tends to be dry, heavy, soft, with an herby or green-olive varietal character. Among bottling wineries are Almadén, David Bruce, Davis Bynum, Chappellet, Chateau St. Jean, Dry Creek, Firestone, Charles Krug, Inglenook, Louis M. Martini, Joseph Phelps, Rutherford Hill, Sonoma Vineyards, Souverain, Stag's Leap Wine Cellars, Sterling, Trentadue, and Veedercrest.

Mission (red): The pioneer California grape, grown from seeds carried by the Mission padres from Mexican vines imported from Spain. It dominated California winemaking for eight decades, until the 1860s, and is still grown on 4,600 acres—in fact, it is even planted from time to time. Despite drawbacks (roughness, poor acidity and color) that make it suitable only for alcoholic Angelica ("hardly a recommendation," sniffed wine authority Frank Schoonmaker) or a poor Port, a few Central Valley wineries bottle it as a varietal table wine.

Muscat of Alexandria (white): A raisin grape second only to Thompson Seedless. Mostly used in cheap Muscatel, it is also used to make a sweet table wine by California Growers, Cresta Blanca, Edmeades, Papagni, Pope Valley, Rutherford Vintners, Sutter Home, and Veedercrest.

Muscat (or **Moscato**) **Canelli** (white): A small Muscat grape of more delicate flavor, also called Muscat Blanc in California and known in France as the Muscat de Frontignan. "One of California's prettiest treats," says Hugh Johnson; the wine is light gold in color, light in body, usually sweet, fresh, with Muscat's daphne-flower aroma and a clean finish. The sweet, pétillant Lancers and Mateus Rosé are popular imports made from this grape. Italy's white sparkling Asti Spumante is also made from this variety. Equally well known are the Christian Brothers' proprietary-named Chateau La Salle and varietal bottlings by Beaulieu, Chateau St. Jean, Concannon, Cresta Blanca, Inglenook, Charles Krug, San Martín, Simi, Sonoma Vineyards, and Souverain. It's meant for drinking with dessert or sipping out on the deck.

Napa Gamay (red and rosé): Also called simply Gamay, this is a grape confused in the past with Gamay Beaujolais. It is now considered the same as the Gamay Noir grape that makes France's Beaujolais. Grown in California's cool areas, it can produce a pleasant dry or medium-dry, fairly light, fruity, spicy-fragrant, tart red or rosé wine, the rosé being drier than Grenache or Grignolino, lighter than Rosé of Cabernet or Zinfandel. Almadén, Bargetto, Inglenook, and Robert Mondavi make Gamay Rosé; Christian Brothers makes it as Gamay Noir; Chappellet, Dry Creek, J. Lohr, Paul Masson, Nichelini, and others make a red Gamay; and it may be the principal grape used in generic rosé. In any case, drink it young.

Petite Sirah (red): A grape of uncertain French origin—probably from the Rhone Valley—but somewhat confused in the past with the more distinguished Syrah, a component grape of Chateauneuf-du-Pape and Hermitage wines. Widely grown in California in both cool and warm areas and widely utilized for its high, stable color in blending generic Burgundy, Petite Sirah has become a popular "big" red varietal: a deep-red, dry, full-bodied, robust, fruity, very tannic, often harsh wine with distinctive peppery-spicy (some say chocolaty) flavor and aroma, capable of smoothing out and developing complexity with bottle age—which is another way of saying a young Petite Sirah may be very unpleasant. Quite a few medium-size and small wineries turn it out, and Field Stone makes a rosé with it.

Pinot Blanc (white): A fine Burgundy grape, confused in quality with Chardonnay and in name with what has been called "White Pinot," which is actually Chenin Blanc. Pinot Blanc grows well in California coastal valleys (two-thirds of the crop comes from Monterey) and produces an underrated wine—Chardonnay always manages to outshine it. A good Pinot Blanc is dry, medium- to full-bodied, rich and fruity in flavor and aroma ("weedy" is the UC-Davis adjective, meant to be complimentary), with a long finish. Tannin makes it likely to turn brown, so it should be drunk soon. Pinot Blanc adds good qualities to generic Chablis and is bottled as a varietal by Almadén, Chalone, Chateau St. Jean, Congress Springs, J. Lohr, Paul Masson, Mirassou, Novitiate, Sebastiani, Shenandoah, Ventana, and Wente Brothers.

Pinot Noir (red): The classic grape in France for red Burgundy and for Champagne. Pinot Noir in California does best in cool climates (most of the crop comes from Napa, Sonoma, and Monterey), but wineries are still trying to make great wines, just as they do in France, succeeding infrequently. Recent opinion is that Napa's cool Carneros district may be the best home for Pinot Noir. At its finest, Pinot Noir is richly colored, dry, full-bodied, robustly flavored ("pepperminty," "mushroomy," and "leathery" are some of the adjectives), fragrant (some say like crab apple or sandalwood), with a soft, velvety finish. But a good many Pinot Noirs are thin, low-colored, fruity, and tart. Being so temperamental, a lot of Pinot Noir is diverted into "Blanc de Noir" table wine and Champagne. The wine is bottled by more than a hundred California wineries and many out of state. The best possibility is a Napa Valley Pinot Noir barrel-aged in French oak at a small winery using traditional methods—but the price may be high. Since the grape is not very tannic, long cellar-aging is not advisable.

Pinot St. George (red): A French grape previously misnamed Red Pinot. The Christian Brothers made it a well-known robust red varietal, even though it has no great varietal distinction, and have been followed by Brookside, Inglenook, Monterey Peninsula, and Pastori. Lately, Almadén planted hundreds of acres in the Salinas Valley; the president of the winery explained that they were putting their money on Pinot St. George, not Pinot Noir, as a grape of the future.

Ruby Cabernet (red): A cross of Cabernet Sauvignon and Carignane, developed by UC-Davis for growing in the Central Valley (acreage there jumped by a factor of 10 in the 1970s), where it retains acidity enough for a nicely colored, light, dry, fruity red wine, generally found in jugs. While it has some Cabernet character (the green-olive or weedy flavor, an earthy feel on the tongue), Ruby Cabernet is scarcely a substitute, and when tasted comparatively is uninteresting. Among coastal wineries that may use Ruby Cabernet grapes grown in cooler vineyards are Almadén, Cresta Blanca, Fortino, Emilio Guglielmo, Hecker Pass, Italian Swiss Colony, Paul Masson (proprietary blend called Rubion), Monterey Peninsula, Novitiate, Ridge, Sonoma Vineyards, and Trentadue.

Sauvignon Blanc, Fumé Blanc, and Sémillon (white): The Sauvignon Blanc and Sémillon grapes are versatile premium varieties that do extremely well in both France and California. In both places they are blended to produce distinctive wines, or can be bottled as varietals. In Bordeaux, a blend of mostly Sauvignon Blanc with Sémillon produces the dry Graves wine; a blend of mostly Sémillon with Sauvignon Blanc, when picked overripe after attack by Botrytis (noble rot), produces the famous sweet Sauternes wine. In the upper Loire Valley, Sauvignon Blanc is used in the crisp dry Sancerre as well as the "smoky" dry Pouilly-Fumé. In California as well, the two grapes are found in combination either in generic "Sauterne" (dry or sweet) or in varietals under one name or the other. Echoing Pouilly-Fumé, dry Sauvignon Blanc is now usually called Fumé Blanc (or Blanc Fumé).

A fine *Sauvignon Blanc,* made from well-ripened grapes, is lemonjuice-colored, medium-bodied, dry, fresh, weedy or spicy in flavor, with an aroma reminiscent of cut grass or new hay, and has a good finish. It can improve with bottle age. Among producers are Almadén, Beaulieu, Buena Vista, Callaway, Caymus, Chateau St. Jean, Christian Brothers, Concannon, Fetzer, Gallo, J. Lohr, Monterey Vineyard, Paul Masson, Parducci, Joseph Phelps, San Martín, Sonoma Vineyards, Spring Mountain, Sterling, Stonegate, Stony Ridge, Trentadue, and Wente Brothers.

Fermented drier and not blended, *Fumé Blanc* is crisper and has been called herbaceous. It is produced by Beckett, Beringer, Davis Bynum, Callaway, Chateau St. Jean, Christian Brothers, Dry Creek,

Fetzer, Foppiano, Geyser Peak, Gundlach-Bundschu, Inglenook, Charles Krug, Paul Masson, Robert Mondavi (who originated the name and style at Krug), Monterey Vineyard, Joseph Phelps, and Souverain.

Sémillon, meanwhile, is a good, nonstandard varietal by itself if grown in cool climates and harvested when sugar and acid are well balanced, producing an appealingly soft, sweetish (though it can be made dry) wine with full body, recognizable aroma (figs or cigars), and good flavor. Varietal Sémillon has been made by Almadén, Barengo, California Growers, Concannon, Fetzer, Emilio Guglielmo, Nichelini, Pope Valley, San Martín, Santa Ynez Valley, Stony Hill, Stony Ridge, Trentadue, and Wente Brothers.

Sylvaner (white): An important grape in the Alsace, Germany, Austria, and Switzerland, growing well where White Riesling doesn't, the Sylvaner has become known as the Franken (from Franconia) Riesling, though it is not a Riesling. Consequently, American wineries can label Sylvaner as "Riesling," though not all do. In California it is grown in both cool and warm districts, but most of the 1,300 acres are in Monterey. Cool-district Sylvaner is greenish white, dry or semidry, light-bodied, tart, and fruity, and should have a delicate but distinct varietal flavor and aroma. Among wineries producing this pleasant but not popular wine are California Growers, Emilio Guglielmo, Gundlach-Bundschu, Hoffman Mountain Ranch (HMR), Monterey Vineyard, Parducci, Pope Valley, and Sebastiani.

White (or Johannisberg) Riesling (white): The classic grape for the Rhine and Moselle wines but not superior in California. Grown on 8,300 acres, mostly in Monterey and the North Coast districts, the grape produces a wine comparable to German *auslese* only in the coolest vineyards with "late harvest" (Botrytis) conditions. Unfortunately, the California crop mostly ripens early, and the large quantity of wine doesn't have the sugar-acid balance to make a Riesling that has so-called "steely" elegance; it is sweetish, fresh, with complex and delicate fruity-floral honeysuckle-like character, and is not too alcoholic. Too often, the product is "fat" in flavor and alcohol but simple in character. As with Pinot Noir, winemakers keep trying to meet an extremely high European standard. Good to better Rieslings in the past have been turned out by Beaulieu, Caymus, Chappellet, Chateau St. Jean, Firestone, Franciscan, Freemark Abbey, Heitz, Hoffman Mountain Ranch (HMR), Charles Krug, Louis M. Martini, Robert Mondavi, Sebastiani, Sonoma Vineyards, Stag's Leap Wine Cellars, Stony Hill, and Trefethen. André Tchelistcheff, Beaulieu's longtime winemaker who now advises other wineries, thinks the best Rieslings will tend to come from the coolest Santa Barbara and Temecula microclimates and from Washington State (Ste. Michelle is the big winery up that way).

Zinfandel (mostly red): Last but far from least, "Zin" is California's own grape. The story for the last century was that Colonel Haraszthy imported it from Hungary in 1861, but UC-Davis believes it's the same as the Primitivo of Italy. In any case, it's a productive grape that grows well in warm and cool areas, and is found in every district, though half the crush comes from around Lodi in the Central Valley. Extremely versatile, Zinfandel is used for generic reds, for a range of varietal reds (from heavy-bodied, sweet, late-harvest "essence" down to fairly light *nuevo*, a Beaujolais-like wine for drinking young), and even for rosés and blancs. (We haven't heard of a Zinfandel Champagne, but who knows?) A good varietal Zinfandel from a cool coastal district might be dry, medium-bodied, well colored, fresh, with a distinctive berry-like (some say raspberry) aroma and flavor. "Big" Zins are turned out by some small wineries for long cellar-aging, and many wine columns will probably be written as the Zinfandels of the 1960s and 1970s are opened in the next century. When buying a Zinfandel from any of 150 or so wineries, determine what "style" you're seeking.

GOING WINE TOURING

When you visit California Wine Country, you will find that the big wineries and a good many of the small ones will give you free tastes. The tastes are almost always of varietals but sometimes only of a minor red like Gamay Beaujolais, a rosé, and a minor white like Gray Riesling or Sylvaner, or if Cabernet Sauvignon or Chardonnay, lesser vintages. If you are certain that you will buy some quantity, such as a case (12 bottles), make that fact known to the salesperson so that you can taste some of the more expensive wines. Remember, though, that the production at boutique wineries is tiny, and the wines may sell out at retail prices on the premises, so that winemakers will be reluctant to pour their best. At some of the larger wineries, you may be hurried off on the tour before you get any tastes, unless you indicate a desire to go directly to the salesroom; stress that. You shouldn't have to pay for tasting at any winery.

The hard part in visiting wineries is making the tasting effective. Wineries don't provide spitting (or even pouring-out) facilities except perhaps to touring professionals, so you have to make sure that too many different samples don't make you happy but undiscriminating. A good picnic lunch and some bites from a loaf of sourdough French bread during the afternoon will inhibit tipsiness. Beyond that, it's wise to stick to one group of wines—all reds, for example—and compare them from winery to winery. There's a lot to be said for taking some organized notes. Wineries like serious visitors.

Incidentally, don't expect a winery's retail prices to be automatically lower than a liquor store's. The end of "fair-trade" pricing in California in 1978 meant price cutting among liquor stores—but not at wineries.

The best time to visit any winery is during the harvest, when grapes are being brought in in carloads, crushed, and pumped into fermentation tanks. At other times, visitors don't observe much more activity than winemakers peering into casks and keeping things very clean. Harvest in the Central Valley starts as early as June, in North Coast vineyards as early as August, with the most activity in September and October. Wineries don't crush every day, however, and if you want to be sure to see the crush, telephone ahead.

Here's a North Coast Wine Country calendar:

January: Hills greening but vineyards barren; vines are pruned. In the winery, some fermentation continuing; "spring" wine may be bottled.

February: Vines dormant; more soaking rains; more pruning. Wines are clarifying, maturing, being racked into new barrels.

March: Sap is flowing, vines budding; plowing, grafting, more pruning. Wines for release this year are being blended, bottled.

April: Vines begin leafing; cultivating, putting out new vines, cordon or trellis training; spraying for spring frost. In the winery, more finishing operations.

May: Vines are growing, buds are tiny, acidic berries; weeding, spraying for pests.

June: Grape clusters forming nicely; selective pruning, irrigating; first wines may be released.

July: Lush leafing, grapes swelling.

August: Grapes coloring, near ripening.

September: Sugar content of grapes rapidly increasing; first harvesting, crushing, fermenting.

October: More harvesting; some wines finish fermenting, are racked.

November: Late harvesting; lots of fermenting; vineyard turns autumn colors.

December: New wines maturing; vines lose leaves; earth lies fallow.

And now, off to enjoy the good-weather aromas of the Napa and Sonoma valleys, the distinctive countryside, the interest and complexity of the winemaking process, the heavy-bodied air of prestige at well-known wineries, subtle educational propaganda, and even a spicy, flavorful picnic from a Wine Country deli.

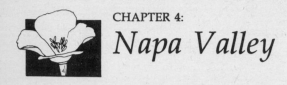

CHAPTER 4:
Napa Valley

HIGHLIGHTS

Wineries:
Christian Brothers
   (Mont La Salle) / 113
Trefethen / 113
Domaine Chandon / 114
Robert Mondavi / 114
Inglenook / 115
Beaulieu Vineyards / 115
Nichelini / 115
V. Sattui / 115
Heitz Cellars / 116
Louis M. Martini / 116
Beringer / 116
Christian Brothers
   (Greystone Cellars) / 117
Charles Krug / 118
Pope Valley Winery / 118
Freemark Abbey / 118
Schramsberg / 119
Hanns Kornell / 119
Cuvaison / 120
Sterling / 120

Chateau Montelena / 120

Other Attractions:
Napa / 121
Yountville / 121
Vintage 1870 / 122
Oakville, Rutherford / 122
Lake Berryessa / 122
St. Helena / 123
Silverado Museum / 123
Wine Country Shopping / 123
Pope Valley Parachute Center / 124
Bale Grist Mill / 124
Bothe-Napa Valley State Park / 124
Calistoga / 125
Spas / 125
Calistoga Steam Railroad / 125
Calistoga Soaring Center / 126
Petrified Forest / 126
Mt. St. Helena / 126
Robert Louis Stevenson State
   Park / 126

The Napa Valley produces some of the best wine in the world, and is worth visiting for that reason alone. But more than that, because it is the most geographically coherent of the several North Coast wine areas, the Napa Valley should be first on the serious wine drinker's itinerary.

For those who are happier bibbing dry martinis, Napa is fortunately an agricultural area that could grow rutabagas and still look pretty and compact. The 35-mile-long valley has some attractions other than ivy-covered wineries (whose aging cellars are, at least, a cool refuge on a hot day): an antique steam railroad, Victorian houses, a Robert Louis Stevenson museum and associated literary landmarks, spas in which to take mud baths, interesting shopping, a petrified forest, a 60-foot "old faithful" geyser, and some exciting sky sports—parachuting, hot-air ballooning, and soaring.

Geography and Great Wine

We wish you had the three-dimensional plastic relief map of California that we have on our office wall so you could understand better what the Napa Valley is and why good wine comes from here. South of Mendocino the features of the Coast Range are quite parallel: At San Francisco Bay, while the hills divide and go on either side of the bay, the intervales—the Petaluma, Sonoma, and Napa River valleys—widen and join as a marshy plain at the northern end of the bay, which is actually a drowned valley.

Now, anybody who visits California in June or July may well swelter in Sacramento but shiver in San Francisco. The proximate reason for putting on a windbreaker is the famous San Francisco fog. Natural air-conditioning, natives call it. The fog is apparent as leaden skies through summer mornings from Oregon to Hearst Castle; at noon the sun breaks through; at four or five in the afternoon the fog comes rolling in off the ocean again. The reason for the fog is that the dampness in the west wind condenses when it hits the cold California current, and the coastal terrace and first ridge of the Coast Range become swathed in cold grayness, which spills over the ridge at some low points and into some of the valleys.

But at the Golden Gate the fog sweeps right into the bay and toward the Carquinez Strait, drawn inland by the hot air. On the way it is gulped by the mouths of the valleys whose rivers feed into the north end of the bay. Thus fog often fills the lower valley lands until the sun dissipates it.

The result of all this is that a substantial part of the growing season for grapes (which is, generally, April 1–October 31) is cool. That's good, for some varieties won't develop good acidity and varietal flavor if the sun is ferocious, as in the Central Valley. But the summer can't be too cool, for the grapes still need the sun to grow juicy and sweet.

The winters are cool and moist, with low temperatures hovering around 32° F., ensuring dormancy for the vines. Any threat of frost can be headed off by turning on the sprinklers: it has been learned that freezing water generates heat, and once there is a covering of ice on the vines, they don't get much colder than 28° F. (Evergreens in the Sierras similarly collect snow on their branches as insulation.)

The soil is important but not as crucial as climate. The soil in the Napa Valley is fine sandy and gravelly loam on the valley floor, stony loam on the hillsides. Drainage is good and underground water supplies adequate, making extensive irrigation unnecessary. The Israeli drip-irrigation system is used, and in the hotter areas the new overhead mist irrigation system modifies the heat and sun's rays when necessary.

A lot of wine lovers who know about the problems of viticulture wish that grape growers would plant more hillside land, in the Napa and other valleys. Here's the reasoning: Wine quality—intensity of color and varietal flavor, at least—seems correlated with small berry size, which unfortunately translates as low yield. Up on the slopes, where the microclimates are cooler and the soil is thinner and perhaps not irrigated, vine growth is naturally controlled and may well produce grapes for superb wine. But crops are heavier in the deeper bottom soils, especially if irrigated in the summer. Indeed, a vineyard can grow "rank" or luxuriant, but the big grapes may make less than great wine. Most vineyardists would rather make red wine than red ink, and have to strive for a high yield commensurate with high quality.

A delicate balance is required. Where the balance is upset—which happens—and the vintage is poor, the art of the winemakers is put to the test. Napa Valley wines are rarely undrinkable.

The Napa Valley is actually not one place. Different varieties do grow better in different areas. Hugh Johnson and Bob Thompson (the one an Englishman extremely knowledgeable about the world's wine-growing regions, the other a California wine critic) have outlined five vineyard districts:

- The Carneros district, between Napa and the marshy bay lands, is the coolest of the five. Chardonnay and Pinot Noir seem to do the best on the 2,000 acres of vineyards.
- The central Napa Valley district extends from Napa

approximately to St. Helena (or south of the town). This is a
warmer area than Carneros and grows the best Cabernet
Sauvignon in the valley, along with good Chardonnay, White
Riesling, and Pinot Noir. This is the most productive part of
the valley.

- The northern Napa Valley district extends from St. Helena
  through Calistoga. It's warmer yet, but overhead mist
  irrigation enables the growing of good Chenin Blanc and
  Zinfandel along with Merlot, Pinot Noir, and Chardonnay.

- The tree-covered west hills (a branch of the Mayacmas
  Mountains, peaked by Mt. Veeder and Diamond Mountain
  among others) contains pockets of vines—the Mont La Salle,
  Mayacamas (extra *a*), Stony Hill, and Spring Mountain
  vineyards. With thin soil, eastern exposure, and coolness that
  comes with the extra 1,000 to 1,500 feet of elevation, these
  vineyards (not visible from Highway 29) produce
  Chardonnay, White Riesling, Gewürztraminer, and other
  white varieties.

- The somewhat bare east hills (another branch of the
  Mayacmas, principal summits including Stag's Leap, Howell
  Mountain, and the Palisades) are drier and have thinner soil,
  with vineyards in pockets or on slopes with less exposure. The
  few vineyards—Chappellet and Burgess, primarily—grow
  better Zinfandel, Petite Sirah, and some Cabernet Sauvignon.

North to the Napa Valley

The Napa Valley wine road is one of the best day-excursions from San
Francisco. The Golden Gate Bridge is a wonderful gateway to anywhere. Then there's a long, increasingly rural drive on Highway 101
through Marin and on Highway 37 across the northern bay lands (the
water area hereabouts is actually San Pablo Bay). Then, when it seems
that, like the fog, you are being drawn into the Sonoma Valley—Jack
London's "Valley of the Moon"—you turn east and cross another
ridge of the Coast Range and drop down into the Carneros district of
the Napa Valley.

Highway 29 bypasses downtown Napa. Napa is a nice city, a proto-
typically wholesome American small city. Unlike Beaune or Bordeaux,
it plays no great role in the wine trade. Then, for the next 27 miles to
Calistoga, the road goes straight up the flat valley floor. An aerial view
of the valley from this, the south, end (which you can get by making a
hot-air balloon ascent over Yountville) will show a diminishing or nar-

rowing perspective: a stretch of vineyards and scattered orchards, held in line by forest-covered hills that rise a couple of thousand feet on either side and finally close the valley off at Calistoga, at the foot of Mt. St. Helena. The view from the north end (which you can get by taking an aerial tram up to Sterling's knoll-top winery) is the opposite: the carpet of vines gradually disappears into the summer haze. Landlubbers who want a good view can simply turn off Highway 29 and take a potholed lateral up to the Silverado Trail (a highway), which follows the eastern slope and offers a continuous vista view.

There's a special feel to this valley. In the growing season the air is permeated—no, not with the smell of vines or wines, but of oak trees and farm-country dust. Afternoon summer heat is soft, aromatic, lazy-making. The valley's peaceful character insinuates itself, calms city nerves. You want to live here. (You're not the only one. Napa Valley luminaries—present or recent past—include Arthur Hailey, M. F. K. Fisher, Francis Ford Coppola, Allen Drury, Jessamyn West, some titled Europeans, and by long tradition, bright San Francisco socialites.)

The commercial signs along the highway will seem familiar: you've seen the names on labels in the wineshop or liquor store—Beaulieu, Inglenook, Christian Brothers, Charles Krug, Louis M. Martini, Beringer, Robert Mondavi (these are the big seven), Hanns Kornell, Schramsberg, Sterling. Visiting one winery is a must; visiting two or three different ones is better. Wineries like Sterling and Inglenook are big corporations in artful disguises; the facilities are apt to be efficient and modern, and the people running them are maybe a little slick, not fitting the "little old winemaker, me" image very well. But some of the wineries with well-known names are small, very personal businesses. Hanns Kornell, for example, is a real person, a half-Jewish German who escaped, penniless, from Germany (from Dachau, in fact) in 1939 and, in the Napa Valley in the early 1950s, continued the family tradition of making sparkling wine. His place looks modest, functional. You may find Hanns Kornell himself pushing a broom, cleaning out a cask, or guiding visitors around his two-million-bottle Champagne cellars. It's not a tiny business—he's turned down a $6 million offer from a Japanese steel company. All the "boutique" wineries—most of them new since the 1960s—are much like Kornell's, though not as prosperous and certain in their reputation.

Turn into the parking lot of Louis M. Martini or Charles Krug to see the kind of medium-size, new-old winery that occupies the middle ground. Both are family-run companies that send their wine into national distribution. Both have some of the new cool-fermentation equipment, which looks very industrial and impersonal, but they also have lots of big redwood barrels and small oak casks that are, in their cool aging rooms, sweating wine into the air. The Martini whose name is on the label, the late dean of California winemakers, built perhaps the plainest buildings in the valley, beginning in the 1930s, but there's a friendly air about them. Charles Krug is the valley's oldest winery (1861), and has the most interesting complex of old aging cellars and new buildings with the latest equipment. The Mondavis, who have run Krug since the 1930s, are right out of a tumultuous Italian family saga about feuding brothers and rivalry in making good wine.

Napa Valley Yesterday

The Napa Valley wine industry actually dates back to before Charles Krug, although he was the pioneer of commercial winemaking. The Indians—Wappos and Patwins, mostly, who numbered in the thousands until decimated by diseases—lived well off the land, but grew no grapes. The first white settlers, including George Yount after 1831, transplanted cuttings from mission vineyards and produced a little California eye-popper for their own use. The grapes were dumped in cattle-hide troughs and crushed with bare feet or mashed with clubs, then fermented in leather bags. The Mission grape was the only grape in Napa Valley until 1852, when two brothers named Thompson planted some cuttings from European varieties south of Napa.

Though the Gold Rush created a big demand for wine, Sonoma's vineyards and those around Los Angeles were the important producers. The Napa Valley's commercial potential wasn't discovered until the 1860s and didn't flourish until the last quarter of the century. The pioneer was Charles Krug, an immigrant from Prussia who met Colonel Haraszthy in San Francisco in 1852, became interested in winemaking, and bought a 20-acre vineyard in Sonoma. In 1858, on John Patchett's ranch near St. Helena, Krug produced some wine, apparently using Mission grapes, an old cider press, and some European methods, and offered it for sale as Napa Valley wine. Three years later he started his own winery north of St. Helena. One stone wall of that winery is incorporated in the present Krug winery, which is a state historical landmark. Krug became the county's first viticultural commissioner, trained Carl Wente, Jacob Beringer, and other early winemakers, and made wine that became known in Europe before his death in 1892. A second pioneer of the 1860s was George B. Crane, who introduced Riesling grapes.

By 1867 the valley had a thousand acres in vines, including some of the premium varieties that Haraszthy had brought back from Europe in 1861. The 1870s were not happy, with economic depression and the arrival of the phylloxera pest, but the valley was well established as wine country because of its ideal climate and satisfactory soil. By 1881 the valley had more than 11,000 acres of vines in more than 400 ownerships, by 1891 more than 17,000 acres in more than 600 ownerships.

Prohibition gradually closed most of the wineries, and vineyards were put to uses other than growing fine wine grapes. It was nearly a fatal blow to the California wine industry. The winemaking tradition was barely alive by the time Repeal came, and it took some new winemakers, such as Louis M. Martini, to revive Napa Valley's fortunes. (Even with the tremendous growth of the wine industry in recent years there are fewer wineries, 50 plus, in the Napa Valley today than there were before Prohibition.)

Today the 23,000 acres of vineyards are prosperous and well tended, producing mostly the best varietals that command the best prices. Growers and winemakers are still learning where all the "microclimates" are and which varieties do the best. With the latest agricultural technology and research, they are finding out how to produce the very best wine. Though the city of Napa has sprawled, and there is a threat of development on unincorporated county land near the Carneros area, most of the vineyards are within the 1968 agricultural preserve that restricts building to one residence per 20 acres.

WHAT TO SEE AND DO

To avoid diluting the product, we're dividing this section into "Wineries" and "Other Attractions." Both are organized linearly, following Highway 29 from south to north.

Area code: 707, unless otherwise noted. Zip codes: Calistoga 94515, Napa 94558, Oakville 94562, Rutherford 94573, St. Helena 94574, Yountville 94599.

WINERIES

Following are just a few of the principal wineries that have tasting, tours, or sales, as noted. A very few that are not generally open except by appointment have been included here for their architectural value. The wineries are in south-north order, on and off Highway 29 (also called St. Helena Highway). Standard hours are daily from 10 or 10:30 to 4, sometimes to 5. Most are closed on major holidays. All groups should book in advance. "By appointment" need not intimidate wine novices.

The Christian Brothers Mont La Salle Vineyards and Winery,** 4411 Redwood Rd., Napa (8 miles northwest of Napa, off Highway 29), 226-5566. Tours, tasting, sales, daily 10:30-4. The Brothers of the Christian Schools, a Roman Catholic teaching order, make wine (and pay all taxes) to support their educational endeavors. Since 1882, the brothers have been California winemakers, basing their wine business in the Napa Valley after World War II, when they purchased the 1903 stone winery built by Theodore Gier and made it their novitiate, winery, and headquarters, with principal vineyard right outside. Today they have an extremely modern crushing and fermenting plant next to the Martini winery south of St. Helena, while north of town the Greystone Cellars (see p. 117) is used for aging and for making Champagne. Under the direction of Brother Timothy, cellarmaster since 1940, the Christian Brothers run the largest winery in the valley (20 million gallons of storage capacity) and are one of the largest vineyard proprietors: 2,400 acres, including 1,500 Napa Valley acres spread from Mont La Salle north to Calistoga, and 900 acres in the San Joaquin Valley, where dessert wines and brandy are produced. As described in Chapter 2, the Christian Brothers traditionally haven't vintage-dated their wine; even their finest varietals are usually blends of not only different varieties but also different vintages and the wine from different vineyards. Among their varietal, generic, and other types of wine, well known are the Cabernet Sauvignon, Pinot St. George, Chateau La Salle (a light sweet white Muscat table wine), Pineau de la Loire (Chenin Blanc), and Pinot Chardonnay. Their brandy is the top seller in the U.S. The Christian Brothers are notable collectors of winemaking items and art, and together with their distributors, Fromm and Sichel, operate the Wine Museum in San Francisco. Many treasures are on display here and at Greystone Cellars.

Trefethen Vineyards,* 1160 Oak Knoll Ave., Napa (13 miles north of Napa on Highway 29), 255-7700. Open weekdays by appointment. The Trefethen family has owned 600 acres and operated a winery since 1968. For a while they were growing grapes and producing sparkling wine for Moët and Chandon (see next entry) until the French firm finished its own building. Trefethen is located in one of the few remaining wooden wineries in the valley, a three-story pumpkin-colored building constructed of redwood in 1886 by architect Hamden McIntyre. Wines produced on a limited basis are Chardonnay, Cabernet Sauvignon, and White Riesling, and other varietals are in the experimental stage.

Domaine Chandon,** California Drive, Yountville, 944-2280, 944-8844. Tours, tasting (about $1.50 per glass), sales, Thurs.-Mon. 11-5:30 (and Fri.-Sat. 6-9 P.M.); restaurant (944-2467) open for lunch and dinner Thurs.-Mon. Specializing in sparkling wine, Domaine Chandon is a new (1977) California branch of Moët and Chandon of Épernay, France, makers of real Champagne. "Champagne" is a term they refuse to apply to their bottle-fermented California products: Chandon Napa Valley Brut (cuvée about 66 percent Pinot Noir, 33 percent Chardonnay) and Chandon Cuvée de Pinot Noir (cuvée of that variety gathered from various parts of their 900-acre valley vineyards). The visitors center has antique Champagne-making artifacts on display.

Robert Mondavi Winery,*** 7801 St. Helena Hwy., Oakville, 963-9611. Tours, tasting, sales, daily 10:30-4; group meals by appointment. Robert Mondavi started this winery after leaving the family operation up the road, the Charles Krug Winery, in great anger. Most recently he bought back the interest Rainier Brewing had purchased in this winery after having sold his own interest in the Krug winery. All these dealings made the San Francisco papers. Located in an attractive California mission-style building with a tower and a dramatic archway (Cliff May, 1966) in the middle of 750 acres of valley-floor vineyards, the Mondavi winery has the latest equipment and produces fine premium wines, as indicated both by tasting the wine and looking at the price. Mondavi himself is widely credited with leading the California wine industry to greater maturity and sophistication, qualities that visitors will recognize in his wine. In early 1980 Mondavi officially announced that he and Baron Philippe de Rothschild, owner of the Chateau Mouton-Rothschild, will jointly produce a Bordeaux-style wine, mostly from Cabernet Sauvignon grapes. The first vintage was produced in 1979 but won't be released (at a price of $25-30 a bottle) until 1983 at the earliest. With a $3 million investment Mondavi-Rothschild may also buy 25 acres in the valley and put up a separate winery so the product will be a true "estate bottled" product. Mondavi's own wines are a well-known Cabernet Sauvignon (especially the Private Reserve), also Fumé Blanc, Chardonnay, Pinot Noir, and several other varietals, and plainly labeled quality generics (Red Table Wine, for example, which is notably more astringent and Cabernet-like than common jug wines). The tour is educational. On several summer Sundays you can picnic on the lawn and listen to (mostly) jazz (information and tickets: Mondavi Summer Festival, Box 106, Oakville 94562).

Inglenook Vineyards,* 1991 St. Helena Hwy., Rutherford, 963-7184, 963-2616. Tours, tasting, daily 9-5. Operating vineyards here since 1879, Inglenook has been part of the United Vintners (Heublein-owned) empire since 1964. The old reputation, which began in the 1930s when Inglenook led the way toward exclusively varietal production, is now being stretched over mass production. "Cask Selection" estate-bottled varietals are at one end of the line of products, inexpensive Navalle-brand generics at the other. A complex of new buildings has joined Captain Gustave Niebaum's romantic, ivy-draped winery of Eastern European design (1887) amid some of the 2,800 acres of Inglenook vineyards. The Niebaum house and other vineyards are owned by *The Godfather's* millionaire director, Francis Ford Coppola.

Beaulieu Vineyards,** 1960 St. Helena Hwy., Rutherford, 963-2411. Tours, tasting, sales, daily 10-4. Long one of the valley's famous wineries, "BV" was founded by Georges de Latour in 1900 and remained in his family until, like Inglenook, most of it was sold to Heublein. However, the operation has not been changed as much as Inglenook's, and its premium varietals (particularly the Private Reserve Cabernet Sauvignon) remain as well regarded as when produced by one of the valley's best-known winemakers, André Tchelistcheff, from 1938 to 1973. The stone visitors center, part of the Rutherford Square complex, was reassembled from an 1880s winery building.

Nichelini Vineyard, Chiles Valley Road, St. Helena (11 miles east of Rutherford off Highway 128), 963-3357. Tours, tasting, sales, also picnicking, weekends 10-6. Founded by Anton Nichelini in 1890, this family winery is small and friendly, and uses much traditional equipment to produce Sauvignon Vert, Chenin Blanc (both specialties), Cabernet Sauvignon, Zinfandel, Napa Gamay, and Petite Sirah, a couple of generics, and a rosé. The grapes are grown on 200 acres here in the Chiles Valley, which is 900 feet higher than the Napa Valley.

V. Sattui Winery, St. Helena Highway at White Lane, St. Helena (south of town), 963-7774. Tasting, sales, some informal tours, and picnicking (deli on premises), daily 10-5:30 (closed early in week, in winter). The winery was founded in San Francisco's Mission District in 1885, foundered during Prohibition, and was revived and rebuilt in 1965 in the Napa Valley by the founder's great-grandson, Daryl Sattui. The modest, 100-percent varietal wines are either made here from purchased grapes (Cabernet Sauvignon, Zinfandel) or bottled here from purchased valley wines (White Riesling, Chardonnay, other varietals), all vintage-dated, some vineyard-named.

Heitz Wine Cellars* tasting room, 436 Main St., St. Helena (south of town), 963-3542. Tasting, sales, daily 11-4:30; no groups. A former professor of enology, Joe Heitz since 1961 has made an enviable reputation as one of the best winemakers in California, for his fine Cabernet Sauvignon (particularly the Martha's Vineyard-labeled Cabernet) and Chardonnay. Remarkably, he grows only 30 acres of grapes and purchases not only the rest but sometimes another winery's wine. Other wines: Pinot Noir, Zinfandel, Barbera, Grignolino (one of the few of this varietal made), Ruby Cabernet, White Riesling, a generic or two, Port, Sherry, and every now and then a special wine. Only the inexpensive varietals are likely to be available for tasting: the best vintages sell out quickly.

Louis M. Martini Winery,*** 254 St. Helena Hwy., St. Helena (south of town), 963-2736. Tours, tasting, sales, daily 10-4:30. Founded in 1934 by a northern Italian and now operated by the second and third generations, the Martini winery is located in unpicturesque cement-block buildings but gives visitors a good welcome and interesting tour. Varietals include a good Cabernet Sauvignon, Pinot Noir, Merlot, Zinfandel, Napa Gamay, well-known Barbera, one-of-a-kind Folle Blanche, Johannisberg Riesling, Chardonnay, and Gewürztraminer. Moscato Amabile is sold only at the winery, as are occasional special lots of Cabernet and experimental wines. Popular generics—Mountain Red and Mountain White—are produced at the Monte Rosso Vineyard in the Mayacmas overlooking the Sonoma Valley. Other family vineyards (total of 1,100 acres) are near the winery and in the Carneros area, in the Chiles Valley, and near the Russian River at Healdsburg.

Beringer Wines,** 2000 Main St., St. Helena (north of town), 963-4812, 963-7115. Tours, tasting, sales, daily 9:30-4 (open later in the summer); groups by appointment. The very Gothic Rhine House (William Mooser, 1876) has been a Napa Valley landmark for a cen-

The Rhine House at Beringer Wines. (Wine Institute)

tury, ever since Jacob and Frederick Beringer established what became Los Hermanos estate here. The German-born brothers, who spent some time in Médoc learning Bordeaux winemaking, hired Chinese laborers to tunnel a thousand feet into the hillside to create cool (58°F.) wine cellars. The Beringer winery survived Prohibition by selling sacramental wine, later developed good Rhine-type varietals. The family sold out in 1970 to Nestlé, which began an expansion program to put Beringer wines into national distribution. Later, while keeping land and buildings, Nestlé had to sell the winemaking operation, now in the hands of the Labruyere family of France. Wines include standard Cabernet Sauvignon, Pinot Noir, and Pinot Chardonnay; Bärenblut (blend of Pinot Noir and Grignolino), Traubengold (a Riesling), and other nonstandards; also generics (cheapest are Los Hermanos-brand jug wines), dessert wines, brandy. The Beringer vineyards total 2,500 acres here and in Sonoma County. The visitor is certain to be charmed by Rhine House (a state historic landmark), if not by the wines.

Christian Brothers Wine and Champagne Cellars,*** 2555 North Main St., St. Helena (north of town), 963–2719. Tours, tasting, sales, daily 10:30–4; groups weekdays by appointment. Another Napa Valley landmark, the Greystone Cellars (Percy and Hamilton, 1889) was built by the San Francisco water company and goldmine million-aire William Bourn (whose city house, Peninsula country house, Grass Valley mine residence, and Irish estate are all open to the public). Several owners later, in 1950, the imposing three-story sandstone building came into the hands of the Christian Brothers, who age their Mont La Salle (see p. 113) wine here, make Champagne by the Charmat (bulk) process on the third floor, and display part of cellarmaster Brother Timothy's vast corkscrew collection to visitors.

Charles Krug Winery,*** St. Helena Highway, St. Helena (north of town), 963-2761. Tours, tasting, sales, daily 10-4. This is one of the most historic wineries in the valley: Krug made the first commercial wine in the valley in 1858, opened this winery in 1861. The winery (a state landmark) was sold by Krug's heirs in 1943 to Cesare Mondavi, whose family (minus Robert, who left in 1966) continues to run it, using buildings and equipment both old and new to produce premium varietals (no fewer than 20) and, under the "CK" label, good jug wines, mostly from grapes grown on their 1,100 acres at Oakville and in the Carneros area. Like Robert Mondavi, the Krug Mondavis sponsor musical events on summer evenings (August Moon Concerts, Box 535, Napa 94558).

Pope Valley Winery,* 6613 Pope Valley Rd., St. Helena (12 miles east of town; turn right on Deer Park Road), 965-2192. Tours, tasting, sales, also picnicking and hiking; weekends 11-5. Operational 1909-59, this unusual three-story gravity-flow winery was reactivated by the present owners in 1972. The redwood building (of timbers from an old mine) was built against a hillside. Grapes went in on the third floor and were crushed and fermented on the second floor, and the wine was racked by gravity flow into barrels and later bottled on the first floor. Wines include Cabernet Sauvignon, Gamay Beaujolais, Sémillon Blanc, Blanc de Blancs (made from Sauvignon Vert and French Colombard), House Burgundy, and Rosé of Zinfandel.

Freemark Abbey Winery, 3022 St. Helena Hwy., St. Helena (north of town), 963-9694. Tours (limited), sales, daily 11-5; restaurant (963-2706) open for lunch and dinner. The handsome 1895 stone building, called Freemark Abbey since 1938, has been operated as a winery by the present partnership since 1967, with fermenting and other operations on the lower floor, cellaring and visitor operations in an adjoining new building; the second floor of the old structure houses the Hurd candle factory, a gourmet shop, and the restaurant, all very popular with tour-bus groups. Wines (all varietals made with traditional methods such as fining, not filtering) include Cabernet Sauvignon (vineyard-named), Chardonnay, Pinot Noir, Johannisberg Riesling, and Petite Sirah.

Schramsberg Vineyard,* Schramsberg Road, Calistoga (off Highway 128), 942-4558. Tours and sales by appointment only. Some say Jack Davies makes the best sparkling wine in California. It is, at any rate, expensive, and is the Champagne that President Nixon took to China in 1972 and served at White House dinners. The Napa Valley's first hillside winery, started by Jacob Schram in 1862, Schramsberg was vividly described in a chapter in Robert Louis Stevenson's "Silverado Squatters" (see p. 126) and was a famous winery until shut down by phylloxera in 1911. Davies bought and revived it in 1965. Except for Cuvée Nature, a still white wine from which sparkling wine is made, Schramsberg produces only bottle-fermented Champagne, including Blanc de Noir (the most expensive; gold-colored, made mainly from Pinot Noir), Blanc de Blancs (less expensive; light gold, made from Chardonnay and Pinot Blanc), and, least expensive, Cuvée de Gamay (a salmon- or peach-colored sparkling wine that is briefly fermented with the skins). Schram's (now Davies') hillside Victorian residence is a state landmark.

Hanns Kornell Champagne Cellars,** 1091 Larkmead La., Calistoga (just off Highway 29, north of St. Helena), 963-2334. Tours, tasting, sales, daily 10-4:30. Third (with Domaine Chandon and Schramsberg) of Napa's sparkling-wine specialists, Hanns Kornell is unusual in several respects. First, Kornell doesn't grow his own grapes, instead buys both carefully selected grapes and base wine from other valley producers to make bottle-fermented sparkling wine for his own label— and for other firms. Second, his best white Champagne is not made from the traditional Pinot varieties of France but from the White (Johannisberg) Riesling of Germany. Third, the whole operation, while large (two million bottles in the cellar), seems small and friendly, with a style and architecture in complete contrast to Domaine Chandon. Kornell, a third-generation sparkling-wine maker, started making Champagne here in 1952, and bought the square, cupola-topped Larkmead Winery (1880s) in 1958. Kornell sparkling wines, all bottle-fermented (which means each bottle is handled 150 to 200 times), range from bone-dry Sehr Trocken through Brut, Extra Dry, Sec, and Demi-Sec, to Muscadelle de Bordelais, Pink Rosé, and Sparkling Burgundy.

Sterling Vineyards,*** 1111 Dunaweal La., Calistoga (south of town, east off Highway 29, 7 miles north of St. Helena), 942-5151. Tours (self-guided), tasting, sales, daily 10:30-4:30; access by aerial tramway ($2.50 charge rebated with wine purchase). A new winery with a spectacular setting, Sterling was begun in 1964 by a partnership of families who controlled the Sterling International paper company. They bought 425 acres of valley vineyards, in 1969 produced their first vintage, and in 1973 opened the gleaming white Greek monastery-like building (designed by Martin J. Waterfield) on an oak-covered hill. They had some success with early wines—at least enough to tempt giant Coca-Cola of Atlanta into buying it in 1977 for an estimated $12 million. The corporate plan is to have Sterling turn out a limited number of fine varietals (Cabernet Sauvignon, Merlot, Chardonnay, and Sauvignon Blanc, the most critically received of the eight previously produced) while Coke's Monterey Vineyard makes modestly priced premium wines and, at Monterey Vineyards, the Taylor Wine Company of New York fills up low-priced jugs with "California Cellars" wine (the big Franzia jug winery is owned by the Coca-Cola Bottling Company of New York). Meanwhile, the winery is one of the most exciting to visit. You ride yellow gondolas from the parking lot and take an enlightening self-guided tour around the winery—unfortunately, one level above the winemaking equipment and casks—and end up in the tasting and sales room. Sterling has stained glass, fountains, sculpture, and a panoramic view of the upper Napa Valley—and it also has the eight recast eighteenth-century bells of St. Dunstan's, which peal in the key of F major.

Cuvaison, 4560 Silverado Trail N., Calistoga (south of Dunaweal Lane), 942-6100. Tasting, picnicking, and, by appointment only, tours, Thurs.-Mon. 10-4. This decade-old (1970) small winery is located in a nicely designed California mission-style building. New ownership has sold the vineyard, intending to concentrate expert efforts in making only Cabernet Sauvignon, Zinfandel, and Chardonnay from purchased grapes.

Chateau Montelena,** 1429 Tubbs La., Calistoga, 942-5105. Tours by appointment only, sales, daily 10-4. Another new winery (under present ownership since 1972) in an old building (a compact stone castle of the 1880s), producing well-received Cabernet Sauvignon, Zinfandel, Chardonnay, and Johannisberg Riesling under an old label (1882). Along with the winery building, the grounds are of certain interest: the five-acre water gardens, three islands with small red pavilions, half-moon bridges, weeping willows, etc., were put in by some former owners, a Chinese family.

This catalogue scarcely represents all of the Napa Valley's wineries. We list 20 of the most visited, most interesting-looking, and most famous—but there are another 40 that could be sought out by the indefatigable.

OTHER ATTRACTIONS

Napa,* the county seat at the San Francisco Bay end of the Napa Valley, is ideal for the American Victorian domestic architecture buff. Whole streets are still lined with **Italianate houses.** See in particular the area around 5th, Division, and Randolph streets, as well as around Oak, Coombs (named for Nathan Coombs, who laid out the town in 1848), and Brown, Everything is enhanced by an air of quiet and lots of trees. The **town square** has a clock tower with carillon. The **Napa County Court House**** (Samuel and Joseph Newsom and Ira Gilchrist, 1878), Brown between 2nd and 3rd, presides over the center of town. At 508 Coombs is a Queen Anne–plus building (ca. 1880) that houses the **Napa County Historical Society.** Not far away, at 486 Coombs, is the **Churchill House*** or Cedar Gables Inn (Ernest Coxhead, late 1890s), a mixture of classical and shingle. At 1333 3rd St., the Victorian Gothic **First Presbyterian Church**** (R. H. Daley and Theodore Eisen, 1874) is a state landmark. The Napa Community Redevelopment Agency, 1600 1st St., and Napa Landmarks, 1834 1st St. (Box 702, Napa 94558), have brochures on **Victorian walking tours** in Napa, Yountville, St. Helena, and Calistoga.

New in Napa is the **Wine and Culinary Center,** 3415 Solano Ave. (224-7811), which has a London-style wine-tasting bar, sells wine, gourmet food, and cookware, and offers wine appreciation and cookery classes. A summer concert series was planned in the center's 500-seat outdoor theater (252-0180 for information).

Leaving Napa you will find Highway 29, a mini-freeway, an inauspicious entry to the wine country. Luckily, the freeway ends in the vicinity of the old **Veterans Home of California** (1884), south of **Yountville.**** Yountville was named for the Napa Valley's first American settler, George Yount, who was granted the 11,000-acre Rancho Caymus and constructed a one-of-a-kind Kentucky log blockhouse in 1836, an adobe residence the next year, and gristmill and sawmill in the next decade. A monument near the Napa River on Yount Mill Road north of town marks the building sites. Yount, who came west with the Wolfskill party in 1831, died in 1865 and is buried in the town cemetery, Jackson and Washington (picnicking adjacent in the town park).

The present attraction in Yountville is shopping in several antique shops and in **Vintage 1870** (closed Monday), a miniature Ghirardelli Square shopping gallery in the old brick Groezinger winery (ca. 1870, modernized 1954 and after). Along with little shops selling wood sculpture, wurst, pipes, Mexican imports, bath soap, etc., there are two little restaurants, a "compleat winemaker" shop, the **Wine Tours International** office, and the **Vintage Theater,** erstwhile summer home of two major Northern California repertory companies.

Tony enough, Vintage 1870 has an unfortunate neighbor, **Vintage Railroad Co.,** a collection of shops in old Southern Pacific boxcars. Nearby are the **Napa Valley Railroad Co. Depot** (1868), now a restaurant, and the **Magnolia Hotel** (1873), a recently revived inn and restaurant. Yountville is a nice gateway to the Napa Valley if it doesn't get too much more touristy. A Yountville walking-tour map is available from Napa Landmarks (address above) or at Vintage 1870.

Two companies will take you up in a balloon over the valley: **Adventures Aloft** (255-8688) and **Aerostat Renaissance** (255-6356); cost is about $150 for two daredevils, including brunch on the ground.

Highway 29 narrows somewhat as it dashes between the vines, which do not at the moment seem to be adversely affected by auto pollution. **Napa Valley Cheese Co.,** on the left, has wine too. **Oakville** is tiny but the **Oakville Grocery** is a worthwhile stop for picnic fixings. **Rutherford** isn't much bigger but is dominated by the Beaulieu winery and its offshoot, **Rutherford Square** (shops, eating and drinking places). After Beaulieu, the wineries come one right after another; nearly every one that wants visitors has hung out a sign.

At Rutherford, Highway 128 shoots off to the east, crossing the Silverado Trail (the hillside route in the Napa Valley) and climbing the last hills of the Coast Range before the Central Valley. You can make a quick detour to **Lake Hennessey,** where there's picnicking in the county park, beneath interesting-looking **Conn Dam.** The highway crosses the **Chiles Valley,** which is a small wine valley, and then follows the west shore of **Lake Berryessa,** a 25-mile-long federal reservoir with several resorts, boat ramps (water-skiing plus fishing for steelhead, black bass, bluegill, and crappie), and **Oak Shores** public park, which is under development after a federal government effort to wrest back control of prime areas from trailer parks. The lake is held back by **Monticello Dam,** near Highway 128 at the Solano-Napa county line.

Returning to the floor of the Napa Valley, continue north on Highway 29 to **St. Helena**** (pronounced heh-LEE-nuh). Founded in 1855, St. Helena can be called the wine capital of California, if such appellations are necessary. An attractive farm town, with little old winery-worker cottages on the east side, better houses on the west, it seems like a nice, nineteenth-century place to live and tend a backyard patch of vines. Note several good examples of Victorian commercial architecture, including the **Ritchie Block*** (1892), 1331 Main St., and **IOOF Building** (1885), 1352 Main St. The **First Presbyterian Church,** 1428 Spring St., dates to 1874, and the **Catholic Church,** Tainter and Oak, to 1889, though it was rebuilt after a fire in 1946.

The Elsie and George Wood Public Library, 1492 Library Lane, in a new vine-surrounded building opened in 1979, houses two of St. Helena's principal attractions. One is the **Napa Valley Wine Library,*** a 1,200-title book collection begun in 1961 at the instigation of the well-known food writer M. F. K. Fisher, a Wine Country resident. The Wine Library Association (Box 328, St. Helena 94574), membership in which costs $10 per year, has a newsletter listing wine events, and runs a members-only wine-tasting in August. In another wing of the public library is the **Silverado Museum,**** formerly located at the old stone Hatchery on Railroad Avenue. The Silverado Museum is devoted entirely to the life and works of Robert Louis Stevenson, displaying first editions, photographs, and memorabilia collected by St. Helena resident Norman Strouse, former chairman of the J. Walter Thompson advertising agency. As visitors to Monterey know, Stevenson spent several months in California in 1879–80, not so much by design as for love. Meeting a married American woman, Fanny Osbourne, in France, he followed her to America and spent a penniless, feverish winter in Monterey, San Francisco, and Oakland while waiting for her divorce. They married May 19, 1880, in San Francisco, spent a few days at a Calistoga spa, then stayed through July at the defunct Silverado Mine on Mt. St. Helena (see p. 126). The museum, 963-3757, is open Tues.-Sun. 12-4, free.

St. Helena has some shopping in its small downtown. **Napa Valley Olive Oil Co.,** 835 McCorkle Ave., sells home-crushed olive oil for low prices, also cheese and other lunch items. **The Bottle Shop,** 1321 Main St., appropriately run by an heir of the Beringer Brothers, has the best selection of local beverages. Also in town, at 699 St. Helena

Hwy., is a branch of **Ernie's,** the complete wine warehouse, in case you want a fine Bordeaux for comparison purposes. The place to uncork and to snack is **Crane Park,** east end of Grayson Avenue, which has picnic tables under the oaks.

Strangely, St. Helena isn't touristy. Road travelers all seem to accumulate at **Freemark Abbey,*** two miles north of town, where there's a tour-bus restaurant (the Abbey), gift and gourmet shop (wine books, too), and **Hurd Beeswax Candles,** where you can watch dipping, cutting, rolling, and coloring—all somewhat different from the winemaking that goes on downstairs. Along Lodi Lane is **Barrel Builders,** in the business of repairing old wine barrels and making new ones (also redwood hot tubs).

The roads that wander north by northeast from here go up Howell Mountain, past the 1882 **Pacific Union College,** and down into **Pope Valley,** where you can find what appears to be the only parachuting resort in the world, **Pope Valley Parachute Center** (965-3400), and arrange to leap from an airplane ($75 for lesson, equipment, and skydive).

About three miles north of St. Helena, after the Beringer winery, watch for a left turn to the **Bale Grist Mill State Historic Park.**** Dr. Edward Bale, an English surgeon (and drunk), was wrecked off the Monterey coast in 1837, married into the Vallejo family, and in 1839 was granted the 9,000-acre Rancho Carne Humana(!) in the northern Napa Valley, abutting Yount's spread. His adobe was south of St. Helena. This photogenic grist (flour) mill, originally powered by water running in a flume from Mill Creek over the top of the 36-foot overshot wheel, was built in 1846 and turned for the next 25 years. Restored in the 1920s by the Native Sons of the Golden West, the mill became a county park in 1941, a state park in 1974. Open daily, 10-6 in summer, 9:30-4:30 in winter. Free. Picnicking seems to be on again, off again. Information: 942-4575.

A mile farther along the highway is another left, into **Bothe–Napa Valley State Park.*** The 1,242-acre park was owned by Dr. Charles Hitchcock (whose daughter Lillie Hitchcock Coit was the toast of San Francisco's firemen, whom she honored with Coit Tower). The doctor's ranch house, "Lonely," burned down after 1929 when this land became a campground. It has been a state park since 1960 and offers camping (35 sites, about the only camping in the valley), picnicking, summertime pool-swimming, hiking into the stands of Douglas fir and coastal redwood (perhaps the most easterly redwoods). Near the southern boundary of the park at the highway is the old **Pioneer Cemetery** and site of Napa County's first church (1853). Information: 3601 St. Helena Hwy., Calistoga 94515 (942-4575). Cars (with picnickers) pay entry fee. Ticketron is best for campsite reservations.

North of the state parks the Napa Valley begins narrowing. On a forested knoll to the right at Dunaweal Lane is the Sterling Vineyards winery (see p. 120), accessible by aerial tramway; Sterling commands a beautiful view south over the vineyards.

Calistoga,** at the northern end of the valley (only 200 feet higher than the bay end), has been a locally well-known spa since Sam Brannan, the Mormon pioneer journalist and sometime millionaire, discovered potential profit in its hot mud baths, mineral springs, and geysers (see p. 161). Brannan thought the place should be California's Saratoga (hence the coined name), bought a square mile, planted 160 acres of vines, started a profitable grocery store in 1859, built a Moorish spa hotel in 1866, and convinced railroad financiers to build a line up the valley in time for a grand opening in 1868. Unfortunately, Brannan went broke and the resort, never very successful, later burned down. One remaining cottage has been moved to 1311 Washington St., opposite City Hall and next door to the **Calistoga (Sharpsteen) Museum.*** Open Sat.-Sun. 12-4, the cottage has period furnishings, the museum dioramas, shadow boxes, and murals of old Calistoga as well as a stagecoach. **Brannan's grocery store** still stands at Wappo and Grant, and the 1868 **Calistoga Depot** has shops and a café.

Until the $20-million, 400-room **Calistoga Falls** resort goes up on 50 acres off the Silverado Trail, half a mile from downtown, Calistoga's several **spas** are the main drawing card. At most of them (see Calistoga listings, p. 284) it costs only about $15 for a full mudbath and Jacuzzi treatment. If colonic irrigations are not your thing, there's always the **Old Faithful Geyser,** 1299 Tubbs La. (942-6463), a 60-foot hot-water geyser that erupts about every 40 minutes. Open daily, 8 A.M. to sundown, (a small admission is charged). Picnicking. Calistoga Water is, by the way, commercially bottled and competes with Perrier.

Calistoga has two transportation adventures. The tamer one is the one-third-scale **Calistoga Steam Railroad,** Silverado Trail (a quarter-mile off Highway 29), 942-5353. Locomotive No. 1913, a 4-6-2 that pulled passengers around San Francisco's 1915 Panama-Pacific Exposition, takes visitors (for little cash) on a 15-minute, 2.25-mile loop through fields, up an oak-covered hillside, and back to the depot (snacks, books) and turntable. Open Tues.-Sun., 12-5 in summer, weekends 12-5 the rest of the year; departures every half-hour. The second adventure is not for the fainthearted or the tipsy: the **Calistoga Soaring Center,** Airpark, 1546 Lincoln Ave. (942-5592), will take you sightseeing in a sailplane (otherwise known as a glider) for $15, and if you get hooked you can pay $700 or so for 50 training flights. Sailplanes take advantage of the valley's thermal drafts and "ridge waves" and have glided as far as Bakersfield (yes, but who wants to go there?).

Just over the Sonoma County line southwest of Calistoga, on Petrified Forest Road, is—surprise—the **Petrified Forest** (942-6667), a 542-acre commercial operation that the state wants to buy. The forest has redwoods that were petrified when covered with volcanic ash some time ago, maybe six million years. The "Queen of the Forest" is 12 feet in circumference, 80 feet long; the "Monarch" is at least 126 feet long and getting longer as they uncover more of it. Open daily, 9-5 (longer in summer), small admission. Picnicking.

At the head of the Napa Valley, with its 4,343-foot summit in Sonoma County, is stately **Mt. St. Helena.** The mountain is not the vent or cone of an inactive volcano, only a peak of folded volcanic flows. The mountain was perhaps named for a Russian princess, or for her patron saint, or for a Russian ship—none of these being unlikely, for the Russians were established at Fort Ross, on the Sonoma coast (33 beeline miles away) for three decades until 1841. The undeveloped **Robert Louis Stevenson State Park*** occupies the foothill area at the junction of the Napa, Sonoma, and Lake county lines. In May-July 1880, Stevenson and his wife Fanny honeymooned 2,000 feet up on the southeast slope at what remained of **Silverado,** site of the Calistoga Gold and Silver Mine, which had operated 1872-77. A steep trail went up a canyon to the abandoned mine shaft, where there was a platform with a decrepit three-story bunkhouse. One biographer says the Stevensons' seven or eight weeks here were more like a camping trip "with the help of a shed-roof and a cookstove." In any case, under the good summer sun, with views down the valley (now obscured by trees), with the help of venison and cream-topped rum punch, and with opportunity for excursions to Schramsberg and other wineries, Stevenson, who had been ill during the winter, recovered some of his health and scribbled the draft of what became "The Silverado Squatters" ("The scene of this little book is on a high mountain," it begins). James D. Hart has noted that RLS romanticized everything—pines became "spires," the nearby mountainside inn was the "Castle of Indolence"—but probably because he was happy. Historian George R. Stewart, identifying California elements in *Treasure Island,* found that Mt. St. Helena contributed to the description of Spyglass Hill, with Long John Silver evolving from "Juan Silverado," the mountain's personification.

Biographer J. C. Furnas, who visited all but one of the places in the world where Stevenson lived, wrote that, "perhaps because of the special immediacy and pungency of his writing about it, one feels more Stevenson in the air at Silverado than anywhere else in the world except in Edinburgh and environs." Take winding Highway 29 north of Calistoga up to the park, and walk to the site of the mine, where there is a monument, an open book inscribed with a stanza beginning "Doomed to know not winter, only spring. . . ." Of the rough park trails, one goes four miles to the summit. Picnicking but no fires.

PRACTICAL INFORMATION

Getting There, Getting Around

Gray Line and other tour buses visit the valley, but the most practical means of winery-hopping is a slow drive by car up Highway 29 on the valley floor, where the most accessible wineries are. Parallel to 29 on the eastern slope is the Silverado Trail (highway); a dozen county roads connect the two arteries. Connection with the Sonoma Valley is difficult because of the Mayacmas Mountains. If you don't take Highway 12 between Napa and Sonoma towns, you may want to try the Oakville Grade (aptly named) between Oakville and Glen Ellen. If you want to loop north through the Napa Valley to Calistoga, then south through the Sonoma Valley, take Petrified Forest Road from downtown Calistoga south to Calistoga Road, which joins Highway 12. See Chapter 5 for details. You can also take Highway 128 straight through Calistoga and into the Alexander Valley, ending at Geyserville, bringing you to the northern Sonoma Wine Country. It's wise to have a good road map; see "Sources of Information" (p. 164).

Bicycles are more and more popular. The valley-floor Highway 29 is flat and has good shoulders, but you'll breathe car exhaust. The Silverado Trail is more tolerable, but there aren't many wineries. Take your pick. Meanwhile, the connecting roads to Sonoma are mostly daunting. Silverado Country Club, Magnolia Hotel, and Napa Lodge all rent bikes to guests, while Hauschild's Ice Cream, 1255 Lincoln Ave., Calistoga, not only rents bikes but will sell you any of 40 flavors. For bike routes, see *The Grape Escape* (Sally Taylor and Friends, 756

Kansas St., San Francisco 94107; $2.95) or *Bicycle Rides In and Around the Napa Valley* (Napa Family Bike Club; $2 at shops in the valley).

Greyhound runs buses six times a day from San Francisco (sometimes via Oakland and Berkeley) through Vallejo to Napa, and five times from San Francisco to Napa and up the valley, with stops at Yountville, Oakville, Rutherford, St. Helena, and Calistoga. Napa has a **bus** service (707/255-7631) and there's a weekday **Dial-A-Ride** service in populated areas (707/224-2351, 963-4222).

Gray Line's nine-hour wine-country tour departs from San Francisco's Trans-Bay Terminal at 9 A.M. three times a week Mar.-Nov. 15, visits one winery, stops at either Freemark Abbey or Vintage 1870, and includes lunch. We have a low opinion of such hurried cattle drives, but it's less than $20 per adult. If you have more capital, try a private guided tour: **D'Vine Wine Tours,** 2699 Silverado Trail, St. Helena 94574 (707/963-2164), and Napa Valley Doubledecker Wine Tours, 3050 Jefferson St., Napa 94558 (707/255-1000). **Wine Tours International,** Pier 39, San Francisco 94133 (415/391-1374), runs one-day group tours for $35 per person, or private three-day tours for $125 per person, going to three wineries (picnic at one) not usually open to the public. The **Napa Valley Wine Library Association** offers three-day summer-weekend wine appreciation courses. Write Box 328, St. Helena 94574.

If you're **flying** from Bordeaux or elsewhere, land at San Francisco International Airport and try to find a commuter airline to Napa County Airport (National Rent-a-Car), or take an Evans Airport Service van (707/255-1559) from SFO to Napa (Hertz, Avis, etc.).

Where to Stay and Eat

Accommodations (including camping) and restaurants are listed in Part IV under these headings: Calistoga/Northern Napa Valley; Lake Berryessa/Napa Highlands; Napa; St. Helena/Central Napa Valley; and Yountville/Southern Napa Valley.

CHAPTER 5:

Sonoma and Mendocino

HIGHLIGHTS

Wineries:
Buena Vista / 134
Sebastiani / 135
Hanzell / 135
Chateau St. Jean / 136
Russian River Vineyards / 136
Korbel / 136
Landmark / 137
Sonoma Vineyards / 137
Hop Kiln / 138
Foppiano / 139
Dry Creek Vineyard / 139
Simi / 139
Johnson's / 140
Souverain / 140
Nervo / 140
Pedroncelli / 141
Geyser Peak / 141
Italian Swiss Colony / 141
Cresta Blanca / 142
Parducci / 143
Weibel / 143

Other Attractions:
Sonoma / 144
Sonoma State Historic Park / 145
Lachryma Montis / 147
Jack London State Historic Park / 149
Sugarloaf Ridge State Park / 150
Hood Mountain Regional Park / 150
Annadel State Park / 151
Marin French Cheese Co. / 151
Petaluma Adobe / 151
Petaluma / 152
Santa Rosa / 153
"Church Built from One Tree" / 154
Luther Burbank Gardens / 154
Apple Country; Farm Trails / 155
Russian River Region / 155
Canoeing / 156
Armstrong Redwoods / 157
Austin Creek SRA / 157
Guerneville / 158
Healdsburg / 160
The Geysers / 161
Asti / 162
Clear Lake / 162
Ukiah / 162

Various descriptions of Sonoma County are apt to sound as though they were written about entirely different places. There's a diversity that is easy to describe or catalogue, but generalizations don't come readily. Sonoma County is, however, all north of San Francisco, and is a good day-trip destination for out-of-staters.

Starting with the Russians

The history of the county has diverse elements. To start with, Russians were the first white settlers. They established an otter-hunting outpost at Fort Ross in 1812 (see Chapter 7 for more on the Sonoma coast), and gave a name to the Russian River—Slavianka ("Slav woman"), though the Mexicans later called it the Rio Ruso. To counter such Russian influence physically, the Mexican governor suggested that the Franciscan missionaries move the San Francisco and San Rafael missions to the Sonoma frontier. Those two missions stayed put, but a new one, Mission San Francisco Solano, was established in 1823. It turned out to be the twenty-first and last of the Franciscan missions, lasting 11 years before secularization.

In the rancho period Sonoma became virtually a fief of General Mariano Guadalupe Vallejo. He planned Sonoma town and ruled his domain (and commanded Northern California) from La Casa Grande on Sonoma Plaza and his big ranch house near Petaluma. The California equivalent of the Boston Tea Party occurred at Sonoma Plaza in 1846, when a band of landless Yankees, at John C. Frémont's instigation, seized Vallejo and declared the "California Republic"—a month before the U.S. took possession of the province at the beginning of the Mexican War.

Interesting events, but anomalies, for Sonoma has never been in the mainstream of California history. Nonetheless, Fort Ross, the Sonoma Mission, portions of three of Vallejo's ranch houses, and Sonoma Plaza all survive as tourist attractions, and the bear flag of the "one-town, one-month republic" is now the state's official banner.

The county's geography is diverse as well. The windy, bluff-lined coast and the dark groves of coastal redwoods seem far removed from the warm, peaceful agricultural valleys inland. The major river, the Russian, seems more like two rivers. The upper river drifts from Mendocino County south into the Alexander Valley, meanders aimlessly near Healdsburg, straightens out, then, just when it should follow the

Santa Rosa or Cotati valley into San Francisco Bay (as it once did), it cuts through the Coast Range ridges to the ocean. If you go down the fairly narrow canyon of the Russian River, you will see that at Jenner it widens considerably at the mouth but seems to end in a lagoon, for a beach sandbar blocks the river a lot of the time.

Two natural phenomena don't fit in with the general softness of the landscape. One is the Petrified Forest near the Napa County line, the other the world's largest geothermal energy field, The Geysers, in the hills above the Alexander Valley. These and the many hot springs are testimony to Sonoma County's volcanic past.

Agriculturally, Sonoma is a big winegrowing district but is also the state's leading producer of apples (8,000 acres), an important dairy-farming area (look for Sonoma Jack cheese), and a leading sheep-ranching county (the ranches are on the green but largely waterless coastside hills). Both the wine roads and the mapped Sonoma Farm Trails are popular with visitors. The fertility of Sonoma was also discovered by America's "plant wizard," Luther Burbank, who found the Santa Rosa Valley "the chosen spot of all the Earth as far as nature is concerned," and conducted all his experimental horticultural breeding here from 1875 until he died in 1926. His gardens are now a public park in Santa Rosa.

Some of the oddities in the county no doubt influenced Robert L. "Believe It or Not" Ripley, who was born and is buried in Santa Rosa. The "Church Built of One Tree" in Santa Rosa is a Ripley museum.

Sonoma's most renowned literary figure was Jack London, who won fame for his adventure stories about the Klondike but who then chose to lead a less-adventurous life as a farmer-rancher and writer in the upper Sonoma Valley, near Glen Ellen. His Beauty Ranch and the ruins of Wolf House are a state park. He is the Sonoma counterpart of Robert Louis Stevenson, whose ghost wanders the Napa Valley.

Sonoma Wine Valleys

Vineyards and wineries seem to be everywhere, making Sonoma Wine Country less convenient for touring than the Napa Valley. Korbel's champagne cellars and vineyards are surrounded by coastal redwoods in the Russian River resort area near Guerneville. Sebastiani's vineyards include those first planted in 1825 by the mission fathers near Sonoma Plaza. Vineyards have now spread into the upper Russian River Valley, which is called the Alexander Valley, and into the valley of a tributary, Dry Creek; they have also taken over former apple orchards around Sebastopol.

The history of winegrowing in Sonoma is discontinuous and erratic. The mission fathers and General Vallejo had many acres of vines. Agoston Haraszthy introduced many premium varieties from Europe at his Buena Vista vineyards and helped Sonoma become, with Los Angeles, the leading wine-producing county in the last century. Earlier than the Napa Valley, Sonoma became a place for rich gentlemen farmers, on the pattern of Bordeaux aristocrats. In the 1880s two U.S. senators, George Hearst of California and James G. Fair of Nevada (both mining millionaires), owned Sonoma vineyards, Hearst's in the Sonoma Valley, Fair's on the Petaluma River. (California's other senator at that time, Leland Stanford, owned a vineyard at Mission San Jose.)

But in time Sonoma was eclipsed by Napa. Phylloxera was a serious blow. The Buena Vista Winery partially collapsed in the 1906 earthquake and was closed for the next 40 years. Prohibition closed dozens of other wineries. After Repeal most of the older wineries produced bulk wines for sale under other labels; even Sebastiani, the oldest in continuous ownership and tradition (since 1904), did not release wine under its own name until the 1950s. The majority of today's wineries have opened since the 1960s, the decade in which the first vintage-dated Sonoma varietal wines were produced.

Although Sonoma now has more vineyard acreage than Napa, its wines do not have the collective reputation of those from the neighboring valley, but they are gaining fast. Many of the wineries you can visit may lack long tradition but compensate for that with an amazing capability to make some of the finest California wine. Sonoma's success has most recently led to the opening of the Ukiah and other Mendocino valleys as a premium wine district. Three Ukiah Valley wineries are included in this section for convenience.

The traveler in Sonoma County will notice many signs not only of historical, geographical, and economic diversity but also of social diversity. With the San Francisco Bay metropolitan area slowly sprawling north through Novato, Petaluma, and Santa Rosa on Highway 101, Sonoma County has gained a lot of city and suburban folk, but still has a good many people whose outlook is definitely rural. The counterculture and San Francisco gay population have outposts here and there, around Sonoma town and in the Russian River resort area, and the retired are a large constituency in the Sonoma Valley and around Santa Rosa. The well-to-do have a 10-mile stretch of coastline at the Sea Ranch for expensive vacation homes, and every summer the very rich and powerful, up to and including presidents, attend the "encampment" at exclusive Bohemian Grove on the Russian River.

All of which is a peculiar mix that has caused, among other things, some long-standing struggles between developers and environmentalists, such as the 20-year battle (ending with an environmentalist defeat in 1979) over the Warm Springs Dam, which will create Lake Sonoma in the hills west of Geyserville; the availability of water will open the dry, hilly, largely unpopulated northwest quarter of the county to development.

Iron Fronts and Rhododendrons

If you don't believe us by this time, these five attractions may convince you of Sonoma's interesting diversity: delightful, iron-fronted Victorian commercial buildings in Petaluma; a century-old French cheese factory; a town in the trees, Occidental, whose most apparent industry is three large, very popular, family-style Italian restaurants; a coastal rhododendron reserve; and a photogenic fishing village. The Sonoma coast is covered in Chapter 7; everything else is below. A triple-A map is a must for exploring.

WHAT TO SEE AND DO

As with the Napa Valley we have divided this section into "Wineries" and "Other Attractions." Winery listings begin with those in the Sonoma Valley, then skip over to the lower Russian River and trend north into Mendocino; visiting the wineries in this or any order would be a trial. "Other Attractions" are those in or near the Sonoma Valley or somewhere along the Highway 101 corridor, with some requiring considerable detours.

Area code: 707, unless otherwise noted. Some zip codes: Geyserville 95441, Glen Ellen 95442, Guerneville 95446, Healdsburg 95448,

Kenwood 95452, Petaluma 94952, Sonoma 95476, Windsor 95492, Ukiah 95482.

WINERIES

Wineries are generally open daily from 10 to 4 (at least) and closed on major holidays. "By appointment" is not to discourage you, only to control hordes of wine buffs.

Sonoma Valley

Buena Vista Winery*** (Haraszthy Cellars), 18000 Old Winery Rd., Sonoma (1 mile east of Sonoma), 938-1266. Tours (self-conducted), tasting, sales, daily 9:30-5; picnicking for retail sales customers only. This was Colonel Haraszthy's old place, the first big commercial winery of the North Coast. After growing grapes in Wisconsin and at San Diego, he planted European vines near San Francisco's Mission Dolores but, finding they wouldn't ripen in the summer fog, he transplanted them to San Mateo County and, finally, to Salvador Vallejo's vineyard here in 1857. It wasn't until 1863, two years after his European vine-collecting tour, that Haraszthy had the two sandstone Buena Vista cellars built and supervised the digging of the hillside tunnels. He competed with General Mariano Vallejo in making good wine (the general's collected more medals), oversaw his son Arpad's attempts to make Champagne (the fizz wasn't vintage), and entered into high-financial dealings with San Francisco's William C. Ralston to make Buena Vista big and prosperous (it was the former but not the latter). Haraszthy's career was brief, for he was driven out of Buena Vista in 1866 and emigrated to Nicaragua, where he died in 1869. His sons, Arpad and Attila, who had married two of Vallejo's daughters, were left in charge. Though Arpad's "Eclipse" Champagne finally succeeded, the enterprise wasn't financially healthy, and was killed by the twin blows of phylloxera and the 1906 earthquake. United Press International executive Frank Bartholomew bought it at auction and revived it in the 1940s. He sold out to Young's Market Company of L.A. in 1968 and went next door to start Hacienda Wine Cellars. Young's hired a grandson and a great-grandson of the Hungarian colonel (they've now set up their own operation) and started expanding production by a factor of 10. A West German wine and liquor import-export firm bought Buena Vista in 1979. Buena Vista now has a new winery and 600 acres (of 700 total) in the Carneros district, just across the Napa line, and is striving to regain the reputation it had in the nineteenth century. Varietals (17 in all) include Cabernet Sauvignon (cask-numbered labels), Pinot Noir, Zinfandel (Haraszthy is falsely credited with bringing this one from Europe), Sylvaner, Green Hungarian, and Gewürztraminer, plus sparkling wines, Sherry, and Port. The winery buildings in the eucalyptus grove here at Sonoma are state landmarks, and one can walk through four of the six original limestone-tunnel aging cellars that either did not cave in during the earthquake or were later restored.

Sebastiani Vineyards,*** 389 4th St. E., Sonoma, 938-5532. Tours, tasting, sales, daily 10-5. Sebastiani has been a mainstay of the Sonoma town economy since the early part of the century, and "Sebastiani" appears on winery and nonwinery buildings alike. Samuele Sebastiani immigrated from Italy about 1892, moved to Sonoma, and by quarrying and hauling building stone earned enough money to buy a small winery and the vineyards that the missionaries had planted in the 1820s and Vallejo had later owned. The winery survived Prohibition by making altar wine and an alleged medicine called wine tonic. Now run by his three grandsons, the winery switched in the early 1960s from selling bulk wine to bottling some of the distinctive varietals that Sebastiani has become well known for. Barbera, Johannisberg Riesling, Green Hungarian, Gamay Beaujolais, Gewürztraminer, Pinot Noir (plus a Blanc "Eye of the Swan"), and Cabernet Sauvignon. Generics, Vermouth, and dessert wines are also produced. Sebastiani led in the production of premium varietals in half-gallon jugs in the early 1970s, and in 1972 started bottling and releasing in the fall a Nouveau Gamay Beaujolais, on the French model. The visitor will enjoy a visit here for the combination of old and new, solid tradition; be sure to see some of the 35 carved wine casks and barrels and the new Indian museum. The 400 acres of vineyard are mostly in the valley near town but the winery also buys grapes from Sonoma, Mendocino, and Lodi growers.

Hanzell Vineyards,* 18596 Lomita Ave., Sonoma (off Highway 12 north of town), 996-3860. Tours and sales by appointment. Started in 1948 but officially founded in 1956 by the late James D. Zellerbach, wealthy executive of San Francisco's Crown Zellerbach and ambassador to Italy. Hanzell has since had a number of owners but continues the tradition of Burgundian winemaking nearly pioneered in the U.S. by Zellerbach: in the 1950s he made the interesting discovery that aging wine in French oak (which is a different species from American oaks) accounted for the "complexity" that connoisseurs said American wine lacked. After Zellerbach's death in 1963, the Napa Valley's Joe Heitz purchased the inventory for further aging and eventually reached a wider audience. The use of French oak, meanwhile, has caught on everywhere, especially among small wineries. The façade of the Hanzell winery (Porter and Steinwedell, 1957) was modeled on the Clos de Vougeot, a Burgundian monastery, but inside, the latest technology coexists with French oak cooperage. Hanzell produces only Chardonnay and Pinot Noir (a Cabernet will be made in the future) from its 20 or so acres around the winery.

Chateau St. Jean,* 8555 Sonoma Hwy., Kenwood (near Highway 12), 833-4134. Tours by appointment; tasting, sales, daily 10-4:30; also picnicking. One of the most successful of the new wineries, Chateau St. Jean (pronounced Saint Jeen) was founded in 1974 by two brothers who owned Central Valley vineyards and wanted to produce premium wines. With a partner they purchased a 200-acre estate with a white 1920s French-Mediterranean villa (used as the tasting room), started constructing a new winery (completed in 1977), produced a 1974 vintage with leased equipment and purchased grapes, and quickly started collecting medals. Chateau St. Jean is specializing in small lots of vintage-dated varietals, mostly white, many vineyard-designated.

Russian River Valley

Russian River Vineyards,* 5700 Gravenstein Highway (Highway 116), Forestville, 887-1562. Tours, tasting, sales, by appointment; restaurant open for dinner Thurs.-Sun. Founded in 1964, under the present ownership since 1975, the winery is in an extremely photogenic prestressed concrete and redwood building modeled on Fort Ross and the hop kilns one still spots in Sonoma, set in the 27 acres of vineyards four miles from the Russian River. The winery is making vintage-dated Chardonnay, Cabernet Sauvignon, Petite Sirah, and Zinfandel, plus generics.

F. Korbel & Bros* (Korbel Champagne Cellars), River Road, Guerneville (east of town, near Rio Nido), 887-2294. Tours, daily 9:45-3:45; tasting, sales, daily 9-5:30. Korbel, like Sebastiani, has been a rock in the turbulent history of Sonoma wine. Francis Korbel and his two brothers immigrated from Czechoslovakia to post-Gold Rush California and came to the Russian River Valley in the 1860s, when logging was the industry and Guerneville was "Stumptown." They bought 6,000 acres, cut down trees, tried dairy farming and growing alfalfa, experimented with tobacco and prunes, and finally decided in the late 1870s to grow grapes on the bottomland, which is cooled by moist ocean air during the summer. Since grape prices were low at the time of their first vintage, they produced their first wine in 1881. Succeeding with that, they planted more vines and in 1886 started constructing half of the present brick winery building, which was joined later by a common roof to a twin distillery building. A Norman tower (modeled on the prison tower where Francis had spent some time) was built to house a brandy still. The Korbels made their first Champagne in 1898 and started making it better after Pilsen-trained Jan Hanuska was hired. The next generation of Korbels didn't want to continue and, in 1954, sold the winery to another trio of brothers, the Hecks, who were German Alsatians with a couple of generations of winemaking tradition. Korbel in the 1970s expanded production to include vintage-dated varietals but now, once again, is concentrating on its sparkling wines: bone-dry Natural, Brut, Extra Dry, Sec, Rosé, and Rouge, all bottle fermented but riddled and disgorged with the use of some modern gadgetry. Outside the complex of buildings are 400 acres of vines on both bottomland and hillsides; another 200 acres are leased. Only recently were some of the vines of the 1890s replaced, and grapes are still harvested from 40-year-old vines.

Landmark Vineyards, 9150 Los Amigos Rd., Windsor (on freeway frontage road), 838-9466. Informal tours, tasting, sales, Wed. and Fri. 12-5, Sat.-Sun. 10-5, or by appointment; also picnicking. Another new winery, founded in 1976, Landmark is located on an estate formerly owned by shipping heir William Matson Roth, now owned by the Mabry family. The offices and tasting room are in the late 1920s mansion at the end of a cypress-lined drive, and the winery is in a new building. Prune orchards are giving way to vines nearby. The 67 acres of Landmark vineyards include vines near Vineburg and in the Alexander Valley; another 16 acres are leased. Varietals include Johannisberg Riesling, Gewürztraminer, Chardonnay, Pinot Noir, and Cabernet Sauvignon, all vintage-dated.

Sonoma Vineyards, ** 11455 Old Redwood Hwy., Healdsburg (3 miles north of Windsor exit from Highway 101), 433-5455. Tours by appointment; tasting, sales, daily 10–5; group lunches and dinners by arrangement; picnicking. What is now known as Sonoma Vineyards, a large maker of increasingly better varietals, with 2,600 acres of vineyards, began in 1961 as a smaller bottler, wineshop, and tasting room in a former boardinghouse, a two-story frame building, in Tiburon, across from San Francisco. Its founder, Rodney Strong, led it through a phase in which it catered, by direct mail and direct sales, to customers who wanted wine with personalized labels. Soon Strong took over the old Windsor Winery (1898) and began expanding, but got into a financial bind and, in 1976, surrendered control to Renfield Importers. Since then, it's all been up. The vineyards—Alexander's Crown, Robert Young, River West, Chalk Hill, LeBaron—provide Chardonnay, Johannisberg Riesling, Cabernet Sauvignon, and Pinot Noir grapes in large quantities for the vintage-dated, vineyard-designated, medal-winning wines. (A second label, Windsor Vineyards, is used for a line of wine sold by mail order.) In 1980 plans were announced for a $6 million joint sparkling-wine venture with France's Piper-Heidsieck. The first bottles of Piper-Sonoma will be released in late 1982. The winery building (Richard Keith and Craig W. Roland, 1969–70) is both pyramidal and cruciform, with rectangular working areas around a central space; the visitor overlooks wine operations from a second-story gallery above the modern crushers, fermenting tanks, and oak cooperage. A former Broadway dancer and choreographer, Strong was quick to start a summertime music and dance series (Summer Concerts, Box 368, Windsor 95492, 736-9711).

Hop Kiln Winery** (Griffin Vineyard), 6050 Westside Rd., Healdsburg (6.5 miles southwest of town), 433-6491. Tours, tasting, sales, Sat.–Sun. 10–5 and by appointment; picnicking for sales customers. Dr. L. Martin Griffin and his family bought the old Sweetwater Springs Ranch with its 65 acres of Russian River vineyards in 1960, then set about restoring the turn-of-the-century hop kiln, with its three distinctive square towers, opening it as a winery in 1975. Visitors can learn something about what goes into beer, for the furnace and tall hop press remain in the winery, which is a state historic landmark. Vintage-dated varietals produced are Petite Sirah, Zinfandel, Gamay Beaujolais, Johannisberg Riesling, and French Colombard, plus "One Thousand Flowers" (a Riesling-Colombard blend) and "Marty Griffin's Big Red" (made from several unknown black grape varieties found growing in a far corner of the vineyard).

Foppiano Vineyards, 12781 Old Redwood Hwy., Healdsburg (2 miles south of town), 433-7272. Tours by appointment; tasting, sales, daily 10–4. John Foppiano started making wine in 1896 and his grandson and great-grandsons are still at it. Production was once mostly bulk wine, with some "country jug wine" sold at the door, but since the Sonoma wine boom, some vintage-dated varietals (Zinfandel, Cabernet Sauvignon—both strong and Italian—Pinot Noir, Petite Sirah, French Colombard, and Sonoma Fumé) and jug generics are coming out of the post-Prohibition winery building.

Dry Creek Vineyard, 3770 Lambert Bridge Rd., Healdsburg (3 miles from Dry Creek Road exit off Highway 101), 433-1000. Tours, tasting, sales, daily 10–5. David and Gail Stare of Boston started their small winery in the early 1970s with the intention of establishing a Médoc chateau in the Dry Creek Valley. They haven't done that yet, but they've been successful with some of their early wines—Chardonnay and Chenin Blanc—and are trying with their Fumé Blanc, Gamay Beaujolais, Zinfandel, Petite Sirah, and Cabernet Sauvignon. Four of those varieties grow in the 50 acres; other grapes are purchased. The winery building is modestly designed.

Simi Winery, * 16275 Healdsburg Ave., Healdsburg (north of town), 433-6981. Tours, tasting, sales, daily 10–5. Simi is another old-new winery. It dates back to 1881, when a pair of brothers from the Piedmont of Italy shifted winemaking from their San Francisco home to the present fieldstone winery building (1890), where they produced bulk wine for sale under other labels. One of the Simi daughters and her husband carried the business into this century and through Prohibition, after which British winemaker George Remington helped them establish a Simi label and a Hotel Del Monte Selection and carried off gold medals from the state fair. Then the business slipped: too much wine was made, too little sold. In 1969 the winery was sold to Russell Green, an oil company executive with vineyards in the Alexander Valley. He found the winery filled with casks of old, partially spoiled wine, along with outmoded equipment for making new wine. After starting a modernization and expansion program he sold the winery to a British winemaking firm which then sold it, in 1976, to Schiefflin and Company, the importers. While there's not much Sonoma-Italian winemaking tradition left, Simi under its new direction is starting to turn out well-received varietals: Chardonnay, Johannisberg Riesling, Chenin Blanc, Gewürztraminer, Rosé of Cabernet, Gamay Beaujolais, Zinfandel, Pinot Noir, and Cabernet Sauvignon. The present winemaker and her predecessor are two of the few women in the field. Russell Green, who had successfully petitioned for an Alexander Valley appellation of origin, sells his grapes to Simi.

Johnson's Alexander Valley Wines* (Rancho Sotoyome), 8333 Hwy. 128, Healdsburg (southeast of Jimtown), 433-2319. Tours, tasting, sales, daily 10–5. The three Johnson brothers (one of whom is a Sonoma County supervisor) started making wine on the family ranch in 1975, picking up where some of the original owners had left off in the 1890s. Rancho Sotoyome makes an interesting visit, not only to sample the wine but to see the 30-pipe theater organ that appears on the wine label (organ concerts are given at a monthly open house) and to see the ranch house, which has no studs and no frame: it is held together by vertical redwood boards inside, horizontal ones outside.

Souverain Cellars,** 400 Souverain Rd., Geyserville (Independence Lane exit off Highway 101), 433-6918. Tours, tasting, sales, daily 10–4; restaurant open for lunch and dinner (reservations, 857-3789). Souverain dates back either to 1943 or to 1973. Lee Stewart founded Souverain Cellars at Rutherford, Napa Valley, in 1943, but sold it to Pillsbury when he retired in 1970. That company started a Sonoma operation, Souverain of Alexander Valley, before getting out of the wine business in 1976. Souverain of Alexander Valley—winery and name—went to North Coast Cellars, a grape-growers' partnership, while the Napa Valley winery—minus the name—was sold to another partnership. Souverain's new owners are now establishing a reputation with varietals—Johannisberg Riesling and Colombard Blanc, in particular, but also Gray Riesling, Green Hungarian, Chenin Blanc, Fumé Blanc, Cabernet Sauvignon, Pinot Noir, Petite Sirah, Gamay Beaujolais, Zinfandel, Pinot Noir Rosé, and a generic red. Before they sold out, Pillsbury hired John Marsh Davis, the original architect of the barn-style winery at Rutherford, to design this winery, which resembles a stretched-out Sonoma hop barn: two towers (one a restaurant-theater, the other offices) are connected by the low-rise winery building. It's good-looking, and one can take a tour before lunch or dinner, which is served inside and on a terrace overlooking the winery's own six acres and a vista across the Alexander Valley. Souverain has started a summer drama series (Summer Theater, Box 528, Geyserville), has art shows, and throws a country Christmas fair after Thanksgiving, when the vineyard foliage has turned.

Nervo Winery, 19585 Redwood Hwy. S., Geyserville (Independence Lane exit off Highway 101), 857-3417. Tasting, sales, daily 10–

5; also picnicking. Frank Nervo built this winery in 1908. His heirs sold it in 1973 to the Schlitz brewing company, which was the new owner of nearby Geyser Peak Winery. Nervo and Geyser Peak winemaking have been combined, but Nervo remains open as a salesroom and picnic spot.

J. Pedroncelli Winery, 1220 Canyon Rd., Geyserville (west of town), 857-3619. Tours by appointment; tasting, sales, daily 10–5. Giovanni Pedroncelli bought the old Canata winery (1904) in 1927 and slowly expanded a hobby into a vocation and turned out good country-jug wine. His two sons took over in 1955 and gradually abandoned bulk wine for varietals under their own label, and are turning out some reputable Chardonnay, Zinfandel, and Pinot Noir as well as Cabernet Sauvignon, Gamay Beaujolais, Zinfandel Rosé (first in California), Johannisberg Riesling, Gewürztraminer, and Chenin Blanc with good varietal flavor plus generics. They grow 135 acres of grapes here and buy from Dry Creek and Alexander Valley growers.

Geyser Peak Winery,* 22281 Redwood Hwy. N., Geyserville (Canyon Road exit off Highway 101), 433-6585. Tours, tasting, sales, daily 10–5; picnicking and hiking. Geyser Peak was a bulk-wine and vinegar company from 1880 through several ownerships until sold by the Bagnani family to Schlitz in 1972. It has changed dramatically since then. First, a shake-roofed, fieldstone-and-redwood winery complex (Richard Keith, architect) was built into the hillside over some of the 600 acres of vines; a red barn remains as a symbol of the old days. Second, Schlitz hired as winemaker the man who had expanded Almadén's production 33-fold. Third, the Schlitz marketing people decided to try some new ideas, such as selling jug wine in a plastic-lined box with a spigot. The winery produces inexpensive generics and varietals in bottles, jugs, and boxes under the Summit label and mid-priced, nonvintage-dated varietals under the Geyser Peak label. In terms of quality, Geyser Peak isn't breaking any new ground yet, and Schlitz reportedly may sell out. Meanwhile, the winery launched one of the most varied of summer festivals, with jazz, opera, dance, humor, ballet, chamber music, Gilbert and Sullivan, folk, theater, and bluegrass (Geyser Peak Arts Festival, Box 66, Geyserville; 707/857-3302).

Italian Swiss Colony,*** Asti (next to Highway 101, between Geyserville and Cloverdale), 894-2541. Tours, tasting, sales, daily 10-5. It's a good old name, but it's not quite the operation one might expect. The name and part of the facility here date back to the 1880s when an altruistic Italian, Andrea Sbarboro, gathered the capital to establish the

Italian Swiss Agricultural Colony for the purpose of employing many recent Italian and Swiss immigrants who were out of work during the depression of the 1870s. Such enterprises never have bright futures, and the early years were rough: the first grapes were harvested when the market price was too low to sell, so the Italian Swiss decided to make wine instead—but it turned to vinegar. But, in time, with a remarkable winemaker named Pietro Rossi in charge, the Italian Swiss produced a Golden State Extra Dry Champagne that bested French Champagne in at least one competition in Europe, and for years Tipo Chianti, in the traditional straw *fiasco,* was an extremely popular California wine (it is still produced—at great cost, since *fiaschi* are more expensive than wine). Organizationally, Italian Swiss Colony has far outgrown its origins. It became a regular business, owned by Sbarboro and Rossi, off and on affiliated with or part of grape-growers' syndicates, until it was sold by Rossi's sons to National Distillers in 1942. At the time it was the third largest American winery. In 1953 it became part of the United Vintners empire (now the second largest wine company); in 1968 UV was gobbled up by Heublein, the liquor firm, though the U.S. government is now suing to force divestiture. Many descendants of the original Italian Swiss, including Rossis, still work here at Asti, but the facility is regarded as one of six units of United Vintners (the six have a storage capacity of 95 million gallons), and at the moment is turning out jug wine under the Inglenook label and Champagne under the Lejon label, while Central Valley units produce wine under the Colony label. Still, they give a good Italian Swiss welcome to 400,000 visitors each year.

Mendocino

Cresta Blanca Winery, 2399 N. State St., Ukiah (north of town), 462-0565. Tours (weekdays), tasting, sales, daily 9–5; also picnicking. Cresta Blanca was founded by a newspaperman, Charles Wetmore, beneath a white cliff *(cresta blanca)* south of Livermore in Alameda County in 1882, and within the next decade carried off some Grand Prix at the Paris Exposition, the origin of the double gold-medal neck ring on the wines today. Cresta Blanca made it through Prohibition and might today be one of the state's very best premium wineries if Wetmore's heirs hadn't sold to Schenley distillers in 1940. Not only did quality slip away but the winery was moved here and there, ending up in a corner of the Roma winery in Fresno, where it was when Schenley sold it all to Guild, the big Central Valley winery, in 1970. Guild decided to make it a good premium producer once again and, starting afresh, put the name on a modernized co-op winemaking facility built in 1946 in the bulk-wine country of Mendocino. Varietals include well-received Zinfandel and Petite Sirah, also Grignolino, Gamay Beaujolais, Cabernet Sauvignon, Pinot Chardonnay, and Sylvaner, plus dessert wines, Champagne, and brandy, not all produced here. The winery has 10 acres of its own and buys other North Coast grapes. Bottling is done at Guild's Lodi winery. Cresta Blanca has a while to go before gold-medal quality is achieved again.

Parducci Wine Cellars, 501 Parducci Rd., Ukiah (north of town off Lake Mendocino Drive), 462-3828. Tours, on the hour 10–4; tasting, sales, daily 9–6; also picnicking. Adolph Parducci, raised around his father's wineries in both Tuscany and the Santa Clara Valley, built a winery at Cloverdale in northern Sonoma about 1917 only to see it burn down during the late 1920s. Beginning again in the Ukiah Valley in 1931, Parducci made bulk wine until turning the business over to his sons in 1960. They expanded and modernized and switched to varietal wines. The two brothers sold majority interest in 1973 to a teachers' investment fund but continue to manage the winery. They specialize in producing husky Mendocino and Lake County red varietals (not oak-aged)—Zinfandel, Pinot Noir, Petite Sirah, Cabernet Sauvignon—plus French Colombard (first in California), mostly from the winery's own 400 acres.

Weibel Champagne Vineyards, 7051 N. State St., Calpella (6 miles north of Ukiah), 485-0321. Tasting, sales, daily 9–6; also picnicking. Weibel is another new arrival in Mendocino: it is home-based in Leland Stanford's old winery and vineyards near Mission San Jose (in southern Alameda County, last survivor in an urbanized wine district). Rudolf Weibel and his son Frederick founded the business there in 1939. After his father's death, in the 1960s, Frederick bought 100 acres here and started building a big producing winery (finishing and bottling are done at Mission San Jose). The tasting room and gift shop are housed in something that looks like an empty Champagne glass— appropriately, for Weibel still prides itself on bottle-fermented Champagne.

OTHER ATTRACTIONS

As we mentioned, you can spend some good time in Sonoma County without even going near a winery.

Sonoma Valley

After you leave Marin County, cross the improbably elevated Petaluma River bridge, and traverse the flat, green, and wet bay lands of Sonoma, you have to look sharp or you'll miss the turnoff on to Highway 121 into the **Sonoma Valley.***** It's not hidden—hundreds of new residents manage to find their way every year—but it is inconspicuous, which helps keep down the crowds.

Sonoma*** (pop. 5,725), which is in the middle of the peaceful, 17-mile-long valley, will never, let us hope, become the victim of its own appeal as a quiet town of great charm and romantic history. The town plaza, a perfect picnic spot, is surrounded by historic buildings, including the restored mission, and there are a few shops of interest.

The most northerly of the Franciscan endeavors, **Mission San Francisco Solano**** was established July 4, 1823, by Father José Altamira. He had wanted to close down the missions at San Francisco and San Rafael and consolidate activities at Sonoma, a move favored by the Mexican governor of Alta California, who wanted a presence to counteract Russian influence. Building of the mission was halted for a time while Altamira's superiors protested about this political interference, but construction was resumed when a compromise was reached. The Russians, as it happened, contributed some furnishings to the new church, a whitewashed wooden structure dedicated in 1824.

The mission wasn't successful during this twilight period for the padres. Altamira was cruel to the Indians and was forced to flee to San Rafael. His successor, Father Fortuni, was kinder but wore himself out by the time the mission was secularized in 1834. Meanwhile, the first church was replaced in 1827 by an adobe structure east of the long, low, tile-roofed padres' quarters. With secularization, General Mariano Vallejo became temporal authority in the area, laid out Sonoma Plaza diagonally from the mission, built soldiers' barracks and other buildings, and set the mission Indians to work on his 175,000 acres of Sonoma land. He took over the mission vineyards, and later competed with Colonel Haraszthy in winemaking. But the mission itself had no missionaries and fell into disrepair. Vallejo demolished the collapsing adobe church in 1841 and built the present small chapel at the west end of the priests' quarters, about where the 1823 building stood. This served as a parish church for the next 40 years.

While the mission ruled for barely 11 years, Vallejo's era lasted only about 12. The dominance of the California rancheros was rudely broken in 1846, initially at Sonoma. On June 18 of that year, 30 or 40 rowdy Americans, under the influence of both frontier rotgut and John C. Frémont, decided that the U.S. government was too slow in its attempts to annex California and that they would take it over. Seizing the main buildings around Sonoma Plaza, they raised a hastily made white flag decorated with a brown bear, a red star, a broad red band, and the words *California Republic*. They arrested Vallejo and his brother Salvador and sent them off to Sutter's Fort in Sacramento. The Bear Flag Republic ended July 9 when Commodore John D. Sloat, who had just seized California at the outbreak of the Mexican War, sent a young lieutenant (Paul Revere's grandson, Joseph Warren Revere) riding north to raise the Stars and Stripes. The crude banner's design was adapted for the official state flag, but the original was unfortunately lost in the San Francisco fire in 1906.

Vallejo was released in August and returned to Sonoma to find his ranching empire somewhat diminished. Not bitter, always pro-American, Vallejo became an honored citizen, was a delegate to the California constitutional convention in 1848, and built a new home a mile from the plaza.

State Historic Park

The settings for Sonoma history were adobe buildings built during the 1830s, '40s, and '50s, mostly on the north side of the plaza. Together with the mission, which was well restored by the state after acquisition in 1903, they comprise **Sonoma State Historic Park.***** The mission, on East Spain Street at 1st Street East, is severe in atmosphere but rich in modern, accurate historical displays, in contrast to those California missions still run by the Catholic Church, which are homey, cluttered, and informal. Across 1st Street East are the principal state-owned park buildings. On the corner, still under restoration at the time of this writing, is the **Sonoma Barracks,*** a two-story, wide-balconied building probably started in the mid-1830s and completed about 1840–41. Because Sonoma was Mexican California's northern frontier headquarters, the barracks were a base for some 100 not always bloodless pacification expeditions against the Indians. These operations were led by Vallejo, his brother, and a Suisune chief who took the name Francisco Solano. The barracks were later occupied by American troops and in 1860 became Vallejo's winery. Next door is the **Toscano Hotel,*** a small, two-story frame building dating to the 1850s. It was for a time an inexpensive hotel called the Eureka, but turn-of-the-century Italian immigrants changed the name. It has been restored with period furnishings of the 1890s.

In the middle of the block, facing the plaza, was Vallejo's principal home in the pre-American period. **La Casa Grande,** an L-shaped building with a three-story corner tower, was completed about 1840, and 11 of Vallejo's children were born here. A girls' school after 1854, La Casa Grande burned in 1867, leaving only the original servants' wing, still standing in the rear. To the west of the big house, at 16–18 W. Spain St., is the **Swiss Hotel** bar and restaurant, identified as an 1850 adobe belonging to Salvador Vallejo. Salvador probably lived in a house at the corner, now gone, but his name is still attached to the building diagonally opposite, at 411 1st St. W., a two-story building known as the **El Dorado Hotel,** which may date to 1836–46; it now houses a restaurant. South on the same side of the street is one more original building, the **Jacob Leese House,** built about 1846 by Vallejo's brother-in-law (an original settler in Yerba Buena) and later occupied by General Persifor F. Smith, military governor of California in 1849.

Back on the other side of the plaza, at 133 E. Spain St., is the **Blue Wing Inn,** * one of the earliest hostelries in northern California. It was built by Vallejo to accommodate travelers, among whom, one can believe, were the future Civil War generals Grant, Sherman, and Hooker, John Frémont and Kit Carson, and, one cannot believe, the imaginary bandido Joaquin Murieta and his sidekick, Three-Fingered Jack. A state-owned building, it now houses shops, a collection called **El Paseo de Sonoma.**

The small park-entry fee is necessary for only a couple of the buildings at Sonoma but also covers nearby Lachryma Montis, Petaluma Adobe, Jack London Park, and Fort Ross. Information: Sonoma State Historic Park, 20 E. Spain St., Sonoma 95476 (707/938-4779).

In one corner of shady **Sonoma Plaza***** is the **Bear Flag Monument*** (1915), a heroic bronze figure with unfurling flag, and in the middle is the stone Mission Revival **City Hall** (H. C. Lutgens, 1906). This is one of the many Northern California buildings constructed of Sonoma Stone, as well as one of several Sonoma structures that winemaker Samuele Sebastiani helped erect. The plaza, with lawn, trees, duck pond, and playground, is good for a picnic. (Fixings can be obtained at the **Sonoma Cheese Factory,** 2 W. Spain St., north of the plaza; don't miss sampling fresh Sonoma Jack cheese.)

Just south of the plaza, at 579 1st St. E., is one more original building, the **Nash-Patton Adobe** (1847). The other downtown buildings date from after the 1850s but fit the scale if not the feeling of the historic buildings. One block north of the plaza, in the old railroad depot, 285 1st St. E., is the local historical society's small **Depot Park Museum** (938-9765), open Wed.-Sun., 1–4:30.

Away from the Plaza

A short walk past the mission on East Spain Street, then up 4th Street East will bring you to the big **Sebastiani Winery,** while a few miles to the east (East Napa Street to Old Winery Road) is Haraszthy's 1857 **Buena Vista Winery** (see "Wineries" above for details). A short walk or a drive west of the plaza, along West Spain Street and up 3rd Street West, will take you to General Vallejo's second Sonoma home, **Lachryma Montis***** ("mountain tears," from the hillside spring). A tree-lined driveway leads to a magnolia-shaded Carpenter-Gothic Victorian house, built in 1851–52 of wood over brick (for summertime coolness), still furnished with Vallejo's possessions. Among the outbuildings are a cute teahouse and the "Swiss Chalet" warehouse (1852) that houses Vallejo memorabilia and exhibits. Vallejo lived here for 35 years into the American period, spending much time reading (his library had 12,000 volumes) and writing a five-volume history of Spanish-Mexican California. He died in 1890. Lachryma Montis is open daily 10-5 for a small admission fee. Picnicking is good here.

South of the plaza, on Broadway (Highway 12 into town), is **Train Town,** a 10-acre park that is home of the Sonoma Gaslight & Western Railroad, a one-fourth-size "mountain division," complete with 2.5-percent grades up miniature mountains, trestles, bridges, a tunnel, a two-acre lake, and "Lakeville," a dollhouse village with replicas of the Wells Fargo office in the gold-country town of Columbia and other historic buildings. The scaled-down Hudson-type steam locomotive hauls around open-carloads of tourists every 20 minutes 1:30-5:30 daily in summer, weekends and holidays from Labor Day to mid-June. Small admission fee. Information: 938-3912.

Around harvest time (the end of September), Sonoma puts on a two-day **Vintage Festival,** starting with a blessing of the grapes in front of the mission and running through historical playlets (the two Vallejo

The ranchhouse where Jack London wrote 1,000 words a day from 1911 to 1916 is now open to the public. (Redwood Empire Association)

daughters wedding the two Haraszthy sons, and the Bear Flag incident), a Spanish Ball, wine tasting, parade, etc.

If it's possible that you don't like wine, but like beer, and want to visit a brewery, give Jack McAuliffe a ring at 938-4263 and see if his **New Albion Brewing Co.,** 20330 8th St. E., is open and brewing. After a hitch with the U.S. Navy in Scotland, McAuliffe decided to try his hand at making English-style beer—that is, pale (light) and dark (strong) ale or bitters, dry and sweet stout, and porter. In 1977 he opened this, the tiniest licensed brewery in the U.S. (San Francisco's Anchor Steam Beer brewery is now second smallest), and promptly found he had difficulty meeting demand. If McAuliffe has none of his brew for sale here, the Sonoma Cheese Factory, Plaza Liquors, and other local shops stock it.

Into the Valley of the Moon

Highway 12 (West Napa Street) goes out of Sonoma and up the valley, past such former resort towns as El Verano, Boyes Hot Springs, Fetters Hot Springs, and Agua Caliente—which saw their heyday long ago—and into the vine-laden upper Sonoma Valley, now officially named the **Valley of the Moon.*** That's a nice name, but it's Jack London's poetic mistranslation of "Sonoma." The best authority is that the name *Sonoma* comes from the local Indian word for "nose," perhaps one chief's distinguishing feature.

The area around **Glen Ellen** is where Sonoma's literary romance is to be found. In the hills above the village is **Jack London State Historic Park,*** site of his Beauty Ranch and several buildings in which he lived and worked once he settled down. Born in San Francisco January 12, 1876, but raised in Oakland, Jack London was a sailor, waterfront rowdy, political activist (socialism filled his writings, which is one reason he's so popular in Russia), Klondike gold-seeker, journalist, wanderer, and "superb meteor" who wrote dozens of best-sellers before committing suicide at age 40 in 1916. With the proceeds from *The Call of the Wild* (1903), London bought his first acreage here in 1903. He had become attached to the Sonoma Valley while courting his second wife, Charmian Kittredge, whom he married in 1905. After a 27-month voyage in a ketch, the *Snark*, in the South Seas, the Londons returned to Glen Ellen in 1911 and started Beauty Ranch, which London wanted to work on a scientific basis (he was thus inspired by Santa Rosa's Luther Burbank). Not everything was scientific: London built a two-story stone tower, the "pig palace," for his swine. While living in an L-shaped, rambling, shingled cottage (built in 1862 by Jackson Temple, later a state supreme court justice), he churned out 1,000 words a day without fail (how else do you produce 43 books in 16 years and become the first American millionaire-novelist?).

And he started building a huge house that would symbolize the rugged world of action, emotion, and virility he wrote about. **Wolf House*** (Albert Farr, 1911–13) was a magnificent redwood and lava-boulder house with 26 rooms, nine fireplaces, and a courtyard with a reflection pool. But it was not to be occupied. In 1913, just before its completion, Wolf House mysteriously burned, perhaps as the result of arson. Three years later London, troubled by alcoholism and collapse of spirit, killed himself (official cause of death was uremic poisoning). In 1919 the widow Charmian built a unique, extremely solid-looking 100-foot-long house of stone and big beams, the **House of Happy Walls,*** half a mile from the empty walls of Wolf House, and lived there until her death in 1955.

After she died, 48 acres of the ranch and some buildings were given to the state; in 1978 the state purchased another 35 acres and plans eventual acquisition of another 700 acres. The House of Happy Walls is today a very visitable Jack London museum, while Wolf House is a set of sad, what-might-have-been ruins; between the two on a 1.25-mile round-trip walk is London's hillside **grave,*** marked by a single boulder. The 1978 acquisition included the **ranch house**** London lived and wrote in (restored, it was opened to the public in 1980), along with several farm buildings. His heirs will continue to run a vineyard here, as London himself would probably be doing. The state park is open daily 10-5 for a small admission fee. Information: 938-5216.

On Arnold Drive, the road paralleling the highway between Sonoma and Glen Ellen, is **London Glen Village,*** a small shopping gallery with a restaurant in an old mill and winery. Across the street, the **Jack London Bookstore*** has new, used and first editions of his books for sale and memorabilia on display. A bar in Glen Ellen is said to have been one of London's hangouts.

State and County Parks

North of Glen Ellen, in the Sonoma Mountains between Santa Rosa and Kenwood and in the Mayacmas Mountains between Kenwood and St. Helena, are two more state parks and two county parks that should interest hikers and riders in particular, picnickers and fishermen as well. **Sugarloaf Ridge State Park,**** Adobe Canyon Road off Highway 12 north of Kenwood, is 2,200 acres of chaparral-covered ridges that lead up to Bald Mountain (2,729 feet), along with trees and meadows in the Sonoma Creek drainage. Spring or fall are the best times to go out on the 25 miles of trails. Sprinkling the meadows in spring are the usual poppies, lupine, cream cups and buttercups, and farewell-to-spring, plus scarlet larkspur, Indian warrior, western azalea, shooting star, coral root, and many flowers without those vivid common names. The largest big leaf maples in California can be found here, along with madrone, laurel, coastal redwood, Douglas fir, and several oak species. Watch for cliff swallows and meadowlarks, but watch out for poison oak and rattlesnakes (both easily avoidable). The park has 50 campsites. Car entry fee. Information: 833-5712.

Across Bear Creek is **Hood Mountain Regional Park,*** at the end of Los Alamos Road a couple of miles east of Santa Rosa on Highway 12. Hikers and riders can tackle the rugged trail to the summit of volcanic Hood Mountain (2,730 feet, highest in this range), which is nine miles round-trip with a partial loop from the peak, or settle for the first few miles of the Santa Rosa Creek Trail (quiet fishing in the creek) which will take them to the walk-in Azalea Creek Camp. There's a small admission charge to this 1,968-acre county park. Information and campsite reservations: 527-2401.

Across the Valley of the Moon is **Annadel State Park,*** a mostly undeveloped, day-use park, with its entrance on Channel Drive E. off Highway 12. The 5,000 acres of the former Annadel Farms have a network of 40 miles of trails, mostly over gentle hill and dale and through woodlands and meadows. Steve's S Trail is a bit steeper but it goes past Lake Ilsanjo, where black bass up to eight pounds and blue-gill are angling prizes. A marsh at the eastern end of the park is good for bird-watching. No camping; everybody out an hour after sunset. Bring water. Information: 539-3911.

Adjoining Annadel Park is another county park, 314-acre **Spring Lake Regional Park,** with nonmotorized boating, bicycling, hiking, fishing, and picnicking. Information: 539-8092.

Highway 12 quickly runs out of the Valley of the Moon and into the outskirts of Santa Rosa, the spreading county seat about which we'll say something below.

Redwood Highway

Highway 101, **Redwood Highway,** is Sonoma's main artery. We'll describe destinations off the highway more or less according to where the turnoffs are.

North of the Marin line, take the Petaluma Boulevard exit to Red Hill Road and turn south in a couple of miles to the **Marin French Cheese Co.,**** founded in 1865 by Jefferson Thompson, an Illinois cheddar maker. His descendants still produce Rouge-et-Noir brand Camembert and other cheese—more than 2,000 pounds daily—from their Ayrshire herd. The setting, with pastures around a pond and old farm buildings, is just right for a picnic, which is made easier by all the deli items and fresh buttermilk you can buy with the cheese. Open daily for tours (10–4). Information: 762-6001.

From Highway 101 take the Highway 116 exit to Casa Grande Avenue and **Petaluma Adobe State Historic Park.***** Twenty minutes east of Sonoma Plaza, this was General Vallejo's big hacienda in the original 100-square-mile Rancho Petaluma, which he started working in the 1830s, though it was not granted to him officially until 1843–44. Between 1834 and 1844 he built what is still one of the biggest, grandest adobe residences in Northern California, a hollow square (now missing the east wing) with wide verandas running completely around the second story. In the enclosed patio and in the outbuildings, California and Indian workers tanned leather, made candles and adobe bricks, practiced carpentry and blacksmithing, cured meat, and did everything else necessary for self-sufficiency on the Sonoma frontier. The adobe has period furnishings and equipment, with working displays of typical rancho activities. **Old Adobe Days** is a big event the third Sunday in August. Picnicking anytime. The adobe is open daily 10-5, with a small admission fee (entry by the same ticket as the Sonoma, Jack London, and Fort Ross state parks). Information: Petaluma Adobe, 3325 Adobe Rd., Petaluma 94952 (762-4871).

Petaluma

Petaluma** (pop. 31,700) is known to "Peanuts" readers as the wrist-wrestling capital of the world (cartoonist Charles Schulz lives in nearby Santa Rosa), to old Californians as the "Egg Basket of the West," and to Victorian architecture buffs as home of many of the best remaining Victorian iron-fronted buildings in the U.S. It also has a claim to fame in legal history, as will be explained, but here's more on the **iron fronts.** These were in fashion in the 1880s at the same time "gingerbread"—cornices, medallions and cartouches, columns and pilasters, arched and triangular hoods over doors and windows—was standard even on stables. To economize and speed up construction, and to make buildings more fire-resistant, some builders had entire façades either cast in iron or molded from sheet metal in foundries (San Francisco was a flat-bottomed-boat ride down the Petaluma River and across San Pablo Bay), then attached to the front of wooden or brick structures, mostly three-story commercial buildings.

Petaluma has retained a remarkable number of iron fronts in its small, homogeneous, somewhat quiet downtown. A good grouping is on Petaluma Boulevard North, Kentucky Street, and the Western Avenue cross street. A prize example is the **McNear Building***** (1886), with façades on both Petaluma Boulevard and 4th Street; the style is Italianate with Beaux Arts touches, such as the faces over the arched windows. The **Masonic Building***** (1882), Western Avenue, has a mansarded cupola with original Seth Thomas clock. The **IOOF Building**** (1880), 111 Petaluma Blvd., is Second Empire with a curved mansard roof. Of the row of iron fronts on Western between

Petaluma Boulevard and Kentucky Street, the **Mutual Relief Association Building***** (1885) would be a magnificent example even if it was not made wonderful by the paint job. And there are more.

There's also some good residential architecture in the downtown area. Walk around several blocks between 3rd and 5th, B and F. On 5th Street, at C and B streets, respectively, are two churches of interest, the Shingle Style **St. John's Episcopal Church*** by Ernest Coxhead (ca. 1890) and the Gothic Revival **Evangelical Free Church** (1880). Between these two areas, at Petaluma Boulevard and B Street, is a tourist center, the **Great Petaluma Mill**** (1876), a large, two-story, yellow-stone building that was a feed and grain mill and now houses 35 shops and restaurants. It backs on the Petaluma River, a reminder that the town was once a busy grain-shipping center. Opposite the mill is a small shopping gallery, the **Lan Mart** (1911). You can pick up a walking-tour brochure at the **Petaluma Museum,** located in the old Carnegie library at 4th and B; open Mon.-Sat. 11–4. Heritage Homes of Petaluma (c/o Chamber of Commerce) sponsors a springtime house tour.

The **World's Wrist-Wrestling Championship,** incidentally, is held in the Veterans Memorial Building in October.

Around Petaluma, and we mean all around, you can see what has led to the town's place in legal history: bedroom subdivisions that at night twinkle to the south, west, and every other direction, reaching north toward Santa Rosa's sprawl. Development was running at 18 percent annually until 1972, when the "Petaluma Plan" set a limit of 500 new houses a year—a growth of about 6 percent—to prevent undue strain on municipal services. The Sonoma construction industry took Petaluma all the way to the U.S. Supreme Court, which in 1976 endorsed the right of Petaluma and other towns to put such reins on runaway development.

Santa Rosa

So perhaps it will take a little longer for Petaluma to blend in with Santa Rosa up the highway. **Santa Rosa** (pop. 73,500), the county seat, is an attractive all-American town, featured as such in many movies—*Pollyanna,* for one. While unfortunately cut in two by a freeway and having a downtown that was rundown enough to have to be redeveloped, it nonetheless has some fine examples of Victorian architecture and a creditable renewal area. Some of the best old houses are along and off B Street between 8th and 11th streets, on Cherry Street, and on McDonald between 12th and 16th streets. A classic is the **McDonald** (or Mableton) **House*** (1877–78), in a city block with gardens still preserved. The renewal area south of 4th Street mixes old and new.

Among tourist attractions is the **"Church Built from One Tree,"*** a 1902 Baptist church at 490 Sonoma Ave. on the edge of shady Juillard Park. Built from a single 300-foot redwood log, with a 70-foot tower and seating 300 people, the building is, believe it or not, the **Robert L. Ripley Memorial Museum.**** Ripley (1890–1949) was born and raised and is buried in Santa Rosa; when famous he resided between his foreign jaunts in Mamaroneck, N.Y., where his beloved possession was the door from his childhood home. Open daily 11–4 (summertime until 5) for a small admission fee. Information: 545-1414.

A block away, at Santa Rosa Avenue and Tupper Street, facing Juillard Park, is the **Luther Burbank Memorial Gardens,**** preserving the home, greenhouse, and gardens of the famed horticulturalist. Born in Massachusetts in 1849, Burbank as a youth was a market gardener when he began plant-breeding experiments, happening on the Burbank potato at the age of 23. Selling the rights to that for $150, he moved to California in 1875, found his way to the Santa Rosa Valley, and got a job as a nurseryman. In 1877 he bought a plot east of the present garden and embarked on his long career. Experimenting with thousands of plant varieties, Burbank developed new and improved varieties of prunes, plums, raspberries, blackberries, apples, peaches, nectarines, tomatoes, corn, squash, peas, and asparagus, not to mention the Shasta daisy and a spineless cactus that can be fed to cattle. In later years most of his work was carried out at experimental farms near Petaluma and Sebastopol. The "plant wizard" died here at 77 in 1926 and is buried at the foot of a cedar of Lebanon (lit up at Christmastime). The gardens were renovated and dedicated in 1960 as a public park but Burbank's widow was still living in the secluded, two-story house at the time of this writing. The gardens (528-5115) are open daily, free. The Luther Burbank Rose Festival and Parade is in May.

If you are around here over Labor Day weekend, drop in at the **Scottish Gathering and Caledonian Games** at the Santa Rosa Fairgrounds. Sponsored by the Caledonian Club of San Francisco for well over a century, the games include bagpipe, highland dancing, and pipe and drum competitions along with the traditional caber tossing, putting the stone, and hammer-throwing contests, which usually feature a number of world and American champions. What's a caber? A log up to 19 feet long and 120 pounds that one man must hoist and flip over one end to land at a perfect "12 o'clock" position. You should see the size of the champion caber-tosser.

Sebastopol Apple Country

At Santa Rosa you can take Highway 12 east into the Sonoma Valley or west into what we will dub Sonoma's **apple country.**** While most of California's agriculture is conducted in fairly dull countryside, this area, with many small farms and nurseries, is an exception, so we'd encourage out-of-state visitors to take a drive. The **Farm Trails** map (see "Sources of Information," p. 169) makes it easy to find sources for homemade raspberry jam, goat cheese, fresh prunes, elephant garlic, apple pics, goldfish, spices, cider, smoked turkeys, organic beef, llama wool, worms, and boars, as well as dozens of varieties of apples (the fall Gravenstein is Sonoma's best apple), peaches, berries, pears, cherries, and vegetables. There are also several vineyards.

The main town is **Sebastopol** (pop. 4,810). Though five California towns (Yountville was another) were once named for the Crimean port besieged in 1854-55, this is the only one so named today. Tradition says that Pine Grove (1853) was renamed after the loser of a fight, one Hibbs, tried to take refuge in the crossroads store, which became known as Hibbs' Sebastopol. A present-day attraction is the **Enmanji Buddhist Temple,** 1200 Gravenstein Hwy. S., originally built for the 1932 Chicago World's Fair as the Manchurian Railway exhibit.

Sebastopol has an apple-blossom festival in April. West along winding roads is **Occidental,** home of three big family-style Italian restaurants (Negri's, Fiori's, Union Hotel) and the Land House Activities (handgoods shop and other things), which are run by dedicated followers of the Russian mystic Gurdjieff. Two of the roads through apple country, Bodega Highway and Coleman Valley Road, will take you down to the coast, which is not only particularly scenic but has numerous state beach access points (see Chapter 7).

Russian River Resort Region

Back on Highway 101, vineyards start predominating north of Santa Rosa. Five miles along the freeway, look for the exits for both Mark

West Springs Road, which you can take east to the Petrified Forest, Calistoga, and Mt. St. Helena (see pp. 125–6 for details), and River Road, a very scenic road which will take you west into **Russian River Resort Region***** (Gravenstein Highway through Sebastopol is an alternate route).

The Russian River, lined with enormous, wonderfully fragrant coastal redwoods, has been a resort area for claustrophobic San Franciscans ever since local redwoods helped build all those closely spaced Victorians on narrow lots. Lumbering, from the 1860s into the 1890s, overlapped with tourism after the railway came in 1876. Trains tooted from the Sausalito ferry up to the river, dropping off entire families and their baggage for extended vacations in the many cottage colonies and campgrounds between Mirabel Park and Duncans Mills downstream. The railroad stopped running in 1935, but some of the depots are still in use—one at the Korbel Champagne Cellars, another at the Duncans Mills campground (see below).

What usually happens to old resorts happened to the Russian River area: except for the Bohemian Grove, it got old and decrepit. Buildings deteriorated and weren't rebuilt, the river got too polluted, dopesters and violent motorcycle gangs started hanging out. The area got a poor reputation and lost its middle-class support. The nadir was reached in the 1960s—but it's all gone up since then. The visitor in the 1980s will find a century-old resort area in rebirth, still a little on the old and funky side and lacking razzle-dazzle and centers of attention, but with compensating attractions and recreational opportunities.

Probably the most popular activity (not counting relaxing) is **canoeing.***** W. C. "Bob" Trowbridge started renting canvas canoes in the 1940s and now has the largest fleet of rental canoes—600 Grumman aluminum canoes—in the U.S., and runs trips on the American, Sacramento, and Colorado rivers as well. On the 60-mile Russian River, one-day trips of 5 to 16 miles on the upper river (Cloverdale to Alexander Valley, 16 miles total), middle river (Alexander Valley to Healdsburg, 12 miles), and lower river (Healdsburg to Monte Rio, 25 miles) are most common; two-day trips are from Cloverdale or Asti to Healdsburg and from Healdsburg to Guerneville or Monte Rio, with overnight camping. Four- or five-day group trips down the whole length are possible. The lower river area is our suggestion for out-of-state visitors because the banks are well forested, with redwoods a constant background, and here and there a summer cabin peeking through. Trowbridge provides canoe (capacity—three adults or two adults and two kids), life jackets, and paddles, plus shuttle transport between starting and ending points, at a cost per canoe of under $20 for one day, a bit more than $30 for two days. Trowbridge offers a special dinner at Sonoma Vineyards. Canoeing season runs approximately from Easter through October, during which Coyote Dam, at the headwaters, releases a steady flow of water. The river is busiest in the cool spring. Bring suntan lotion, sunglasses and hat, water, sleeping bags, etc. No children under five. Reservations: Trowbridge Recreation, Inc., 20 Healdsburg Ave., Healdsburg 95448 (433-7247).

There are other things to do. **Fishing** is popular year-round, with an open season on black bass (best in summer), bluegills, catfish, American shad (which run in April and May), silver salmon, steelhead (mostly in the tidewater area to Duncans Mills November and December, later in pools and riffles), striped bass, and sturgeon, and, from the end of April to mid-November, trout. Tourist authorities have details on fishing. Nearly all the **swimming and beach play** is at the numerous private resorts, some of which (Johnson's Beach in Guerneville, for example) are free to all. Northwood Lodge has a nine-hole golf course; other resorts have tennis courts.

Armstrong Redwoods and Austin Creek

And, of course, there's hiking, riding, camping, fishing and picnicking in the hills, including **Armstrong Redwoods State Reserve***** and adjacent **Austin Creek State Recreation Area,** on Armstrong Woods Road north of Guerneville. The area around Guerneville, once called Big Bottom, was rich in big coastal redwoods—once. The biggest were cut down in the last century. One of the broadest measured 23 feet (one man spent two years cutting 600,000 shingles from it), and one of the tallest was said to be 367 feet, which would today rival the world's tallest tree in Redwood National Park. One lumberman, Colonel James Armstrong, cut in the Big Bottom but decided in the 1870s that some of it should be preserved in its virgin state. He set aside land on upper Fife Creek and was planning, with Luther Burbank, an arboretum and botanical garden when he died. His daughter sold the 680-acre parcel to Sonoma County in 1917, and it became a state park in 1934. The state acquired the 4,200-acre Austin Creek SRA in 1964.

Armstrong Redwoods is still what the local Pomo Indians called "the dark place," where weather, soil, and topography have combined to create a cool redwood jungle. From the entrance parking lot (which accommodates horse trailers) interlinked roads and trails lead to the **Parson Jones Tree,** 13.8 feet in diameter, 310 feet tall, and on to the **Luther Burbank Circle.** Go around the circle and backtrack to the **Redwood Grove** picnic area, where you'll find the **Colonel Armstrong Tree,** 14.5 feet in diameter, 308 feet high. The Jones and Armstrong trees are both well over 1,300 years old.

To explore Austin Creek SRA, continue past Burbank Circle on the Pioneer Trail (or parallel road) along Fife Creek to the picnic area. Dirt roads (some for hiking and riding only) carry on to **Horsehaven,** a horse group camp, and the **Redwood Lake** family camping area, where the road from the entrance terminates. From here there's only hiking and riding in wooded and open country—good Sonoma scenery. There's a primitive trailside camp on Thompson Creek.

Information: 1700 Armstrong Woods Rd., Guerneville 95446 (869-2015).

Russian River Towns

Guerneville (pronounced GURN-vill) is the local metropolis, a town of several streets settled in 1860 and named for a Swiss lumbermill owner in the 1870s. Most of its history concerns either floods or fires. A history of the county written in 1880 observed in romantic terms that the Russian River "rushes seaward with relentless fury, and everything in its pathway is swept into the broad bosom of the Pacific." This seems to happen every two years. As for fires, most of the town burned down in 1923, and individual landmarks have been lost through accidents or arson since then. Guerneville serves tourist hordes on three-day holiday weekends and cabin residents on vacation in the summer and, increasingly, all year, as this area becomes a rural suburb of Santa Rosa. Guerneville is a market town for backwood Sonoma's countercultural cottage industries and more recently a thriving resort area for Northern California's substantial gay population. (Fife's, 16467 River Rd., was one of the first gay resorts and was even pictured in *Newsweek;* straights are welcome.) But the descendants of the San Franciscans who pioneered this resort area are still coming, making Guerneville a weekend melting pot.

The town draws one kind of folks to the **Russian River Rodeo** and **Stumptown Days Parade** in June, another kind to the **Russian River Jazz Festival** in September (Count Basie, Stan Getz have performed).

Details and tickets from the Chamber of Commerce (see page 169). (A former September event was the Pageant of Fire Mountain, a corny Indian love story.) There are occasional concerts at the amphitheater in Armstrong Redwoods.

Among the other resort towns, **Cazadero** (Spanish for "hunting place") has an active sawmill and the famous **Berkeley Music Camp,** 5385 Cazadero Hwy. (632-5285), which offers summer concerts under the redwoods by Austin Creek. **Duncans Mills,** on the floodplain at the head of the Russian River tidewater, has some shops and, in the restored depot, a small museum. Clan Parmeter Livery Stable, 865-9982, rents horses for rides into the hills.

Bohemian Grove

Monte Rio is principally the turnoff for the very private, very exclusive **Bohemian Grove,** midsummer scene of what Herbert Hoover is said to have called "the greatest men's party on earth." It is a two-week "encampment" in rustic but comfortable surroundings, a period of hell-raising, elaborate rituals, lakeside talks by governors and defense secretaries, amateur theatricals called "Jinks," the traditional urinating on the trees, and even some illicit sex (the big scandal in 1971 concerned "jumping the river" to red-light establishments). It is a fraternity party under the redwoods attended by the rich and powerful, the influential and famous—not only presidents of corporations but presidents of the U.S., the elite of business, politics, the professions, entertainment, and academia—all men, mostly Republican. Guests are allowed: George Schultz brought his friend Helmut Schmidt here in 1979. Surprisingly, there are many unknown people in attendance, the artistic and literary talent responsible for the entertainment. Establishment artists, they are allowed associate membership in San Francisco's exclusive Bohemian Club, which owns the grove.

The club was founded in 1872 by Ambrose Bierce and four other journalistic and artistic types who would not be allowed in today (Bierce would in any case be happier outside, sneering in). Partially planned by Golden Gate Park's John McLaren, the 2,700-acre grove, which stretches east along the south bank of the Russian River, has been the club's rural retreat since 1880.

While the club's motto, Weaving Spiders Come Not Here, is an admonition not to talk politics and business, the grove is the scene of a lot of that. Traditionally, financiers and industrialists find it a good place to examine new government officials, who, in turn, use lakeside talks to float trial balloons. In 1942 atomic scientists made some of the key decisions on the Manhattan Project in a secret meeting here; Nixon and Reagan had a preconvention session here in 1967. One of the interesting aspects of this summer camp for adult men is that there are clubs within the club: 129 cabins and lodges with their own memberships, specialties, and traditions. The most exclusive of these is Mandalay, whose membership in 1968 included Stephen Bechtel Sr. and Jr., Edgar Kaiser, Leonard K. Firestone, former CIA Director John McCone, and the presidents of Wells Fargo and the Bank of America. (Conspiracy web-spinners, look not here.)

The precincts of the grove were penetrated figuratively and literally in the mid-1970s by two mortals, one, G. William Domhoff, a psychologist interested in ruling-class cohesiveness (*The Bohemian Grove and Other Retreats,* New York: Harper & Row, 1974), the other, John van der Zee, a journalist who disguised himself as a waiter (*The Greatest Men's Party on Earth,* New York: Harcourt Brace Jovanovich, 1974).

Back to more mundane aspects of the Russian River region, we'll sum up by observing that the Russian River does run to the coast, which is described in Chapter 7. Highway 116 is a very attractive riverside drive to the mouth of the river and the junction with coastal Highway 1. An alternative route in the hills is Cazadero Highway–Fort Ross Road to old Fort Ross or continuing on Seaview Road to Salt Point State Park.

Northern Sonoma

Back on the Highway 101 freeway, past the turnoff to the Russian River resorts, you will pass several wineries starting at **Windsor,** which was named at the suggestion of an Englishman because of the resemblance between the rolling oak countryside and the grounds of Windsor Castle. The big town in this area is **Healdsburg*** (pop. 6,575), settled in 1852 and now both a wine town and a separate Russian River vacation town. Well-spruced **Healdsburg Beach Regional Park*** (fee required) has facilities for swimming, picnicking, and canoeing. **Healdsburg Museum,** 133 Matheson St., is open (free) Tues.-Sun. 1–4. The plaza is the site of the **Russian River Wine Festival** in mid-May. A nice drive out Matheson Street from the plaza takes you past some solid Victorian houses to pretty **Fitch Mountain,** around which the river makes a narrow turn, a road loops, and a July Fourth footrace is run; there's a park on the lower edge of the mountain.

South from Healdsburg **Westside Road** will take you to the **Hop Kiln Winery,** a three-towered remnant of the hop-growing industry of Sonoma. The industry withered after World War II, when American breweries started using fewer hops to give beer its bitter taste. The winery preserves some of the old kilns and equipment. The most recent Lassie movie, with James Stewart playing a winemaker, was filmed here in 1977. Westside Road goes here and there along the west bank of the Russian River and joins River Road.

The Geysers

At Healdsburg, ignore the freeway and take Healdsburg Avenue north and east into the **Alexander Valley,** the biggest new vineyard area in Sonoma. At Jimtown the road meets Highway 128 between Calistoga and Geyserville. Go left on 128 for 2 miles to Geysers Road, which takes you another 16 miles to **The Geysers,**** a natural curiosity that powers the largest geothermal generating plant in the world.

Discovered in 1847, The Geysers were one of those nineteenth-century tourist attractions that drew Grant, McKinley, Theodore and Franklin Roosevelt, Mark Twain, Horace Greeley, John Muir, the Prince of Wales, Henry Ford, and many others. What they came to see at the "Gates of Hell" in the Big Sulphur Canyon was steam continuously issuing forth from the earth (not, however, any hot water ejected like Yellowstone's Old Faithful and its namesake at Calistoga. In the 1950s a consortium (Magma-Thermal-Union) drilled some steam wells between 400 and 1,000 feet deep, near natural vents. Pacific Gas and Electric was persuaded to buy the steam, which was run through large-diameter pipe to a building housing a 1924 turbine brought from Sacramento. Unit 1 generated only 11,000 kilowatts, but it was successful. By 1979 the 15 units could generate 908,000 kilowatts. Later units were connected to 7 to 15 steam wells drilled deeper than the first ones, to between 2,000 and 7,000 feet. There are more than 220 wells in the 120-square-mile geothermal field. PG and E will add three more units in the 1980s, for a total of 1,248 megawatts (that's about 10 percent of PG and E's thermal capacity, not counting hydroelectric), and the state's Department of Water Resources plans its own geothermal unit across the Lake County line.

As energy facilities the Geysers are pretty dramatic. In mid-1980 PG and E, whose investment totals about $400 million, and the steam suppliers were renovating the old Big Geysers Resort for use as a full-fledged visitor center so that they can show off the power of geothermal.

Geyserville and North

Continuing through the vineyards of the Alexander Valley, Highway 128 meets 101 at Geyserville, which is of no particular importance. When Lake Sonoma is created behind the planned Warm Springs Dam a few miles west of town, this will no doubt be a busier place. If you're interested in a very long and winding road to the coast, take the Skaggs Springs Road to Stewarts Point, south of the Sea Ranch development (see p. 214).

North of Geyserville the Geyser Peak Winery (see under "Wineries") has constructed Panoramic Trail, a signposted, 40-minute-long path that should be good in the spring, when the winery plants California poppies to create a hillside carpet of gold, and River Trail, a short stroll through the vineyards down to the Russian River. Picnicking.

Asti was named in the 1880s by the Italian Swiss Colony for the Piedmont wine town, home of the sweet white sparkling wine called Asti Spumante. The Italian Swiss Colony winery, which is a very popular tourist stop, built the nearby El Carmelo Catholic Chapel* (1907) to resemble half a giant wine barrel.

Lake and Mendocino Counties

Crossing the Mendocino County line you enter the Ukiah Valley, a principal Mendocino wine district. At Hopland, Highway 175 goes east over the Mayacmas Mountains into Lake County and to Clear Lake, a greenish body of water that is the largest natural lake entirely within California (Tahoe is partially in Nevada). The lakeshore is mainly lined with resorts and vacation cabins, but there is 500-acre Clear Lake State Park, on two miles of shoreline. Lots of water sports, especially boating, water skiing, swimming, and fishing (crappie, black bass, catfish), and camping and hiking (nature trail). Information: Box 33, Kelseyville 95451. In Lakeport (pop. 3,580), the county seat, the Lake County Museum (707/263-2276) has Indian artifacts and other things. Open Mon.-Fri. 1-4, Sat. 11-4, free.

Ukiah (pop. 12,000), Mendocino County seat, has the three Mendocino wineries we listed above. The Victorian **Held-Poage House,** 603 W. Perkins St., houses the Mendocino County Historical Society, which has some exhibits; open Tues. and Sat. 2–4. The **Sun House** (1911), 431 S. Main St., is a memorial and museum to a well-known Indian portraitist, Grace Carpenter Hudson. Open, for small fee, fourth Sat. of each month; gift shop open Wed.-Fri. 10–3. The county museum is further up the road in **Willits,** inland terminus of the "Skunk Train" (see p. 227).

PRACTICAL INFORMATION

Getting There, Getting Around

Santa Rosa (Sonoma County Airport, nine miles north of the city) is served by three **commuter airlines,** two of them from San Francisco.

Greyhound buses run on the following Bay Area—Sonoma County routes: Napa—Sonoma (once daily), San Francisco—San Rafael—Sonoma (twice), Sonoma—Glen Ellen—Santa Rosa (three times), San Francisco—Santa Rosa—Mark West Springs—Petrified Forest—Calistoga—Lakeport (once), San Francisco—Santa Rosa—Windsor—Healdsburg—Geyserville—Asti—Cloverdale and north (six times), Santa Rosa—Sebastopol—Forestville—Mirabel Park—Rio Nido—Guerneville—Monte Rio (once). Information: 415/433-1500 (San Francisco), 707/542-6400 (Sonoma County).

Local bus service is more extensive but not that convenient. Golden Gate Transit has frequent, multistop service from San Francisco and Marin points to Petaluma, Santa Rosa, and Sebastopol. Information: 415/332-6600, 707/544-1323. Santa Rosa Transit (707/528-5306) has buses around that area daily. There is weekday minibus service in Petaluma (707/762-2783), and weekday, daytime minibus service in Sebastopol (707/823-7863).

Bicycling is something else. As in the Napa Valley, you can pedal from winery to winery in two areas. In the Alexander Valley an 18-mile loop begins in Healdsburg, goes out Healdsburg Avenue to Lytton Springs Road, under the 101 freeway to Geyserville Avenue, then north to and past Geyserville to Canyon Road, over to Dry Creek Road, and south back to Healdsburg, taking in these wineries: Simi, Souverain, Trentadue, Nervo, Geyser Peak, Pedroncelli, and Dry Creek. Around Sonoma itself the bicycling on town streets is very easy.

While it's all uphill from Sonoma to Glen Ellen, you can avoid high-way traffic by taking Arnold Drive. There's an easy loop between Glen Ellen and Kenwood. In the Russian River Resort Region, it's an easy trip from Guerneville into Armstrong Redwoods State Park (6.5 miles round trip) and from Duncans Mills or Monte Rio up to Cazadero along Austin Creek (21 miles maximum). You have to be in good condition to pedal to the coast through the Coleman Valley (from Occidental the coast is 26 miles away) or along the coast. But it's all great countryside. See Phyllis L. Neumann's *Sonoma County Bike Trails* (self-published; 50 Crest Way, Penngrove 94951, 1978).

For guided wine-tour possibilities, see p. 128.

Where to Stay and Eat

Accommodations (including camping) and restaurants are listed in Part IV under these headings: Clear Lake/Lake County; Guerneville/Lower Russian River; Healdsburg/Upper Russian River; Petaluma/Cotati Valley; Santa Rosa; Sebastopol/Apple Country; Sonoma/Sonoma Valley; Sonoma Coast; and Ukiah/Inland Mendocino.

SOURCES OF INFORMATION—WINE COUNTRY

You can get around the North Coast Wine Country and learn more about wine with only this chapter and a map in hand, if you want, but we're listing many other sources of information below.

First-time visitors to the Napa Valley, Sonoma County, and other California wine districts should first write to the Wine Institute, 165 Post St., San Francisco 94108 (415/986-0878) and ask for *California's Wine Wonderland,* a directory of member wineries and facilities, hours, and map directions. The maps, unfortunately, are inadequate. The AAA's Sonoma-Napa and Mendocino-Lake county maps are better. Other road maps are available from the other travel information sources below.

Wine Periodicals

Books are essential for formal wine education but periodicals are necessary for learning more, for keeping up with wine-industry news and the ever-changing trends, for keeping score among thousands of wine offerings every year, and for assistance in stocking a good cellar effi-

ciently and economically. Here are some of the newsletters and maga-
zines, most of which will send a sample for $1 and a SASE:

Bacchus Data Services (J. D. Kronman), Box 6861, Burbank
91510. Newsletter 10 times a year has tasting notes;
computerized index of tasting-session results.

Bottles Up (Fred Cherry), 470 Columbus Ave., San Francisco
94133. Periodic newsletter with lots of anecdotes and antic
notes, also tasting-session results. There's a subscription
charge, but on the other hand, reproduction in any form is
encouraged.

Connoisseurs' Guide to California Wines, Box 11120, San
Francisco 94401. Bimonthly. Each issue rates 200 wines of a
particular variety. Informative features for oenophiles.

Robert Finigan's Private Guide to Wines, 100 Bush St., San
Francisco 94104. Monthly newsletter with comparative
tasting notes (for example, 1976 Beaujolais, 1974–76
California White Rieslings, Cabernet Sauvignons under $5)
and some features, all filled with details about and
descriptions of many wines. Written by an opinionated expert
for real buffs.

Robert Lawrence Balzer's Private Guide to Food and Wine,
12791 Newport Ave., Tustin 92680. Informal but well-
produced newsletter by a well-known gourmet. Each issue
rates about 40 wines in one category.

Wine Discoveries (Arthur Damond and Nick Scott), 7474
Terrace Dr., El Cerrito 94530. Small bimonthly newsletter
with tasting notes and recommendations on wines costing less
than $4, with indication of Bay Area and Wine Country
availability. For the local buff with a budget.

Wine News Letter, Box 279, Franklin Lakes, N.J. 07417.
Newsletter with retrospective and comparative tastings (for
example, 1971 Hocks and Moselles, Ports from Portugal).
Best for East Coasters and foreign-wine fanciers.

Wine Scene (John D. Movius), Box 49358, Los Angeles 90049.
Newsletter published 10 times a year, stresses comparative
blind tastings using elaborate scoring methodology, with 80 to
100 wine comparisons per issue. Also has detailed features.
Best for the systematic wine buyer and collector.

Wine Spectator, 305 E. 53rd St., New York, N.Y. 10022.
Semimonthly tabloid-size newsletter with general-interest
wine news, including grape harvest reports, tasting results,
winemaker profiles, etc.

Wine & Vines, 703 Market St., San Francisco 94103. Monthly
magazine for the wine trade but of interest to wine students.
No tasting notes. Like the Wine Institute, not critical in any
way.

WINO (Wine Investigation for Novices and Oenophiles), 13910
La Jolla Pl., Garden Grove 92640. Unfortunately named
wine-appreciation group whose chapters (mostly in Southern
California) have dinners, tastings. Newsletter (Jerry Mead)
has chatty chapter-tasting and social notes.

These newsletters cost $15 and up. No one publication seems to have
the right combination of both comparative-tasting/buying-guide notes
and wine news for the interested-but-still-learning buff.

Wine Books: General

Turning to books about wine, the variety is amazing. If you wish to go
further into wine than this guidebook, check the food and wine paperback section at your local bookstore or write to The Wine Group (1930
Hornblend Ave., San Diego 92109) for a list of books in stock.

Adams, Leon D. *Commonsense Book of Wine.* 3rd ed. Boston:
Houghton-Mifflin, 1975. As the title says. An easy read.
————. *The Wines of America.* 2nd ed., rev. New York:
McGraw-Hill, 1978. A thorough, state-by-state survey and
history that devotes 245 pages to California, 254 to the other
states plus Canada and Mexico, and the other 81 to general
history and such. Adams, founder of the Wine Institute, has
been an authority for a long time, and is a defender of wines
made from *Vitis labrusca* and other native American grapes.
Amerine, Maynard A., and Roessler, Edward B. *Wines: Their
Sensory Evaluation.* San Francisco: W. H. Freeman, 1976.
Just one of the authoritative works by Professor Amerine,
California wine's chief academic writer, and a colleague at
UC-Davis. Wait until you see the statistical measures for
judging wines.
————, and Singleton, Vernon L. *Wine: An Introduction.* 2nd
ed. Berkeley: University of California Press, 1976. Soberly
written and authoritative, but not academic. Hardcover and
paperback.
Bespaloff, Alexis. *Guide to Inexpensive Wines.* New York:
Simon & Schuster, 1976. Try to get a recent edition of this or
Sichel's book.

Broadbent, Michael. *Wine Tasting*. Rev. ed. London: Christie Wine Publications, 1974. Written for the amateur and the connoisseur by the head of the wine department at the auction house. Less technical but more informative than Amerine and Roessler.

Henriques, E. Frank. *Signet Encyclopedia of Wine*. New York: New American Library, 1975. Companion paperback to Bespaloff's. Brief entries.

Johnson, Hugh. *Pocket Encyclopedia of Wine*. New York: Simon & Schuster, 1977. Vinyl-covered portable on thin paper is encyclopedic on a country-by-country basis, making it just right for helping you while examining labels in a wineshop or the choices on the wine list at a restaurant. A little marvel.

————. *Wine*. Rev. ed. New York: Simon & Schuster, 1974. Text-only survey, a companion to Johnson's other books. Very readable but no maps.

————. *The World Atlas of Wine*. 2nd ed. New York: Simon & Schuster, 1978. Well-regarded, best-selling, large-format atlas with lots of information, color pictures, beautiful maps (some ground-breaking), wine labels. This and Lichine's encyclopedia should be the first two reference books for budding bibbers. The first edition came out in expensive hardcover, moderately priced paperback.

Lichine, Alexis. *New Encyclopedia of Wine and Spirits*. 2nd ed., rev. New York: Knopf, 1976. The best one large fat volume on the subject, with worldwide scope but sharp focus on France. Good introductory material, then detailed, digressive entries, also a good index. Pronunciation list. Some maps, no pictures. Lichine is both a wine merchant and winegrower.

Robards, Terry. *The New York Times Book of Wine*. New York: Avon, 1977. Alphabetical but readable.

Schoonmaker, Frank. *Encyclopedia of Wine*. 7th ed. New York: Hastings House, 1978. Many entries but short ones, with pronunciations along the way. Better than Robards or Henriques. Less detailed than Lichine (for example, no write-ups on reputable California wineries), but also less intimidating. The late author, an American, was a wine importer who singlehandedly got wineries here to lessen their dependence on appropriated generic names and start using varietal names.

Sichel, Peter M. F., and Ley, Judy. *Which Wine?: The Wine Drinker's Buying Guide.* New York: Harper & Row, 1975. Even if a revised edition isn't available, a useful guide for consumers. Extensive blind tastings that involved professionals and amateurs resulted in comparisons of, for example, Bordeaux wines and California Cabernet Sauvignons, with jug wines getting a fair chance to be judged on their merits. Sichel is a wine importer.

Wine Books: California

Californians will, of course, note that their wine gets short shrift in all of the books above except Adams' *Wines of America.* Here's a list for California Wine Country visitors, for people who expect to drink mostly California wine, and for chauvinistic natives.

Benson, Robert L. *Great Winemakers of California.* Santa Barbara: Capra Press, 1977. Large-format book with extensive profile-interviews of 28 California winemakers. Technical but informative. Author is a law professor and champion of wine consumers.

Brennan, John M., ed. *Buying Guide to California Wines.* 3rd ed. San Diego: Wine Consultants of California (Box 15238, San Diego 92115), 1977. Includes travel guide to North Coast wine regions.

Thompson, Bob, and *Sunset* editors. *California Wine.* 2nd ed. Menlo Park: Lane, 1977. Well-done coffee-table paperback: good pictures, explanations, etc. for the newcomer to wine.

————— and Johnson, Hugh. *The California Wine Book.* New York: Morrow, 1976. Thompson, *Sunset's* wine man and a newspaper wine writer, seems to have written most of this book, with Hugh Johnson, a Briton and all-round wine expert, looking over his shoulder and tasting glass. This is an encyclopedic survey, though it leaves out many small wineries, and has comparative tastings of varietals and generics, winery by winery, vintage by vintage.

Vintage Image. *Napa Valley Wine Book* (rev. ed.). *Sonoma & Mendocino Wine Book. Central Coast Wine Tour.* St. Helena: Vintage Image (1335 Main St., St. Helena 94574), 1977–79. These three companion volumes, in both large format hardcover and small format paperback, comprise a guide to all the wineries, big and boutique, in three premium wine districts. Each winery gets two (sometimes four) pages, one with a good pen-and-ink drawing by Sebastian Titus, the other with an uncritical, often badly written write-up. The revised *Napa Valley Wine Book,* by Richard Paul Hinkle, is the best of the three. Chapters on food and lodging are in the *Wine Tour* guides. While the titles make it clear that these are tour guides, they would be better if they were more educational on the subject of wine.

Wine Education

University extension and adult-education centers in major cities usually have a wine-appreciation course for $50 or so. Designed to educate mind and palate, such courses use tuition money to good advantage and let you taste far more wines than you could otherwise afford. The Society of Wine Educators, 499 Hamilton Ave., Palo Alto 94301, can refer you to members (though the society has no certification procedures yet).

Wine Country Travel Information

General: Redwood Empire Association, 360 Post St., Suite 201, San Francisco 94108 (415/421-6554). Information for coastal area from San Francisco north to Josephine County, Ore., including Napa, Sonoma, Mendocino and Lake counties. Ask for comprehensive visitor's guide.

Napa: Napa Chamber of Commerce, 1900 Jefferson St., Box 636, Napa 94558 (707/226-7455). St. Helena Chamber of Commerce, 1508 Main St., St. Helena 94574 (707/963-4456). Calistoga Chamber of Commerce, 1139 Lincoln Ave., Calistoga 94515 (707/942-6333).

Sonoma: Sonoma County Economic Development Board, 2300 County Center Dr., Santa Rosa 95401 (707/527-2406). Santa Rosa Chamber of Commerce, 1st Street and Santa Rosa Avenue, Santa Rosa 95404 (707/545-1414). Sonoma Valley Chamber of Commerce, 453 1st St. West, Sonoma 95476 (707/996-1033). Russian River Region, Inc., 14034 Armstrong Woods Rd., Box 331, Guerneville 95446 (707/869-2584). Petaluma Chamber of Commerce, 314 Western Ave., Petaluma 94952 (707/762-2785). Also chambers in Healdsburg, Geyserville, Cloverdale. See also this section in Part II.

Mendocino: County Chamber of Commerce, 331 N. School St., Box 244, Ukiah 95482 (707/462-3091). See also this section in Part II.

Lake: County Chamber of Commerce, George G. Hoberg Vista Point, Highway 29 and Lakeport Boulevard, Lakeport 95453 (707/263-6131).

The special thing to do in Sonoma besides wine touring is visiting farms, which have organized themselves as Sonoma County Farm Trails, Box 6043, Santa Rosa 95406. They'll send a nice map if you send a SASE.

Part II

COAST

MARIN, SONOMA, MENDOCINO

Now here is Minot, North Dakota, population 32,290. One searches for something to say, and here it is: Minot is near Rugby, the geographical center of North America. Which is to say, it is nearly as far to the Arctic Ocean or the Gulf of Mexico as to the Atlantic or the Pacific. Perfectly inland. Flat enough to encourage membership in the Flat Earth Society. It would be as incredible to see people having a hotdog roast on an ocean bluff in Minot as it would be to see a stranded whale on 1st Avenue outside the Minot Farmers Elevator. If one of the good people of Minot wants to breathe salt air, he must add a teaspoon of Morton's Salt to a cup of warm water. Or travel two or three days on the interstate to Puget Sound.

Imagination is necessary for such inlanders. North Dakota, after all, has prairie until you don't believe it anymore: 19 million acres of wheat and flax, and on a windy day (lots of those there), the fields churn and ripple like the sea, and from the land emanates the same enormous heady smell. There's a similar "huge sameness," as Robert Louis Stevenson, crossing our Great Plains, put it. The pioneers navigated this land in, appropriately, prairie schooners.

Yet the prairie doesn't represent freedom. The horizon, noted RLS, is "mocking, furtive," a "prison-line." Over the curve of the sea, however, lie Bali and Macao, Tangier and Buenos Aires. So perhaps only hardy souls can live inland. Twentieth-century refugees must live on the coast and cling to that vanity left over from the nineteenth century: the idea that we can always throw everything aside and take ship, like Ishmael.

But let us not be unfair to North Dakota. The ocean has too much of itself, it can be deadly boring when not being merely deadly; it is always wet; and it makes people seasick.

The alternative to a trip either to North Dakota or the Bermuda Triangle is happily halfway between sea and land: the California coast. You don't have to travel all 1,072 miles of it, just enough to appreciate the amazing variety and sense the differing impact and presence of all that ocean out there. Start with the California coast north from San Francisco to beyond Mendocino: it astonishes with its continuous beauty, which begins with the Golden Gate Bridge and hardly lets up.

This stretch of coast has 10-mile strands, fogged-in stretches of rocky shore, postcard towns, bold cliffs that plunge into the sea, offshore stacks and arches, pocket beaches where beachcombers delight in finding seaworn driftwood or shiny bits of rounded gemstone, marshlands that serve as stopping-off places for migrating birds, tiny villages that were once lumber "dog ports" (big enough for a dog to turn around in), river-mouth lagoons, award-winning vacation-home architecture, expanses of tidal flats dotted with weekend clam-diggers, cavorting sea lions and migrating gray whales, wildflower-sprinkled meadows, twisting panoramic highways that dip from redwood valleys to wind-blown ridges, rhododendron reserves, pastureland where sheep or cows graze just beyond the sea spray, old towns where Victorian gingerbread is plentiful, some stretches where summer cottages uglify the landscape, fishing piers, vast dune areas, and some quiet rocky places where the only action is in the tide pools.

That's a long catalogue. This chapter gives you the whole length of coastal Highway 1 and some inland detours too. Frankly, though, you would need stamina to travel along Highway 1 from San Francisco to Mendocino in a day. And no matter which route you take, the roads have enough twists, zigs, ups, turns, zags, and downs, and hug the coastal cliffs so tightly, to make you wish for either a stronger stomach or a low-slung red MG so you can really enjoy the driving. A relatively comfortable day trip can be made from San Francisco to Point Reyes, but for any driving into Sonoma and Mendocino, it's best to plan an overnight stop somewhere.

There's slow, bumper traffic southbound on parts of Highway 1 Saturday and Sunday afternoons, when people are returning from day trips.

This shore has beaches but most would not be for swimming even if the water were Malibu-temperate. Except as noted here and there, these North Coast beaches are for beachcombing, picnicking, fishing, tide-pool study, running, and playing Frisbee. Good advice is to never turn your back on this ocean. Do bring warm clothes even if it's blazing hot inland—the coast is famous for its summertime fogs and chill.

And don't forget a camera.

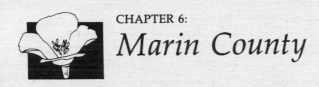

CHAPTER 6:

Marin County

HIGHLIGHTS

Marin Headlands / 179
Kirby Cove / 179
Rodeo Lagoon / 180
Bayside.
Sausalito / 181
Houseboat Colony / 182
Tiburon / 183
Richardson Bay Wildlife
   Sanctuary / 183
Belvedere / 184
Larkspur Landing / 184
San Rafael / 185
Marin Civic Center / 185
Coastside:
Mill Valley / 188

Mt. Tamalpais / 189
Dipsea Trail / 189
Muir Woods / 190
Muir Beach / 192
Stinson Beach / 192
Audubon Canyon Ranch / 192
Bolinas / 192
Point Reyes / 193
Earthquake Trail / 194
Drake's Bay / 194
Bear Valley Trail / 202
Tomales Bay State Park / 203
Inverness / 203
Samuel P. Taylor State Park / 204
Tomales Bayshore / 204

When you visit Marin County—indeed, as soon as you cross the Golden Gate Bridge and land on the dramatic Marin Headlands—you will understand why people pay handsomely, in rents, house prices, taxes, and such occasional hardships as water shortages, to live here. One of the richest counties in the U.S., Marin has some of the most gorgeous countryside in California, with rolling hills dotted with cattle and oak trees, brooding Mt. Tamalpais, foggy valleys with tall coastal redwoods (who doesn't know Muir Woods?), a cliff-lined ocean shore that sometimes borders on the melodramatic, bayside hill towns like sybaritic Sausalito, secluded pockets of rustic dwellings, small dairy industry towns, and at least one destination that makes a journey, Point Reyes National Seashore.

The Coastal Range, which includes the Marin Headlands and Mt. Tam, divides Marin into two sections: the part with the people, who have the bay to look at, and the part with the cows, who have the coast to look at.

Eastern or bayside Marin is the part with most of the population, in prosperous, woodsy suburbs on either side of Highway 101 (Redwood Highway). As symbolized by the painted rainbows on Highway 101's Waldo Tunnel, this is the land at the end of the rainbow: "marvelous Marin," a mythical country where you're OK and I'm on a trip and anything goes, birthplace of the hopelessly hedonistic hot-tub culture, a place where everyone jogs and plays tennis, guzzles Perrier by the case, owns a BMW or a Mercedes (ski racks on all summer, of course), strokes each other with peacock feathers (if you believed NBC's "I Want It All Now" documentary), and talks to each other in continuous streams of psychobabble (if you believe Cyra McFadden's book and movie, *The Serial*).

Many Marinites, the ones who claim to work all day long and go to PTA meetings at night, don't believe Marin is all that marvelous. Skeptics, however, may want to peruse the five pages of hot-tubs listings in the Marin yellow pages, including the ad for the Truck-a-Dub-Dub, a van outfitted with hot tub, stereo system, and skylight (stargazing for navel-gazers).

By contrast, western or coastal Marin, the part with the cows, is sparsely populated, with the scattered rich residing in hill-hugging glass and wood structures, agriculturalists on large, luxuriant dairy farms, and counterculturalists in a few coastal villages and hidden valley towns that they would prefer not be publicized. This part of Marin, served by narrow, winding, two-lane Highway 1 (Shoreline Highway), is marvelous in quite a different way: it includes a long, glorious stretch of publicly owned shore, part of the Golden Gate National Recreation Area and Point Reyes National Seashore, the geological "island in time" where Sir Francis Drake perhaps landed in 1579 to make England's first claim to America.

WHAT TO SEE AND DO

When you cross the Golden Gate Bridge, you're theoretically on both Highways 101 and 1, but no one is paying much attention. There are some distracting things, such as the international orange-colored bridge itself, the superb views of The City behind you, and, looming ahead on the left, the Marin Headlands, on which the northern end of the bridge is well anchored.

Like highways 101 and 1, which split just north of the headlands, this chapter is divided into two parts: bayside Marin, with excursions off Highway 101 into Sausalito, Tiburon, Belvedere, and San Rafael; and coastal Marin, with detours to Mt. Tamalpais and Muir Woods off a Highway 1 drive from Stinson Beach past Point Reyes and north along Tomales Bay.

Marin Headlands

The **Marin Headlands***** have escaped being covered with the homes of architects, *Playboy* readers, wealthy conservationists, et al., only because the army occupied them first in the name of national defense in the last century. Until the missile age it was feared that enemy fleets could sail into San Francisco Bay and shell the Bank of America with impunity unless hindered by coastal artillery fire. Thus the army moved into the Spanish Presidio and built Fort Point on the southern side of the Golden Gate and established **Forts Cronkhite, Baker, and Barry** on the northern point. The army is keeping some of the land for the time being, but has turned 1,073 acres over to the Golden Gate National Recreation Area and opened to scrutiny the deserted **artillery emplacements*** on the hilltops (they're fascinating but inscrutable in their design). To get to these outposts and the headlands vista road, take the Alexander Avenue exit off Highway 101 just north of the bridge. Ignore turn-offs until a left marked for the GGNRA. That takes you through a one-way tunnel governed by a light. Go past some Fort Baker married-personnel housing. Turn left off Bunker Road and up Conzelman Road. At a Y junction, another left will take you up next to one of the Golden Gate Bridge's towers (and back to Highway 101 when you're ready to return). The **view of San Francisco***** is incomparable. From the principal artillery emplacement a road for walkers and bicycles only winds a mile down to **Kirby Cove,**** worthwhile particularly for photographers, who can get a pine-framed shot of the city under the bridge, complete with fishermen on the beach and sailboats on the bay. Back at the Y the headlands road goes up another gun emplacement to a popular **vista point,***** where the road ends. Here all the tourists go ooh and ahh at the view of The City above and between the towers of the bridge.

Now go back along Conzelman and McCullough roads to Bunker Road and turn left. You're in Fort Barry and heading toward Fort Cronkhite, which is a set of ugly barracks located at **Rodeo Lagoon and Beach.*** Here you can find restrooms and a ranger station (415/561-7612). Rangers lead walks into the chaparral, along the beach and lagoon, to the old coastal defenses. There's also bird-watching (that's **Bird Island** offshore), combing the beach for colored pebbles, sunbathing, and picnicking. Behind the ranger station, the **Marine Mammal Rehabilitation Center** rescues seals, sea lions, and other ocean creatures and cares for them, at an average cost of $1,500 each, until they can be returned to their environment. Open to the public; call 415/561-7284 for information. The army's 100 or so buildings on the headlands may someday be part of a national energy center with, it is hoped, displays of unusual energy technologies.

Trails on the Headlands

At several points on the Marin Headlands you can pick up the first segment of the new **Pacific Coast Trail,** which will in time be mapped and signposted all the way to Tomales Point (northern tip of the Point Reyes Peninsula). Among the shorter hikes on the headlands: **Wolf Ridge Loop,** five miles, starting from the Rodeo Lagoon parking lot, along the Pacific Coast Trail to the Wolf Ridge Trail, the Miwok Trail, and back to the beginning. **Miwok-Bobcat Trail Loop,** five miles, from trailhead on Bunker Road a mile west of the tunnel, taking the Miwok, the Bobcat, then the Miwok again. **Kirby Cove Trail,** two to three miles round-trip, from Battery Spencer on Conzelman Road, winding gently down to the cove. Some of these trails run exclusively on old military roads or fire roads; the vegetation is typical coastal scrub, with oaks and madrone here and there and, in the spring, displays of poppies, lupine, paintbrush, morning glory. You'll see hawks and an occasional deer. And the views are easily worth two blisters.

Another GGNRA hike of interest to visitors is the **Tennessee Valley Trail,** two miles, which starts at the end of Tennessee Valley Road, signposted off Highway 1 just after that highway leaves 101. You walk through eucalyptus groves, through meadows and past bucolic ranches, and out to Tennessee Valley Cove on the Headlands. You can ride if you call Miwok Horse Rentals, 701 Tennessee Valley Rd., 415/383-1056.

Marin Headlands information: 415/556-0560, 561-7612.

To leave the headlands, you have two choices: south and north. Conzelman Road will take you to Highway 101 south, if you're returning to The City. Bunker Road and the one-way tunnel go back to Alexander Avenue. Follow signs back to 101 north to reach, first, the turnoff to Marin's Shoreline Highway, and second, the several bayside towns on either side of 101, including Belvedere, Tiburon, and San Rafael. Otherwise, take Alexander Avenue down into Sausalito.

Bayside Marin

Sausalito** is the first community north of the Golden Gate. With a fleeting resemblance to a Mediterranean coastal village, it climbs from the sail- and houseboat-lined docks up the steep, green hillsides to Highway 101. Named from the Spanish *sauce,* "willow," the townsite of Sausalito ("little grove of willows") was a 19,000-acre rancho given to Captain William Richardson of Yerba Buena (San Francisco) in 1838. Before the Golden Gate was bridged in 1937, Sausalito was the terminus for rail and ferry traffic between the North Coast and The City. Once Sausalito was inhabited by some genuine artists; when living costs soared, most departed. Sausalito today is populated by commuters who can afford the lofty rents of apartments and mortgages on houses that command sparkling bay and city views, by those who run the tourist industry, and by many less-than-affluent houseboat dwellers. During the summer and on most weekends, traffic backs up on Bridgeway and other streets as tourists from everywhere try to get into the shopping, dining, and strolling district along the waterfront.

Shopping is the backbone of Sausalito's economy. One of the oldest and most popular shopping galleries is **The Village,** a multi-storied collection of specialty and import shops and restaurants. A long-time gathering place is the **no-name bar.** Heath Ceramics, 400 Gate 5 Rd., has made-in-Sausalito items; the Industrial Center displays other local art. The **Sausalito Art Festival,** once again displaying works of other than the crashing-wave school of painters, takes place in September.

After—or before—you tire of shopping, go for a walk along the waterfront and up onto hillside Sausalito to get some of its flavor. Across from the town center, Plaza Viña Del Mar, are some municipal steps that lead up the hill to the woodsy residences above the hubbub. Or go to the south end of Bridgeway, up Richardson about four blocks, and walk along Central, San Carlos, Harrison, or Bulkley, then maybe up the hill via Glen to Currey and Toyon. Notable houses include **60 Atwood Ave** (Joseph Esherick, 1950), built on the foundation of one of William Randolph Hearst's imported castles; **Sausalito Women's**

Club (Julia Morgan, 1913), Central and San Carlos; **St. John's Presbyterian Church,** (Coxhead and Coxhead, 1905), 100 Bulkley; and the oldest, Gothic **Gardner House** (1869), at Cazneau and Girard.

Sausalito has several points of interest along the long waterfront area. A string of small parks on Bridgeway have superb bay views, and offer fishing and picnicking areas. The **Boardwalk and Plaza Area*** is a short walkway overlooking a yacht berthing, with an adjacent landscaped plaza open to restaurant and other commercial activity. Bicyclists might like to try the 3.2-mile ride along the bay from Sausalito to Mill Valley.

Sausalito's most unusual attraction is the U.S. Army Corps of Engineers' **San Francisco Bay and Delta Model,**** in a warehouse at 2100 Bridgeway, at Spring. Spread over an acre and a half, the model gives you a bird's-eye view—from the equivalent of 12,000 feet, and in a mere 14 minutes—of a 24-hour cycle of tides and currents in the 11,000 square miles of salt and fresh water in the bay and delta. Engineers can watch the effect of droughts, floods, and other events, with three and a half model-days equal to one year of actual water flow. The model is open, free, weekdays and the first and third Saturdays of each month, 9–4. Call 332–3870 to see if the tides and currents will flow for you.

Risking the wrath of the residents, we also list the **Waldo Point houseboats**** as of interest to visitors. The colorful, feisty waterdwellers are a controversial community within Sausalito. Many of the 500 residents of Gates 3, 5, and 6 pride themselves on living on relatively low incomes—perhaps $5,000 or less a year, which is no mean trick anywhere in the U.S. but is made easier if rent is nothing or very little. Free life-styles, however, are one thing, but the fact that houseboat sewage goes directly into the bay has offended Marin County officials and residents—Marin is, above all, the most conservation-inclined county in the state. The houseboaters' life-style protective association fights county planners, modern development, higher berth fees, the threat of tourism, and Marin trendiness. In 1977 some 36 were arrested after they threw themselves in front of the bulldozers of would-be developers of Gate 5; things have become only a little less noisy since then. The major gathering of houseboats, at Waldo Point Harbor, numbers more than 200 boats, about 85 percent owned by their occupants. Some are funky bohemian pads that are barely afloat (federal housing loans are available to bring them up to code), others are $100,000 palaces on the bay.

Parts of "Marvelous Marin": Angel Island (foreground), Tiburon Peninsula, and Sausalito (background). (Redwood Empire Association)

Sausalito is served by ferry and Golden Gate Transit (GGT) buses 2, 3, 5, 10, 20, and 62.

Tiburon and Belvedere

More swank and snobbish than Sausalito, Tiburon and Belvedere are adjacent Marin suburbs situated on a peninsula directly across from Angel Island.

Tiburon wraps along the mainland around Richardson Bay and San Francisco Bay. Pricy modern homes, condominiums, and apartments spread over adjoining hills, and a small town-center on the waterfront offers restaurants and shops catering mostly to visitors. En route from Highway 101 on Tiburon Boulevard, watch for a tall Victorian Italianate mansion in a cypress grove on the right. Marin's oldest Victorian (1874), **Lyford House** was moved from Strawberry Point and is now the Audubon Society's **Richardson Bay Wildlife Sanctuary** headquarters. Winter finds a hundred harbor seals and sea lions, and 350,000 birds of 200 species (residents and migrants from as far away as Siberia) enjoying life in the 11 onshore and 900 tideland acres. Any season is good for bird-watching and walking here, but picnics are not allowed. Visitors are welcome Wed.-Sun. 9–5; small admission charge. Sundays are busy: at 9 early risers can go on a two-hour bird walk with a naturalist; at 3 is a wildlife program; from 1 to 4 Lyford House is open for tours. Information: 415/388-2524.

Running along the bay's edge are a series of parks and open spaces. Bicyclists and joggers like the **Shoreline Park,** which stretches 5,000 feet beginning near the wildlife sanctuary; a path continues into Tiburon center. Signs indicate entry points along Tiburon Boulevard, and several large natural parks have splendid views. **Shoreline Path** extends another 1,500 feet along San Rafael Avenue on Belvedere's shoreline, and is great for strolling.

In Tiburon center is the **Boardwalk,** adjacent to the ferry slip and extending over the bay. The views of San Francisco are good, of Angel Island excellent. On a hill above Alemany and Esperanza streets is **Old St. Hilary's Church,** a Carpenter Gothic Victorian (1888), now the **Landmarks Society Museum;** it is surrounded by a live wild-flower display. Open 1–4 Wed., Sun., Apr.-Oct.; information: 415/435-1853. Tiburon is served by ferries from The City plus buses 8, 9, 10, and 11.

Belvedere, perched on a hilly subpeninsula—once an island—is one of the Bay Area's most exclusive residential districts. Beautiful homes are nestled among old cultivated groves of pine and eucalyptus with twisting streets, garden paths, and lagoons. The **town square** has some Bay Area brown-shingle landmarks, the Belvedere Land Co. (1905) and cottages and an apartment house (Albert Farr, 1906). Two paths that are fun to explore are Woodwardia Lane and Pomander Walk. Three of the many gorgeous homes are **Moffitt House** (1900), 8 W. Shore Rd., which was cut in two and moved from 1818 Broadway in San Francisco in 1962; **Rey House** (Willis Polk, 1893), 428 Golden Gate Ave.; and **Blanding House** (ca. 1900), 440 Golden Gate. Belvedere buses: 8 and 9.

Larkspur and Landing

Larkspur, a town with suburban houses climbing up the hills over Corte Madera Creek, is of interest to out-of-state visitors for **Larkspur Landing,** a $50 million complex of offices, apartments and condos, shops, and restaurants next to the Larkspur terminal of the Golden Gate Transit ferry. The site, a former rock quarry, could have been spectacularly utilized, but the quarry walls are actually a stark backdrop for the instant village on the bayfront. Taking better advantage of location is nearby **Wood Island,** two hilltop office buildings enveloped in an oak forest; corporate headquarters of the Victoria Station restaurant chain are here. East of Larkspur Landing is Marin's least admirable building and least wanted institution: **San Quentin** state prison. In the lee of **Point San Quentin,** perhaps at Larkspur Landing, Sir Francis Drake may have beached his ship for repairs in 1579; the debate is discussed below, under Point Reyes.

Larkspur Landing and the ferry terminal are reached by Sir Francis Drake Boulevard East off Highway 101; by ferry from the foot of Market Street, San Francisco; and by GGT buses 1, 15, 19, 25, 29, 31, 37, 41, 51, and 61.

San Rafael

Marin County's seat and principal city, **San Rafael** was founded as a mission in 1817, twentieth in the series the Franciscan fathers strung from San Diego to Sonoma. **Mission San Rafael Arcangel,** 1104 5th Ave., is, however, a 1949 replica, for the original was knocked down for its timber in 1860. Old San Rafael has similarly disappeared, leaving not much more than several buildings on B Street, including the **Marin Historical Society,** at 1125 B St., in the gatehouse (1879) of the Boyd Estate. Open Wed.-Sun. 1–4. Another historic building is **Falkirk,** the Robert Dollar mansion, 1408 Mission. Built in 1879 with a multitude of dormers, gables, rounded and slanted bay windows and porches, the 17-room house was sold to shipping magnate Robert Dollar in 1907. When threatened by a developer in 1972, Falkirk was saved by San Rafael's citizens, who rallied, purchased it, restored the house and gardens, and opened it as a community center. Information: 415/457-6888. Incidentally, *American Graffiti* director George Lucas, who lives in Marin, found his small-town American Main Street on 4th Street, San Rafael; after the success of *Star Wars* Lucas decided to build a film center in the Marin hills.

San Rafael buses: 26, 30, 34, 36, and 50 from San Francisco; 1, 25, 37, 41, and 51 from the Larkspur ferry terminal.

Of considerable interest to architecture buffs, and even ordinary people, is the **Marin Civic Center**** three miles north of San Rafael off

Frank Lloyd Wright's Marin Civic Center dazzles and shocks; Marinites show it off to visitors. (Redwood Empire Association)

Highway 101, on North San Pedro Road. This is one of Frank Lloyd Wright's most dazzling creations, a slender, extremely stretched-out structure with two long arms, the Administration Building and the Hall of Justice, on either side of a small dome; some say it's a 10-story building lying on its side. The circle is the motif, but shallow arches seem more dominant on the outside, with three levels of arches of decreasing size topped by a fourth level of circular windows; the bottom arches are underpasses for three access roads. The gallery corridors, courtyard elements, and many furnishings are also circular. The exterior colors—brown stucco, blue roof tiles—harmonize with the summer-burned Marin landscape. This was Wright's only municipal complex, and it incorporates his only commission from the federal government, a small post office. The master plan was completed in 1957 but the first phase of the main structure wasn't finished until

1962, after Wright's death. A separate building, the **Marin Center,** includes an auditorium. Around the buildings is the **Marin County Civic Center Park and Fairgrounds,** 80 acres that include a lagoon for bird-watching, expansive lawns, picnic tables and benches, and on occasional weekends fairs and festivals. Buses. 1, 34, and 35.

To reach **China Camp State Park** and the relatively undeveloped area of bayside Marin, continue east on North San Pedro Road past the Civic Center. China Camp State Park takes in 1,600 acres of bayshore, marsh, hillsides, and what remains of a Chinese fishermen's village. In the 1880s as many as 3,000 Chinese lived here, supported by shrimp fishing. After the 1906 earthquake, six cases of bubonic plague reported in San Francisco's Chinatown led to the evacuation of 10,000 Chinese by boats and junks to tents on the hillsides above China Camp. In 1910 bottom-net shrimping was banned following complaints by sports fishermen: the nets caught all fish, including bass. The Chinese population was more than decimated, but the Quan family stayed on, and Quan Hok Quan designed the (legal) conical shrimp net; his descendants run the decrepit pier, café, cottages.

China Camp is a recent state acquisition, and is going through a lengthy planning process. Some locals worry that it could become cutesy and overdeveloped, a Chinatown-by-the-bay attracting thousands daily. We don't think this is likely, but some reconstruction and building of new facilities would be desirable. Information: 415/456-0766.

North to Novato

The Marin countryside reappears on either side of Highway 101 about three miles north of the Civic Center: there are a few golden hills that don't have hilltopping office complexes and condominiums. But there are threats to the remaining dairy ranches and expanses of open space up this way. One is **Hamilton Field,** or, shall we say, the absence of the air force, which flew planes in and out of the field from World War II until the base was declared surplus in the 1970s. Some Marinites want to convert it into a commercial airport (indeed, both San Francisco and Oakland International airports have proposed making Hamilton a satellite facility). Some want to make it an industrial park—but clean industry only. Some want to suburbanize it, perhaps into a model "solar village." It now looks as if the government will break it up, devoting part of it to a wildlife sanctuary.

The other threat is **Novato,** a weed of a town that is by no means too distant to be considered one of San Francisco's bedroom communities: just ask one of the many San Francisco cops who live there.

Most travelers have no reason to stop north of the Civic Center, but two turnoffs from the highway should be noted. **Lucas Valley Road** winds west into the hills and past Nicasio Reservoir before joining the coastal road at Point Reyes. The other, at Ignacio, is Highway 37 east toward the Sonoma and Napa valleys.

Off Highway 37 the Blackpoint oak forest is the site of the annual, original **Renaissance Pleasure Faire** on six weekends from mid-August to late September. The fair, sponsored by the nonprofit Living History Center, has a costumed, paid cast—Queen Elizabeth and her court, minstrels, jesters, and jugglers, a good many lusty, busty maids, and so forth—and the audience is encouraged to come dressed for the occasion (patterns are available, classes held in the months before). Behind the Elizabethan façade is, essentially, a crafts fair with the usual (and some unusual) food concessions, but admission (steep: adult—$7.50, child—$2.95) gets you a day of good fun . . . once. Information: Box 1112, Novato 94947; 415/892-2166, 883-2473. A mid-July event at the fair site is the **Blackpoint Oldtime Music Festival,** with blues, country, Cajun, and bluegrass performers, also square-dancing, country barbecue, etc. The Living History Center wants to make the Blackpoint forest a permanent fair site, but Novato is resisting.

If you don't leave Highway 101, you will soon enter Sonoma County south of Petaluma. We cover this area in Chapter 5.

Coastside Marin

On Highway 101 north of the Marin Headlands and Sausalito, visitors who want to drive along the coast should be alert for freeway exit signs for Highway 1 (Shoreline Highway) to Muir Woods and Stinson Beach. The turnoff is not far north of **Marin City,** which is Marin County's particular pocket of nonaffluence, a redeveloped World War II housing project for shipyard workers that is now a mini-ghetto. Near the turnoff a big parking lot is the congested weekend site of a flea market.

At Tam Junction you can detour to a prototypical Marin town, **Mill Valley,** which really did once have a mill and sweaty millworkers but now has about 15,000 laid-back dwellers in homes ranging from funky to posh (the town is favored by rock stars) but all woodsy and superexpensive. A right turn at Tam Junction will take you along Miller Avenue to the villagey downtown at about Blithedale and Throckmorton. (If Mill Valley ever wanted to change its name to something more apt, Blithe Dale would be it.)

Highway 1 winds up around one side of Mill Valley's own looming mountain, **Mt. Tamalpais.***** The name, Indian for "bay-mountain," which it certainly is, is pronounced *tam-ull-PIE-iss* but is usually called by its first syllable, Tam. The 2,571-foot mountain rises grandly from both the ocean and the bay to beautiful heights with views in all directions. In 1898 you could have ridden up eight miles of the "crookedest railroad in the world," whose 281 curves and loop-the-loops of track thrilled passengers (especially in the gravity ride on the way down) until 1930. Nowadays, twisting **Panoramic Highway** serves the same function as it goes nearly over the top and down to Stinson Beach.

Tam has traditionally been a day-use wilderness area, a place for city and suburban folk to escape to. Hiking on Tam's slopes and peaks is popular year-round, and grand views forever can be seen from West Peak (2,560 feet), Middle Peak (2,490 feet), and East Peak (2,571 feet). These three peaks are beads strung on Ridgecrest Boulevard. Hikers enjoy 30 miles of trails within the 6,000 acres of the state park, but these connect 200 more miles of trails in adjacent Muir Woods, Stinson Beach, the 10,000-acre Marin Municipal Water District watershed, and Golden Gate National Recreation Area lands.

About 10 trails start at park headquarters in the Pan Toll area, and at the ranger station a detailed hiking map can be purchased. One of our favorite hikes is the **Dipsea Trail,** which you can start either in Mill Valley (the long version, 6.8 miles) or next to Muir Woods (slightly shorter route, about 6 miles one-way). This hike takes you through the whole range of Tam's diverse environments—redwood forests, oak glens, waving grass hillsides, chaparral-covered and rocky ridges, and Pacific Ocean sandy beaches. Each year on the last Sunday in August thousands of runners fly or stumble along this trail in the **Dipsea Race,** quite an uphill jog for the first half from Mill Valley. We prefer a more leisurely hike with time to enjoy the views and our picnic lunch. Having a car at each end gives you all day to relax or take a one-day hike. For other trails, see the books mentioned below under Muir Woods.

Mountain Theater is a natural amphitheater with seating for 5,000 on serpentine and peridotite rock seats laid by the Civilian Conserva-

Muir Woods is just across the Golden Gate from San Francisco; go early to avoid the crowds. (Redwood Empire Association)

tion Corps in the 1930s. Here open-air amateur theatrical productions have been mounted yearly since 1913. The picnic areas are at **Boot Jack** (tables, stoves, water, restrooms) and **East Peak** (tables, no fires due to fire danger). Camping is at **Pan Toll,** where the 16 walk-in campsites have tables, stoves, drinking water, and nearby restrooms. Day hikers enjoy refreshing themselves at two small, woodsy inns on Tam. **West Point Club,** Mt. Tamalpais Hwy., built in 1904, serves lemonade, tea, and coffee, and now allows overnight stays. The Teutonic **Tourist Club,** in German called *Die Naturfreunde,* has beer *natürlich,* as well as wine, candy bars, and peanuts. Their long driveway turnoff is 2.2 miles beyond the Muir Woods–Highway 1 split from Panoramic Highway.

Information: Mt. Tamalpais State Park, 801 Panoramic Hwy., Mill Valley 94941; 415/338-2070. Buses: 62 and 63.

Muir Woods

From either Panoramic Highway or Shoreline Highway it is only a couple of miles to one of the best-known redwood forests in the world, **Muir Woods National Monument.***** Since these are the closest coastal redwoods to San Francisco, and consequently the most frequently visited, you can easily get there by tour bus from The City.

In Muir Woods you can stroll or hike through virgin groves of *Se-*

quoia sempervirens, the tall trees that so love the coastal fog and protected valley environment. The introduction to Part III explains how to
tell coastal redwoods from their mountain cousins, the Big Trees or Giant Sequoias.

Spread over 502 acres, Muir Woods has trees more than 240 feet
high; a few are 1,500 years old. Most of the land was a gift to the country from Congressman William Kent and Elizabeth Thatcher Kent in
1908. In making the donation they asked President Roosevelt to name
the park for John Muir, whom they greatly admired but had not met.
Muir was still alive and was able to visit and enjoy the park.

The main and most heavily traveled walking route in Muir Woods
is the **Redwood Creek Nature Trail,** a 2.5-mile stroll along a paved
path complete with educational signs and a booklet describing 20 interesting things about the redwood forest's plant and animal life. Within
the main area are several fine groves of redwoods, some named for in-
dividuals or groups who assisted in the park's establishment, including
Pinchot Memorial, Bohemian Grove, Cathedral Grove, and Kent Memorial.

Another six miles of less well-beaten paths take you into quieter
parts of Muir Woods and surrounding Mt. Tamalpais State Park and
connect to hundreds of miles more. Inquire at the Visitor Center for
maps and routes. Or follow a route in the Sierra Club's *To Walk with
a Quiet Mind,* Margot Patterson Doss' *Paths of Gold,* or Dorothy
Whitnah's *An Outdoor Guide to the San Francisco Bay Area.*

Try to arrive at Muir Woods before 8 A.M. to enjoy the forest qui-
etude before the crowds arrive on tour buses about 9 or 9:30. Some
eight million visitors come yearly, but most of them stick to the paved
Redwood Creek trail. Park hours: 8 A.M.-sunset, though you can actually enter before 8 (and, as a reward, avoid paying). Admission fees are
small. The **Visitor Center** has exhibits, books, brochures, postcards,
and a snack stand. Picnicking and camping are not allowed in Muir
Woods, but are allowed in Mt. Tamalpais and at Stinson Beach. Redwood forests can be cool, so bring a sweater.

Information: Muir Woods National Monument, Mill Valley 94941;
415/388-2595. Bus: 61 (from Larkspur ferry terminal).

And Down to the Shore

Back on Highway 1 after the Panoramic Highway turnoff to Muir
Woods and Mt. Tam, the narrow road plunges down into **Green**

Gulch, a Zen retreat and nature reserve (open for enlightenment Sunday at 8.30 A.M.). At sea level there's a turnoff to **Muir Beach** (mostly sunbathing) and beyond that another road back to Muir Woods. Now Highway 1 climbs Mt. Tam again, passing a left exit to the **Muir Beach Overlook,*** then dips in and out of gulches to **Stinson Beach,*** which is both a small town and a popular beach that is now part of the GGNRA and, therefore, free. This beach continues for a couple of miles to **Sea Drift,** one of those locked-gate communities that fenced off parts of the coast until the 1972 coastal initiative liberated at least the sandy shore. Stinson Beach has some of the only so-called warm swimming water around, and lifeguards, so naturally is popular with families. It can be windy, however. Information: 415/868-1922.

North of the town the highway follows the shoreline of **Bolinas Lagoon,*** a remarkably flat-looking body of water and mud that is popular with birds. About 3.5 miles from Stinson Beach look on the right for the **Audubon Canyon Ranch,*** a sanctuary (headquartered in a charming white Victorian house) for nesting great blue herons and great egrets in the spring, and other birds all year. Trails in two canyons take you to overlooks *above* the nesting birds. List-keepers can watch for some of the 55 species of waterfowl, 90 of land birds hereabouts. Open free (but donate, please) 10-4 weekends and holidays March-July 4. Information: 415/383-1644.

Not much more than another mile along Highway 1 is a turnoff right to the **Fairfax-Bolinas Road,*** a twisty mountain road that winds up in Fairfax on the way to Highway 101. Up on top of **Bolinas Ridge** is the very scenic **Ridgecrest Road***** south to Pan Toll (trailhead for Mt. Tam) and Panoramic Highway.

Bolinas

At the Fairfax-Bolinas Road junction is a turnoff left to a place many people would rather we didn't mention: **Bolinas.**** While in many towns it's the newcomers who want tourists and industrial parks and subdivisions, in Bolinas they want to keep everyone else out. Back-to-the-landers, country craftsmen, well-to-do escapees from San Francisco—collectively the "laid back"—quadrupled the town's population to about 2,000 before realizing Bolinas wouldn't long remain a rustic village 27 miles from San Francisco if any more people arrived. So now— Sea Drift revisited—they rip down the highway signs to discourage anybody else, including passersby. Well, it's okay to visit the "People's

Republic of Bolinas" for a time. Wharf Road, with a few shops and an ice cream parlor, dead-ends at the ocean, so park on the main road and walk as much as you can.

If you follow town roads vaguely west 1.5 miles to **Agate Beach** (at the end of Elm Road), you can get to the fabulous **Duxbury Reef,** ** on which you can wander a half-mile offshore when the tide is out. You can't take anything but sportfish but the tide-pool watching is great. The reef was named for a ship that hit it in 1849.

Mesa Road north of town goes to the **Point Reyes Bird Observatory,** * said to be the only full-time ornithological research station on the continent. Listmakers have counted 193 species in one day; 361 species have been spotted all told. Exhibits. Closed Monday. Information: 415/868-1221. Outside is the **Palomarin trailhead,** giving access to the Point Reyes trails from the south. From here you can walk on the edge of America for 16 miles to the Limantour trailhead.

Point Reyes—"Island in Time"

Bolinas is at the southern end of the **Point Reyes Peninsula.** On a map the peninsula looks out of place: it's oddly shaped, too triangular and pointy for a coast that has few bumps and dents, and the extremely long, slender Tomales Bay almost cuts the peninsula away from California. Point Reyes is out of place; in fact, it is a geological feature that, 40 million years ago, was perhaps 350 miles south of here and has drifted north. The reason is right under you as you drive the nine miles from Bolinas to Olema on Highway 1: the **San Andreas Fault** slashes the earth in a straight north-south line along Olema Valley and Tomales Bay, which is a drowned valley.

The famous San Andreas Fault, 20 miles deep, 600 miles long, is the same "strike-slip" fracture whose sudden movement in 1906 caused so much new construction in San Francisco and elsewhere along the coast. It is not only California's major fault but also the joint between the Pacific Plate and the North American Plate. These giant pieces of the earth's crust—this is a field called plate tectonics—have been slipping past each other over the millions of years, at the rate of two inches a year. In umpteen million years, this slippage will bring about the merger, with a crunch, of San Francisco (on the North American Plate) and Los Angeles (on the Pacific Plate).

Point Reyes is, in this area, isolated on the Pacific Plate. It is thus an island in time and in nature: Point Reyes and Bodega Head (north of here) have the only granite bedrock along the North Coast; bishop pines (and some unique flora) are found only on Point Reyes, redwoods only on the "mainland." Inverness Ridge, along the west side of Olema Valley, keeps Point Reyes fairly cool, as you will find out when you turn off the highway on to the peninsula.

If you're interested in physical evidence of this earth slippage, take the self-guided mile-long **Earthquake Trail***** from behind the Point Reyes Seashore Headquarters at Olema; you'll pass through a fence that was offset more than 15 feet by the ought-six shake. Because the long movement measured as much as 21 feet locally, Olema is usually named as the epicenter of that earthquake.

Only 35 miles north of San Francisco, **Point Reyes National Seashore***** makes even the most intense urban existence bearable. The peninsula, still the location of dairy farming, has always been a recreational destination but wasn't public parkland until 1962, when a battle between developers and conservationists resulted in legislation establishing the National Seashore, and 1969–70, when a second confrontation led to the appropriation of enough funds to buy out the dairy farmers (who remain on the land during their life). And what the public has gained! Miles of ocean bluff, several miles of broad beach, dozens of tiny coves, two dramatic points (Tomales and Point Reyes itself), lagoons, lakes, and *esteros* (as estuaries or inlets were called by the Spanish), moorland and rolling pastureland, steep ridges and hills, more than a hundred miles of trails through deep woodland and along the ocean bluffs, and, not least, a controversial historical site, or nonsite: **Drake's Bay,** where Sir Francis Drake may have careened his *Golden Hind* for repairs, built a fort, and sojourned for 34 days while on a voyage of exploration and plunder.

Drake's Landing Site

The controversy over just where Queen Elizabeth I's favorite admiral came ashore in California has been around for nearly 200 years, and has fairly raged for the last 100. It generated a lot of noise and paper in the last few years before the quadricentennial celebration in June 1979. If the controversy is ever resolved, we would know where to put an unequivocal historical marker, and we would know whether Drake discovered San Francisco Bay in 1579 or whether it lay hidden behind a foggy Golden Gate for another 200 years, until Gaspar de Portolá's land expedition stumbled upon it in 1769 (they were looking for Monterey Bay) and Juan de Ayala's *San Carlos* sailed into it in 1775.

A secondary controversy has been over the authenticity of the most tangible purported evidence of Drake's stopover: a flat, thin, 5 x 8–inch piece of brass with an inscription that is either California's most historic relic or a hoax perpetrated by some Berkeley undergraduates in the 1930s.

We have our opinions on the major questions, but here's a review of both Drake's fabulous voyage (which everyone agrees on) and the evidence on where he might have anchored.

In 1577 Drake, in his midthirties, was a sea dog of experience, wealth, and fame who already had African slaving and Caribbean piracy behind him. With what may have been the permission of Queen Elizabeth to make trouble for her rival, the king of Spain, Drake mustered a fleet of five ships and sailed from Plymouth on November 15, 1577. By the time he reached the Pacific by way of the Strait of Magellan, his fleet was reduced to his flagship, the 100-ton, 18-gun *Pelican*. He renamed it the *Golden Hind* after the crest (a hind trippant or) of one of his sponsors—a political act, for Drake had just beheaded the patron's former secretary.

Drake raided ports along the South American coast and captured a fully loaded galleon on its way from Peru to Panama. Armed additionally with Spanish charts and pilots, El Draque, whom the Spanish called the "master thief of the unknown world," continued north in search of the (mythical) Strait of Anian, or Northwest Passage.

According to contemporary documents, mainly varying narratives based on notes by the ship's chaplain, Francis Fletcher, Drake sailed as far north as Oregon or Washington—latitude 48° north—then backtracked to California waters to find a sheltered place to repair the *Golden Hind* and take on water and victuals before attempting to cross the Pacific.

Fletcher wrote that such a "conuenient and fit harborough" was found about latitude 38° north on June 17, 1579 (June 27 by our calendar). The crew erected an earthen fort and careened the *Golden Hind* to scrape the barnacles off the hull and caulk the leaks. Noting the resemblance of "the white banks and cliffes, which lie toward the sea" to those of Dover, Drake named the land Nova Albion (New England). And he met the local residents, who have been identified as Coast Miwoks, a tribe located in what is now Marin and the southern part of Sonoma. In true meeting-of-two-cultures fashion, the Indians fell to their knees and worshipped Drake, later holding a ceremony to crown him king and "freely offer" to surrender their land and become vassals of the Virgin Queen. As a pioneer imperialist, Drake accepted. There was singing and dancing, and a good time was had by all.

Except for the damnable weather, which by Fletcher's account seems worse than anything England could offer. "Most uile, thicke, and stinking fogges" blotted out sun and stars for 14 days straight, and Drake's crew and Indians shivered alike.

The ship being repaired by July 23 (August 2 by our calendar), preparations were made to depart. Drake evidently decided to abandon a small unseaworthy Spanish frigate he had seized 3,000 miles south. And because of overcrowding aboard the *Golden Hind* he possibly even decided to leave behind 13 or 14 crewmen. This was not, for Drake, an unusual thing to do—he had done it before and was to do it again—but at least one of the men requested to be left behind, possibly fearing a cross-Pacific voyage. Two hundred years later, early white settlers heard an Indian tradition that Drake's men traveled to warmer parts of Marin and became amalgamated with the tribespeople. Father Juan Crespi, who explored the Bay Area in 1772, found many Indians who were "rubios, blancos y barbados"—that is, blond, fair-skinned or white, and bearded. We don't know anything more than this; there is no further evidence.

"Before we went from thence," Fletcher's narrative in *The World Encompassed* (1628) continues, "our Generall caused to be set vp a monument of our being there, as also of her maiesties and successors right and title to that kingdome; namely a plate of brasse, fast nailed to a great and firme post; whereon is engrauen her graces name, and the day and yeare of our arriuall there, and of the free giuing vp of the prouince and kingdome, both by the king and people, into her maiesties hands: together with her highnesse picture and armes, in a piece of sixpence current English monie, showing itselfe by a hole made of purpose through the plate; vnderneath was likewise engrauen the name of our Generall, etc."

Captain General Drake and the *Golden Hind* then sailed off across the Pacific and around the world (only Magellan's expedition preceded them in this feat). They arrived back in Plymouth in November 1580. Elizabeth was pleased that he brought so much booty back with him; she awarded him enough to make him rich and used the rest to pay off much of England's foreign debt, and later knighted the sea dog. On the other hand, she may have wanted to hush up aspects of the trip that might have made the Spanish unhappy, for she seized Drake's logs and other papers, which haven't been seen since. The *Golden Hind* was displayed at Deptford on the Thames until broken up in the next century. Eight years later Drake sailed to victory against the Armada, and in 1596 died of dysentery on a Caribbean expedition.

Quite an adventure, quite a vivid personality. That alone would account for the interest in Drake's California sojourn. But historians, navigators, archaeologists, and anthropologists have also been interested in what was England's first claim to North America, in England's first structure and "colony" in the New World, in the first land exploration of California north of Ventura, and in the fantastic possibility that San Francisco Bay escaped all notice during 230 years of coastal exploration. Naturally, the principal question is, Where did Drake actually find his "faire and good Baye"?

Pinpointing the location would be easy if the logs or any on-site sketch maps existed. The principal evidence—*The World Encompassed* and similar accounts, most of them based on Fletcher's notes, along with Jodocus Hondius' crude 1595 "Portus Nova Albionis" map and a few other inspired maps—does not conclusively point to any one of dozens of possible landing sites in an area as far north as Oregon and as far south as San Luis Obispo. The three sites with the most active proponents at the moment are Drake's Bay (or Drake's Estero, an inlet off the bay) at Point Reyes; San Quentin Cove, in the lee of Point San Quentin at the outlet of Corte Madera Creek in San Francisco Bay; and Bolinas Lagoon.

The Drake's Bay advocates, led by Raymond Aker of the Drake Navigators Guild (Admiral Chester Nimitz was honorary chairman and spokesman), say that only Point Reyes has the remarkable Dover-like cliffs facing the sea, is both a "faire and good Baye" for careening a ship and a "conuenient and fit harborough" for watering and victualing, has the most noticeable difference between shore area and inland, and, most crucially, has the longest, most depressing summertime fogs.

The Bolinas Lagoon contingent, a smaller party, is led by V. Aubrey Neasham, a professional historian who has been regional historian for the National Park Service, among other positions, and has actually been excavating for Drake's fort, at one site or another, since 1947. At a gathering of Drake scholars during the quadricentennial, Neasham revealed what he has turned up at the latest site on the lagoon's west shore half a mile from Bolinas town: several badly corroded wrought-iron spikes, burned or decomposed (tent) pegs, and a hardpan layer

The White Cliffs of Point Reyes may have attracted Drake as they attract present-day visitors. (Redwood Empire Association)

that could have been the floor of an earthen fort. Found in layers above were Coast Miwok artifacts and nineteenth-century items. If this is Drake's fort (Neasham hasn't absolutely stated that it is, and digging continues), it would be the oldest English-built structure in the Western Hemisphere, six years older than Fort Raleigh on Roanoke Island, N.C., site of the "Lost Colony," whose disappearance has as much mystery and controversy as Drake's lost harbor.

The Point San Quentin proponents, led most vociferously by Robert H. Power, part-owner of the Nut Tree restaurant and a former president of the California Historical Society, say that the cove is an even better harbor, could have had sky-blotting fogs during the "little ice age" in Elizabethan times, and shows the closest correspondence to the Hondius map under sophisticated computer analysis. Furthermore, the plate of brass was found nearby.

Aha, a red herring.

"Plate of Brasse"

The scandal of the plate of brass began in 1936 when a young department-store employee named Beryle Shinn, whose veracity has never been seriously questioned, spotted a rectangular piece of tarnished metal in the ground near Greenbrae, 1.5 miles from Point San Quentin. Cleaning revealed an inscription:

BEE IT KNOWNE VNTO ALL MEN BY THESE PRESENTS
IVNE. 17. 1579.

BY THE GRACE OF GOD AND IN THE NAME OF HERR
MAIESTY QVEEN ELIZABETH OF ENGLAND AND HERR
SVCCESSORS FOREVER I TAKE POSSESSION OF THIS
KINGDOME WHOSE KING AND PEOPLE FREELY RESIGNE
THEIR RIGHT AND TITLE IN THE WHOLE LAND VNTO HERR
MAIESTIES KEEPEING NOW NAMED BY ME AN TO BEE
KNOWNE VNTO ALL MEN AS NOVA ALBION.

G FRANCIS DRAKE

In the lower right is a ragged hole, empty of sixpence. A famed University of California historian, Herbert E. Bolton, excitedly submitted it to lab tests and proclaimed it Drake's long-lost "plate of brasse"—which, coincidentally, he had always told his students to be on the lookout for.

The find seemed conclusive proof that Drake had sailed into and anchored in San Francisco Bay, if not in San Quentin Cove. But then stepped forward a man named William Caldeira, formerly a chauffeur for a vice-chairman of the Bank of America. Caldeira said that in 1933 he had found just that piece of metal while his boss was hunting—at Point Reyes, in the vicinity of the present seashore headquarters. Not finding a use for it, he tossed it away—half a mile or so from where Shinn found it later. That evidence pointed back to Drake's Bay. Although the plate is what archaeologists would call a portable artifact, it was generally accepted as the find of the century and put on display in Bancroft Library on the Berkeley campus, as the university's most prized possession.

It wasn't until 1974 that the plate was subjected to its harshest attack in decades. In the second volume of *The European Discovery of America,* the late Samuel Eliot Morison questioned the findings of the metallurgists in the 1930s, said the Elizabethan lettering was all wrong, and stated outright that the plate was "a hoax perpetrated by some collegiate joker." It was then reported that the president of the university in the 1930s had suppressed a secret report from a Princeton chemist who challenged the plate's authenticity. British scholars followed Admiral Morison in attacking the inscription, both wording and engraving. And in 1975 the university itself sent samples of the plate to labs at Berkeley, MIT, and Oxford. Two years later the reports came in: the metal had too much zinc and too little copper and lead for six-teenth-century brass; the plate in fact seemed like standard No. 8-gauge brass, made by the modern rolling-machine method rather than the sixteenth-century hammering method; and the plate appeared straight-cut with a modern guillotine shear, not with a chisel.

Stating that the tests for authenticity were "essentially negative," the Bancroft Library left the plate on display as an "item of interest." But Robert Power, with his argument in favor of San Quentin Cove par-tially hinging on the plate, remained unswerving in his belief in it. He contended that the labs did sloppy research and ignored contrary evi-dence of authenticity, such as the existence of other sixteenth-century brass with high zinc levels.

The library resubmitted the plate to more tests, including X-ray and light diffraction, and in May 1979, a month before the Drake quadri-centennial, reaffirmed the 1977 conclusions. James D. Hart, the li-brary director, admitted that "we can perhaps never say for certain that the plate is a hoax unless the perpetrators of the forgery come for-ward," but went on to say that "it is clear that the weight of scientific examination of the plate indicates beyond all reasonable doubt that it is of recent origin."

The revelation that the plate is akin to Piltdown Man and the Vin-land Map is merely the end of a single false trail: the question of where Drake anchored is still open.

Not surprisingly, no official body answered the question before the anniversary celebration. The California Historical Resources Commis-sion declared by a three-to-one vote that it was impossible to determine the landing site under the strict criteria of the landmarks law; the one nay-voter favored Drake's Bay. At a later meeting the irresolute com-mission members voted on three issues: two to two, with one absten-tion, defeating a motion to authorize a plaque; three to two in favor of a resolution stating the probability that Drake anchored in Drake's Bay; and five to nothing to rescind all action taken and postpone fur-ther decisions. The separate Sir Francis Drake Commission decided on vaguely worded plaques at two sites. On the anniversary, a huge stone boulder with a plaque of brass was unveiled at Drake's Bay by the bishop of London and the chief of the British naval staff; and a second plaque was dedicated, with less fanfare and fewer dignitaries, at the Vista Point on the north side of the Golden Gate Bridge.

If historians and politicians couldn't decide, could a lawyer, using rules of evidence from the courtroom? Taking on this challenge, San Francisco lawyer Warren L. Hanna, in *Lost Harbor* (Berkeley: University of California Press, 1979), reviewed the evidence in 17 categories—such as flora and fauna, the fogs, the white cliffs, navigation, and artifactual evidence—and the claims made for the three candidate sites. Without reaching a verdict himself, Hanna awarded 11 points to Drake's Estero (Drake's Bay), 9 to San Quentin Cove, and 4 to Bolinas Lagoon. But in 13 of the categories, Hanna found that the evidence didn't favor one site to the exclusion of the others.

So there it is. Or there it isn't. If you believe travel-guide writers, Drake's Bay is the place—but it really is a matter of belief.

Point Reyes never had much settlement. The Coast Miwoks, who had dozens of villages on the peninsula at one time, disappeared when the white man came. The first ranches weren't established until the early nineteenth century, and Point Reyes was left in its splendid rural isolation until recently. Even now, parts of the peninsula—mostly the southern area, south of Limantour Road—are so wild that there is some noise over designation of an official wilderness area, which would thwart the National Park Service in some of its plans for development.

Visiting Point Reyes

Near Olema is the **Point Reyes National Seashore Headquarters,** ** a good place to stop for information and a look at the exhibits. It's also the trailhead for the Bear Valley and most other trails (see below). The principal road in the park leaves Highway 1 farther north, at Point Reyes Station. **Sir Francis Drake Highway** goes past the town of Inverness on the shore of Tomales Bay and out to the point of the peninsula itself, serving Point Reyes Beach and Drake's Beach. Past Inverness there's a turnoff on **Pierce Point Road** to Tomales Bay State Park and on to McClure's Beach and the trail for Tomales Point. The third road is shorter: from park headquarters, take Bear Valley Road to **Limantour Road,** which leads you to the natural areas around Limantour Spit. Details on all these places follow.

Near the park headquarters, along with the previously mentioned **Earthquake Trail***** and the **Woodpecker Nature Trail*** (both self-guided), is the **Morgan Horse Farm*** where the National Park Service raises the smallish, intelligent, calm, Vermont-originated Morgans as pack and trail animals for rangers going into remoter parts of the park. Conveniently, the public gets a chance to observe horseshoeing, feeding, and so forth. New colts begin their four-year training in the spring. You can't ride a Morgan, but Five Brooks Stable (three miles south of Olema, 415/663-1510) and Bear Valley Stables (a mile north of headquarters on Bear Valley Road, 415/663-1570) will rent you other riding horses for about $20 for the day and give you directions for rides along the seashore.

A mile's walk from headquarters is **Kule Loklo**** ("bear valley"), a re-creation of a Miwok village that includes redwood and willowpole huts thatched with tules, a dance house, a sweat house (the Spanish called them *temescals*), and granaries. Miwok Archaeological Preserve volunteers show how to make stone tools, fish traps, and baskets.

Bear Valley and Coast Trails

One of the most popular trails in the Bay Area leaves from the trailhead parking lot near the headquarters: the **Bear Valley Trail,***** a 4.4-mile walk (or bike ride) that wanders across meadows and in the well-forested creek valley until it comes to the open, scrub-covered bluffs above the sea. Curiously, while the stream does come down to the sea, the walk or ride back inland is mostly downhill. Second most popular is the **Coast Trail,***** 13.3 miles from Palomarin (near Bolinas) to near Limantour Spit. Four trail camps (two on the coast, two on Inverness Ridge) are for hikers only; see "Marin Coast" in Part IV for details.

The peninsula is rather fine naturally, with many different habitats. Of the 72 mammal species, two of the most interesting were introduced: the fallow deer (from Europe and Asia) and the spotted axis deer (from India and Ceylon). The deer can be seen in the open meadows from the Estero and Muddy Hollow trails and are most easily spotted in October. There's controversy here, too: some believe the deer are too numerous, or should be removed as nonnative exotics.

A favorite pastime during the winter, particularly when the weather breaks nicely in February, is to sit on the ocean bluffs along the Coast Trail or out on the point and watch the California gray whales migrate south. Binoculars are handy.

Flower season begins in February, and can extend into July.

Beaches

Those with cars have an easier time exploring the beaches, which are all open to the public except for the Headlands Research Natural Area. The most amazing waves and surf, with an unsurprising absence of swimmers and waders, are at **McClure's Beach**** (Pierce Point Road 9 miles north of Drake Boulevard) and along the knife-edge-straight, 10- or 12-mile-long **Point Reyes Beach*** (access mainly from parking areas 11 and 14 miles from seashore headquarters). McClure's has tide pools at low tide, Point Reyes Beach nothing but a vast and lonely and windswept strand, good for jacket-clad solitude and for beachcombing after a storm. Near the shore RCA, AT and T, and the coast guard have big overseas receiving antennas. Picnickers and other gregarious visitors will do better at some of the little beaches on the Tomales Bay shore, particularly **Heart's Desire Beach**** in **Tomales Bay State Park**** (off Pierce Point Road, 415/663-1140), which has a parking fee, or **Drake's Beach***** (two miles off Drake Boulevard), which has a snack bar. You might even see a sunbather. Here are the white cliffs that may have reminded Drake of Dover.

The very end of Drake Boulevard is at the **Point Reyes Light Station,***** or, rather, above it, for you'll have to walk down no fewer than 304 steps, or maybe 429 steps, to see the thousand-faceted, pineapple-shaped, second-order Fresnel-lensed light that since 1870 has been warning ships that this is one of the foggiest, most dangerous shores in America. When the fog is too dense, rangers even close the stairs. Captain Sebastian Rodriguez Cermeno's *San Agustin* in 1595 had the dubious honor of becoming the California coast's first recorded shipwreck when it hit rocks near Drake's Beach. The heroic Cermeno and his crew fabricated a launch from the pieces on Limantour Spit and sailed down to Mexico. Lighthouse information: 415/669-1534.

Now, that hints of the one problem with Point Reyes that keeps it from being as popular as Fisherman's Wharf: the weather, which is mostly awful, especially in the summer, when the coastal fogs (which make San Francisco so photogenic) clamp down and make not only a sweater but a warm coat very desirable. Remember that while inland points, even only a few miles away on Highway 101, can have record-breaking summertime heat, the coast can be cold and foggy, as Drake and his men found. Ironically, some of the best weather—sunny and clear—is during the winter.

Point Reyes Seashore information: 415/663-1092, 669-1250.

Towns, Too

The towns hereabouts are small (**Olema** is so small we're not sure it exists) and peaceful (even **Point Reyes Station,*** West Marin's commercial center). **Inverness,***** on Tomales Bay, is a hideaway-vacation village with some unusual attractions: the best Czech restaurant around, Manka's (see "Marin Coast" in Part IV); **Johnson's Oyster Farm,** Sir Francis Drake Blvd. (415/669-1149); and one of the two Shaker furniture workshops in the U.S., **Shaker Workshops West,** at 5 Inverness Way (669-7256; catalogue for $1). Inverness gives its name to a **music festival** every summer, the concerts being held here and elsewhere in Marin (information: 415/457-3750).

Samuel P. Taylor State Park

Just a couple of miles east of Olema, on the other side of Bolinas Ridge, is a redwood park, **Samuel P. Taylor State Park,*** whose campsites are much in demand because they're among the only ones so close to San Francisco. The redwoods grow in the dark creek bottom while the park's more open woodlands and meadows are on the canyon's dry north side.

Park information: 415/488-9897.

Tomales Bay

Continuing north on Highway 1 you'll follow the shore of the drowned mouth of a rift valley, **Tomales Bay.***** A 16-mile-long fjordlike bay, it is remarkable for its many redwood-fenced commercial oyster beds, salt marshes, and mud flats. You can tour the **Tomales Bay Oyster Company** (415/663-1242) Wed.-Sun. 9-5. A few small towns, like **Marshall,** summer homes on piers, and **Miller County Park** (launching ramp, picnic area) are the only attractions in miles of countryside below Bolinas Ridge until the highway bends inland to **Tomales,** where a side road goes to the summer colony at **Dillon Beach.** From there is an unpaved toll road to **Lawson's Landing,** a resort known for the clam-rich bars that are exposed at low tide; call 707/878-2443 for information on clamming trips. Tomales Bay boaters should watch for fog and "sneaker waves."

The Marin Coast ends at the Estero Americano, which is the Sonoma County line.

PRACTICAL INFORMATION

Getting There, Getting Around

Marin is both suburban and rural, but you need not have a car to get there and, within reason, get around with efficiency. There's good ferry service from San Francisco to three Marin points popular with tourists, and there's regular bus service (at least on weekends) from The City to the Marin Headlands, Muir Woods, Mt. Tamalpais, Stinson Beach, Bolinas, Point Reyes National Seashore Headquarters (shuttle from there), Point Reyes Station, and Inverness. Details below.

Air: San Francisco International Airport, though 20 miles away, is Marin's airport too—at least until the fate of Hamilton Field is decided. The **Marin Airporter** bus runs between SFO and Sausalito, Greenbrae, Terra Linda, and Novato. Information: 415/461-4222.

Buses: The main bus system is run by **Golden Gate Transit,** using tolls from the Golden Gate Bridge. GGT is largely geared to commuters, but tourists can certainly take advantage of frequent service between San Francisco and Marin and Sonoma counties. Fares range from 50 cents to $2.25, based on a six-zone system. Information: 1011 Andersen Dr., San Rafael 94901; 415/332-6600 (San Francisco and southern Marin), 415/453-2100 (northern Marin), 707/544-1323 (Sonoma). The major GGT transfer point is San Rafael (4th and Hetherton); the Larkspur Ferry Terminal is a major focal point. (See below under "Ferries" for bus-ferry connections.)

- *64*, a major route of tourist interest, runs twice daily on weekends and most holidays, from San Francisco Zoo (46th Avenue and Sloat)–Sloat Boulevard–19th Avenue–Golden Gate Park (stopping at Lincoln Way and at Fulton)–25th Avenue Lincoln Boulevard–toll plaza, then Highway 101 across Golden Gate Bridge to Marin City and Greenbrae, then Sir Francis Drake Boulevard through San Anselmo–Fairfax–Woodacre to Samuel P. Taylor State Park–Olema–Point Reyes Seashore HQ–Point Reyes Station–Inverness. It's two hours from the zoo to Inverness. Catching the first bus from the zoo or another city stop to Point Reyes Seashore HQ (where there's a shuttle to the trailheads and Drake's Beach) and catching the last bus back would give you seven hours at Point Reyes.
- *63* runs 11 times a day on weekends and most holidays from Marin City–Manzanita parking lot–Tam Junction–Mountain Home–Boot Jack–Pan Toll (these three stops are on Mt. Tam)–Stinson Beach Park HQ, continuing four times a day to Audubon Canyon Ranch and Bolinas.
- *61* runs weekends and most holidays from Larkspur Ferry Terminal (connecting with ferry arrivals/departures)–Tam Junction–Muir Beach Junction–Muir Woods visitors' center.

- *62,* a commute route, runs once in the morning from Bolinas-Stinson Beach-Pan Toll-Tam Junction-Marin City-San Francisco Civic Center, the other direction in the evening.

San Francisco's **Muni** has a new bus, 76-Fort Cronkhite, running hourly on weekends from spring into fall from Southern Pacific depot (4th and Townsend)-3rd Street-Sutter-Van Ness-Lombard-Golden Gate Bridge-Marin Headlands-Fort Cronkhite, with the first run from the City about 9:30 A.M., last run from Fort Cronkhite at 7:30 P.M. Fare: 50 cents (cheap). Information: 415/673-MUNI.

As mentioned, the **National Park Service** has been running a shuttle bus from Point Reyes Seashore HQ to major trailheads and Drake's Beach. Information: 415/556-0560 (San Francisco), 415/663-1092 (Pt. Reyes).

A firm called **Traveler's Transit** has service nine times daily between San Rafael (4th and Hetherton) and Richmond (BART and Greyhound depot) across the bay. Information: 415/457-7080.

Ferries: Marin has three ferry terminals:

- Larkspur: **Golden Gate Ferry,** which is also supported by bridge revenues, speeds between the San Francisco Ferry Building (foot of Market) and the Larkspur Ferry Terminal 13 times daily during the week, 4 times a day weekends and most holidays. Connecting Golden Gate Transit buses: 1 (basic all-day route), 19 (connects with ferry arrivals/departures), 61 (likewise, but only on weekends and most holidays, going to Muir Woods), and the commute-period 15, 25, 29, 31, 37, 41, and 51. Fare: $1.50. Information: see GGT bus information numbers above.

- Sausalito: **Golden Gate Ferry** has a separate run between the Ferry Building in San Francisco and the Sausalito Ferry Terminal (Humboldt Street) nine times daily on weekdays, eight times daily weekends and most holidays. Connecting GGT buses: 3, 5, 10. Fare: $1.50. Information: see GGT bus information numbers above.

- Tiburon: **Harbor Carriers** (Red & White Fleet) has two Tiburon routes: commuter service to the San Francisco Ferry Building weekdays during commute periods; tourist service to Angel Island and to Fisherman's Wharf (Pier 41) daily in summer, weekends and most holidays all year. Fare: $4 round trip. Information: 415/546-2815. Connecting GGT buses: 9 and 11 (Tiburon Ferry Terminal), 8 and 10 (Tiburon Boulevard and

Main). **Tiburon-Angel Island Ferry,** a smaller operation, sails daily in summer, weekends and most holidays all year. Information: 415/435-2131.

Conducted tours: The Sausalito–Muir Woods bus tour is probably as popular as a cable-car ride. **Gray Line,** 415/771-4000, has a 3½-hour tour twice a day, March into November, from the Trans-Bay Terminal in San Francisco, for $7.25 per adult, about half as much for a child. Following in the exhaust of the Gray Line: **Muir Wood Tour Co.** (415/775-5200); **Great Pacific Tour Co.** (415/929-1700); and **In-Sights,** Box 984, Larkspur 94939 (415/924-2272), which is a personalized guide service to anywhere you want. **Commodore Helicopters** (415/332-4482), will take you up over the Golden Gate Bridge and Marin Headlands for a few minutes and a few bucks.

Bicycling: You can pedal across the Golden Gate Bridge (east sidewalk only) from the south and north Vista Points 6 A.M.-9 P.M. or so; it's a breezy, noisy ride; be careful of pedestrians. Northbound bikers can continue down into Sausalito. The Richmond–San Rafael Bridge is closed to biking but Traveler's Transit buses (see above) have bike racks. The safe, scenic long-distance route from Marin is on Caltrans' Pacific Coast Bicentennial Route: Golden Gate Bridge–Sausalito lateral–Bridgeway–Highways 101 and 1 bike paths–Casa Buena Drive–Tamalpais Drive–Magnolia Avenue–College Avenue–Sir Francis Drake Boulevard–Highway 1. Information and route booklet: 415/557-1840 (San Francisco) and other Caltrans offices. Hardy bike tourists are allowed along the 101 corridor, either on the roadway or on a separate pathway next to it. Many loop tours are possible in Marin. Best areas: Sausalito, Strawberry Point, Tiburon Peninsula, Angel Island (ferry from San Francisco and Tiburon), Point San Pedro past China Camp, Point Reyes Seashore, and many West Marin farm roads. The Marin Headlands, Mt. Tamalpais, and Muir Woods are hilly and roads are narrow-to-dangerous. Bicycle rental: Viking Ventures, Blackfield Drive and Tiburon Boulevard (Cove Shopping Center), Tiburon (415/388-0800).

Where to Stay and Eat

Accommodations (including camping and hostels) and restaurants are listed in Part IV under these headings: Marin Coast; Mill Valley/Mt. Tamalpais; San Rafael/Northern Marin; and Sausalito/Bayside Marin.

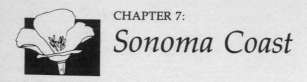

CHAPTER 7:

Sonoma Coast

HIGHLIGHTS

Bodega / 209
Bodega Bay / 209
Sonoma Coast State Beaches / 210
Russian River Mouth, Jenner / 211
Fort Ross / 211

Salt Point State Park / 213
Kruse Rhododendron
  Reserve / 213
Sea Ranch / 213
Gualala Point Park / 214

The coast of Sonoma County is the coast pure, unsophisticated, scenically dramatic, not much adorned with population or development, except near Bodega Bay. It can be traveled for the spectacular and steep coastal bluffs, offshore sea stacks, and hidden pocket beaches—many of them in the necklace of Sonoma Coast State Beaches. There are some individual sights of great interest, such as Fort Ross, Russia's imperial outpost in California in the last century; a rhododendron reserve; a giant statue to peace by San Francisco's late left-wing sculptor and wildman, Benny Bufano; and several picturesque villages. The Sonoma coast was where another crazyman artist, Christo, ran his Running Fence into the sea in 1976. And many people seem to know that Bodega Bay was the scene of the 1962 filming of Alfred Hitchcock's scary *The Birds*. All very interesting and quite, quite photogenic.

WHAT TO SEE AND DO

Having continued on Highway 1 north, you left Marin County a few miles after leaving Tomales Bay. Crossing the Estero Americano, you'll enter the dairy-farming community of **Valley Ford,** where the high-

Sonoma Coast near Timber Cove as photographed by Ansel Adams for the Redwood Empire Association.

way—always two-lane and probably to remain so—bends toward the sea again. In a few miles, detour a bit to the right on Bodega Highway to the town of **Bodega,** named for Lieutenant Juan Francisco de la Bodega y Cuadra, who in 1775 charted the bay that also bears his name. As usual, the Spanish place-names often honor those who merely pass through. It was not the Spanish but the Russians who tried to settle this windy shore. Close to the present Bodega was the Russian settlement of Kuskov, founded by Captain Ivan Kuskov sometime after he and his band of Aleut fur-hunters landed in 1808. Crops grown in this area for 30 years were shipped to other Russian outposts in Alaska. Both Captain Kuskov and his town have disappeared. Bodega has two fine churches and the very good-looking old **Potter School,** now housing an art gallery. Look also for the **Yesterdays' Museum,** Bodega Highway, displaying Americana. Farther off Highway 1 is the old **Watson District School** (1856), a small county park with picnicking.

Bodega Bay

Continue on Highway 1 five miles to the coast, past the unfortunate **Bodega Harbour** subdivision into the unfortunately developing **Bo-**

dega Bay** town. This is on silt-clogged Bodega Bay, which is ringed by a superb system of marshes, mud flats, and other biologically productive wetlands. The bay is almost enclosed by a narrow sandspit containing **Doran County Park*** and a wider, rocky headland, on which are **Westside County Park**** and the **Bodega Marine Life Refuge.** The tip of the headland has the "hole in Bodega Head," famous for an environmental controversy. In the early 1960s Pacific Gas and Electric dug a 72-foot-deep hole into the granite bedrock for a proposed nuclear power plant but reluctantly abandoned it after a couple of years of protest and the revelation that the San Andreas Fault is only a quarter of a mile away. It is now "the world's most expensive duck pond." You can visit the University of California's **Bodega Marine Laboratory** (707/875-3511) Fridays 2-4 p.m.

The bicycling is good on the side roads around Bodega Bay, but Highway 1 can be a bit choked on weekends in the summer. Both the county parks (small user-fees) have boat ramps and camping, while Doran has a beach and clamming and Westside has fishing. Park information: 707/875-3540. Bodega Bay's **piers and 200 fishing boats**** (it's the busiest fishing harbor between San Francisco and Fort Bragg) are good subjects for photographers; party fishermen unload and clean between 1 and 2:30. The **Bodega Bay Fisherman's Festival** is in April (information: 707/875-3836).

Sonoma Coast State Beaches

Squeezing your way out of town to the north, you'll come to the first segment of the **Sonoma Coast State Beaches,***** Salmon Creek Beach; 14 miles north, at the mouth of the Russian River, is the fifteenth segment, Goat Rock Beach, on a spit of land opposite Jenner. Most of the beaches can't be seen from the road, so you'll have to do some walking down the cliffs, on marked trails. Some of the beach names are charming: Schoolhouse, Portuguese, Blind, Arched Rock, Goat Rock. Photography and fishing are the principal attractions, but there is camping (at two locations), picnicking, and beachcombing. State Beaches information: 707/875-3483 or -3382. Try to ignore the summer homes that local authorities allowed to be built on some bluff edges before the California Coastal Commission started putting a stop to that sort of nonsense in 1973.

Highway 1 follows the edge of the coastal shelf north to the mouth of the **Russian River,***** which Captain Kuskov named the Slavianka.

At the mouth is the small town of **Jenner,** * built on a coastal hillside. Up the river, around Guerneville and Monte Rio, is a busy summer resort area (see Chapter 5 for details); its main road, Highway 116, is the principal Sonoma County road to the coast. The Cazadero Highway–Fort Ross Road is a quieter, more hilly way to get from the 101 freeway to the coast, but you'd miss the dramatic cliffside road between Russian Gulch, north of Jenner, and Fort Ross.

Fort Ross

We've avoided talking much about the Russians because we wanted to get to **Fort Ross,** *** the main historical attraction along this coast. Here is the main site of Imperial Russia's attempt from 1812 to 1841 to establish a California foothold from its bases in Alaska (Sitka and Kodiak). In 1806, the czar's chamberlain, Count Nikolai Rezanov, found the Russian colonists at Sitka suffering from scurvy and fever, and decided to seek a permanent source of food in some fertile country to the south. He sailed to San Francisco to negotiate a trade agreement with the Spanish authorities. He was successful—but here the travelogue must be interrupted for a historical romance.

In San Francisco Count Rezanov also won the heart of Concepción (or Concha) Arguello, daughter of the San Francisco Presidio's comandante. Rezanov left for Russia, where he was to try to obtain dispensation to marry Concha. He never returned; Concha waited. She turned away suitors, and finally joined an order of nuns to care for the poor and sick during travels up and down Alta California. In Monterey, while attending a dinner for the visiting manager of the Hudson's Bay Company, Concha learned that Rezanov had died in 1807 in Siberia. Here is how Bret Harte—one of many writers who have used the tale—ended his verses:

> . . . the formal speeches ended, and amidst the laugh and wine,
> Some one spoke of Concha's lover—heedless of the warning sign.
> Quickly then cried Sir George Simpson: "Speak no ill of him
>   I pray!
> He is dead. He died, poor fellow, forty years ago this day—
> Died while speeding home to Russia, falling from a fractious horse.
> Left a sweetheart, too, they tell me. Married, I suppose,
>   of course!
> Lives she yet?" A deathlike silence fell on banquet, guest,
>   and hall,
> And a trembling figure rising fixed the awe-struck gaze of all.

Two black eyes in darkened orbits gleamed beneath the nun's white hood;
Black serge hid the wasted figure, bowed and stricken where it stood.
"Lives she yet?" Sir George repeated. All were hushed as Concha drew
Closer yet her nun's attire. "Señor, pardon, she died, too!"

Concha didn't die until 1857, aged 66, a Dominican sister, at the convent in Benicia.

Meanwhile, because of the success of Rezanov's trade mission, in 1809 Captain Kuskov of the Russian-American Fur Company arrived on the Sonoma coast for the purposes of otter hunting, crop growing, and trade. Fort Ross (the word is derived from *Rossiya*) was started in 1812, and became the center of activities. On the bluff above tiny Fort Ross Cove, the Russians erected a strong, 14-foot redwood palisade, two blockhouses (one eight-sided, the other seven-sided), quarters for the commander, a chapel, and seven other buildings, and installed 40 guns. Outside the fort were perhaps 50 other buildings. The original colony numbered 100 Russians and 80 Aleuts, and it grew to a total of perhaps 400. The seas were harvested for otter pelts, the river valleys for grain and vegetables. In time, both the Mexican authorities and the American government in Washington grew worried over the Russian presence but it was, in the end, gophers in the fields, the extermination of sea otters, and the lack of profit that led to the fur company's decision to evacuate the Sonoma coast. They sold Fort Ross to John A. Sutter, the Swiss-American who had built his fort and trading post at Sacramento, and in 1841 sailed back to Sitka. Only 26 years later the Russians sold Alaska as well, to the U.S.

What the Russians left behind suffered from neglect and destruction. Most buildings fell down, the chapel collapsed in the 1906 earthquake. The state took it over that year and started restoration in the 1950s. Two arson fires in 1970 and 1971 (rumoredly linked to the issue of Jewish immigration from Russia) destroyed the reconstructed chapel and damaged the commander's quarters, seven-sided blockhouse, and stockade. Again there was restoration (some blueprints from archives in Moscow were used) and the historic park reopened with fanfare in 1974. It makes an interesting visit. Don't neglect the museum exhibits (spartan) and a look down the bluff at Fort Ross Cove; try to imagine how men managed to load lumber and offload cargo. There's picnicking but it can be very breezy here. Fort Ross information: 707/847-3286.

North of Fort Ross

Just north of Fort Ross, as the road becomes rather more tame than it was south of the fort, is **Timber Cove,** where the Timber Cove Inn gives refuge to an eight-story **sculpture of Peace*** by San Francisco's late Beniamino Bufano. Frankly, the sculpture sticks out, inappropriately vertical (not to say political) for this setting. There are two more coves: **Stillwater Cove,** site of a county park (picnicking, fishing, skindiving; 707/847-3245), and **Ocean Cove,** where you can pay a so-called trespass fee to get to the water—how nice.

Don't bother trespassing, for only a mile north is the rapidly developing 4,100-acre **Salt Point State Park.***** West of the road the park covers 3.7 miles of coastal shelf, headlands, tidepools, and some small beaches (snorkeling, scuba diving, beachcombing, rock fishing, camping); east of the road are uplands and a bishop pine forest. Salt Point information: 707/847-3221. Adjoining Salt Point to the north is the **Kruse Rhododendron Reserve**** (be alert for the entrance about three miles from Salt Point), a 300-acre state park set aside for the native California rosebay (*Rhododendron macrophyllum*), the pink-flowering (April to June) shrub that differs from the creamy white-flowering *R. occidentale* (western azalea), which is also to be found in this neighborhood (the Azalea State Reserve is near Arcata in Humboldt County). No picnicking, just strolling on the nature trail beneath arches of 20-foot-high rosebay bushes. Information: 707/865-2391.

The Kruse Ranch road continues into the hills, where at the town of Plantation it runs into Seaview Road, which runs into Fort Ross Road, which leads to Cazadero and the Russian River. County roads, like these, while scenic, are not always terrifically maintained. Farther along, at the diminishing village of **Stewart's Point,** once a busy lumber port, is the turnoff on Stewart's Point Road; this will take you to Skaggs Spring Road, a tortuous 45-mile route all the way to Geyserville, on the 101 freeway, or to Annapolis Road, a 20-mile semicircle through the uplands and backwoods back to the coast near the Sea Ranch.

Sea Ranch

The Sonoma coast does not end happily except for architecture buffs: the last 10-mile stretch of Highway 1 to Gualala is occupied by the

largest second-home development on the North Coast, **Sea Ranch.****
The authors admit to a great deal of prejudice against Sea Ranch and
most other residential development on the coast; one of us went to work
for the Coastal Commission as editor of the *Coastal Plan* (1975), just to
play some role in controlling the ruinous development of the coast typi-
fied by Sea Ranch. Ruinous? Such award-winning architecture? Such
design controls? Such Beautiful People decorating the highway with
their BMWs and Jaguars and Sevilles? Such public-spirited generosity
from a developer as the donation of 150 acres for a county park? Well,
yes. Without the controls exerted by the Coastal Commission, the public would be denied access to 10 miles of public tideland (that's a sizable percentage of the physically accessible tideland on the entire
coast); many of the 300,000 trees, when mature, would block views
from along a public highway; the subdivision, if built to 5,200 houses,
would so clog Highway 1 with even more Mercedes as to create both
bumper-to-bumper traffic and the need to widen the highway or build
a new lateral through the hills from the 101 freeway; and build-out
would threaten the quality of coastal water.

On the credit side, the developers, Oceanic California (Castle and
Cooke), when starting up in the 1960s, retained landscape architect
and city planner Lawrence Halprin to draw up a master plan and numerous design restrictions—all-underground utilities, well-designed
homes or condominiums to be clustered or individually sited, half the
area to be kept in natural open space, etc. Most of the 1,765 lots sold
until 1975 were to those who could well afford architectural services,
and they hired such prominent firms as Moore and Turnbull and Joseph Esherick's to design many of the first 350 houses and condos, most
of them in the Cut-Out Vertical Box or Grain Elevator Modern style.
The *Guide to Architecture in San Francisco and Northern California*
provides a helpful map and a list of 30 of the most notable buildings;
the authors of that guide especially admire the 10-unit **Condominium
1**** (Moore, Lyndon Turnbull, Whitaker, 1965). The most visible
structure to the passing motorist is the complex housing the **Sea Ranch
Lodge, restaurant, general store, and land office**** (Esherick, 1965;
additions 1970). Sea Ranch information: 707/785-2411.

As mentioned, the developers donated **Gualala Point County
Park**** (visitors' center with exhibits, also fishing, picnicking, camp-
ing), just opposite the town of Gualala, which is in the next chapter.
Park information: 707/785-2377.

PRACTICAL INFORMATION

Getting There, Getting Around

There is virtually no public transportation and, as hinted, there's only one major road, Highway 1. It's wide enough for ordinary cars, and experienced touring bicyclists have been known to dare the curves south of Fort Ross (best to ride north so you're on the rocky inside, not the empty outside). The only numbered lateral highway to and from the coastal road is Highway 116 along the Russian River from the mouth, at Jenner. Several local roads go inland, and make good excursions for those with time. See a county map.

Sea Ranch has an airstrip. Of course.

Where to Stay and Eat

Accommodations (including camping) and restaurants are listed in Part IV under the heading Sonoma Coast. See also Marin Coast; Gualala/Southern Mendocino Coast; and Guerneville/Lower Russian River.

CHAPTER 8:

Mendocino Coast

HIGHLIGHTS

Gualala / 218
Point Arena / 219
Manchester State Beach / 219
Navarro River Valley / 219
Hendy Woods State Park / 220
Boonville / 220
Heritage House / 220
Pygmy Forest / 220
Van Damme State Park / 221
Mendocino / 221
Mendocino Headlands / 223

Russian Gulch State Park / 223
Caspar / 224
Jug Handle Creek / 224
Botanical Garden / 225
Noyo Flat / 225
Fort Bragg / 225
Skunk Train / 226
Georgia-Pacific Mill / 227
Ten-Mile Beach / 227
MacKerricher State Park / 228
Westport / 228

The visitor to Mendocino may feel the frontier as strongly as he feels the wind. The look of the frontier is exemplified by the false-fronted buildings that line the wooden sidewalk on Main Street in Mendocino village. The spirit of the frontier is evident in the people who live in these parts: for sheer orneriness and fractiousness, they match the Dodge City cowpokes who were always trying to get Marshal Dillon's goat.

The loggers of Fort Bragg, for instance. Driving their enormous redwood lumber rigs to or past the speed limit on public highways (even ones with R-shaped turns) must be the perfect exercise of freedom; on the private logging roads the lack of speed limits and weight restrictions is perhaps made more thrilling by driving on the left. On weekends, they lean against their campers—the ones with the "Sierra Club Kiss My Axe" bumper stickers—and, Coors in hand, look sardonically at strangers.

Hiding in free-form constructions in the backwoods of Mendocino are several thousand of the century's romantic outlaws: back-to-the-land counterculturists who have fled the wickedness of San Francisco and Los Angeles and New York and now resist public health officials and building inspectors who would interfere with their rugged, free lives, which are unhampered by flush toilets and other conveniences of the twentieth century. They grow so much marijuana that the local agricultural commissioner included pot in his official 1980 crop report. The children of these outlaws are named Strawberry and Joshua and Sunshine.

Even the conservatives around here are of a peculiar stripe: city artists who rode into dilapidated Mendocino town some years ago, brightly painted some of the weather-beaten gray Carpenter Gothic houses, and now shoot verbal bullets at outlanders—that is, *city slickers*—who tear into town on weekends to disturb the isolation and—what's worse—encourage development. The bumper stickers that *they* have say "Don't Carmel-ize Mendocino."

One is not surprised to learn of the 1974–75 Mendocino secession movement. Although founded with a declaration containing bitter comments about the Sacramento bureaucrats (the Coastal Commission is, however, in San Francisco) who "eat away our tax money and initiative," the secession's opening shot was a beer-blast at the Heeser Fishing Access.

Dislike of outsiders is about the only thing the Fort Bragg lumbermen and the Mendocino artists (those are labels) have in common. As one acerb resident has written, "Telephone prefixes are very important on the coast . . . Fort Bragg is the 964 prefix. This indicates stability, steady employment, short haircuts, trimmed lawns, whist, bingo, and cribbage. Mendocino's 937, on the other hand, implies long hair, smoking of pot, too many accounts-receivable, and the playing of guitars while hawking cheap jewelry on Main Street."

Recently, people in Mendocino were greatly exercised again—and divided again—on the subject of sidewalk artists and vendors. One side was claiming that tourists were attracted by uniqueness, while the other side was asserting that "the cashmere sweater type of tourist" was being driven away by all the public peddling. The county board of supervisors sided with the establishment shopkeepers and banned the vendors.

With such divisiveness the Mendocino secession movement was thus bound to fail.* Luckily, Mendocino and its coast are still part of California, for it does provide a different experience. And there are many who hang out the welcome sign for those who come from foreign parts to sample the comfort of country inns and the good eating, the giant redwoods and steelhead fishing holes, the picture-taking opportunities across sheep-dotted coastal meadows toward an ocean that angrily smashes against sea stacks, browsing in shops and galleries in Mendocino city, walking and bicycling up the Little River and Russian Gulch, the long drive from the lighthouse at windy Point Arena north to the ghost town of Rockport, picnicking and beachcombing, and visits to both an "ecological staircase" and a pygmy forest.

WHAT TO SEE AND DO

The Mendocino Coast stretches from the Gualala River north to Point No Pass. **Gualala*** town, like nearly every other North Coast settlement, was once a lumber port, and like many, had a lumber mill. Until the advent of logging trucks in the late 1930s, lumber was transferred from the coastal bluffs to waiting schooners in small coves either by means of greased slip-chutes or wire chutes. Set up for each ship, a wire chute was a cable along which was winched a sling holding as much as an entire wagonload of lumber. You can still see the remains of these contraptions here and there. Historical anecdotage along this coast largely concerns some aspect of the journey of wood—redwood, Douglas fir—from the forest to the lumber mill to the ships. Each locality's story ends dismally: eventually, the forest was logged out, the mill was closed and dismantled, and the ships didn't call again; sometimes the town burned down. Gualala survives as a minor tourist town, with restored Victorian hotel and an art center. In the town is the turnoff onto the **Ten Mile—Iverson—Old Stage Road,** which takes you through the lower Coastal Range elevations to Point Arena.

Small **Anchor Bay** has a camping resort that provides one of the

---

* The local state senator has authored legislation to split California into North and South, but Mendocinans like San Francisco about as much as Los Angeles.

only accesses to the shoreline in this stretch of tree-obscured coast. Off Anchor Bay are the **Fish Rocks,** often populated by sea lions.

Point Arena

Ten miles along Highway 1 the coastal shelf broadens into big dairy pastures around **Point Arena**, a town now largely divorced from the sea since its unprotected harbor is no longer a busy lumber port. A left turn into Lighthouse Road takes you out past another sea lion habitat, **Sea Lion Rocks,** to **Point Arena**** proper, a 40-foot-high headland surmounted by the 115-foot-high **lighthouse** (open weekends, holidays). This is one of the windiest spots in the U.S. (on this coast one awful night, November 20, 1865, no fewer than 10 ships met some form of misfortune), so the lighthouse, established in 1870, has one of the most powerful lights on the coast. PG and E abandoned plans for a nuclear power plant here because of earthquake hazard but may build something more appropriate: a wind-powered generating station.

Beyond Lighthouse Road is a turnoff right on **Mountain View Road,** a zigzagging alternative route to Boonville and Ukiah.

One of the largest state beaches in the area runs seven miles north of the lighthouse. The road to windy **Manchester State Beach** (picnicking, camping, surf fishing) is in the missable town of **Manchester**. About a mile north of Manchester the San Andreas Fault goes out to sea, leaving California behind. The road is not interesting for the next seven miles, past the **Irish Beach** vacation home subdivision, to the nifty village of **Elk,**** which has a rustic café that never seems to be open, also two inns, the first of many good ones on this part of the coast.

Navarro River Valley

From Elk, and from the Navarro River mouth six miles north, are parallel roads to Philo and Hendy Woods State Park. **Greenwood Road** is a twisting 18 miles but more interesting is **Highway 128**** along the Navarro River and through Boonville to Highway 101.

The valley of the Navarro River (good steelhead and salmon fishing in fall and winter) is still rich with redwoods, but Navarro and Philo are no longer active lumber towns. **Navarro's** mill had a thousand workers but closed in the 1930s; fire later razed much of the town, whose present population is quite scattered. Near **Philo,*** which is a small art colony and market town, are two redwood parks: 15-acre **Indian Creek State Reserve*** (picnicking, walking) and 605-acre

Hendy Woods State Park** (picnicking, camping, swimming, fishing, hiking in the groves, riding). Park information: 707/895-3141. Eight miles south on Highway 128 is the biggest town hereabouts, **Boonville,*** a farming and ranching center that hosts several events but is more generally known for its local parlance, a funny language called Boontling, which originated in the 1880s lumber camps. Some Boont words are appropriated (a big moustache is a "Tom Bacon" after one wearer of a legendary handlebar), some are telescopings (a rail fence is a "relf"), and some are of whole cloth (coffee is "zeese" and good food is "bahl gorms"). The county Chamber of Commerce has published an official Boontling cookbook-vocabulary so Boonters won't try to put on tourists. South of Boonville is **Mailliard Redwoods State Reserve** (picnicking only).

Little River Area

The more populated part of the coast begins at **Albion,*** a small fishing-harbor town to be found below the highway. It was named by an Englishman, William A. Richardson, Yerba Buena's first settler, but Albion has more recently been called "Little New York"—because of the accents of some of the latter-day escapees from city to country.

Just a mile north of Albion, at what must be the finest single site on the whole coast, is **Heritage House,***** most expensive of the several inns in the **Little River** area. Lunch or dinner here, not terribly expensive, provides a good excuse to stroll around the well-landscaped grounds. Except for one scene the movie *Same Time Next Year* (1978) was entirely filmed at Heritage House.

Look for a sign on the right near Little River pointing to the Mendocino County Airport, and take that road 3.5 miles to the **Pygmy Forest,***** part of Van Damme State Park. Here, because of the incredibly leached, hard, white-gray soil that the Russians called *podsol*, the underlying hardpan that keeps roots from going deep, and the poor drainage, vegetation is "bonsai-ed," or kept dwarf by nature. A 60-year-old Mendocino cypress, which outside the park can be 50 feet high, here may be only a foot high and a quarter of an inch in diameter. Many of the cypresses (*Cupressus pygmaea*, found only here and near Anchor Bay) are more than 100 years old. Intermixed are dwarf Bolander pines that are perhaps as high as 10 feet, rhododendrons, bishop pines, and dwarf manzanita. The environmental threat here is an ironic one: rich sewage from nearby houses may make the trees grow! A guide pamphlet to the short nature trail is available. Stay on the trail.

Go back to Highway 1, past the **Little River** settlement and **Little River Inn*** (the 1853 Silas Coombs House), to get to the main entrance of **Van Damme State Park,***** which comprises nearly all the watershed of the Little River. Because the area was logged by 1893, nearly all the redwoods and Douglas fir are second-growth, but nonetheless attractive. The **Fern Canyon***** nature trail (walking and good bicycling) shows you where the log ponds and skid trails were, but they may not be apparent under the lush cover of ferns (western sword, five-finger, lady, goldback licorice, stamp, wood, bird's-foot, and deer ferns), red alders, madrone, tan oak, chinquapin, rhododendron, huckleberry, and other flora. Van Damme has camping and picnicking and, at the river mouth, a beach. Park information: 707/937-0851. Van Damme is closed mid-Sept. to mid-May.

Big River is good for canoeing and kayaking—you can go upstream with the tide; Catch A Canoe, Box 686, Mendocino (707/937-0273) rents 15- and 17-footers.

Mendocino

Just a mile on, across Mendocino Bay and Big River, is your first view of **Mendocino***** ("city" or "village" are often appended to distinguish it from the county), a collection of Victorian wooden buildings clustered on a green headland. One glimpse at the quaintness of this fine location, and you can't be surprised that it attracted city-bred artists a couple of decades ago. Particularly since the founding of the Mendocino Art Center in 1959 the town has had a rebirth that sometimes threatens to consume it.

But there's lots of irony hereabouts, for the town was founded in exploitation: a rapacious pioneer San Franciscan, Harry Meiggs, sent a party north in 1851 seeking salvage from a stranded vessel carrying oriental silk; when they brought back word of rich redwood forests, Meiggs assembled mill machinery and lumber workers and sent them to establish a mill on the Big River. ("Honest Harry" later had to leave suddenly for South America; the movers and shakers of the last century were a different breed.) The town grew on lumber—it had a population of 700 by 1865, predominantly New Englanders but including as many as 200 Chinese—and was built of redwood. Along with eight hotels and 21 saloons, they built some fine New England saltboxes and

MacCallum House is one of the Victorian residences in Mendocino that is now an inn. (Redwood Empire Association)

Carpenter Gothic Victorians on the four principal streets of the town: Main, Albion, Ukiah, and Little Lake. Most of the sawing and other operations eventually were consolidated eight miles north, at Fort Bragg, but Mendocino town stayed alive until it was rediscovered in a state of suspended animation.

You can pick up a guidebook to the town at the restored **Kelley House***** (1861), Main Street, headquarters of Mendocino Historical Research; museum and library (707/937-5791). Among other notable buildings are the white, asymmetrically steepled Gothic Revival **Presbyterian Church**** (1868), Main Street, a state historical landmark whose front door is in the rear, where the old coast road once was; two 1975 restorations, the **Mendocino Hotel**** (1878), Main Street, and the **MacCallum House**** (1882), Albion Street, both of which are inns (it is the gingerbread-encrusted MacCallum House that is on the other side of the world's most photographed **duck pond,***** next to the Kelley House); the sun-faded red **Joss House,**** Albion Street, a Chinese temple-in-a-Victorian-cottage kept by a third-generation Chinese resident; and the **Masonic Hall**** (1865), Ukiah Street, which the Gebhard architectural guide thinks is a peculiar building because it has a "wavy-line verge-board and a cupola vaguely modeled on the Choragic Monument of Lysicrates surmounted by a wooden sculptural group—Father Time hovering over a strange little girl."

Many of the houses have deliberately been kept unrestored (remodeling is controlled by the Mendocino Historical Review Commission), the streets are bumpy, mostly sidewalkless, and public facilities are few, so the town still has a patina of unspoiled weather-beaten frontier charm. Facing the sea, Main Street, which, uniquely, has buildings only on the landward side, is the principal tourist thoroughfare, with shops and galleries upstairs, downstairs, and in back of most of the buildings. The shops, of course, cater to tourists, not purists among the town's residents, who may prefer the old **Mendosa general store,** garages, and other functional stores on Lansing Street. If you need a destination, head for the **Mendocino Art Center,*** Little Lake Street, which has a small theater, exhibitions, and summertime courses in pottery, design, weaving, jewelry, painting, stained glass, photography, and printmaking. Information: 707/937-5818. **Crown Hall,** Ukiah Street, is home of the local Gilbert and Sullivan troupe.

Mendocino Headlands

Probably the worst threat to the town is in the past: Boise-Cascade, once the largest developer of vacation homes in the state, gobbled up the 52 acres between Main Street and the sea; in 1972 the state, luckily, forestalled the subdivision, and the land remains open meadow. The **Mendocino Headlands State Park*** takes in most of the bluffs and beach from the Big River Bridge around to the Heeser Fishing Access. This undeveloped state park is good for strolling, casual picnicking, and picture-taking. Beneath you are wave tunnels, one of them calculated to be 700 feet long; legend says these contain the wrecks of many ships. Nothing remains of any of the harbor structures in the beautiful cove except for some of the metal parts of the wire chute system used to load lumber onto ships. Among the best bicycling routes is the headlands road (Main Street to Heeser Street and Heeser Drive, around to Lansing Street, which takes you back to Main); it's short but worthwhile. You can clamber down to the water at Heeser Access.

If you have a feeling of déjà vu in and around Mendocino (as in many other places in California) it's because you've seen it in the movies: scenes for *Johnny Belinda, Frenchman's Creek, East of Eden, The Russians Are Coming,* and *Summer of '42* were filmed locally.

Russian Gulch State Park

Mendocino is, thankfully, off Highway 1, which now becomes quite wide and runs straight up to Fort Bragg. Two miles along, take a left into **Russian Gulch State Park***** (picnicking, camping, etc.), which is among our favorite state parks. Like Van Damme, it follows a stream up through a once-logged area, now thick with second growth. The trail system, however, is more extensive, with not only a 2.5-mile hiking and biking trail along the stream but a trail up on the slope and a loop trail for another 3.5 miles to 36-foot **Russian Gulch Falls**** and back. This state park also includes the headlands on either side of the stream-mouth beach below the highway bridge; on the north headlands, in the middle of a peaceful meadow, is the **Devil's Punch-bowl,***** a frightening boiling pot. It's a 100-foot-wide, 60-foot-deep blowhole, formed when the roof of the wave tunnel, this one 200 feet long, collapsed. Park information: 707/937-0497.

Just after the park entrance, leave Highway 1 on Point Cabrillo Drive to undeveloped **Caspar Headlands State Reserve** and **State Beach.***

Like the other headlands, there's a coastal meadow here, along with wave tunnels, and a blowhole or two; those convey the power of the sea well, but the white octagon of the **Point Cabrillo Lighthouse*** is also a reminder of what a dangerous coast this has been, and still is, for shipping. Another left from Highway 1 across Caspar Creek takes you to **Caspar.**** Site of a lumber mill until 1955, Caspar barely exists except for the white-spired **Four Square Lighthouse Church,*** a funky inn, and a couple of New England-style houses; the setting of this tiny village is as perfect as Mendocino's, but it looks as if it's asleep forever.

Jug Handle Ecological Staircase

The next creek along, **Jug Handle Creek,** is well known among environmentalists in California because it is an entire ecosystem in miniature; a fascinating series of different biocommunities arranged on what has been called the **ecological staircase.***** Rising from the sea are five successive marine terraces, each between 75 and 175 feet higher than the previous one, each formed at different times over the last 500,000 to one million years. The soil is, naturally, different on each terrace. The consequence of all this is that in only four crow's-flight miles, the creek and the trail you may walk on traverse or pass near six marine and salt-spray communities (between the open ocean and the cliff), five coastal, terrace, and dune communities, and four ridge, canyon, and aquatic communities.

The best part of the staircase is preserved in either Jackson State Forest (the upland parts) or **Jug Handle State Reserve,** which was created in 1975 after efforts that began in the early 1960s and continued with numerous purchases by the Nature Conservancy, Save-the-Redwoods League, and Sequoya Challenge. In the role of activist were John Olmsted, proponent of several cross-California trails that would take in an amazing range of ecological communities, and his John Muir-inspired California Institute of Man in Nature (Box 392, Berkeley 94701).

A walk up the staircase, preferably with a knowledgeable guide, is essential to appreciate the interrelationships between plant and animal life, geology, and soil formation over the last years. Inquire at the ranger station south of the parking lot near the Jug Handle Creek Bridge on Highway 1; at the state parks office at Russian Gulch State Park, 707/937-5804; or at Jug Handle Farm (Box 17, Caspar 95420; 707/ 964-9912, or 415/332-2110 in Sausalito). The farm, an educational center located east of the highway, south of the bridge, has been conducting five-hour tours Sundays at 10 A.M.

There's more nature to come: a mile farther on the highway are the private **Ocean Bluff Fuchsia Gardens*** (Pacific Way, off Ocean Drive; 707/964-2190), with hundreds of varieties of fuchsias, and, another mile onward, the **Mendocino Coast Botanical Garden**** (707/ 964-4352), 47 acres of rhododendrons (April-May), and dahlias (summer and fall). Picnicking. Open daily, 8:30–6. Admission: adult— $1.75, children—75 cents and $1.25. There's an August concert series.

Nearby, **Highway 20** goes through **Jackson State Forest**, a forestry methods laboratory, to Willits, 39 miles away on Highway 101. North of the turnoff, Highway 1 passes high over the Noyo River, with a side road going down to **Noyo Flat,**** a photogenic fishing village used as a setting in the movie *The Russians Are Coming*. Noyo has party fishing boats, some seafood restaurants, and such fish-processing facilities as ice houses, custom canneries, and smokehouses.

Fort Bragg and the "Skunk"

Noyo is part of, shall we say, metropolitan **Fort Bragg,*** which with a population of 5,150 is the biggest place on the coast between San Francisco and Eureka (the inland Mendocino County seat, Ukiah, is twice as large as Fort Bragg). Frankly, compared with this scenic coast, Bragg is ugly: a lumber-company town laid out in a checkerboard, its main street the highway, strip development north and south. The economic health of the town almost entirely relies on the old Union Lumber mill that occupies the land west of the highway.

The California Western Railroad "Skunk" trains haul tourists and lumber. (Redwood Empire Association)

At 321 Main St. is a historical reminder that there once was a *fort* here, founded by an artillery lieutenant in 1857 and named for the same General Braxton Bragg as the military post in Georgia; sometimes an army private, with orders written for Fort Bragg CA, instead of GA, shows up here, looking for a fort that was abandoned in 1864. The only remnant of the fort is the lumber-mill museum. The town wasn't founded until 1885, when a mill was started at a harbor site served by a wharf instead of a wire chute.

A railroad was completed in 1911 from Bragg along Pudding Creek and the Noyo River to Willits, 40 miles of track through country not accessible to autos. The California Western Railroad is perhaps better known as the **Skunk,***** and it's the most popular tourist attraction in this neck of the woods. Originally the train hauled lumber and passengers, connecting with the overnight Northwestern Pacific train down to Sausalito on San Francisco Bay, whence ferryboats paddled to the city. The Northwestern Pacific doesn't haul passengers any longer but CWRR does: in fact, it's the only scheduled standard-gauge steam train in the west. What's more, it's not a toy tourist train: it still carries lumber too. The passengers go on either the yellow railcars, which were nicknamed "skunks" because of the smell of their gasoline-powered motors, or the "Super Skunk" train, which consists of an old steam locomotive (either a 2-8-2 Mikado or a 2-6-6-2 Mallet) or a conventional diesel engine pulling red passenger coaches.

The Skunks' summer schedule offers (1) once-daily steam train round trips from Fort Bragg to the halfway point, Northspur, where you can picnic under the redwoods, (2) once-daily diesel round trips from Willits to Northspur, (3) Bragg-Willits (or vice versa) round trips, diesel one way, steam the other, and (4) once-daily Bragg-Willits round trip by Skunk railcar. Only the railcar runs in the off-season. Round trips now cost $8.20 (adult), and $4.10 (child); the Northspur excursion is $5.75 (adult) and $3.25 (child). All train departures are around 9 A.M. Make your reservations well in advance: CWRR, Box 907, Fort Bragg 95437 (707/964-6371).

Willits, on Highway 101, has standard motels, restaurants, and shops. The **Mendocino County Museum,*** 400 E. Commercial, has Pomo and Yuki artifacts, turn-of-the-century period rooms, and so forth, and in July and August the Mendocino Quilt Show. Open daily in summer 10-5 for token admission. Information: 707/459-2736.

If you can't get aboard the Skunk, you may want to take the free 45-minute tour of the **Georgia-Pacific Mill.**** Beginning at the company museum (open weekdays 8-5), 90 W. Redwood, near the Skunk Depot, tours run several times on summer weekdays, at 2 P.M. only on weekdays in winter. Very exciting is the Bellingham debarker, which uses hot-water jets exerting 1,500 pounds per square inch to strip bark up to a foot thick off the redwood logs—in only a few seconds. Fifty-foot band saws then cut the big "cants" and they go to the "green line" for cutting into lumber of various sizes. The company, which runs the Skunk and owns 180,000 acres of Mendocino timberland, is quick to talk about its reforestation; it grows 2.1 million seedlings a year in a nursery at Bragg. The opulent redwood **Johnson House** (1892), built by the pioneer lumber-miller, was a Georgia-Pacific guest house and will become a museum. Information: 707/964-5651.

Fort Bragg has a couple of antique and crafts shops and art galleries you may want to look for. The big event in town, **Paul Bunyan Days**, occurs over Labor Day weekend.

Ten-Mile Beach

Georgia-Pacific has one more goody for the public: on weekends it opens up its logging road, which runs right next to the shore along

Ten-Mile Beach** to a closed gate at Ten-Mile River (they cut trees up that way). The road offers wonderful access to fine coastal meadows, tide-pool areas, beaches, and dunes, and bicycling is great. Unfortunately, it's difficult to get from the logging road into **MacKerricher State Park,**** which is three miles north of Bragg, with entrance off Highway 1. The park has camping, picnicking, hiking, rock and surf fishing, skin diving (for abalone), beachcombing on the black-sandy beach, and nonpower boating and water play on a land-locked lagoon called **Lake Cleone.*** Park information: 707/964-9112.

Once past the state park the coast is as pastoral and deserted as below Elk. Lumber-mill towns like Cleone and doghole ports like Newport are ghost towns, and even the most visible settlement, **Westport,**** looks as if it may slip into history one day soon, either because people will forget about it or because it will run out of water. For the time being, Westport has some New England saltbox houses and a couple of casual cafés good for a short stop before proceeding. North of town is 2.5-mile-long **Westport-Union Landing State Beach,** good for surf fishing (for smelt) but not much else at the moment.

North of **Rockport,** which *is* almost gone, Highway 1 also disappears: it bends inland and becomes the Hollow Tree Road, then terminates at Leggett on Highway 101 (the Redwood Highway). North of Rockport, extending nearly to Eureka, is the largest undeveloped section of coastline in California, if not the contiguous United States. Much of it is included in the **King Range National Conservation Area**, accessible by rough roads, beginning with Usal Road, which is not shown on ordinary highway maps. See pp. 241-3 for details.

PRACTICAL INFORMATION

Getting There, Getting Around

As described above, the Skunk trains run once a day (twice in summer) between Fort Bragg and Willits, but that's not really transit. B&H Transportation, 222 E. Redwood, Fort Bragg (707/964-9574), has buses between the two towns as well. Greyhound runs buses four or five times a day on Highway 101 from San Francisco into Redwood Country, with stops at Willits, but has one daily bus between San Francisco and Fort Bragg, by way of Cloverdale, Boonville, Philo, Navarro, Albion, Little River, Mendocino, Caspar, and Noyo. The MTA, which around here is the Mendocino Transit Authority (405 W. Perkins, Ukiah, 707/462-1462), has a number of minibuses with infrequent service on such routes as Fort Bragg–Gualala, Bragg–West-port, Ukiah–Mendocino, Bragg–Mendocino–Little River, Mendocino–Bragg–Cleone. Fares are low—only $1 between Point Arena and Bragg.

The county airport in Little River is occasionally served by commuter airlines.

As described in the text, there are many good bicycle excursions. For touring bikers, Highway 1 is narrow and sometimes has no shoulders, but traffic is mostly light and the terrain is gently rolling, with one steep stretch (southbound) near Elk and longer hills (both directions) south of Rockport. Long excursions are on the logging road north of Fort Bragg (see text), on the old coastal road between Russian Gulch and Jug Handle Creek (five miles), and on the old road and the highway from Mendocino and Jug Handle (seven miles).

Where to Stay and Eat

Accommodations (including camping) and restaurants are listed in Part IV under these headings: Fort Bragg/Northern Mendocino Coast; Gualala/Southern Mendocino Coast; Mendocino/Central Mendocino Coast. See also Sonoma Coast; Garberville/Southern Redwoods; and Ukiah/Inland Mendocino County.

SOURCES OF INFORMATION—COAST

General: Redwood Empire Association, 360 Post St., Suite 201, San Francisco 94108 (415/421-6554), is the visitors' bureau for the region across the Golden Gate.

Marin County: Golden Gate National Recreation Area (GGNRA), Fort Mason, San Francisco 94123 (415/556-0560). Marin County Chamber of Commerce and Visitors' Bureau, 30 N. San Pedro Rd., Suite 150, San Rafael 94903 (415/472-7470). Marin Coast Chamber of Commerce, Box 94, Olema 94950 (415/663-1244, 663-8494). Also chambers in Sausalito, Tiburon, San Rafael, and most other towns.

Sonoma coast: Bodega Bay Area Chamber of Commerce, Box 146, Bodega Bay 94923 (707/875-3407). Russian River Chamber of Commerce, Box 331, Guerneville 95446 (707/869-2584).

Mendocino coast: Fort Bragg–Mendocino Coast Chamber of Commerce, Box 1141 (332 N. Main St.), Fort Bragg 95437 (707/964-3153). South Mendocino Coast Chamber of Commerce, Point Arena 95468. Mendocino County Chamber of Commerce, Box 244 (331 N. School St.), Ukiah 95482 (707/462-3091).

 *Part III*

REDWOOD COUNTRY

Once, when we were visiting a redwood state park on California's North Coast, a tour bus pulled up and disgorged a group of healthy-looking souls—Swedes, it turned out—who chattered their way up the path to a particularly magnificent redwood, formed a circle, and began singing hymns.

Now that seemed like an appropriate thing to do in a redwood grove. As in a Gothic cathedral, the light in a redwood forest is filtered or even dim, and the structure towers over you, occasioning feelings of smallness; you stop, look around and up, and think it would be grand to see a stately procession march up the forest path while a choir—the Mormon Tabernacle Choir—sends a mighty paean soaring to the heavens. Our hymn-singing Swedes fulfilled the wish.

The Tallest, the Biggest, the Oldest

California is blessed with three botanical wonders: the world's tallest living thing (the *Sequoia sempervirens*, or coastal redwood), the world's largest living thing (the *Sequoiadendron giganteum*, or Sierra redwood or Big Tree), and the world's oldest living thing (the *Pinus aristata*, or bristlecone pine). We'll compare briefly the two types of redwoods, and then cover in more detail the northern domain of the coastal redwood, from Leggett north to the Oregon border.

Some 100 million years ago, a tree that was the ancestor of the two types of present California redwoods grew throughout the Northern Hemisphere. Over the millennia, for the coastal redwood the natural habitat shrank to a 30-mile-wide strip along Oregon's southern coast and California's northern and central coast, and for the Sierra redwood, isolated sections of the southwestern Sierra Nevada.

Both trees are members of the swamp cypress family *Taxodiaceae*, which the coastal redwood was first classified as in 1824. However, they are each in a separate genus. The coastal redwood is in the genus *Sequoia*, so named in 1847 by the Austrian botanist Stephan Endlicher in honor of the Cherokee Indian Sequoyah, who developed the first alphabet used by that tribe. The Sierra redwood is in the genus *Sequoiadendron*; *dendron* is Greek for "big tree." It was so classified in 1939 by Professor John T. Buchholz after much dispute by botanists. In addition the trees have a species name—*sempervirens* (Latin, "evergreen") for the coastal redwood, *giganteum* (Latin, "giant") for the Sierra redwood.

Both species are known for their extreme size. The coastal redwood is the world's tallest, with the record presently held by a 367.8-foot tree in Redwood National Park north of Eureka. As a means of imagining how tall this tree is, here is a comparison: it's taller than the Hyatt Hotel–Union Square in San Francisco (355 feet) and the State Office Building (350 feet) in Boston; it is fully half as tall as the Citibank Building (741 feet) in New York, the IBM Building (695 feet) in Chicago, the First International Building (710 feet) in Dallas, and the Security Pacific National Bank Building (738 feet) in Los Angeles. The Sierra redwood, on the other hand, is the world's biggest in terms of bulk, with the General Sherman Tree in Sequoia National Park judged the largest. The General is 272 feet tall, has a circumference of 83 feet, 11 inches at an adult's chest level, weighs 2.5 million pounds, contains 600,000 board feet, and could be used to build 40 houses—if it were not protected and its wood were not so brittle.

There are ancient specimens of both species. The average age of old coastal redwoods is 500 to 700 years, though a few have lived over 2,000 years, and one judged the oldest (2,200 years) was for some reason cut down in 1934 (perhaps we don't like to be reminded of the superiority of a *vegetable*). The Sierra redwoods make their coastal cousins look youthful in contrast. It is estimated that the oldest living Sierra redwood, 2,700 years old, is the Grizzly Giant in Yosemite National Park, though older ones are always hunted out; several of the giants are 1,500 to 2,000 years old.

Survival of the Redwood

Several factors allow the coastal and Sierra redwoods to achieve such size and longevity. Redwoods generally outcompete their neighboring plants—e.g., oak, maple, hazel, laurel, fir, spruce, and hemlock—for the available sunlight, air, moisture, and soil nutrients; the coastal redwood can grow up to 2.5 feet each year for a century. Plants that do co-exist well with the redwoods are various ferns—such as sword, bracken, lady, maidenhair, chain, and licorice—which love the shady, cool, damp forest floor with its rich soil. Walking through a redwood and fern forest you feel as if you've stepped back several million years in time, when the giant Taxodiums and huge ferns spread throughout the hemisphere and all was quiet. Another factor that contributes to the redwoods' growth is their protective bark. On both types the bark is much like our skin, keeping out undesirable organisms—though for these trees the bark may be from four inches to three feet thick. The thick bark also behaves somewhat like asbestos and makes the trees resist fire; only if the fire is severe enough will it burn away the protective bark and reach the wood. The rich reddish-brown bark, as well as the wood interior, inspired the name *redwood*. Both the bark and wood contain bitter chemicals called tannins that discourage attacks by insects and fungi. It is a combination of all these factors that makes the redwoods grow as well for so long, and it is mainly man who now both threatens and protects them.

California's redwoods have a foreign cousin native to China called *Metasequoia*, or dawn redwood. It was thought to be extinct until 1941, when a Chinese forestry professor identified specimens from Szechuan in central China. Botanists have determined that its main distinctions are its natural location and smaller size; it is also deciduous rather than evergreen, as the California redwoods are. Examples of the *Metasequoia, Sequoia*, and *Sequoiadendron* have been planted in many places around the world, though their natural habitats are still those described above.

Coastal redwoods are unique among the conifer (cone-bearing) trees because they are able to reproduce both by seeds and by sprouting from the roots or stump of a parent tree. Male cones mature from December through February and release their pollen, which is windblown to the female cones. These female cones mature and release their seeds from October through January. Though the seeds germinate easily, their roots frequently cannot reach through the thick organic cover on the forest floor, and thus they do not live. On the other hand, when sprouts develop from the root or stump of a mature or cut tree, they do much better because they have the already established life-support system to give them the required water, minerals, and nutrients to grow. Thus, much reproduction of coastal redwoods comes through the root and stump sprouts.

Roots, Bark, Trunk, Crown

Sequoia sempervirens, like its cousin in the Sierras, has a root system that is broad and shallow, without any central tap root. Because the most sensitive part of the root system lies just a few inches under the soil, disturbances around the base of a tree can harm its growth. Putting low fences around the base of many redwoods in well-traveled forests has decreased vehicle and foot traffic and has thus prevented compacting of the soil, which disrupts the drainage and flow of nutrients.

The coastal redwood's reddish-brown, thick fibrous bark differs from the Sierra redwood's in that it may form small to large burls, or protrusions. A burl is a natural growth, a mass of undeveloped or dormant buds that can be compared to a benign tumor. Burls vary from walnut size to a hefty 50 tons. Commercial firms will cut burls off unprotected trees and accentuate the twisted, beautiful grain in making curios, bowls, tables, veneers, and paneling, most of which are tacky. A burl placed in a pan of water will sprout into a tiny redwood tree, short-lived but beautiful.

There are few branches until near the tree's top. This self-pruning is a result of the competition for light, which in a mature forest is mainly at the treetop level. The needles of the coastal redwood are arranged along both sides of the twigs and form flat, green sprays that look somewhat like white fir and smell very pungent.

Animal life and birdlife may seem sparse on the floor of the coastal redwood forest. The deep shade limits growth of many varieties of flowers, fruits, seeds, and insects for the wildlife to live on. Birds that may be spotted, however, are the crested, or Steller's, jay in particular, plus owls, brown creeper, pygmy nuthatch, chestnut-backed chickadee, varied thrush, winter wren, and golden-crowned kinglet. The animals that live in the coastal redwood forest are typically the Trowbridge shrew, Sonoma and Townsend chipmunk, western gray squirrel, Douglas squirrel, chickaree, raccoon, and mountain beaver. At home in the Prairie Creek State Park and some other redwood forests in the far north are Roosevelt elk.

Most visitors to California experience coastal redwoods in places like Muir Woods, Big Basin, and Redwood National Park. The coastal redwood grows in the fog belt, climbing from near sea level up the

Coastal Range to an elevation of about 2,000 feet, but staying within the fog belt with its cool dampness, much appreciated by the trees during the summer.

Discovery of the Redwood

Redwoods were first reported by European travelers in October 1769, when Juan Crespi, a Franciscan missionary with the Portolá expedition, called them *palo colorado* ("red tree"). The coastal redwoods then covered almost 2 million acres of land. Today redwoods still cover 1.5 million acres, but only 155,000 acres are virgin (uncut) stands—7.75 percent of the original—of which 75,000 acres are protected within parks and 80,000 acres (as of 1978) are in private hands and are being cut at a rate of 10,000 acres a year. A total of 233,000 acres of virgin and second-growth coastal redwoods are protected within parks.

As the early settlers found, the coastal-redwood lumber is valuable, useful, and popular. It is durable, resists rot and termites, does not warp, is straight-grained and lightweight, holds nails and finishes well, acts as a good insulator, is easy to work, and is quite strong. Most of the Victorian homes in San Francisco and elsewhere were built of redwood, allowing the beautiful and elaborate decorative millwork characteristic of this style of architecture. Logging began in the 1820s and has continued nonstop. Rather than just log, though, the timber companies—the three biggest today are Georgia-Pacific, Simpson, and Arcata Redwood—are expected to also plant seedlings, which are harvestable in 50 to 100 years, conserve, and manage the forests they own or lease. However, the timber companies and conservationists obviously do not share the same goals, and conflict is inevitable, especially concerning virgin stands around parks.

It is due to the conservationists' unflagging efforts over the last century that the 75,000 virgin acres that are inside parks do exist at all, given the value of the lumber (each virgin tree is worth about $125,000 in 1978 dollars). The coastal redwoods began to be protected in 1900 when the Sempervirens Club brought attention to the trees at Big Basin near Santa Cruz. Two years later the California legislature created the first state park, California Redwood Park, at Big Basin. Muir Woods was donated to the federal government by Congressman William Kent in 1908; it is now a national monument visited by eight million people each year. A few stands were thus protected but the rest were disappearing rapidly because of California's growth. In 1918 the

Save-the-Redwoods League was formed to save trees all over the state. The league also pushed to have the State Park Commission and California State Park System established in 1927; the State Park system now supervises more than 250 units covering one million acres across the state, including 28 redwood parks. Since 1918 the league has raised over $23 million in matching funds to add more than 135,000 acres and 280 memorial groves to the park systems.

The struggle continues to preserve the remaining old-growth redwoods, with controversial Redwood National Park the focal point of bitter disputes since the 1960s (see p. 262). In 1978, before Congress approved funds to add 48,000 more acres to this park, some sick individual killed 18 giant redwoods in five groves—Smithe, Richardson, Pioneers, Federation, and Founders—in three state parks. The trees died after their delicate life-supporting cambium tissue was cut by a chainsaw in a ring around the trees. The criminal was never found. The trees were cut down and the lumber used in park fences.

The redwood country in California's far north is a perfect region for a family vacation. Camp under the towering coastal redwoods, hike and bike and horseback-ride through the forests, fish in crystal-clear streams and in the Pacific Ocean, beachcomb and picnic along beaches and bluffs, explore charming towns like Ferndale and cities like Eureka, relax at a resort with all the luxuries. The way of life is slower-paced than elsewhere in Northern California. Plan to spend at least five days to appreciate the great beauty.

We have divided Part III into three chapters: "Southern Redwoods," stretching from Leggett to Scotia; "Eureka Area," including the surrounding region from Ferndale north to Dry Lagoon State Park; and "Northern Redwoods," extending from Orick at the southern end of Redwood National Park north to the Oregon border.

CHAPTER 9:

Southern Redwoods

HIGHLIGHTS

Leggett / 240
Standish-Hickey State Recreation
   Area / 240
Smithe Redwoods State
   Reserve / 240
Richardson Grove State Park / 240
Benbow Lake State Recreation
   Area / 241
Garberville / 241

King Range National Conservation
   Area / 241
Humboldt Redwoods State
   Park / 243
Avenue of the Giants / 243
Rockefeller Forest / 244
Founders Grove / 244
Scotia / 245

The Southern Redwoods area starts at the small town of Leggett and runs north along Highway 101 to the lumber town of Scotia. En route is one of the country's best state parks—Humboldt Redwoods, with the famous Avenue of the Giants and 79 dedicated memorial groves of virgin trees. The 33-mile-long avenue, which is the old two-lane Highway 101, is an unimaginably nice place to bicycle, walk, or jog, beneath towering giants and beside creeks and rivers. If you cannot drive the whole distance from San Francisco to Redwood National Park, Humboldt Redwoods Park makes an excellent destination by itself. Explorers will like the challenging King Range, a mountainous expanse of coast off the beaten track. Camping is superb inside the state parks, while resorts and motels offer other accommodations.

Driving north to the beginning of this redwood area directly from San Francisco can be time-consuming and tiring. Plan to stop at least one night in the Southern Redwoods. San Francisco to Leggett is about 186 miles on Highway 101. For the more scenic way to Leggett, take Highway 1 along the spectacular Sonoma and Mendocino coastline as far as Rockport, then go inland on Highway 208. You might give yourself as many as three days to enjoy the coastal route to Leggett (see Chapter 5).

WHAT TO SEE AND DO

Leggett to Garberville

Leggett, at the junction of highways 208 and 101, is the gateway to the Southern Redwoods. It is at an altitude of 860 feet and at the confluence of the Hollow Tree Creek, Eel River, and Cedar Creek, with fishing in all. Leggett has a few simple cafés and stores, a flea market in mid-August, and that's about it.

Standish-Hickey State Recreation Area* is a mile north of Leggett. Most of the area is covered with second-growth (as opposed to virgin or first-growth) coastal redwoods and Douglas fir. The few first growths include the **Captain Miles Standish Tree,** named after the *Mayflower* ancestor of Mr. and Mrs. S. M. Standish, donors of some of this land. Hike along, swim and fish in the Eel River. At the entrance to the park is a planted *Metasequoia,* the dawn redwood native to China. This recreation area has 162 camping sites.

Smithe Redwoods State Reserve,* another four miles north of Standish-Hickey, has a beautiful stand that is almost exclusively redwoods, situated on both sides of the highway and the banks of the meandering south fork of the Eel River. Bright meadows break the forest occasionally. Picnic, fish, swim, and walk.

Continue north on Highway 101 another 12 miles to more redwoods.

Richardson Grove State Park** straddles the highway 17 miles north of Leggett, 9 miles south of Garberville. The 831-acre park was set aside and named in honor of Friend Richardson, former publisher of the *Berkeley Gazette* and the state's twenty-fifth governor (1923–27). Families and others like this park's educational exhibits, museum, summertime campfire program and guided nature walks, picnicking, fishing and swimming (lifeguards are present) in the Eel River, and numerous (185) campsites. Also open in the summer are the gift shop and post office. An easy stroll on the **Grove Trail** takes you from the park entrance to the south fork of the Eel River. Other walking and hiking trails are the Lookout Point, Settlers, Woodland, and Toumey, which go through the trees and to nearby scenic viewpoints. Information: Richardson Grove State Park, Garberville 95440 (707/247-3318).

On the west side of Highway 101, six miles north of Richardson Grove, is **Benbow Lake State Recreation Area.** The small lake is about 1.5 miles long and .5 miles wide, and offers swimming, water skiing, boating, and canoeing. For day-use only, the lake has picnic sites, a boat-launching ramp, and makes a pleasant pre-lunch swim.

Also in this vicinity is the **Benbow Inn,** a six-story Tudor-style resort on an elbow of the south fork of the Eel River. See Part IV, Garberville/Southern Redwoods. For in-town accommodations, visit Garberville.

Garberville is the small (pop. 1,000) headquarters town for the southern part of the Humboldt County redwood country. It was named for Jacob Garber, who moved west from Virginia and settled here in 1871. Facilities include a nine-hole golf course, small airport, stores, post office, restaurants, and motels. The Garberville rodeo may be mid-June. The tenth largest but illegal cash crop in California—*sinsemilla* (female marijuana plant)—has roots among other places in the mountains around Garberville, where its estimated value ranges from $186 million to $1 billion. Farmers are "at war" with local, state, and federal officials over their lucrative business.

Based in Garberville is the **Squirrel,*** a half-open-air sightseeing bus that runs June to September, going north to various memorial groves, Pacific Lumber Company, Founders Grove and Rockefeller Forest in Humboldt Redwoods State Park. Boarding points are: 9:30 A.M., Hartsook Inn; 9:35, Richardson Grove; 9:50, Benbow Inn; 10:00, Garberville. The Squirrel stops for lunch in Scotia and returns to Garberville and elsewhere after 5 P.M. Fare: adult—$7.50, child under 12—$3 (not including lunch). Information: Box 353, Garberville 94440 (707/986-7526).

Just north of Garberville is a turnoff west to the nearby town of Redway, about three miles. Continuing west via the narrow winding Briceland Thorne Road for another 22 miles, you can reach the remote King Range.

King Range National Conservation Area

For years the **King Range**** was called California's "lost coast." The chain of King Range mountains abruptly and dramatically rise from the Pacific Ocean to heights of 3,000 to 4,000 feet, with just a few roads and trails allowing access to the interior and coast. However, because of its proximity to Garberville, this area did not escape the attention of real-estate developers, who particularly liked the Shelter Cove area. Here some 40 miles of access roads were built to connect 5,000 lots, which were sold in the 1960s. In the process the geologically unstable cliffs were bulldozed to try to prevent landsliding, but to little avail. Less than a hundred homes were built, thanks to limitations imposed by the California Coastal Commission to protect this fragile coast.

After a series of studies of the King Range by the Department of Interior from the 1920s to 1960s, some 54,200 acres were declared a national conservation area by Congress in 1970, under the direction of the Bureau of Land Management. About 17,000 acres are still privately owned, and while 7,000 acres have already been purchased with federal funds, another 10,000 are yet to be bought. Further funds are being used to develop about 21 miles of trails, four semideveloped camping areas, and access roads.

The area is beautiful for hiking, exploring, camping, and fishing. Mountains to climb include **Kings Peak,** which at 4,087 feet is the highest point on the continental U.S. shoreline. The 16-mile-long **King Crest Trail** goes to its summit, as well as to North Slide Peak (3,512 feet). **Chemise Mountain Primitive Area** is a special 3,941-acre wilderness that is closed to all vehicles but is accessible through a five-mile trail within the area and to the peak.

Hiking in the summer may be cooled by coastal fogs, while winter brings scores of inches of rain (an average of 100 inches yearly at nearby Honeydew). Exploring by car, a two-hour drive over the paved and "all-weather" roads takes one from the Punta Gorda Beach in the north of the conservation area to Four Corners in the far south, winding through sides and ridges of the King Range en route. Camping is at four semideveloped sites: Wailaki (16 units), Nadelos (14), Tolkan (9), and Horse Mountain (9), each of which has table, grills, water, and basic toilets. Fishing is possible in both salt and fresh water. Ocean fish include salmon, bottom fish, rockfish, surf perch, ling cod; halibut, cabezon, smelt; you can also catch abalone and clams. The Mattole River is very fine for salmon and steelhead, mid-November through February, while streams provide trout fishing.

Shelter Cove, in the subdivision, has a small private-plane landing strip, rental fishing boats, grocery store, nine-hole golf course, summertime restaurant, and picnic and camping facilities. Skin divers here wear wet suits because of the chilly water. Tide-pool exploring and beachcombing are captivating along the miles of unusual black sandy beaches. Occasionally dune buggies may bug you, but the Bureau of Land Management is thinking of ways to separate them from hikers and others.

King Range information: District Manager, Bureau of Land Management, 555 Leslie St., Ukiah 95482 (707/462-3873).

You can return to Garberville on Briceland Thorne Road or you can explore some of the lovely, undulating countryside that has attracted back-to-the-land folk by taking the Etterburg–Honeydew–Wilder Ridge rough roads to Honeydew, then the Mattole and Bull Creek roads to Dyerville and Highway 101.

Humboldt Redwoods State Park

One of the glories of the state park system, **Humboldt Redwoods State Park,***** is shaped oddly—like a bulb bulging west of Weott, with long tendrils coming out to head north and south along old and new highways 101, covering some 38 miles and 46,146 acres. Its highlights are the Avenue of the Giants, Rockefeller Forest, and 79 memorial groves including Founders Grove. Base a family camping vacation here for hiking, biking, fishing, swimming, jogging, and strolling through the 25,000 acres of gorgeous virgin redwoods. The park and surrounding county were named for Alexander von Humboldt, an explorer of the West and South America in the early nineteenth century.

The **Avenue of the Giants***** begins about six miles north of Garberville, where old 101 leaves the new 101 freeway to begin its meander north through the scores of groves and along the Eel River. This 33-mile-long, two-lane parkway is maintained as a low-speed scenic drive that crisscrosses the freeway. Along it are more memorial groves, the main section of the park, and many pullout areas for gentle walks through the forest to the south fork of the Eel River, Bull Creek, and other streams. Picnic areas with tables are in the Lane Memorial, Garden Club, and California Federation of Women's Clubs groves. We recommend visiting the Avenue of the Giants in the early morning and late afternoon when traffic is light. Bring your own bike, a picnic lunch, and try the ride (an 18-mile round trip) from Myers Flat to Rockefeller Forest.

At the junction of the Eel River and its south fork, north of Weott about two miles, is the turnoff to Bull Creek Flats Road and **Rockefeller Forest.***** With a generous donation from John D. Rockefeller, Jr., this old-growth forest was purchased and preserved. Extensive logging and fires in the 1940s and 1950s severely hurt the upper Bull Creek watershed, and the floods of 1955 and 1964 turned the creek into a 300-foot-wide, gravel-filled destroyer, pulling down trees from the Rockefeller Forest and elsewhere in its path. However, 700 acres of original Rockefeller forest still remain, and, to prevent future disasters, the park has been expanded to include the whole Bull Creek watershed. The tallest tree in the Rockefeller Forest is 359.3 feet high and is about five miles from the highway at the parking spot for "Tall Tree Area."

On the opposite side of Highway 101 is **Founders Grove,***** established in honor of the founders of the Save-the-Redwoods League. As we have mentioned, the league has been instrumental in saving 135,000 acres of redwoods, and in this park alone helped purchase 25,293 acres with $8.6 million. A short, pleasant, educational self-guided nature trail takes you to **Founders Tree** (1,300 to 1,500 years old), a fire-scarred walk-through tree, the **Dyerville Giant** (over 358 feet tall), the **Fallen Giant** (over 200 feet), and describes other plants and features in this old-growth redwood forest.

There are ample camping facilities inside the park, though a reservation through the park system or Ticketron is always advisable in the summer. Most facilities are open May 30 to Labor Day. Sites are located at Hidden Springs, 1 mile south of Myers Flat (155 sites); Burlington, 2 miles south of Weott (58 sites); Albee Creek, 6 miles northwest of Weott on Bull Creek Flats Road (32 sites); and Cuneo Creek/ Horse Camp, 8.5 miles northwest of Weott, 2.5 from Albee Creek Camp, same road, then turn off onto .5-mile gravel road (for groups with horses, as well as others). Hidden Spring and Burlington have nature programs in the summer, and hot showers, and all campgrounds are on or close to the river or creek for swimming and fishing.

Information: Humboldt Redwoods State Park, Box 100, Weott 95571 (707/946-2311).

At Dyerville is the turnoff west via Bull Creek Flat Road and Mattole Road to Honeydew—then south to King Range (see above), or north to the tiny coastal towns of Petrolia and Capetown and inland to Ferndale (see Chapter 10) and back to Highway 101. This is an alternative route north to Eureka, going through beautiful, isolated farming and ranching country and by Cape Mendocino, the most westerly mainland point on the Pacific Ocean coast south of Alaska. The approximate mileages are Dyerville-Honeydew—23, Honeydew-Petrolia-Capetown-Ferndale—45, Ferndale-Highway 101—5. The route is windy and narrow, so give yourself time to enjoy the sights if you decide to take this mountain and coast route.

Scotia

Back on Highway 101, leaving Humboldt Redwoods, you reach the turnoff to **Scotia*** (pop. 1,000), a company town that is owned and operated by the Pacific Lumber Company, and is built out of redwood, naturally. The lumber company was started by some farmers-turned-loggers who purchased 6,000 acres of land on the Eel River in the late 1850s for about $1.50 an acre. In 1886 a Nova Scotian named Simon Jones Murphy took over control of the mill and founded the town, naming it Scotia in honor of that Canadian province. Two buildings of note are the **Winema Theatre,** an overgrown log cabin built in 1920, with 10 redwood trunks as columns in the front; and the **Visitors Center,** another 1920s creation in the classical Roman style complete with more tree-trunk columns. The museum is open in the summer, and no admission is charged. **The Pacific Lumber Company mill** allows visitors in for hour-and-a-half self-guided tours 7:30-12, 1-4:30 (closed holidays and most of July), but permits for the tours must be obtained from the main office or the museum. The company's **demonstration forest** is five miles south of town, open 9-6 in summer, and has picnic facilities. Rio Dell and Scotia sponsor Wildwood Days and Peddlers Fair in late August.

PRACTICAL INFORMATION

Getting There, Getting Around

Most people drive to and through the redwood country, but there are other ways to tour the southern section. Highway 101 goes directly from San Francisco and through the redwoods north to Oregon. Highway 1 goes north along the coast through Sonoma and Mendocino counties, with connecting highways east to 101 being 128-253 to Ukiah, 20 to Willits, and 208 to Leggett. We think the most scenic (though longer), drive is along Highway 1 north to Rockport, then 208 to Leggett, then 101 north through the redwoods.

Greyhound also runs buses north through this area. A local redwood tour-bus service, the Squirrel (see p. 241), is based in Garberville.

The nearest main commercial airports are in Fort Bragg and Ukiah, which are sometimes served by commuter airlines. See also "Practical Information" in Chapter 10.

Energetic bicyclists can try the local section of the Pacific Coast Bicentennial Route. From the coast inland to Leggett, Highway 208 is steep-steep, but then Highway 101 is more level, especially along the Avenue of the Giants, a fine local ride.

Where to Stay and Eat

Accommodations (including camping) and restaurants are listed in Part IV under the heading Garberville/Southern Redwoods. See also Eureka/Central Redwood Country; Fort Bragg/Northern Mendocino Coast; and Ukiah/Inland Mendocino.

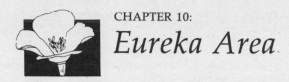

CHAPTER 10:

Eureka Area

HIGHLIGHTS

Ferndale / 248
Alton / 249
Eureka / 250
Eel River / 251
Fort Humboldt State Historic
  Park / 252
Sequoia Park and Zoo / 253
Eureka Boat Basin and
  Harbor / 253
Humboldt Bay / 253

Old Town / 254
Carson Mansion / 254
Victorian Driving Tour / 255
Samoa / 256
Arcata / 256
Azalea State Reserve / 258
Little River State Beach / 258
Trinidad / 258
Patrick's Point State Park / 259
Dry Lagoon State Park / 259

The Eureka area is the major metropolitan cluster in the Redwood Country. Though it does not have many redwoods itself anymore, it is situated between the two forested regions to the south and north. In this section we travel from the Victorian farming community of Ferndale into the county capital and "big city" of Eureka. Here enjoy walking and driving tours, a harbor cruise, fresh-seafood restaurants, history, and architecture. Moving north on Highway 101, we come to Arcata—home of Humboldt State University—and the tiny burg of Trinidad. For recreation there is a string of beaches and parks north of Eureka—Azalea, Little River, Patrick's Point, and Dry Lagoon.

WHAT TO SEE AND DO

Leaving Scotia, which was the last point in the Southern Redwoods section, and driving north on Highway 101, you reach the small community of **Rio Dell,** on the Eel River. Fish, boat, swim, explore Scotia Bluffs' ancient fossil beds. The Rio Dell Fire Department provides a free picnic area. Here also is the turnoff west to the town of Ferndale, about 11 miles via Grizzly Bluff Road and an excellent excursion to include en route to Eureka.

Ferndale

Ferndale*** is a Victorian architectural gem, with enough ornately decorated buildings to please any enthusiast, and to earn the name "Victorian Village." The area was first settled in August 1852 by farming pioneers, who set about cutting down the towering redwoods to clear the land for agriculture. One pioneer, Seth Louis Shaw, named his farm Ferndale, which formed the nucleus of the community. In 1856 Shaw began building his permanent Gothic Revival home, which stands at 703 Main St. Danish and Portuguese dairy farmer immigrants opened the Ferndale, Grizzly Bluff, and Excelsior creameries in the 1890s, and descendants of both groups still farm. The Victorian homes and stores were erected mostly from 1860 to 1880, and today there are many fine specimens, thanks to awareness on the part of the old-time residents and to artists and craftspeople who opened shops on Main Street and settled down.

The largest concentration of Victorians is along Main Street and its cross streets: Washington, Brown, Ocean, and Eugene. **Main Street** is the well-tended commercial district, today blooming with antiques and art galleries. Along Main look for these Victorians starting at the north end: 923 (1880s Eastlake–Queen Anne-style home), 831 (1880s Italianate–Queen Anne-style home), 703 (Shaw's Gothic Revival home), 507 (1880s Eastlake store and office), 475 (1880s Eastlake store), 370 (1880s store), 366 (1880s Eastlake store), Main/Ocean (1880s Eastlake and Italianate). A couple of homes to look for especially include 455 Ocean (1860s Gothic cottage) and one on the northeast corner of Berding and Brown streets (ca. 1894). Three churches to spot are **Church of the Assumption** (1880s), Berding and Washington, **Our Savior Lutheran** (1870s), Shaw near 3rd Street, and **First Congregational** (1881), Lewis/Main. These buildings and more are all described in more detail in the Gebhard architectural guide. The Ferndale Chamber of Commerce, 421 Main St., will send you a free, historic, photographic brochure.

The best way to see Ferndale, as anywhere, is to walk. In this case a four- to six-block stroll will encompass most of the town center. You may want to visit in spring, when there is a week-long art festival including the Great Arcata to Ferndale Cross-Country Kinetic Sculpture Race, or in late July–early August, when the Humboldt County Fair is held nearby. From town, it's a short drive out to Centerville Beach to see the memorial to the 38 who died in the wreck of the *Northerner* in 1860; there's also beachcombing, driftwood collecting, surf-casting for perch, and smelt netting.

From Ferndale, drive north about five miles to return to Highway 101, or take the road back to Rio Dell. From that town a short drive north on 101 takes you to **Alton,** home of the little **Alton & Pacific Railroad,** a two-foot-gauge steam train with a wood-burning engine that toots its way 1.5 miles from, well, here to there and back. Daily runs except Tuesday on the hour 11–6, June–Labor Day. Fare: adult—75 cents, child under 16—50 cents. Located on Highway 36, about half a mile off Highway 101.

Another eight miles north on Highway 101 brings you to Humboldt Bay and the city of Eureka.

Eureka

Eureka*** is nicely situated on Humboldt Bay, one of the largest ports between San Francisco and Seattle. The bay wasn't discovered by Europeans until 1806, when Jonathan Winship dropped the anchor of the *O'Cain*, a Russian-American Company ship. He called the waterway the Bay of the Indians, after those original residents. In time, two more names were given to the bay. Settlement by outsiders took longer, Major P. B. Reading's discovery of gold nearby on the Trinidad River, in May 1849, was important in attracting interest. In December of that year the Josiah Gregg party made a fresh discovery of the bay, which Dr. Gregg called Trinity Bay. In April 1850 the Laura Virginia Company expedition entered the bay and Lieutenant Douglass Ottinger of the ship *Laura Virginia* bestowed Alexander von Humboldt's name on the body of water.

The first town, Humboldt City, was founded on April 14, 1850, by the *Laura Virginia*'s people opposite the bay's narrow entrance. It eventually failed because of poor location and extreme competition. The next town, Uniontown (later Arcata), was founded only five days later by some members of the Gregg party and was better situated to provide overland access to the mountain mines, which drew early gold-seekers. The present Eureka was established and named three weeks after that, on May 13, 1850, by the Mendocino Exploring Company, led by James T. Ryan, after founders of Uniontown agreed to give up their claims to the land. Some stories say that Ryan, as he jumped onshore from a whaleboat, shouted "Eureka!"—Greek for "I have found it"—though he may have been simply repeating the state slogan, adopted the year before. The fourth town, Bucksport, was established in the summer of 1850 by David Buck, a former member of the Gregg party; this town was later absorbed by Eureka. The U.S. Army founded Fort Humboldt on a bluff over Bucksport in January 1853, and an unhappy Ulysses S. Grant was stationed here in 1853–54.

After the area's economic emphasis shifted from mining to logging, Eureka rose to prominence as the shipping center, thanks to its ideal location on the bay. In 1856 it became the county seat, taking that status away from Uniontown. Since then, Eureka has been the dominant city.

Today Eureka has a population of about 24,600 people, which is not only the largest in Humboldt County but the largest north of Santa Rosa—or in the top quarter of the state. Its main industries are fishing, lumber (which accounts for three-fourths of local revenues), and tourism. Gradually there will be a shift away from lumbering as the old-growth redwoods disappear or are protected within state- and national-park boundaries; new-growth redwoods take 40 years to mature. The NWPRR, owned by SP, takes Eureka's rail freight south.

Lumber magnates such as William Carson lived in ornate Victorian homes built of the pliable coastal redwood, and the elaborate Carson Mansion is an historic landmark; some brag that it is "the most photographed house in the nation." More than a hundred of these good old Victorians still stand in Eureka, and federal and local funds have helped spruce up Eureka's formerly deteriorating old downtown into Old Town and a collection of Victorians along 2nd Street.

Walking and driving tours of Eureka, as well as a harbor tour of Humboldt Bay, are the best ways to take in the sights. We suggest you first obtain a map of Eureka from a gas station or the Chamber of Commerce, 2112 Broadway (707/442-3738).

Entering Eureka from the south on Highway 101, you pass the mouth of the **Eel River,** which the highway has followed for many miles. In years of heavy rain the Eel—like other big rivers in this very wet part of California, such as the Smith, Klamath, and Mad—is apt to flood, washing out topsoil, rocks, trees, and even towns on its way to the ocean. Two big flood years were 1957 and 1964.

In the Fields Landing area is a turnoff to the bay point called King Salmon, via King Salmon Avenue. First along here to the left is **Shipwreck,** a commercial maritime museum and marine aquarium located in a replica of a three-masted nineteenth-century ship. It has historical artifacts from Humboldt Bay and shows off the harbor seal, giant octopus, leopard shark, wolf eel, ling cod, black snapper, sea anemone, and other local ocean life. Open daily 8–8 (summer) or 9–5 (winter). Admission: small fee. Next, on the right side of the road, is the **Pacific Gas & Electric Nuclear Power Plant,*** a small one (only 168 megawatts in capacity) due to be decommissioned in the near future. Tours are generally available in the summer. Further along King Salmon Road is a public picnic area built by PG&E. **King Salmon** is a bay- and deep-sea fishing resort area, with boat-rental facilities. Two operators are Captain Ole's (442-8212) and Johnny's Marina (442-2284); usually all the fishing gear and bait is furnished for the daily fishing trips, but bring your own lunch. Catches from piers, rocks, beaches, and boats may include chinook and silver salmon (April through September), crabs, greenling, rockfish, cabezon, ling cod, surf perches, and clams (gaper, Washington, littlenecks, basket, cockles, and geoduck). You need tackle and a license. Write or visit: California Department of Fish and Game, 619 Second St., Eureka (707/443-6771).

Fort Humboldt

Back on Highway 101, in about two miles you come to the turnoff (right on Highland Avenue) to **Fort Humboldt State Historic Park,**** on a plateau overlooking Eureka. Fort Humboldt was established in 1853, when settlers appealed to the U.S. government for help after being attacked by the local Indians—the Hoopas, Yuroks, and Mattoles. The Indians had welcomed trading with the miners and settlers—until the newcomers began taking their village sites and hunting grounds and killing those who resisted. When the Indians defended themselves and retaliated on an eye-for-an-eye basis, the settlers cried for help from the government. The classic how-we-won-the-West story!

Help arrived in 1853, when Lieutenant Colonel Robert C. Buchanan and his men set up a fort on the 40-foot bluff on the east side of the bay overlooking the town of Bucksport. By July 1854 the men had constructed 14 buildings, including officers' quarters, a commissary, hospital, powder magazine, guardhouse, and laundry buildings. These formed three sides around a 260-foot-square parade ground, with the fourth (western) side left open. Later additions were a blacksmith shop, stable, bakehouse, and a newer hospital.

Life was slow and relatively uneventful for this isolated fort, the main purpose of which was to resolve conflicts between the settlers and Indians. One young officer based here for five months in 1853-54 was Ulysses S. Grant, who was so lonely and miserable that he drank too much, and was offered a choice: resign or be brought up on fitness charges. He chose to resign, returned to Missouri to farm, and had his comeback in the Civil War.

Nor were the settlers satisfied with the fort's actions on their behalf, constantly fighting their own skirmishes as illegal "Volunteers." In February 1863 Governor Leland Stanford authorized the formation of the "Mountaineer Battalion" to control the Indians of the Humboldt region, and this group, led by a Colonel Black, succeeded in getting many Indians to surrender. The Hoopa Treaty of August 21, 1864, gave the Hoopa Valley to the Indians. Today this area along the Klamath, Trinity, and many other Humboldt County rivers is the 86,056-acre Hoopa Valley Indian Reservation, largest in the state. Fort Humboldt was abandoned as a military outpost in August 1870, and the land and one remaining building—the hospital—were sold to a Eurekan, W. S. Cooper. His descendants gave it to the city, which in turn gave it to the state in 1955.

Fort Humboldt State Historic Park consists of the restored hospital building, which serves as a state-park district headquarters, and an informative historic logging display on the grounds. The self-guided logging exhibit includes a logger's cabin, specimens of redwood logs and stumps, loggers' tools, and old methods of transportation for the logs, such as the steam donkey and narrow-gauge railroad. Indian artifacts are also shown. Location: 3431 Fort Ave., off Highland (707/443-7952). Picnic facilities. Open daily (except Thanksgiving and Christmas), 8-5; free.

Continuing on Highway 101 a few more blocks, go right on Harris Street and east to Eureka's **Sequoia Park and Zoo,** * located at Glatt and W streets. This 52-acre park has a stand of virgin redwoods, a few survivors of the forest that formerly covered this urban area. There are also flower gardens, a duck pond, playground, hiking trails, picnic areas, and a small museum with the first three fire engines used in the county. The zoo has local and imported animals, and the small petting zoo is open weekends from 1-4 P.M. The park gates are open until dark; the zoo is closed Mondays.

Most of the other attractions and services are located on the north end of Eureka, in the area between 1st and 7th streets, from Broadway to T streets. Here are the commercial waterfront, restaurants, motels, Old Town Square and Victorian districts, and more. The north end of Commercial Street is the **Eureka boat basin and fishing harbor,**** where the small fishing boats dock, a good spot for observing one of the West's busiest fleets. More than half the fish consumed in California are landed in Humboldt Bay, and this activity makes Eureka the state's premier producer of fresh fish and shellfish. There are about 200 commercial vessels registered on Humboldt Bay, as well as visiting boats from other West Coast ports. Fresh fish caught locally can be sampled at restaurants nearby, such as the Eureka Seafood Grotto and Lazio's Seafood, listed in Part IV, Eureka/Central Redwood Country.

Harbor cruises of **Humboldt Bay***** leave from the foot of C Street. Passengers have a 75-minute tour aboard the *Madaket*, built of local timber in 1910 and formerly a ferry until the Eureka-Samoa Bridge opened in 1972. On the way, you see from a distance the Carson Mansion, an egret rookery (part of the planned 8,600-acre Humboldt Bay National Wildlife Refuge), a former Indian village, oyster beds, pelican roosts, sawmills, the 1917 wreck of the U.S.S. *Milwaukee*, woodchip loading docks, pulp mills, and the Eureka boat basin. Tours leave daily Memorial Day weekend to mid-September. Departures are at 2:30, 4, and 7 P.M. Fare: adult—$3, child—$1.50-$2, or free. Drinks are available on board. Information: End C St., Eureka 95501 (707/455-1910).

Fish cannery tours are offered at the Coast Oyster Company at the end of A Street and the Lazio Fish Cannery at the end of C Street. Visitors are welcome when the plants are operating, usually 9-2:30; inquire.

Eureka's Old Town

Also in the waterfront area is the redeveloped shopping and service district called **Old Town*****—formerly a skid row. *Skid row* is a term that reputedly originated around here, after the slovenly settlements that grew like weeds along the skid roads on which redwood logs were

The Carson Mansion in Eureka is one of California's most flamboyant Victorian houses. It is a private club—inside. (Redwood Empire Association)

brought down from the forests. Thanks to federal funds and a $3 million bond issue, the old Victorians have been spruced up, streets landscaped, miniparks built, utilities run underground, period-style lighting installed, shops and restaurants opened, and promenades with bay views established.

In the center of the district, which stretches between A and M and 1st and 3rd streets, is **Old Town Square,** ** at the corner of Second and F streets. Around the corner is the **Humboldt Cultural Center,** 422 1st St., a mercantile store built in 1875 and now featuring shows by artists and crafts people from the Eureka area; open 12-4, Tues.-Sat. Other art collections and sales are at: **Old Town Art Guild,** 329 E St., and **Art Center,** 211 G St. The **Clarke Memorial Museum,** 3rd and E, has a collection of mounted birds and bird eggs, Indian artifacts, pioneer relics, antique machines and dolls, and historical photographs of the Eureka area. Open Tues.-Sun. 10-4, closed Mon. and holidays; free.

At the intersection of 2nd and M is the queen of Old Town and of Eureka, the **Carson Mansion.** *** The splendid 18-room house was built in 1884–86 by Canadian William Carson. Coming here from New Brunswick in 1850 to look for his fortune in gold, he found it instead in the coastal redwoods. To build his home, he hired Samuel and Joseph Newsom as architects, employed hundreds of carpenters, and even imported two woodcarvers from Ireland and Switzerland to do the ornate carving. The predominant style outside is Queen Anne, though many other styles, from Italianate to Eastlake, are represented. Inside are redwood, Philippine mahogany, and South American primavera woods, eight fireplaces including three of onyx, and stained-glass windows with figures in medieval costumes representing music, painting, drama, and science. The dining room, seating 26, was modeled after one in Chapultepec Castle in Mexico City; on the second floor Moorish arches bend over the hallway. The Carson family lived in the mansion from 1886 until 1950, when it became a men's club, the Ingomar. Its male-only policy was being challenged by the state attorney general's office, after a woman California coastal commissioner was denied access on a tour given for all the commissioners. Meanwhile, the mansion is closed to the public, who must be satisfied with photographing its elaborate exterior.

A **driving tour**** that takes in the more than 125 Victorians in Eureka is outlined in a brochure available at the Eureka Chamber of Commerce. It basically goes along 2nd, 3rd, E (the 200-300 and 1900-2100 blocks), F (100-200, 900-1000 blocks), G (900-1100 blocks), C (800-1600 blocks), B (1400-1600 blocks), Hillsdale (200-300 blocks), California (1100-1200 blocks), Grant (200 block), and Clark (200-300 blocks). The standard architectural guide to Northern California lists no fewer than 50 houses, with notes on their style. A five-hour city tour is described below on p. 260.

Indian Island and Samoa

After your Victorian walking and driving tours, you may be ready for a lumber-company tour and old-time camp cookhouse meal in Samoa on the thin Samoa Peninsula opposite downtown Eureka. Go to R Street and head west on Highway 255, crossing over Daby, Woodley, and Indian islands and Humboldt Bay en route. Bret Harte, employed in the late 1850s on the Arcata *Northern Californian*, was driven out of town after he took advantage of the editor's absence to editorially denounce the settlers' massacre of a hundred Wiyot Indian women and children on Indian Island. The 270-acre island's present population, mainly birds, is protected these days as part of the Humboldt Bay National Wildlife Refuge (information on the reserve from Box 1386 or 5th and H streets, Eureka 95501).

Samoa** is an old mill town named for the distant South Seas island group by founder John Vance in the 1890s. Louisiana-Pacific had a redwood sawmill and a bleached kraft pulp-mill in Samoa. The sawmill closed in late 1977. L-P said mill closings and layoffs around Eureka were due to the expansion of Redwood National Park. That was one factor. Others included the increased mechanization of mills and the shift of the forest-products industry from the Pacific Northwest to the South (Texas, Louisiana, Mississippi, Florida, etc.), where trees grow twice as fast, land is flatter, and environmental and regulatory restrictions are fewer.

The main attraction is the **Samoa Cookhouse,*** which claims to be "the last surviving cookhouse in the West." Inside is a small museum with historical logging and lumber tools, banquet rooms and a large main dining room that serves "lots of good food—lumber-camp style." Every logging and lumber camp traditionally had a cookhouse that served its employees three square meals a day (with a light supper on Sunday) for a very nominal price (e.g., 60 cents a day in 1922) so the workers would have the energy to work 12 hours a day, six days a week. The Samoa Cookhouse, first built as the Hammond Lumber Company cookhouse, can give you a feeling of what Samoa was like years ago—and a hearty meal (see Part IV, Eureka/Central Redwood Country).

Leaving Eureka on Highway 101 going north, in about eight miles you come to the turnoff to downtown Arcata.

Arcata

Arcata** (pop. 12,000), the second town founded on Humboldt Bay, was called Uniontown from 1850 to 1860. It served primarily as a mining supply center for the Klamath-Trinity gold-mining camps, and the Jacoby Building, 8th and H, is one of the architectural survivors from this pioneer period. When redwood replaced gold as the economic raison d'être for Humboldt Bay towns, Uniontown was upstaged by Eureka with its superior deep-water port.

Bret Harte, who lived here from 1857 to 1860, when he was in his early twenties, worked as a newspaper "printer's devil" for the *Northern Californian*. One wonders whether he would have achieved his later fame if he had stayed here and written logging stories.

In 1913 the Humboldt State Normal School was established in Arcata. Now Humboldt State University, it has about 7,600 students but is the smallest and most northern of the several state university campuses. HSU is located on 145 acres in the redwoods and runs 306 acres of experimental forest nearby. You may walk around the landscaped grounds, stop in the three galleries, library, administration building, and Wildlife Building, and attend cultural events. Information: 707/826-3011, 826-3928 (events).

Arcata's **Victorian walking/driving tour**** begins at the Chamber of Commerce (which provides a tour map) in the renovated Jacoby Building at 8th and H on the southwest corner of the plaza. The tour takes you around old downtown Arcata, built traditionally around a plaza sporting a flagpole and a statue of President McKinley, on the west side of Highway 101. The blocks and buildings to head for are: F Street (700, 987), 11th Street (630, 11th and G, 11th and H), J Street (927, 1621, 1651), 10th Street (860, 974, 1022), 12th Street (986, 1102 and between J and K), 13th Street (890, 1056), 14th Street (902, 980), and H Street (916, 1378, 1395).

The **Jacoby Building,**** a state landmark, was completed in 1857, solidly constructed of local brick and stone with decorative brick work and iron shutters—as such, one of the few buildings to be well protected from fire and Indian attacks. Its purpose was to store merchant Augustus Jacoby's groceries and goods for shipment by pack mule to the mines in the Klamath-Trinity area. In 1880 another merchant, Alexander Brizard, bought it and by 1907 had added two more stories and a complete wood and glass jacket around the original brick. Today the building has been restored as Jacoby's Storehouse, and in it reside the Chamber of Commerce, a savings and loan, a shopping gallery of more than a dozen stores, and on the upper floors a restaurant and offices.

The **"Pythian Castle"**** (11th and H) was built in 1885 with its delightful witches' caps topping the Knights of Pythias' North State Encampment; it has also recently been restored. The **Northern Redwood Lumber Office** (1102 12th St.), with its charming façade, served the lumberyard of the Arcata and Mad River Railroad, one of the oldest operating railroads on the West Coast and still running along the Mad River to the forests nearby (although it may close as lumber shipments decline). An early August A and MRRR celebration—Annie and Mary Day—is held annually in nearby Blue Lakes. A wonderful arched and spindled front doorway is on the **Bair House** (916 13th St.), built in 1887 by a doctor but later lived in for 40 years by the Bair family; note also the octagonal tower, which is like one on a house at 380 9th St. and has a witch's cap.

Leave Arcata and head north again on Highway 101. In about four miles is the turnoff east on Highway 200 to **Azalea State Reserve,*** about one mile from 101. These 30 acres are best visited in late spring, when the flowers are in full bloom.

Back on 101, in two miles is the next turnoff east to **McKinleyville.** Termed the "county's largest unincorporated city," it boasts a Guinness superlative: the world's tallest totem pole. Carved by locals Ernest Pierson and John Nelson in 1962, the 160-foot-tall totem pole weighs 57,000 pounds, and is topped by a thunderbird with a wingspan of 12 feet. The tall tree was cut in a Pacific Redwood Company forest south of Scotia, and was judged to have been about 500 years old at the time. If you like contests, try McKinleyville for the Pony Express Days in early June or the championship Logging Olympics in September.

First in a chain of state beaches in this area is **Little River State Beach,**** about seven miles north of McKinleyville, twelve miles from Arcata. It is adjacent to Clam Beach County Park. The 112-acre state park offers a beach along the Pacific Ocean, and fishing in the ocean and the Little River. Clam-digging is also a popular activity—determined use of a long, pointed shovel may reward you with a fresh sea meal.

Trinidad

Trinidad** is one of California's smallest incorporated cities, with a population of merely 300, but a history nearly 400 years in the making. The bay was first sighted by foreigners in 1595, when explorer Sebastian Cermeño saw the bluff, now named Trinidad Head. On June 10, 1775, the Bruno de Hezeta expedition entered the bay and named it Puerto de la Trinidad, in honor of that day, Trinity Sunday. The bay disappeared into the fog for another 75 years until 1850, when the town was founded as Warnersville, the first on the north coast. Gold-seekers and settlers came, the population boomed to 3,000, and the city was made a county seat. Bust followed boom when the action shifted south to logging and shipping from Humboldt Bay, and by 1854 the place was nearly deserted. In 1912 someone found that the city charter was still alive, so a city government was refounded and various schemes dreamed up to make Trinidad as great a port as Eureka . . . if only the government would give $7 million or so to make it all happen.

Nothing happened, so today the landmark town overlooks the bay, fishing and pleasure boats bob in the harbor, and visitors appreciate the unspoiled beauty. Sample some of the fresh salmon, rock cod, ling cod, cabezone, sea perch, and other local catches at the small restaurants in Trinidad—ask about the town's mid-June fish fry.

Just north of town is **Trinidad State Beach.*** On this 159-acre coast you may picnic, hike, fish for perch and rockfish, and observe offshore Pewetole Island.

Scenic old Highway 101 goes past Louisiana-Pacific's demonstration forest and Scotty Point to **Patrick's Point State Park,***** the first state park north of Eureka with camping. The 443 acres include tree- and meadow-covered headlands, precipitous cliffs, and a broad sandy beach. Trees that predominate are spruce, hemlock, pine, fir, and red alder. Yurok Indians liked this area for its ocean life, especially abalone and sea lion, fresh water and fish from Penn Creek, forest game and berries. Visitors can hike along old Indian and nature trails in the lush forests and meadows, play and hunt for agates on the beach, fish in the salt and fresh waters, watch for deer, sea lions, and birds, and camp (123 developed sites). Don't be surprised by the summer fogs.

The next in this chain of beaches is **Dry Lagoon State Park,**** three miles north. Its triad of lagoons are just barely cut off from the ocean that they were originally part of. To the east all three—Big, Stone, and Freshwater—are bounded by the private Three Lagoons Recreation Area, owned by Georgia-Pacific Corporation but open to the public for day-use, for boating, fishing, and swimming. Dry Lagoon covers 1,036 acres and eight miles on the west (ocean) side of Big and Stone (and the southwest side of Freshwater) lagoons. A county park is on the south end of Big Lagoon. A finger of Prairie Creek Redwood State Park reaches south to Stone Lagoon's northwest side. Picnic, fish, beachcomb, and swim (chilly!) in the lagoons.

PRACTICAL INFORMATION

Getting There, Getting Around

Arcata Airport, served by Hughes Airwest (707/445-2021) and sometimes by commuter airlines, is the main airport for Redwood Country. Century Airlines (707/445-9677, 445-8446) flies out of Eureka's Murray Field. Ken Tours Travel of Eureka (707/443-1685) has twice-daily, 5–10 seat Cessna flights, S.F.-Eureka-S.F., leaving from

Butler Airport (next to S.F. International). Arcata Airport has car-rental counters.

Greyhound runs through Humboldt County and makes stops in several towns along Highway 101, including Eureka (415 4th St., 707/442-0370).

Local transit does exist. Eureka Transit Service (707/443-8935) serves Eureka Mon.-Sat. Arcata Transit System (707/822-3775) serves Arcata and Mad River Valley West Mon.-Sat. and Blue Lake Mon.-Fri. Redwood Transit System (Humboldt Transit Authority, 707/443-0826) has buses between Rio Dell in the south and Trinidad in the north.

North Coast Redwood Tours (707/677-0334) has Redwood National Park and coastal bus tours from Trinidad and Orick as far as the Klamath River in the summer.

The Eureka Chamber of Commerce (707/442-3738) sponsors a thorough, five-hour "Image Tour" by bus and boat, including Fort Humboldt, Sequoia Park, a sawmill, the commercial fishing fleet, and Clarke Museum, cruising on Humboldt Bay, and lunching at the logger's cookhouse. The tour runs mid-June to October, costs about $7 per adult, $4 per child. Reservations necessary.

Where to Stay and Eat

Accommodations (including camping) and restaurants are listed in Part IV under the heading Eureka/Central Redwood Country. See also Garberville/Southern Redwoods and Crescent City/Northern Redwoods.

CHAPTER 11:

Northern Redwoods

HIGHLIGHTS

Redwood National Park / 261
Tall Trees Grove / 265
Lady Bird Johnson Grove / 265
Prairie Creek Redwoods / 265
Coastal Drive / 267
Klamath River / 267
Klamath / 269

Del Norte Coast Redwoods / 270
Crescent City / 270
Jedediah Smith Redwoods / 273
Six Rivers National Forest / 273
Lakes Earl and Talawa / 274
Smith River / 274
Pelican State Beach / 274

Redwood National Park, protecting the world's tallest trees in one of the most expensive and controversial parks in the U.S., is the focal point of the Northern Redwoods area. This area stretches along Highway 101 from Orick, at the southern edge of the national park, up to the Oregon border. In between are three former state parks—Prairie Creek Redwoods, Del Norte Coast Redwoods, and Jedediah Smith Redwoods—that were absorbed into the national park in 1978; Crescent City, the main populated district; and fine beaches. The Klamath and Smith rivers drain the Six Rivers National Forest to the east, offer excellent fishing and recreation, and empty into the Pacific Ocean.

WHAT TO SEE AND DO

Redwood National Park,*** with a gateway information center in Orick, shelters the tallest and some of the oldest trees in the world, as well as a beautiful coastline that equals the best in the country. This

The tallest tree in the world, 367.8 feet, in Redwood National Park. (Redwood Empire Association)

park has also caused congressmen to introduce controversial legislation, loggers to demonstrate noisily in Eureka and take logging trucks to San Francisco and Washington, D.C., twisted minds to "ring" and kill giant trees, conservationists to campaign for decades, and taxpayers to spend millions. First established in 1968, the park covered 58,000 acres, but was such a patchwork quilt of state, federal, and private land that clear-cut logging was carried on next door to protected giants. It took another 10 years, to 1978, and many acrimonious debates, discussions, and demonstrations, to get the national park expanded to a total of 106,000 acres, including three state parks—Prairie Creek Redwoods, Del Norte Coast Redwoods, and Jedediah Smith Redwoods.

Redwood National Park has two distinct ecological areas—the inland redwood forests along the rivers, and the coastal bluffs and shoreline. The park's redwood forests extend from the southern areas around Orick and Redwood Creek to the northern area above Crescent City. It was the Orick section of the park that was so hotly disputed. Logging began here in the 1850s, but most of the virgin forest was cut in the last 25 years.

Forestry, logging, and lumber have been big business in California. The state's total land area is just over 100 million acres, of which 42.4 million are forest. Of these 42 million, 16.8 million acres—or about 40 percent of the forest land, 17 percent of the total land—is commercial forest where harvesting is allowed. This forest land is in two general areas: the pine region in the Sierra Nevada and other mountains up to Oregon (ponderosa, Jeffrey, sugar, Douglas fir, incense cedar, white fir, etc.), and the coastal redwood region hugging the coast from Big Sur to Oregon.

In the 1970s California's lumber and wood-products industries employed about 50,000 people, including 9,000 in the redwood region of Humboldt and Del Norte counties. Despite the passage of the Redwood National Park extension bill in 1978, redwood industry employment was expected to shrink because the old-growth redwoods have been disappearing, new growth but inferior redwoods mature slowly, and automation steadily removes jobs.

Trees are harvested in at least two ways: by selective cutting and clear cutting. Selective cutting harvests only certain trees above a specified diameter, allowing neighboring trees to grow taller and new trees to sprout from the stumps and roots; except for the fresh stumps, selectively cut forests after a couple of years would not offend most hikers. Clear cutting, however, removes virtually *everything*, regardless of age or size. Theoretically, clear cutting is used in areas where the timber is "overmature" and no longer able to reproduce, where remaining trees would be vulnerable to sun scalding and wind, and where steep slopes could lead to erosion. Clear cutting leaves ugly scars on the land, which, though reseeded by helicopter and replanted by hand, takes years to reproduce to the point of being visually pleasing. Unfortunately, clear cutting was the technique predominantly used by timber companies on the fringes of Redwood National Park around Orick.

Once trees are cut and have fallen onto a softened bed, the branches are removed and the trunk is sawn into shorter lengths, a process called bucking. Yarding is taking the logs with cables and yarder (or a skidder with hooks) to a truck landing. From here, logs go to the sawmill for bark removal, slicing into planks, trimming, grading, air drying, perhaps kiln drying, and storing until shipping for manufacture. Tours of redwood mills are sponsored by various companies throughout the redwood country, as outlined in this chapter (see also the Georgia-Pacific Mill, Fort Bragg, p. 227). A complete list of commercial tree farms, forests, mills and tours of facilities is available through the California Redwood Association, 1050 Battery St., San Francisco 94111. The mill closest to Orick is the Arcata Redwood Company Mill near the junction of Highway 101 and Bald Hill Road, two miles north of Orick; unguided tours weekdays 7:30–3:30.

The dispute over Redwood National Park was a classic "jobs versus environment" struggle: local logging companies and their employees, who felt resentful of and threatened by the existence and expansion of the park, pitted themselves against local and urban environmentalists, who felt the virgin old-growth redwoods should be preserved for later generations. The controversy raged on for decades before the national park was established in 1968—and didn't let up even then. It focused particularly on "the Worm," a narrow, seven-mile-long strip of redwoods on either side of Redwood Creek south of Orick. Here reside the world's tallest tree and trees. But around the Worm clear cutting was leaving the hillsides naked—and thus prone to winter floods accelerating erosion of both the clear-cut and the old-growth areas in the creek's drainage basin. During the years of controversy, the virgin old-growth stands decreased in this area from 32,000 to about 12,000 acres, as the companies were allowed to continue cutting.

In 1977 California Congressman Philip Burton and Senator Alan Cranston proposed expanding Redwood Park by 74,000 acres at a cost of anywhere from $150 to $700 million, depending on the corporations' price tag. A year later, on March 27, 1978, President Carter signed the Redwood National Park Expansion Act. This specified that $432 million was to be spent as follows: $359 million to purchase 48,000 acres (8,990 acres of old-growth redwoods, 39,010 acres of adjacent clear-cut land, with probably another 30,000 acres to be purchased later, with additional funds, as a buffer zone); $40 million to retrain and guarantee income for up to six years for about 920 local redwood lumberworkers affected by the land purchase; and $33 million to rehabilitate Redwood Creek basin lands. Three companies were involved—Louisiana-Pacific, Arcata National, and Simpson Timber. L-P and Arcata contested the payments they were to get, and the issues will be settled in federal court, with the land cost possibly doubling. The total cost of the park expansion may climb to $823 million or more, making Redwood National Park one of the most expensive in the U.S. However, world treasures will be preserved for future generations to enjoy.

Touring Redwood Park

The **southern section of Redwood National Park** is accessible just north of Orick, via Bald Hill Road east of Highway 101. This road goes the half-mile to the trailhead of **Redwood Creek Trail,** a hike of 8.5 miles one way or 17 miles round trip southeast along Redwood Creek to the **Tall Trees Grove.***** This is the site of the **Howard Libby Redwood,** the world's tallest tree—367.8 feet—discovered in 1964 by a National Geographic expedition. The world's third and fifth tallest trees also reside here with other old giants, age 2,000 years or so. Primitive camping is allowed along the riverbank here. Alternatively, a summertime shuttle bus (small fee) leaves every hour from 9–4 daily from the Bald Hill Road parking area, off Highway 101 about 7 miles. After the 6-mile, 30-minute ride through logged land, you can walk a mile to the tallest trees.

Bald Hill Road also provides access to **Lady Bird Johnson Grove,***** a beautiful stand of old-growth redwoods dedicated by President Nixon in 1970 to the former first lady. A half-mile walk across a bridge will bring you to the grove, and a self-guided nature-trail walk brings you back to your car. Bald Hill Road continues east over the mountains, turning into gravel halfway along the 40-mile windy drive to Weitchpec in the Hoopa Indian Reservation.

The coastal and marine parts of Redwood National Park's southern section feature rugged headlands, bluffs rising from the sea, long sandy beaches, tide pools and lagoons, and active bird and sea life. Dress warmly, especially if it's foggy. It's best to explore the terrain on foot, carrying a picnic for sustenance.

Information: Superintendent, Redwood National Park, Drawer N, Crescent City 95531. Park headquarters on Highway 101 in Orick is open 8–8 daily, phone 707/488-3461.

Prairie Creek Redwoods

Continuing north, five miles from Orick on Highway 101 you come into **Prairie Creek Redwoods,***** a state park absorbed into Redwood National Park. This 12,240-acre area is special in having lush Fern Canyon, two herds of Roosevelt elk, and Revelation Trail for the blind, as well as many tall redwoods.

The Prairie Creek region is relatively undeveloped, but once it bustled with activity. Gold Beach and Gold Bluffs derived their names

Fern Canyon in Prairie Creek Redwoods is aptly named: the 50-foot walls are covered with ferns. (Redwood Empire Association)

from the thousands of fortune-seekers who landed here in 1851, hoping to cry "Eureka!" They worked the sands of the beach and the bluffs, but after several thousand dollars in gold was tediously recovered, the diggings were deserted. The virgin redwoods and beautiful beaches were noticed later and not deserted. The Save-the-Redwoods League was instrumental in purchasing parcels here starting in 1921 (many groves are named in honor of donors), and the state began acquisition in 1923. The league's efforts have continued: in 1976 it purchased 280 acres along Boyes Creek for $1.7 million and thus helped enlarge the park's southeast section.

Exploring this park is best done on foot on any of the 21 trails, which are accessible from the three roads (described below) and from park headquarters off Highway 101. The 4.5-mile-long **James Irvine Trail** goes west along Godward and Home creeks, to Fern Canyon and Gold Beach. **Fern Canyon,**** reached from Irvine Trail and Gold Beach Road on a .6-mile loop trail, is a natural cut through the bluffs, caused by water erosion from Home Creek. The canyon's 50-foot-high walls are lushly covered with a profusion of delicate and beautiful five-fingered ferns, while fallen trees are softened by moss. Also off Irvine Trail is the **Elk Refuge,*** though the two herds of Roosevelt elk do stroll all around. After the moose, they are North America's largest deer. Because one of them can weigh up to 1,000 pounds, the elk should be observed from a respectful distance.

Also leaving from park headquarters is .2-mile **Revelation Trail,*** designed for the blind, though sighted people can probably learn something. Rails and rope guide you along the trail to touchable things described on signs and in a Braille handbook available at the headquarters. On the east side of the park is the long rhododendron glen, which is in bloom in spring and is reached on the 5.5-mile **Rhododendron Trail.*** The short .3-mile **Circle Trail**** goes to Big Tree, just off Highway 101 to the east, where most of the redwoods in the park are found.

Three roads run north-south through different sections of the park. Highway 101 goes through the middle, past the turnoff to park headquarters and the beginning of many walking trails, including those to Fern Canyon, Gold Beach, the Elk Refuge, Big Tree, and Corkscrew Tree. The gravel **Davison-Ossagon Road** leaves and then rejoins 101, going west to allow access to Gold Beach and shorter trails to Fern Canyon, Gold Bluffs, and the Elk Refuge; the northern end, Ossagon Road, is usually closed in rainy weather. The **Cal Barrel-East Ridge Road** skirts the east side of the state park, giving shorter access to the Rhododendron Trail and other redwood hiking trails.

Prairie Creek Redwoods offers the visitor facilities for camping, picnicking, hiking, natural history, and fishing. The several creeks contain rainbow and cutthroat trout, and in season salmon and steelhead. Camping is possible at 100 developed sites around park headquarters and near Gold Beach; Ticketron reservations are advised in summer. Park information: 707/488-2171.

Leaving Prairie Creek Redwood on Highway 101, take the turnoff west on Alder Camp Road to the **Coastal Drive***** through the northern tip of Prairie Creek and another section of Redwood National Park in Del Norte County. This eight-mile scenic drive is partly unpaved gravel, with spectacular views and scenery—redwood bluffs hundreds of feet above the crashing surf below. The drive ends up on Beach Road, which goes back to Highway 101 before reaching the Klamath.

Klamath River

The **Klamath River,***** California's second largest, originates in Upper Klamath Lake in the Klamath Mountains in southwest Oregon and flows 265 miles to the Pacific Ocean. Two hundred tributaries feed into the river as it winds through national forests, carves canyons, and meanders through redwood-tree-lined and grassy valleys.

The Yurok Indians lived along the banks near the mouth for generations before the arrival of the white man, living well off the abundant salmon, smelt, crabs, rockfish, and other river and ocean fish, and building huts from the abundant redwood. Their culture was well developed when Jedediah Smith's expedition first crossed the Klamath River on May 25, 1828, hungry and tired as they opened a route to the north. Though the river was named for Smith by the white explorers, it was changed to Klamath in 1851 after the short-lived county of that name, somehow derived from the Chinook Indian word *tlamatl*. Because of the Klamath's long, difficult-to-follow course, it was not traced from its mouth toward its source until 1850, when prospectors tracked it to the junction of the Shasta River in the middle of California.

Like other rivers in the north, the Klamath can rise to flood levels during winter rains and now and then washes out the towns along its banks. During the later spring, summer, and fall, though, the river is favored by fishermen, rafters, kayakers, and canoeists. From Requa, speedy "jet boats" ply upstream (see below).

The fishing on the Klamath was considered excellent until 1978. That was the year of the salmon war between local Indians and government agents, during which 143 Indians were arrested and dozens of nets seized. The issues centered around the commercial fishing rights of the Yuroks, Hoopas, and others along the Klamath and Trinity rivers, particularly those fishing with gill nets. State and federal officials banned all commercial fishing when the salmon's survival was threatened on the two rivers in 1978 and 1979. Causes of low salmon- and also steelhead-trout-count included commercial overfishing in the rivers and offshore in the ocean, antiquated logging and road-building methods silting the streams, two years of drought, and new dams upstream releasing less water. It will take years for the fish to repopulate to previous higher levels. Until conditions improve, each Hoopa and Yurok can fish with one 100-foot anchored gill net for food (not for profit); sport fishing with hook and line and dip nets is allowed. The state has proposed a fisheries restoration program to build more hatcheries, restore spawning grounds, and open up streams clogged by logging waste.

For sports fishers, the season stretches from June to December.

Trout are catchable all along the river from June to November. The first king (Chinook) salmon runs upstream start mid-July and continue through October; the majority of the salmon are caught at the mouth and in the tidewater areas of the river. Silver salmon runs begin in September and continue through November. Steelhead may be caught June to November, with the summer runs really starting in August. Fishing equipment can be bought or purchased in Klamath and Requa towns at places like Benedict's Tackle Shop and Requa Boat Dock. Fish and Game Department regulations should be checked locally for limits and license requirements; ask also for the department's *The Angler's Guide to the Klamath River.*

Northern California companies that offer 2-to-5-day white-water rafting and inflated canoe and/or kayak trips down the Klamath River include (all area code 415, except as noted): All-Outdoors, 2151 San Miguel Dr., Walnut Creek 94596 (934-0240); American River Touring Assoc., 1016 Jackson St., Oakland 94607 (465-9355); Echo, 6505 Telegraph Ave., Oakland 94609 (658-5075); OARS, Box 67, Angels Camp 95222 (209/736-2924); Outdoor Adventures, 3109 Fillmore St., San Francisco 94123 (346-8700); Outdoors Unlimited, 2500 5th Ave., Sacramento 95818 (916/452-1081); Whitewater Voyages, 1225 Liberty St., El Cerrito 94530 (236-7219); and Wilderness Water Ways, 33 Canyon Lake Dr., Port Costa 94569 (787-2820).

Crossing over the Klamath, Highway 101 goes by the turnoff to the town of **Klamath,** located on this new site since the flood in 1964 washed the town away from its site closer to the river. Klamath offers some facilities to the traveler, such as motels, coffee shops, small resorts, equipment rental shops, and the like. The last Sunday in June is the annual Klamath Salmon Festival and salmon barbecue.

From Klamath head north on Highway 101 to the small fishing resort town of **Requa,** whose name may derive from the Indian *re'kwoi* ("creek mouth"). What puts Requa on the map is the **Klamath Jet-Boat Kruise service,*** Box 5, Klamath 95548 (707/482-4191), a 64-mile round trip up the Klamath River into Hoopa Indian territory. Coast guard–inspected "jet boats" leave the Requa boat dock daily at 9 A.M. and return at 3 P.M., May 30–October 15 (reservations encouraged during summer). Cost: $10 adult and $4 child, 4 to 11.

About four miles north of Requa is a tourist trap, the **Trees of Mystery.** Redwoods have been sculpted—with a chainsaw—into grotesque "sculptures" of Paul Bunyan, the Blue Ox, and such. Some trees have actually been left alone in groves. Admission: adult—$2, child—$1. Open daily 8–8.

Del Norte Coast Redwoods

Stretching along the coast is the **northern extension of Redwood National Park,** up through the former state park, **Del Norte Coast Redwoods.***** This is in one of the wettest areas in California. A true rain forest that receives an average of 80 inches a year, these 6,375 acres of redwoods also have some warm sheltered inland campgrounds at Mill Creek, protected by mountains to the west. Rhododendrons and azaleas bloom in April through July, golden-leafed alder in the fall. Mill Creek has trout-fishing and people-swimming. Hiking trails go through the redwoods to the coast, where, on Wilson Beach, you can beachcomb and tide-pool-watch. Two trails in particular: **Damnation Creek Trail,**** beginning at the Henry Solon Graves Memorial Grove on Highway 101 and going west to the ocean at the mouth of the vividly named creek; and **Last Chance Trail,**** which starts off Highway 101, follows old Highway 1 and winds west to bluffs overlooking the ocean. While hiking watch for Roosevelt elk, black-tailed deer, and maybe even a black bear. Camping is in 145 developed sites at Mill Creek. The official entrance is about five miles south of Crescent City on the east side of Highway 101.

Crescent City

Deriving its name from the crescent-shaped bay, **Crescent City*** has had a close relationship with both the sea and the land, though several times the sea has wreaked havoc. The original inhabitants were the Tolowa Indians, who lived near the beach in redwood-hut villages. One of their four major local villages is preserved as a historical landmark on Pebble Beach Drive near the end of Pacific Avenue. You can see where the Indians had their redwood huts, *temescals* ("sweat houses"), ceremonial dancing pit, and burial ground.

The lure of gold brought prospectors by boat and by foot. In 1850 ships anchored in the pleasant harbor, but another two years passed until settlement began when an overland group set up camp on the beach and sent south for supplies and more people. Crescent City was founded by J. F. Wendell in 1953, and a year later it had 300 buildings and hundreds of residents trading with miners in the interior mountains in Northern California and southern Oregon.

Two early shipwrecks left their mark on the town. The steamer

The lighthouse at Crescent City is accessible by foot at low tide. (Redwood Empire Association)

America burned and was wrecked on June 24, 1855, and its cannons are at **Battery Point** at the end of Battery Street at A. The federal government in 1856 built a lighthouse to alert ships to the tricky rocks off Battery Point. Now the **Crescent City Lighthouse Museum,** the building is 200 yards offshore and is accessible by foot a few hours daily at low tide. The museum, run by the historical society, is open, free, daily from March to November when the tides permit. The second coastal tragedy occurred off this rocky coast in 1865. On July 30 the Pacific Mail steamer *Brother Jonathan* was wrecked on St. George's Reef a few miles north, and only 19 of the 232 passengers and crew survived. Many of the victims were buried in the town cemetery at 8th and Pebble Beach Drive, which was renamed **Brother Jonathan Cemetery** and is also a state historic site.

Two buildings in town that give a flavor of the nineteenth century are a museum and a home. The **Del Norte County Historical Society Museum,** 577 H at 6th Street, has exhibits of Yurok and Tolowa Indian artifacts, pioneer days, and the old county jail. Open free, Mon.-Sat. 1–4 (shorter hours in winter). One block away is the **McNulty Pioneer Memorial Home,** 7th at H Street, which has been refurnished in the early pioneer style.

World War II brought another maritime incident, when the *Emidio,* a 10,745-ton tanker, became the first ship attacked by a Japanese submarine off the Pacific Coast, on December 20, 1941. Shelled and disabled about 200 miles north of San Francisco, the *Emidio* was abandoned, drifted north, and broke in two on rocks outside Crescent City's harbor. Portions of the hull lie under the state historic marker at 1st and H Streets in the city's waterfront park, a memorial to the five who died.

Fishing has always played an important economic role in Crescent City, as in Eureka. To affirm support of their fishermen, in 1950 residents donated money, materials, and labor to build **Citizen's Dock,*** on Citizen's Dock Road off Highway 101 south of downtown. The photogenic working wharf is the home of the fishing fleet, two fish-processing plants, lumber shipping, a sports-boat marina, seafood restaurants, and the **Undersea Gardens.** This commercial aquarium has an estimated 5,000 specimens of fish and plant life, as well as entertainment by the Aquamaids and Armstrong the Giant Octopus; an entry fee is charged.

To protect the harbor from the sea, Crescent City in 1958 built a large breakwater. In turn, to strengthen this structure, 1,975 tetrapods—big 25-ton, four-footed things invented in France—were placed on the breakwater's seaward side. A monument was erected to mark the first place in the Western Hemisphere where tetrapods were used. These tetrapods were put to a severe test in 1964, when a devastating tsunami, or seismic sea wave, hit California's coast and particularly Crescent City. That tsunami was generated in the Pacific by an earthquake in the Aleutian Trench, far north near the Bering Sea. Starting small, it gathered strength as it traveled at speeds up to 500 miles an hour across the ocean. When the 21-foot-high wave hit Crescent City it killed 11 people and leveled downtown; in Alaska 107 people died. The tsunami also moved the tetrapod monument from its post to its present location where Highway 101 crosses Elk Creek.

After this disaster, Crescent City rebuilt 21 blocks, including six in the downtown **Mall,** around I and 3rd streets. **Redwood National Park headquarters,** Front and K, has a visitors' center. A half-block away at the Convention and Cultural Center, the visitor can find more information at the Del Norte County Chamber of Commerce. The county fair is in mid-August at the Crescent City fairgrounds. Crescent City is the last "urban" area until Coos Bay, Oregon, 135 miles north.

For an enjoyable picnic, take your lunch to the city park along Scenic Drive at the harbor, or north to **Pebble Beach,**** where you can hike and collect well-worn driftwood. Alternatively, you can head inland to Jedediah Smith Redwoods.

Jedediah Smith Redwoods

Either of two routes from Highway 101 will take you to **Jedediah Smith Redwoods,**** third of the state redwood parks absorbed by the national park: Elk Valley Road to scenic Howland Hill Road (part of the ca. 1858 Crescent City Plank and Turnpike stagecoach road, still mostly unpaved) into the southern section; or Highway 101 to Highway 199 into the northern section. Both will take you to the surging Smith River, crossed by two bridges. By entering via Howland Hill Road you arrive in the original section of the park—**Frank D. Stout Memorial Grove,**** donated to the state in 1929. This grove still has the park's largest tree, 20 feet in diameter and 340 feet high. Gradually the park grew to its present 9,139 acres, about two-thirds purchased with donations (for 18 memorial groves) to the Save-the-Redwoods League.

The park was initially named for the Hiouchi Indians in the area, then, like the river, was renamed for the explorer Jedediah Smith. He reputedly discovered the Rocky Mountains' south pass, was the first to cross the Sierras overland and to traverse the West Coast from San Diego north to the Columbia River near Canada, and led the first party of white men through Del Norte County.

Jedediah Smith Redwoods offers beautiful nature and hiking trails to and through the redwood groves, along creeks, and over the river. The Smith River, one of Northern California's largest, has good trout fishing in late summer, and steelhead and salmon fishing October through February. Sandy beaches and swimming in the Smith are also attractions. Camping is possible in 108 developed sites across the river from the Jensen Family Grove, off Highway 199.

Six Rivers National Forest

Highway 199 goes northeast into **Six Rivers National Forest,**** which covers 968,792 acres in Del Norte and Humboldt counties. The six rivers are the Smith, Klamath, Eel, Trinity, Van Duzen, and Mad, which are fed by hundreds of tributaries and cut through the forests on their way west to the Pacific. Recreation activities center around the forests and rivers—camping, hiking, fishing, swimming, boating, and hunting. Camping is in 15 developed areas and more primitive sites, at least four of which are located off Highway 199 between and near Gasquet and Patrick Creek: Panther Flat, Grassy Flat, Patrick Creek, and Cedar Rustic. Information: Six Rivers National Forest Headquarters, 710 E St., Eureka 95501 (707/442-1721); a regional Forest Service information office is at Gasquet on Highway 199 (457-3131).

If instead you go back to Highway 101 via 199, where the highways join is an exit west to **Lake Earl,*** a 2,000-acre freshwater body, and **Lake Talawa,*** a smaller freshwater lagoon attached to Lake Earl and adjacent to the ocean.

Continuing north on Highway 101, in about 10 miles you come to the **town of Smith River,** named after the river and the explorer, as described above, but situated on Rowdy Creek. Its claim to fame is that it is the "Easter Lily Capital of the World," producing perhaps 90 percent of the nation's lily bulbs and sponsoring an Easter-in-July Festival.

The **Smith River,** like the Klamath, is famous for fishing, with the types of fish available depending on the location—the lower Smith going from the ocean inland to Smith Redwoods, the upper Smith to around Gasquet. At the mouth, the tidewater fish available all year include ling cod, black snapper, cabazone, flounder, perch, and smelt. The river fish vary more, with cutthroat trout June through November, salmon September through December, and steelhead November through March. The upper Smith has trout and steelhead May to November 1, with salmon joining them and being catchable the rest of the year.

About the last point of interest off Highway 101 just before it enters Oregon is **Pelican State Beach,*** five acres of ocean coastline with piles of sea-shaped driftwood and inviting sand dunes.

PRACTICAL INFORMATION

Getting There, Getting Around

Greyhound has buses running between San Francisco and Coos Bay, Oregon, with stops at Klamath, Crescent City, and Smith River.

Small planes can land at Crescent City, Gasquet, and Smith River, but most aviation is conducted at Arcata Airport near Eureka (see p. 259).

North Coast Redwood Tours has summertime bus tours from Trinidad and Orick to Redwood National Park, along the coast and the Klamath River. Information: 707/677-0334.

Where to Stay and Eat

Accommodations (including camping) and restaurants are listed in Part IV under the heading Crescent City/Northern Redwoods. See also Eureka/Central Redwood Country.

SOURCES OF INFORMATION— REDWOOD COUNTRY

General: Redwood Empire Association, 360 Post St., Suite 201, San Francisco 94108 (415/421-6554), is the general visitors' information bureau for Humboldt and Del Norte counties as well as the others north of the Golden Gate.

Save-the-Redwoods League, 114 Sansome St., San Francisco 94104 (415/ 362-2352), is not a tourist bureau but there you can find out anything you want to know about coastal redwoods and their preservation. Please join.

California Redwood Association, 1 Lombard St., San Francisco 94111 (415/392-7880), has a rather different view of the trees, and can tell you about logging and redwood construction.

Chambers of Commerce: Eureka Chamber of Commerce, 2112 Broadway, Eureka 95501 (707/442-3738). Humboldt County Convention & Visitors Bureau, 7th F St., Eureka 95501. Arcata Area Chamber of Commerce, 780 7th St., Arcata 95521 (707/822-3619). Trinidad Chamber of Commerce Scenic/ Main, Trinidad 95570 (707/677-3874). Del Norte County Chamber of Commerce, Box 246 (Front and K), Crescent City 95531 (707/464-3174). Also in most other towns.

Books: *Redwood Empire* by Stuart Nixon (New York: Dutton, 1966) is a pictorial history of the redwood region. *California Coast Trails* by J. Smeaton Chase is a classic (Boston: Houghton Mifflin, 1913). The *California Coastal Plan* outlines in detail the whole California coast and the California Coastal Commission's plans for protecting it (San Francisco: California Coastal Commission, 1975). *The Humboldt Bay Region* by Owen C. Coy is an old history of this area (Los Angeles: California State Historical Association, 1929). *Fine California Views—the Photographs of W. A. Ericson* by Peter Palmquist is a history and collection of photographs of the redwood region (Eureka: Interface California Corp., 1975). *The Last Redwoods and the Parkland of Redwood Creek* by François Leydet is the Sierra Club's superb format book and a moving treatise on this controversial section of what is now Redwood National Park (San Francisco: Sierra Club, 1969). *The Ageless Relics: The Story of Sequoia* by Norman Taylor compares the coastal and Sierra redwoods, and discusses how these giants have affected human history (New York: St. Martin's, 1962). *Exploring the North Coast* by Mike Hayden is an informative guide to the coast from San Francisco's Golden Gate Bridge north to Oregon (San Francisco: Chronicle Books, 1976). Sunset's picture book *Discovering the California Coast* has beautiful photographs that make you want to leave instantly for an extended coastal journey, with about 40 pages on the North Coast redwoods region (Menlo Park: Lane Publishing, 1975).

Part IV

WHERE TO STAY AND EAT

Nothing is so perishable as travel information, especially hotel and restaurant listings. Name, address, telephone, price, cuisine, ownership, management, hours, credit-card acceptance, decor, style—not to mention quality—all change as frequently as the news. Although this book is primarily a sightseeing guide, we would be negligent if we failed to give readers some indication of acceptable places at which to stay and eat. Thus this concise, fallible listing of significant but perishable facts. Call or write ahead to confirm facts of concern to you.

Our emphasis in the listings below is on choice. We believe in that 2,000-year-old maxim of Publius': "No pleasure endures unseasoned by variety." Travel celebrates variety, thrives on it. Not every travel guide reflects this sentiment, and the tourist industry seems to think variety is positively dangerous, possibly un-American. Popular travel guides and the hotel and restaurant industries, like TV programmers, pitch their products to the lowest common denominator among American travelers: the desire to avoid unpleasantness.

The removal of risk from travel has resulted in far too many sanitized motels and wood-grain-Formica coffee shops: a Holiday Inn in every city in America, suburban strips lined with Burger King, Denny's, McDonald's, Long John Silver's, ad nauseam, all across this fair land of ours. Places to stay and eat are indistinguishable, interchangeable; inside or outside, you could as easily be in Birmingham, Michigan, as Birmingham, Alabama.

Too many travel guides reflect this uniformity rather than the variety that still exists. The publisher of the Mobil guides, Rand McNally, sends out teams of college students on vacation to take quantified, objectified, computerized inventory of accommodations ("Ck-out, noon. Coin lndry 10 blks") and restaurants ("Background music. Kiwanis, Lions meet here"). The result is homogenized listings of establishments that meet the avoid-risk criterion. Thus both Mendocino and Little River are mixed with Fort Bragg, and the many little inns that make the Mendocino coast such a good weekend excursion are left out.

Choice certainly means risk. Little inns can have lumpy mattresses; rustic lodges may not have heated pools. But the inn can have individually decorated rooms, and the lodge can offer a friendly home-cooked breakfast in front of the fireplace.

To avoid risk is to forsake most of the possibility of pleasant surprise, most rustic charm, some true comfort and some interesting discomfort, a lot of relaxed communication with real people, occasional adventure, rural detours, unique experiences, and other qualities of individual travel.

Mass tourism may avoid risk. We recommend a risk a day as good for the soul. We think it is better to take a chance on a hotel or restaurant that can be wonderful or dreadful than to go to a place that can never be memorable at all.

But we're not crotchety all the time, not intolerant of Colonel Sanders and Ronald McDonald every day. We list some "surprise-free" accommodations and restaurants because even the most rigorously independent travelers don't feel like taking a risk every night and every mealtime. Even then we list a few more predictable accommodations (because it is always safer to reserve ahead) than cookie-cutter restaurants (because these are too easy to find).

Incidentally, we did not accept any free accommodations or meals, and moved about as anonymously as possible, which isn't difficult. All listings are our responsibility.

PRICE CATEGORIES

The most worthwhile guidebooks tell exactly how much things cost. Unfortunately, in times of double-digit inflation, such books are out of date as soon as they appear in the bookstore. But leaving out any indication of prices makes readers frustrated. After years of struggling with various schemes, we contrived a four-level price-category system based on a simple assumption: *While a hotel or restaurant may raise its prices, so do all its competitors—but, barring complete renovation or refurnishing, or change of cuisine or style, the place keeps the same position relative to its competitors.* Thus the Holiday Inn that charged $25 for a double five years ago may charge $50 today, but it is still moderately priced compared with the Hyatt Regency nearby. What you thought was an expensive restaurant in 1970 is likely to be expensive in 1981. We all have to run to keep up with inflation; somehow we manage, but mental adjustments and revised guidebooks are always necessary.

Here are the four price categories:

$:budget	The least expensive. A sign of welcome for those keeping a close eye on expenses.
$:intermediate	As the term implies, prices are in the middle of the range. For those whose budgets are reasonably flexible.
$:expensive	In most parts of California, though probably not in the San Francisco Bay Area or on the Monterey Peninsula, this signifies the best and most costly rooms and meals.
$:luxury	A special price category, applicable mostly to the super-hotels and super-restaurants of the Bay Area and Monterey Peninsula.

But, you ask, what is this in real money? Here we'll take a chance and give monetary definition to the terms, *based on San Francisco prices in late 1979* (bear in mind that 18-percent inflation has changed this already):

Accommodations

Cost of a **typical double room** (average quality or standard for that hotel, for two persons) for one night in high season; no tax, tips, or extras included:

$:budget	less than $30
$:intermediate	$30–45
$:expensive	$45–70
$:luxury	more than $70

Restaurants

Cost per person for a **complete dinner** (soup and/or salad, average-priced entrée, vegetable, potato or similar, bread and butter, coffee or other beverage); no wine, no dessert; no tax, tips, or parking included:

$:budget	less than $7
$:intermediate	$7–11
$:expensive	$11–17
$:luxury	more than $17

A mixed term, such as $:budget-intermediate, means that the hotel has two or more kinds of doubles or the restaurant dishes are priced over a wide enough range so that you can order in one price category or the other. A mixed term may also mean that the average price was, at this writing, hovering on the border between the categories.

This scale is, to repeat, based on the most expensive place in Northern California: San Francisco. Consequently, accommodations and restaurants there are well distributed over the scale, while away from the big city, in Eureka, say, places to stay and eat tend to be at the less expensive end of the scale. There's a difference in quality, too: a $:budget meal in Sonoma County is probably a better value than a $:budget meal in San Francisco.

We do not put breakfast-lunch places in price categories. The descriptions will hint at possible priciness.

We also do not indicate camping fees. In 1980 the State Parks started charging $5 per developed family campsite; commercial campgrounds typically charge a couple of dollars more.

Credit Cards

> AE—American Express
> CB—Carte Blanche
> DC—Diners Club
> MC—MasterCard
> VI—Visa (BankAmericard)
> Major cards—all of the above are accepted.

Where no cards are listed, there is the strong possibility that MC or VI will be accepted by the time you go there.

Reservations

If you want to be sure of eating anywhere, call ahead for reservations. Accommodations often require a deposit with reservation.

FINDING A PLACE TO STAY OR EAT

Accommodations and restaurants are grouped under the name of a principal town in an area or the name of the area itself (Marin Coast, for example). The towns/areas are in alphabetical order, and an introductory paragraph describes the extent of the area covered and gives telephone area code and zip codes. Under each town or area, listings are nonalphabetical but in rough order according to general quality or style. Descriptive tag lines should make it easy to scan listings.

As a help to travelers who are not familiar with California, here are some map-in-hand ways to find where to stay and eat:

On or near Highway 101 (Redwood Highway) north from San Francisco to Oregon:

Marin County:
  Sausalito / 310
  Mill Valley / 302
  San Rafael / 307
Sonoma County:
  Petaluma / 305
  Santa Rosa / 309 (also:
  Sonoma / 314,
    Sebastopol / 313)

Healdsburg / 295
Mendocino County:
  Ukiah / 319 (also: Clear Lake / 286)
Humboldt County:
  Garberville / 290
  Eureka / 287
Del Norte County:
  Crescent City / 286

On or near Highway 1 on the coast, joining 101 in the redwoods:

Marin Coast / 297 (also:
  Sausalito / 310,
  Mill Valley / 302)
Sonoma Coast / 317 (also:
  Guerneville / 293, Sebastopol / 313)

Gualala / 292
Mendocino / 299
Fort Bragg / 289
Garberville / 290
Eureka / 287
Crescent City / 286

Centers of wine-touring districts:

Napa Valley:
  Napa / 303
  Yountville / 320
  St. Helena / 306
  Calistoga / 284
Sonoma Valley:
  Sonoma / 314
  Santa Rosa / 309

Russian River, Alexander Valley, Ukiah Valley:
  Guerneville / 293 (also:
    Sebastopol / 313, Santa Rosa / 309)
  Healdsburg / 295
  Ukiah / 319

Areas with cozy little accommodations for weekend escapes:

Calistoga / 284
Gualala / 292
Guerneville / 293
Marin Coast / 297
Mendocino / 299

St. Helena / 306
Sonoma / 314
Sonoma Coast / 317
Yountville / 320

Outdoor recreation and resort areas:

Clear Lake / 286
Crescent City / 286
Eureka / 287
Fort Bragg / 289

Garberville / 290
Guerneville / 293
Lake Berryessa / 297
Napa / 303

Restaurants just across the Golden Gate:

Marin Coast / 297
Mill Valley / 302
San Rafael / 307

Sausalito / 310
Sonoma / 314

Calistoga/Northern Napa Valley

Old, rambling, tree-shaded Calistoga somehow doesn't seem like it's at the head of California's sophisticated wine valley, and the accommodations (hot-springs and plain motels, a couple of small ranch resorts) and restaurants (mainly American) reflect the mixed Country & Western/old resort/retired-and-counterculture nature of the place. The planned $20-million, 400-room. Calistoga Falls resort may change Calistoga when it opens. All listed places have a Calistoga address—area code 707, zip code 94515.

WHERE TO STAY

Spas: If mud baths, mineral baths, whirlpools and Jacuzzis, steam massages, chiropractic adjustments, foot reflexology, blanket sweats, and colonic irrigation are your thing, a Calistoga spa may be your place. There are, at last count, seven of them: **Calistoga Spa,** 1006 Washington, 942-6269; **Dr. Wilkinson's Hot Springs,** 1507 Lincoln, 942-4102; **Golden Haven Spa,** 1713 Lake, 942-6793; **Hideaway Hot Springs,** 1412 Fairway, 942-4108; **Nance's Hot Springs,** 1614 Lincoln, 942-6211; **Pacheteau's Original Calistoga Hot Springs,** 1712 Lincoln, 942-5589; and **Roman Spa,** 1300 Washington, 942-4441. . . . None is terribly expensive, being either $:budget or $:low intermediate. All take MC, VI; Golden Haven also takes AE. Dr. Wilkinson's and Golden Haven are the most adequate as accommodations. Pacheteau's is on the site of Sam Brannan's original resort and has kitchens in its old, widely spaced cottages. Hideaway is for adults only.

Latest in-inns: **Calistoga Inn,** 1250 Lincoln, 942-4101, and **Mount View Hotel,** 1457 Lincoln, 942-6877. Both $:expensive.

Quiet motels: **Royal Inn Motel,** 1880 Lincoln, 942-4636. $:budget. MC, VI. . . . **Wardway Motel,** 1202 Pine, 942-6829. $:budget. MC, VI.

Rustic resorts: **Mountain Home Ranch,** 3400 Mountain Home Ranch Rd., 942-6616. $:budget (American Plan also available). MC, VI. 21 rooms in cabins, modern cottages. Tennis, swimming, hiking; lake fishing nearby. Home cooking. . . . **Triple S Ranch,** 4600 Mountain Home Rd., 942-6730. $:budget. Nice little redwood cabins are away from it all. Swimming, hiking. Popular for country-cooking restaurant.

State park camping: Bothe-Napa Valley State Park, halfway between St. Helena and Calistoga on the main highway, is adequate but it's not a wilderness park; it has a pool, even. Ticketron reservations.

RV camping: Calistoga Ranch, 570 Lommel Rd., 942-6565. Off Silverado Trail E of town. Full facilities. Also has cabins. Fishing. . . . Napa County Fairgrounds, Fairway at Oak. Minimal facilities. No reservations.

WHERE TO EAT

Best wine list in town: **Silverado Restaurant and Tavern,** Lincoln/Washington, 942-6725. $:budget-intermediate. MC, VI. Full bar. Standard menu items well prepared, served in the American naugahyde-and-Formica dining room; Wednesday is popular for Zinfandel Beef. What is special, however, is the Napa Valley's most serious wine list, with wine marked up not much over retail, and daily tastings.

Another good one: **Calistoga Inn** (see "Where to Stay"). $:intermediate. MC, VI. Changing menu with emphasis on seafood. All wine only $2 over retail.

There's also: **Alex's,** 1437 Lincoln, 942-6868. Prime rib the specialty. . . . **Mountain Home Ranch** (see "Where to Stay"). Family-recipe meals on weekends for nonguests. . . . **Triple S Ranch** (see "Where to Stay"). More extensive country-cooking menu. Full bar. C&W.

Mexican: **El Faro,** 1353 Lincoln, 942-4400. $:budget. MC, VI. Wine, beer. Flautas and chili relleno are the specialties. Run by the head of the local chamber of commerce. . . . **Palacio,** 1400 Lincoln, 942-5139. $:budget. Frequented by migrant grape-pickers.

Breakfast all day: **Cinnabar Restaurant & Café,** 1440 Lincoln, 942-6989. Omelettes the specialty, also charcoal-grilled hamburgers.

Snacks: **Depot Café,** 1458 Lincoln, 942-5732. The old train station, nicely converted. Sandwiches, salad, soda.

Delis/picnic spots: Get your provisions at Pete's Deli, 1359 Lincoln, 942-6144, and go along to the city's Pioneer Park, Spring and Cedar; Robert Louis Stevenson State Park, 5 miles N of town; or Bothe-Napa Valley State Park (entry fee), 4 miles S. Or wine-tour locally until you see a picnic table (Cuvaison, 4560 Silverado Trail, has some).

Clear Lake/Lake County Resort Area

Every state has resort areas highly popular with people in the state but of lesser interest to out-of-state visitors. Lake County, dominated by green Clear Lake, is one of them. We list a few places to stay, but no restaurants—if you go, you'll find enough Italian and prime-rib places. Area code: 707.

WHERE TO STAY

The big resort: **Konocti Harbor Inn,** 8727 Soda Bay Rd., Kelseyville 95451, 279-4281. $:intermediate. Major cards. Fully equipped resort: 2 restaurants, 2 Olympic-size pools, and so forth. 98 acres, 93 efficiencies. Union-owned.

Motels: **Skylark Motel,** 1120 N. Main St., Lakeport 95453, 263-6151. $:budget. MC, VI. The usual, plus a seaplane ramp, for use when Amanda learns to pilot your Grumman Goose. . . . **Anchorage Inn,** 950 N. Main St. Lakeport 95453, 263-5417. $:budget. MC, VI. . . . Both have efficiencies and weekly rates too.

Cabins and campgrounds: There are 200 resorts and campgrounds ranging from U-Wanna Camp to Ferretti's Linger Longer, from Ski Resort and Cast-Away Houseboats, to Tiki Tiki and Loch Lomond. Please write to the Lake County Chamber of Commerce, 875 Lakeport Blvd., Lakeport 95453, for a list. Clear Lake State Park, 3.5 miles NE of Kelseyville, has 80 sites; Ticketron reservations.

Crescent City/Northern Redwoods

Redwood National Park is the elongated focal point here, stretching from near Trinidad to above Crescent City. Accommodations are generally in motels along Highway 101 around Crescent City and Klamath. Dining is in basic seafood restaurants, mostly.

Area code: 707. Zip codes: Crescent City 95531, Gasquet 95543, Klamath 95548, Smith River 95567.

WHERE TO STAY

Standard motels: **Curly Redwood Lodge,** 701 Redwood Hwy. S., Crescent City, 464-2137. $:budget. Major cards. Central, near boat harbor. Built, it is said, from one huge curly-redwood tree. 36 rooms with functional modern decor, some kitchens. . . . **Royal Inn,** 102 L St. (Front—Hwy. 101), Crescent City, 464-4113. $:budget-intermediate. Major cards. Next to convention center. Good facilities and comfort. . . . **Jack's,** Hwy. 101, Klamath, 482-5911. $:budget. MC, VI. Unfancy.

Resorts: **Ship Ashore Resort,** Box 75 (Hwy. 101), Smith River, 487-3141. $:budget-intermediate. 32 motel rooms, beach cottages, RV/trailer parking, dining room, tackle shop, boat rental. . . . **Patrick Creek Resort,** P.O. Gasquet (Hwy. 199, 20 miles N of Crescent City), tel. Patrick Creek 5. $:budget. MC, VI. Cl. Nov. 15–Mar. 15. Fir lodge from 1920s (replaced stage-stop on old Gasquet Toll Road) at confluence of Patrick Creek and middle fork of Smith River. Main lodge fireplace built from 17 native ores; vine-covered dining room. 17 lodge or motel rooms. 9-hole golf nearby, also pool, fishing.

Camping: In Redwood National Park (Prairie Creek, Del Norte, and Jedediah Smith state park campgrounds) and Six Rivers National Forest, at developed sites around Weitchpec on Hwy. 96 and Gasquet on Hwy. 199. See Chapter 11 for details. Trailers and RVs can find facilities around Crescent City, Klamath, Smith River, and Gasquet.

WHERE TO EAT

Seafood is king: **Harbor View Grotto,** Citizens Dock Rd., Crescent City, 464-3815. $:budget-intermediate. View of fishing and pleasure boats. Fish from sea and river, also steak, prime rib; buffet lunch. Cl. Tues.; Also Oct. . . . **Ship Ashore Galley** (see "Where to Stay"). $:budget-intermediate. Seafood and steaks overlooking the ocean. . . . **Crescent Beach Restaurant,** 1155 Hwy. 101 S., Crescent City, 464-6000. American menu, Pacific Ocean.

Chinese: **Silver Dragon,** 920 L St., Crescent City, 464-5200.

Cafés, delis: **Bee Hive Café,** Hwy. 101, Klamath, 482-5871. Homemade pies, cakes, soups, chili. . . . **The Chalet,** 12 Hague Center, Crescent City, 464-6022.

Mexican/Italian: **Allotta's,** 1193 2nd St., Crescent City, 464-5683.

Eureka/Central Redwood Country

Eureka and Arcata accommodations are mainly motels on or near Highway 101, which can be noisy. Off-season rates are usually available October–May. There's more variety on the restaurant scene, with many in Eureka's Old Town and near the Humboldt State campus. Area Code: 707. Zip Codes: Arcata 95521, Eureka 95501.

WHERE TO STAY

Big downtown inn: **Eureka Inn,** 7th & F, Eureka, 442-6441. $:intermediate. AE, DC, MC, VI. Thankfully away from lumbering trucks in the night, inn has old-fashioned atmosphere with 1922 Tudor architecture (half-timbered high-beamed redwood ceilings in rambling garrets), 150 rooms, Rib Room restaurant. $2.5 million went into recent sprucing up. Rooms and inn have modern comforts. Central.

Motels: **Carson House Inn,** 4th & M, Eureka, 443-1601. $:intermediate.

Major cards. Not an inn but a motel across from famous mansion of same name. 45-room establishment with good Old Town location. . . . **Downtowner Motel,** 424 8th St. (near F), Eureka, 443-5061. $:budget-intermediate. Major cards. 70 soundproofed rooms, creature comforts including bar. . . . **Best Western Thunderbird Lodge,** 5th & Broadway, Eureka, 443-2234. $:budget-intermediate. Major cards. On the highway. 100 rooms, usual conveniences including all-night coffee shop-bar. . . . **Imperial 400** and **TraveLodge** in Eureka, **Ramada Inn** and **Motel 6** in Arcata.

Camping: Difficult for tenters (try Patrick's Point State Park—25 miles N of Eureka). Trailers and RVs can park at Eureka Trailer City, Redwood Camp, Johnny's Marina and RV Park, and KOA around Eureka, and Fortuna Trailer Village in Fortuna.

WHERE TO EAT

Seafood: Eureka is a big commercial-fishing harbor, so be sure to ask what's fresh and in season, such as salmon, abalone, crab, halibut, clams, oysters. . . . **Eureka Seafood Grotto,** 605 Broadway (near 6th), Eureka, 443-2075. $:budget-intermediate. Major cards. Wine, beer. Owned by Eureka Fisheries, which claims that "we catch 'em, we cook 'em, we serve 'em." Specialties: clam chowder, oyster cocktail, smoked sliced salmon, seafood casseroles. . . . **Lazio's Seafood,** foot of C St. on Humboldt Bay, Eureka, 442-2337. $:intermediate. Major cards. Full bar. Fish market and restaurant since 1944. Specialties are whatever's fresh plus calamari, cioppino, sourdough bread. . . . **Anchor Café,** 3500 Broadway, Eureka, 442-7231. Full bar. Cl. Sun.-Mon. . . . **Weatherby's,** 1906 4th St., Eureka, 442-0683. . . . **Captain's Galley,** 109 4th St., Eureka, 443-4835. Another Eureka Fisheries outlet. . . . **Jonah's,** 332 Harris/E St., Eureka, 443-7305. Also a market. . . . **The Waterfront,** 1st/F, 445-2832. . . . **Volpi's,** 6269 Loma, 442-1376. . . . **Fat Albert's,** 312 E St., 443-8887.

Continental: **Eureka Inn Rib Room** (see "Where to Stay"). $:intermediate. Major cards. Old Eureka atmosphere plus prime rib, filet of salmon, and the like, with garnishings and style. . . . **Maxwell's Bistro,** 527 W. Wabash Ave., Eureka, 443-9221. MC, VI. Tournedo chasseur, teriyaki steak, coquilles St. Jacques. . . . **North Town Park,** 752 18th/H St., Arcata, 822-4619. Soup-and-salad bar, brochettes and fresh white meat from the sea.

French: **Le Palais de René,** 507 2nd St., Eureka, 445-5906. $:intermediate-expensive. Specialties: fresh poached salmon, sauteed sole and prawns, roast duckling, milk-fed veal, rack of lamb.

Chinese, which is all Cantonese around here: **Shanghai Low,** 1835 4th St., Eureka, 443-8191. . . . **Kwan's Café,** 29 5th St., Eureka, 443-3651.

T-bones: **Art's Gallery,** 5th/T, 442-5278. $:intermediate. Full bar. Also prime rib, seafood.

Mexican so far north: **Los Panchos,** 409 Opera Alley, Eureka, 442-5651.

In Old Town. . . . **Reyes y Casas Viejas,** 1436 2nd St., Eureka, 442-5072. . . . Both $:budget, both take MC, VI. . . . **Red Pepper,** 856 10th St., Eureka, 822-2138. $:budget. Mexican fireplace for California fog.

Historic place with museum: **Samoa Cookhouse,** 445 W. Washington, Samoa, 442-1659. $:budget. AE, MC, VI. "Last surviving [logging] cookhouse in the west" serves (three) big meals at big tables, lumber-camp style. Genuine, down-to-earth, with no fancy-pants gourmet dining—but be sure to reserve on summer weekends. Logging museum. . . . **Youngberg's,** 3rd floor, Jacoby Storehouse, 781 8th St., Arcata, 822-1712. Varied cuisine in state landmark.

Delis, lunch places: **Waterfront Sandwich Co.,** 1st & F, Eureka, 445-2832. In Old Town. . . . **Plaza Gourmet Delicatessen,** 846 G St., Arcata, 822-1706. . . . **Tomaso's Tomato Pies,** 216 E St., Eureka, 445-0100. That is, Sicilian-style pizza, also spinach pie. . . . **Bun & Bagel,** 603 E/6th St., Eureka, 442-6911. . . . **Christian's Old-Fashioned Ice Cream Parlor,** 1338 Myrtle, Eureka.

Vegetarian: **Whole Earth Kitchen,** 773 8th St., Arcata, 822-1047. . . . **Sprouted Seed,** 1604 G St., Arcata, 822-0360.

Fort Bragg/Northern Mendocino Coast

Fort Bragg, a lumber town on the highway, has an unpretentious, Kansas City-honest style to its motels and seafood-Italian restaurants, contrasting with the studied, San Francisco-commercial charm of nearby Mendocino. Bragg has more to, uh, boast of in the way of fine dining than it did a few years ago.

Area code: 707. Zip codes: Fort Bragg 95437, Westport 95488.

WHERE TO STAY

New-old town inn: **Gray Whale Inn,** 615 N. Main St., Fort Bragg, 964-0640. $:intermediate (incl. breakfast). Handsome weathered-redwood inn was district hospital until 1972; old hospital equipment was creatively utilized in the conversion to a 12-room hotel.

Farmhouse inn: **DeHaven Valley Farm,** Box 128, Westport, 964-2931. $:budget (incl. breakfast). Off the road, in the hills, 2 miles from tiny town. Victorian has 6 rooms, all sharing. Farm-fresh food at dinner Fri.-Sat.

Motels: **Harbor Lite Lodge,** 32951 N. Harbor Dr., Fort Bragg, 964-0221. $:intermediate. MC, VI. Noyo harbor views. . . . **Best Western Vista Manor,** 1100 N. Main, Fort Bragg, 964-4776. $:intermediate. All cards. Hilltop manor with sea vista, indoor pool. . . . **Pine Beach Inn,** Box 1173, Fort Bragg, 964-5603. On Highway 1, 4 miles S of town. $:budget-intermediate. AE, MC, VI. Coffee shop, bar; tennis, and some views. . . . **Surf Motel,** Box 488, Fort Bragg, 964-5361. On Highway 1 at Noyo River Bridge. $:budget. Major cards.

State park camping: MacKerricher State Park, 3 miles N of Fort Bragg, is beachy and big but less appropriate for tents than for RVs (tenters might be happier at Russian Gulch and Van Damme; see Mendocino). Open all year; Ticketron reservations.

RV camping: Tara Campgrounds, 17700 Franklin Rd., Fort Bragg, 964-5378. All facilities in "the sun belt" 3 miles E. of town. . . . Wages Creek Beach Campground, Westport. Creek and ocean location, good for fishermen, abalone divers.

WHERE TO EAT

Place to go: **Sollini's,** N. Hwy. 1, Fort Bragg, 964-3321. $:intermediate. MC, VI. Full bar. Italian, seafood, steak inside or out on deck with ocean view.

Eggs only: **Egghead Omelettes,** 326 N. Main, Fort Bragg, 964-5005. $:budget. No cards. Breakfast and lunch only. Long selection of 3-egg plates, other short-orders after long wait.

Italian-American: **Piedmont Hotel,** 102 S. Main, Fort Bragg, 964-2410. $:intermediate. MC, VI. Full bar.

Bragging about the seafood: **The Wharf,** 780 N. Harbor Dr., Fort Bragg, 964-4283. $:intermediate. No cards. Full bar. Not fancy. . . . **The Dock,** 780 N. Harbor Dr., Fort Bragg, 964-4561. $:budget-intermediate. MC, VI. . . . Both of these are at photogenic Noyo Harbor, which is Fisherman's Wharf with real fishermen.

Skunk Train passengers' delight: **The Restaurant,** 418 N. Main (opposite the depot), Fort Bragg, 964-9800. $:budget-intermediate. MC, VI. Wine, beer. Mostly seafood. Some specialties: stuffed trout with crab and mushrooms; scampi and razor clams. Sunday brunch, too.

And way north in Westport: **Cobweb Palace,** Hwy. 1, 964-5588. Simple but sufficient lunches, dinners for wayfarers. Not cobwebby, just rustic.

Garberville/Southern Redwoods

Accommodations and restaurants are clustered around Garberville, with the range from Piercy to Scotia. The emphasis is on older family-oriented resorts and dining rooms under the redwoods, and newer functional motels and American food on or near the highway.

Area code: 707. Zip codes: Garberville 95440, Miranda 95553, Piercy 95467, Scotia 95565.

WHERE TO STAY

Gracious old-time resort: **Benbow Inn,** Highway 101, 2 miles S. of Garberville, 923-2124. $:budget-intermediate. MC, VI. Famous 1926 gabled, Tudor-style hotel. 6 stories (no elevator), dining room, and 70 rooms preside over the terrace, gardens, and lake. For recreation: nearby 9-hole golf course, fishing, hiking, tennis. For peace: no room-phones, TV. Unwind genteelly. Cl. Dec.-Mar.

Redwood forest resorts: **Hartsook Inn,** Highway 101, Piercy (8 miles S. of Garberville, 247-3305. $:budget. MC, VI. Adjacent to Richardson Grove State Park, Hartsook's 30 acres include 80 rooms in the main lodge and cottages, dining room, putting green, Eel River swimming and fishing. A good place for a family stay-put vacation. Cl. Nov.-Apr. . . . **Miranda Gardens Resort,** Box 186, Miranda (on Highway 101—15 miles N. of Garberville), 943-3011. $:budget. MC, VI. On the edge of Humboldt Redwoods State Park, the motel and cottages are among the redwoods, birch, spruce, madrone, and pepperwood. Swimming in pool and Eel River, games, playground, picnics.

Modern motels: **Sherwood Forest,** Box 537, 814 Redwood Dr., Garberville, 923-2721. $:budget-intermediate. MC, VI. Heated pool, sauna. . . . **Rancho,** 987 Redwood Dr., Garberville, 923-2451. $:budget. Pool. . . . **Singing Trees Resort,** Box 400, off Highway 101, Garberville, 923-2712. $:budget. On the Eel River, with motel, cottages, restaurant. . . . **Whispering Pines Resort,** Box 246, Miranda, 943-3160. $:budget. Major cards. Heated pool and 4 acres located on the Avenue of the Giants.

Camping is pleasant in several state parks and recreation areas: Standish-Hickey, Richardson Grove, and Humboldt Redwoods, as described under these sections in Chapter 9. King Range also has primitive camping. Information and maps: BLM, 555 Leslie St., Ukiah, 462-3873. National Forest campsites are at Mad River on Hwy. 36 via Ruth Rd. (28 tent, 12 trailer sites); Bailey Canyon 2 miles S. of Ruth Dam on Ruth Lake (19 tent, 4 trailer sites), and Fir Cove, 2 miles S. of Ruth Dam on Ruth Lake (13 tent, 8 trailer sites). Information: Mad River Ranger Station, Mad River. Fees: $1/day/vehicle.

Commercial camping: Many facilities at Richardson Grove, Garberville, Redway, Miranda, Myers Flat, and Redcrest.

WHERE TO EAT

Best dining in Southern Redwoods: **Benbow Inn** (see "Where to Stay"). $:intermediate. MC, VI. Full bar. The Tudoresque dining room has antiques, an Eel River view, patio, its own bread, and specialties: baked ham Southern style, prime rib, mushrooms Normande, lobster Mornay, chicken sauté Benbow, chateaubriand, trout amandine. Also breakfast, lunch, and Sunday brunch. Cl. Dec.-Mar. 15.

Redwood resort dining room: **Hartsook Inn** (see "Where to Stay"). MC, VI. Serves all-American breakfasts, lunches, dinners. Cl. Nov.-Apr.

Other Garberville: **The Trees,** 728 Redwood Dr., 923-3837. $:intermediate. American and varied lunches and dinners, including tournedos du boeuf au vin rouge, filet of sole Marguery, veal scallopine chasseur, roast cross rib of beef au jus.

Scotia: **Scotian Room,** Hwy. 101 & Mill St., Scotia, 764-5683. $:intermediate. MC, VI. Full bar. A hotel until 1976, the charming, tidy white building now serves the public only in its restaurant and bar. Specialties: filet mignon, prime rib, broiled lamb chops, Southern fried chicken, Humboldt salmon, fresh biscuits, old-fashioned chicken fricassee. Cl. Mon.–Tues.

Gualala/Southern Mendocino Coast

The lodging and eating on the long, fairly lonely southern stretch of Mendocino coast are mostly found at Gualala, which is on the Sonoma County line north of Sea Ranch (see under Sonoma Coast). The world of TV and telephones is fairly far away from here.

Area code: 707. Zip codes: Gualala 95445, Manchester 95459, Point Arena 95468.

WHERE TO STAY

Built to stay: **St. Orres,** Box 523, Gualala, 884-3303. On Highway 1—2 miles north of Gualala. $:expensive (breakfast included). MC, VI. One-of-a-kind construction (1977) that is Fort Ross Russian, Black Forest Teutonic, Marin County countercultural, and Union Street Victorian all at the same time. 8 in-inn rooms have some handmade furniture, seaview balconies; 2 garden cottages are more luxurious. Built on foundations of old Seaside Hotel on the old St. Orres ranch. Restaurant.

New-old inn: **Old Milano Hotel,** 38300 Hwy. 1, Gualala, 884-3256. $:intermediate-expensive (breakfast included). No cards. An Italian-run hotel (1905) became a Swedish-run fisherman's lodge (1922), then a modernized private house (1940), and has now been restored as a Victorian inn (1978 and continuing). 6 upstairs rooms plus garden cottage and a caboose unit at the moment. Open Apr.–Dec.

Charm is in the eye of the beholder: **Gualala Hotel,** Box 129, Gualala, 884-3441. In town. $:budget. 29 rooms dating from 1903—some still look it, others don't, but none has private bath. Known mainly as a restaurant.

The plain alternatives: **Surf Motel,** Box 595, Gualala, 884-3571. $:budget. . . . **Reed's Motel,** 135 Main St., Point Arena, 882-2000. $:budget.

Coastal houses to rent: **Irish Beach Rental Homes,** Star Route, Manchester, 882-2467. 4 miles N of town. Vacation subdivision has many architect-designed houses, though this isn't Sea Ranch. Rates are for 2 or more nights: $:expensive. You bring the linen.

Camping: Manchester State Beach is not one of the cozier state parks, and tent-campers will feel dwarfed by the RVs; few facilities, and no reservations accepted. Gualala Point County Park is a smaller alternative. Commercial alternatives include the Manchester Beach KOA, Box 266, Manchester, 882-

2375; Anchor Bay Campground, Gualala, 884-9923; and Gualala River Redwood Park, Box 101 (County Road 501), Gualala, 884-3533.

WHERE TO EAT

Distinctive setting, less distinctive dining: **St. Orres** (see "Where to Stay"). $:intermediate-expensive. No cards. Wine, beer. Cl. Tues. Dinner weekdays, lunch and dinner weekends. At the moment, surprise-free menu has Continental standbys and specials of the day, with quiet flair compared to the handcrafted, timbered, domed and multiwindowed dining-room architecture.

Good deal for weary travelers: **Gualala Hotel** (see "Where to Stay"). $:budget. No cards. Full bar. American and Italian. Locals like this old place.

Guerneville/Lower Russian River

Along the meandering Russian River between Forestville and Duncans Mills (where the coastal fog begins) and under the redwoods, Northern Californians have vacationed for generations (the authors' families for four generations). Accommodations and restaurants reflect the uncritical standards of such old-time, simultaneously down-and-out/up-and-coming resort areas. The places we list should pass muster with out-of-staters.

Area code: 707. Zip codes: Cazadero 95421, Duncans Mills 95430, Forestville 95436, Guerneville 95446, Monte Rio 95462.

WHERE TO STAY

The fancier resorts: **Hexagon House,** 16881 Armstrong Woods Rd., Guerneville, 869-3991. $:intermediate. MC, VI. Popular hotel and restaurant, with lodging in motel building (cheaper) or woodsy cabanas. . . . **Northwood Lodge,** Box 100 (River Rd.), Monte Rio, 865-2126. $:budget. AE, MC, VI. Motel in clearing with 9-hole golf course.

Good ol' resorts: **Angelo's Resort,** Box 277 (River Blvd.), Monte Rio, 865-2215. $:budget. . . . **Parker's Resort,** 16220 Neeley Rd., Guerneville, 869-2037. $:budget.

Gay but straights welcome: **Fife's,** Box 45 (16467 River Rd.), Guerneville, 869-0656. $:intermediate-expensive. MC, VI. Riverside cottage colony made over into spacious, very comfortable, nice-looking resort "for all grown-ups, straight and gay, who enjoy themselves and each other." Tolerant straights would not, we think, be embarrassed, though the gay guests will outnumber you. Restaurant and good camping, but many cabins are for midgets.

More like inns: **Ridenhour Ranch House Inn,** 12850 River Rd., Guerneville, 887-1033. $:expensive. B&B within a cork's pop of Korbel. . . . **Village Inn,** Box 56 (20822 River Blvd.), Monte Rio, 865-2738. $:budget-intermediate. No cards. Larger, more like an old-fashioned resort hotel, now modernizing a bit. Good restaurant. . . . **Russian River Lodge,** 7871 Trenton Rd. (off River Rd.), Forestville, 887-1524. $:budget. MC, VI. 3 rooms in 1890s Victorian farmhouse, 6 in new outbuilding. Good vineyard views, but road noise.

Forest lodge: **Cazanoma Lodge,** Box 37 (1000 Kidd Rd., off Cazadero Hwy.), Cazadero, 632-5255. $:budget. MC, VI. Couple of cabins and lodge rooms available on limited basis in old-fashioned lodge in the woods. Mainly a restaurant.

State park camping: In this area, only Austin Creek State Recreational Area, adjoining Armstrong Redwoods Park N of town, has camping; tent and RV sites, also walk-in, ride-in sites. First come, first served; call 869-2015 for info.

Other camping: As old-time resort area, Russian River has commercial campgrounds that even seem friendly to tent-campers. One of best is Duncans Mills Campground, Box 57, Duncans Mills, 865-2573, with full facilities, horse and canoe rentals, beach, trails, and restored old village buildings. Fife's resort (see above) is for tents only, something nice and different. Or try these others: Parker's Resort, 16220 Neeley Rd., Guerneville, 869-2037 (bit on the urban side); Schoolhouse Canyon Campground, 12600 River Rd., Guerneville (near Hilton, 4 miles E), 869-2311; Mirabel Park, Box 681, Forestville, 887-2383; Riens Sandy Beach, 22900 Sylvan Way, Monte Rio, 865-2102.

WHERE TO EAT

Young gourmet: **Village Inn** (see "Where to Stay"), 865-1180. $:intermediate. No cards. Full bar. Attractive, youthful inn-restaurant that is the authors' choice. Delicious mushroom roulade Florentine indicates quality of what comes from the kitchen. Rustic dining room. Entertainment Sat.

Gay place for happy food: **Fife's** (see "Where to Stay"). $:expensive. MC, VI. Full bar. Basic menu but basically excellent food prepared with some style.

For wine-trippers: **Russian River Vineyards Restaurant,** 5700 Gravenstein Hwy., Forestville, 887-1562. $:intermediate-expensive. MC, VI. Wine, changing international menu, Russian River wines on brick patio and in redwood building that resembles hop kiln. Cl. Mon., maybe other days (reserve anyway). Sunday brunch.

Country tavern: **Blue Heron Inn,** Hwy. 116, Duncans Mills, 865-2269. $:budget-intermediate. Full bar. Relaxed, cozy, convivial place with imaginative mostly vegetarian menu, light entertainment. Bargain Tues. community-night dinner, also Sunday Champagne brunch.

Risk-free dining: **Hexagon House** (see "Where to Stay"). $:expensive. MC, VI. Full bar.

The popular steakery: **Buck's,** 4th & Mill, Guerneville, 869-9935. $:intermediate. MC, VI.

French by the Russian: **Le Chalet,** 16632 River Rd., Guerneville, 869-

9908. $:intermediate. MC, VI. Wine. Family-style with choice of country-French entrées, also lobster, bouillabaisse on weekends. Cl. Wed. . . . **L'Omelette,** 6685 Front St., Forestville, 887-9945. $:intermediate. No cards. Wine. More than omelettes but quite a bit less than La Tour d'Argent. Cl. Mon.-Thurs.

German food in American forest: **Cazanoma Lodge** (see "Where to Stay"). $:intermediate. MC, VI. Hasenpfeffer, Wiener Backhuhn, etc. with German trimmings, or rainbow trout, spareribs, etc. with American trimmings. Sunday brunch. Trout pond, waterwheel, trees comprise view.

Mostly Mexican: **Casa de Joanna,** 17500 Orchard Ave., Guerneville, 869-3756. At Vacation Beach. $:budget-intermediate. MC, VI. Wine, beer. Popular weekends. Cl. Mon. . . . **Forestville Inn,** 6625 Front St., Forestville, 887-1242. $:budget-intermediate. Wine, beer. Have a wine cocktail on the patio. Tuesday special, otherwise standard Mexican. Cl. Mon.

No pretensions here: **River Inn,** 16377 Main St., Guerneville, 869-0481. $:intermediate. Beer, wine. American Formica. Everything's on the menu, and everybody's here.

A quick dinner: **Russian River Pub,** 11829 River Rd., Forestville, 887-7932. $:budget. Full bar. Hamburgers, Italian, chili.

A quick lunch: **Northwood Restaurant** (at Northwood Lodge, see "Where to Stay"). Create-your-own burgers and omelettes plus golf-club fare. . . . **The Cheese Merchant,** 25191 Hwy. 116, Duncans Mills, 865-9914. In a restored Victorian shop.

Healdsburg/Upper Russian River

Healdsburg is the charming, small-town center of the upper Sonoma County (Alexander Valley) wine district, and makes a good center for wine-trippers, too. The accommodations are better elsewhere (see Guerneville, Calistoga, St. Helena) but the local restaurant scene rivals Napa Valley's, with much opportunity among the wines and vines.

Area code: 707. Zip codes: Cloverdale 95425, Geyserville 95441, Healdsburg 95448.

WHERE TO STAY

Standard motels: **Fairview Motel,** 74 Healdsburg Ave., Healdsburg, 433-5548. $:budget. Major cards. . . . **La Grande Motel,** 721 N. Cloverdale Blvd., Cloverdale, 894-5705. $:budget. Major cards. . . . Both have pools; Fairview has therapy pool.

Camping: Cloverdale KOA, Box 600, Cloverdale (E of Asti on River Rd.), 894-3337, and Boucher's Liberty Lake RV Resort, 225 Theresa Dr., Cloverdale, 894-5512, allot a third of their sites to tenters, rest to RVs.

WHERE TO EAT

Winery dinery: **Souverain Restaurant,** at Souverain Cellars, 400 Souverain Rd., Geyserville (Independence Lane exit off Hwy. 101), 857-3789. $:expensive. MC, VI. Wine. The cooking is French, the atmosphere is white-tablecloth but not formal, the architecture is modern winery after Sonoma hop kiln, and the view from the terrace (must reserve!) over the vineyards is wonderful. Awkward wait between end of winery tour and first dinner. Wine inexpensively priced. Cl. Mon.-Tues. for dinner, also Jan.

An alternative: **Hoffman House,** 21712 Old Redwood Hwy., Geyserville, 857-3818. $:intermediate-expensive. MC, VI. Wine. 1903 house. Most popular for lunch and Sunday brunch (picnics packed, too), also good for table d'hôte dinner, different each week (reservations necessary). Wineshop specializes in local wines, which are many. Cl. Tues., also Nov.-May.

Big and new: **Wine Country,** 106 Matheson St., Healdsburg, 433-7203. $:expensive. MC, VI. Full bar. Good-looking new (1979) restaurant with Spanish/winery architecture, international menu, long list of Sonoma wines immoderately priced. Lunch, dinner, Sunday brunch.

Good Northern Italian: **Mama Nina's,** 1 mile N of Cloverdale on Hwy. 101, 894-2609. $:intermediate. AE, MC, VI. Full bar. Homemade pasta, prime rib in every room of old house and on deck. Related to the Yountville Mama Nina's, and just as popular. Dinner only. Cl. Mon.-Tues.

Locally popular: **Lockhorn Restaurant,** 134 N. Cloverdale Blvd., Cloverdale, 894-7977. $:intermediate. MC, VI. Full bar. Seafood, Italian, steaks, plus music Fri.-Sat. Cl. Tues. . . . **Healdsburg House,** 25 Grant Ave., Healdsburg, 433-1106. $:intermediate. MC, VI. Full bar. Prime rib, chicken, steaks. Sonoma wines.

And Mexican, too: **Tamaulipeco,** 25 Adeline Way, Healdsburg, 433-5202. $:budget. MC, VI.

Relaxed meals: **Camp Rose Inn,** 2100 S. Fitch Mt. Rd., Healdsburg, 433-4557. $:budget-intermediate. Short, varied menu of dishes that go well with wine (if BYOB, $2 corkage). Decks and views of Russian River below.

Delis/picnic spots: Two Healdsburg delis, Salame Tree, 304 Center St., 433-7224 (daily) and Pic-a-Deli Square, 109 Plaza St., 433-2530 (cl. Sun.), have the fixings; if you're too tired to slice French bread, they'll make the sandwiches for you. Next door to the Salame Tree is Plasberg Liquor Store, but try Dry Creek Liquors, 177 Dry Creek Rd., 433-5529, and Hoffman House (see above) for a good selection of North Coast wines. Nibblies can be obtained at Costeaux French Bakery, 421 Healdsburg Ave., 433-1913 (cl. Mon.-Tues.). Many wineries have picnic areas: Alexander Valley Vineyards, Field Stone, Geyser Peak, Hop Kiln, Italian Swiss Colony, Nervo, Simi, and Sonoma Vineyards. Near the delis are the Healdsburg Plaza and Healdsburg Memorial Beach (fee).

Lake Berryessa/Napa Highlands

Lake Berryessa is the big Bureau of Reclamation lake in the hills northeast of the Napa Valley, an area we have arbitrarily called the Napa Highlands. Some of the small valleys up this way—Pope, Chiles, Wooden—have vineyards, but the main attraction is the man-made lake, where all accommodations are campground resorts frequented mainly by those with RVs and motorboats. Area code: 707.

WHERE TO STAY

Indoor accommodations and camping: **Steele Park Resort,** Rural Station, Napa 94558, 966-2123. Fancier than the campgrounds, with some motel units and cottages, swimming pool, restaurant, full bar.

Camping: Spanish Flat Resort, Knoxville Rd. on lakeshore; Lake Berryessa Marina Resort, Knoxville Rd.; Lake Berryessa South Shore Resort, Wragg Canyon Rd.; Rancho Monticello Resort, Knoxville Rd. Usual facilities plus boat rental, launch ramps. No reservations accepted.

WHERE TO EAT

Something different: **Pope Valley Parachute Center,** 1996 Pope Canyon Rd., Pope Valley, 965-3985. Short orders.

Picnic spots: Oak Shores day-use park, Knoxville Rd., Lake Berryessa, 966-2111; Conn Dam Recreation Area, at Lake Hennessey, Hwy. 128, NE of Rutherford; and the Nichelini Winery, Hwy. 128.

Marin Coast

Thanks to the slowly developing good taste of Marin County residents, West Marin is no longer a place where the gourmet food is found walking in pastures. Point Reyes National Seashore is such a worthwhile place to go that you might take a chance on lunch or dinner.

Area code: 415. Zip codes: Dillon Beach 94929, Inverness 94937, Marshall 94940, Olema 94950, Point Reyes Station 94956, Stinson Beach 94970.

WHERE TO STAY

Cute, cozy, maybe fattening: **Inverness Lodge,** Callendar Way/Argyle St. (go left uphill quarter-mile after Vladimir's), Inverness, 669-1034. $:budget. AE, MC. Genuine hideaway: rustic shingled lodge (ca. 1900) with 9 units—4 rooms with bath upstairs (rooms 1 and 2 share good deck), 5 cottages under the pines, laurels, oaks, and acacias. What's fattening is what is served downstairs in Manka's (see "Where to Eat").

For yachtsmen: **Golden Hinde Boatel,** Box 295 (Sir Francis Drake Blvd.), Inverness, 669-1389. $:intermediate. MC, VI. 37 motel units on Tomales Bay marina; some rooms with fireplaces (good in summer!), decks. Heated pool, unheated bay.

For tennis players: **Inverness Valley Inn & Tennis Ranch,** Box 629 (13275 Sir Francis Drake Blvd.), Inverness, 669-7250. $:intermediate. MC, VI. 9 rooms with fireplaces and kitchenettes, pool and courts outside.

For fishermen: **Lawson's Resort,** Box 97, Dillon Beach, 707/878-2204. $:intermediate, for weekends and weeks. 4 cottages.

Routine accommodations: **Inverness Motel,** Sir Francis Drake Blvd., Inverness, 669-1081. $:budget. . . . **Sandpiper Motel,** Box 208 (Marine Way), Stinson Beach, 868-1632. $:budget. Modern rooms, rustic cabins; some kitchenettes.

For wandering youth: **Laguna Ranch Hostel/Point Reyes Hostel,** Limantour Rd., Point Reyes Seashore, 669-9985; for information, call American Youth Hostels, Fort Mason, San Francisco, 771-4646. Room for 40 card-carrying hostelers for a couple of dollars each.

Walk-in camping: Point Reyes Seashore has 3 hike-in, 1-night-only tent grounds: Sky Camp, 2.25-mile walk; Glen Camp, 4.5 miles; and Coast Camp, 8 miles. Free, but reservations essential; those on waiting list can stand by at headquarters at noon and take place of no-shows. No wood fires. Call 663-1092 or write to seashore headquarters.

State park camping: Samuel P. Taylor State Park, deep and cool in the redwoods on the landside of Bolinas Ridge, off Sir Francis Drake Blvd., has 65 sites, each popular—in fact, very popular, for this is about the closest camping to The City. Ticketron reservations.

Commercial camping: Olema Ranch Campground, Box 175 (Hwy. 1), Olema, 663-1363. Full facilities; 150 open sites. . . . Also: Lawson's Landing, Dillon Beach, 707/878-2443.

WHERE TO EAT

Czech mates: **Manka's Czech Restaurant,** at Inverness Lodge (see "Where to Stay"). $:intermediate. AE, MC. Wine, beer. Perfect country restaurant, with Czech and Viennese cuisine (cubes of veal in subtle paprika sauce, roast duckling in caraway sauce, etc.). Scandinavian smorgasbord for starters, Czech pastries on a cart at the end. . . . **Vladimir's Czechoslovakian Restaurant,** 12785 Sir Francis Drake Blvd., 669-1021. $:intermediate. No cards. Wine, beer. Moravian dumplings, chicken paprika, cold duckling, sweet and sour cabbage. Run by the daughter of the Manka family.

Alternative: **Inverness Coffee Shop,** Sir Francis Drake Blvd., Inverness,

669-1109. $:budget. No cards. Wine, beer. Varied menu includes Drake's Bay oysters, cioppino, Russian pelmeny (ravioli). Popular for weekend breakfast/ brunch.

French country bistro: **Chez Madeleine Restaurant Française,** Hwy. 1, Point Reyes Station, 663-8998. $:intermediate. MC, VI. Wine, beer. Busy, crowded little place on weekends (no reservations taken); romantic, cozy little place during week or off-season. Traditional French items, plus Franco burger! Dinner only. Cl. Mon.-Tues.

Honest American: **Jerry's Farmhouse,** 10005 Hwy. 1, Olema, 663-1264. $:intermediate. MC, VI. Full bar. Can't go wrong with good home-cooked halibut, rock cod, or other fresh fish, chicken, steaks. Cl. Mon. except hols.

Restored rustic: **Marshall Tavern,** Hwy. 1, Marshall, 663-8141. $:intermediate. MC, VI. Full bar. Pre-1906 tavern of uncertain parentage is being beautified. Marshall's best. Mostly seafood and short orders. For lunch or Sunday brunch, try a Skiff. C&W on the jukebox, dancing Fri.-Sat.

Consider the weekend oyster: **Tony's Seafood,** Hwy. 1, Marshall (on the Tomales Bay shore), 663-1103. $:budget. The oysters are barbecued on weekends only. Otherwise, there's usually fish just brought in by the family's commercial fishing business. Plain-Jane.

New French: **Le Printemps,** 7303 Sir Francis Drake Blvd., Lagunitas (near Samuel P. Taylor State Park), 488-9500. $:expensive. MC, VI. Formerly the well-rated Old Viking, still at a good country location.

The only place at Point Reyes Seashore: **Snack bar at Drake's Beach,** intermittently open.

Quick stop: **Station House Café,** A & 3rd, Point Reyes Station, 663-1515.

Mendocino/Central Mendocino Coast

Accommodations (mostly inns without TV and telephones) and restaurants (usually at inns) are concentrated in villagey Mendocino and rural Little River, with a couple at tiny Elk. Quality ranges from funky to fine. Atmosphere is casual everywhere except Heritage House, an establishment that wouldn't be out of place at Pebble Beach. Reservations highly recommended all year for all lodging (two nights sometimes required) and dinner.

Area code: 707. Zip codes: Elk 95432, Little River 95456, Mendocino 95460, Philo 95466.

WHERE TO STAY

Destination by itself: **Heritage House,** Hwy. 1, Little River, 937-5885. $:luxury (but both breakfast and dinner included). No cards. 1877 farmhouse, guest cottages on rolling green lawns on bluff over cove; 50 units total. Quality is high. Dress well here. Cl. Dec.-Jan.

Stained-glass modern: **Mendocino Hotel,** Box 587, Mendocino, 937-0511.

$:intermediate-luxury (breakfast included). 1878 loggers' hotel on Main St. elegantly restored by a native son with part of his Jack-in-the-Box fortune, but antiques have that store-bought look, decor is overfancy Victorian. Dated aspects (several rooms without bath or view) make this far overpriced, too.

Modernized Victorian: **MacCallum House,** Albion St., Mendocino, 937-0289. $:intermediate (breakfast included). MC, VI. Carefully built old house with original decorations and furniture was carefully converted into a 14-room inn. Best of the in-town inns.

Creaky, homey inn: Old part of the **Little River Inn,** Hwy. 1, Little River, 937-5942. $:budget. No cards. Old rooms upstairs in white Maine mansion (1853) are charming, favored by the house cat. Our favorite, too. Well-planted grounds.

Functional with character: **Little River Inn's** newer cottages and motel annex. $:intermediate. . . . **S.S. Sea Foam Lodge,** Box 475, Little River, 937-5516. $:intermediate. MC, VI. 27 units with porches to admire sea view from. . . . **Mendocino Hill House,** Box 625, Mendocino, 937-0554. $:intermediate-expensive. MC, VI. At 10701 Palette Dr., a place of great comfort.

Small, rural, family inns: **Schoolhouse Creek Inn,** Little River, 937-5525. $:budget. The least modern, but congenial and improving. . . . **Glendeven,** 8221 N. Hwy. 1, Little River, 937-0083. $:intermediate (breakfast included). No cards. 6 guest rooms (2 with bath) in 1867 farmhouse that is Victorian here, contemporary there.

Small-town lodges: **Joshua Grindle Inn,** 44800 Little Lake St., Mendocino, 937-4143. $:intermediate (breakfast included). No cards. The house built for Grindle and his bride in 1879 became a 5-room inn 98 years later, with Early American decor. Private baths. . . . **Mendocino Village Inn,** Box 626, 937-0246. $:budget. 1882 doctor's house, now homelike inn; 2 rooms with bath, 3 with fireplaces, 3 with view; no. 8 is best, no. 4 biggest, both are best-equipped. . . . **Headlands Inn,** 44950 Albion St., Mendocino, 937-4431, is new to us.

Mellow on purpose: **Ames Lodge,** Box 207, Mendocino, 937-0811. $:intermediate. 3 miles E on Little Lake Rd. Restaurant and cottages in the woods.

Far from the madding crowd, even from Mendocino's: In Elk, 16 miles S of Mendocino, are two tiny, quality inns. **Harbor House,** Box 167, 877-3203. $:expensive-luxury (dinner, breakfast included). No cards. Handsomer of the two. A duplicate of the Redwood Model Home of the 1915 Panama-Pacific Exposition, built by a lumber company as guest house; the living room is a gem of hand-hewn, beeswaxed redwood. 9 rooms. Congenial, very quiet. . . . **Elk Cove Inn,** Box 367, 877-3321. $:expensive (breakfast, dinner included). Less formal, more intimate, good for gourmets and music lovers. 4 of 7 units are in Sandpiper House half-mile away. . . . New is **Navarro By the Sea,** Navarro Beach Road, 937-0409.

Ranch resort: **Highland Ranch,** Box 150, Philo, 895-3294. Tennis, riding, fishing Mar.-Nov.

State park camping: Russian Gulch (June-Sept.) and Van Damme (all year) are close to coast, villages, while Hendy Woods (all year) is way inland on the road to Philo; reservations are by Ticketron. Paul M. Dimmick Wayside Camp (May-Oct.), closer to coast on Navarro River, is first come, first served.

RV camping: Caspar Beach Trailer Park, 45201 Pt. Cabrillo Dr., Mendocino, 964-3306. . . . Also: Albion Flat Marina, Albion (no reservations).

WHERE TO EAT

Fine fare, good value, but not gourmet: **Heritage House** (see "Where to Stay"). Prix-fixe dinner $:intermediate. No cards. Full bar. Most scenic setting imaginable; atmosphere inside a bit middle-aged, upper-middle-class formal. American-Continental entrées well prepared but not imaginative. But it's not that expensive, and we recommend it.

The leading country French and Italian restaurant: **Ledford House,** at Schoolhouse Creek Inn (see "Where to Stay"), 937-0282. $:expensive. No cards. Wine, beer. Menu changes constantly, depending on what's good and available, with more flair in the offerings than Heritage House. Chef-owner makes own bread. Cl. Sun., also Thurs. in off-season.

Locally popular for good home-cooked food: **Little River Inn** (see "Where to Stay"). $:intermediate. No cards. Seafood dominates menu at this unpretentious inn.

Small and civilized: **Café Beaujolais,** 44835 Ukiah St., Mendocino, 937-5614. $:intermediate-expensive. No cards. Wine. French menu surprisingly long for such a small place, but there's some inconsistency in the kitchen.

Victorian theme restaurant: **Mendocino Hotel** (see "Where to Stay"). $:intermediate. MC, VI. Jack-in-the-Box gone gourmet, which means prime rib, steaks, chicken. Union Street ambiance.

Also: **MacCallum House** (see "Where to Stay"). $:intermediate-expensive. MC, VI. Full bar. Varied menu. Getting a reputation with the carriage trade. . . . **Little River Café,** Hwy. 1, 937-0404. Northern Italian, seafood. Prix-fixe dinner $:expensive. Old house (1862) now a little restaurant.

Reopened, not checked: **The Seagull,** Lansing & Ukiah, Mendocino, 937-5204 burned down, to the dismay of locals, but has now been rebuilt, presumably to their delight. We'll look in sometime. Good for lunch, casual dining.

And way down there in Elk: **Greenwood Pier Café,** Hwy. 1, 877-9997. $:budget. MC, VI. Drop in for breakfast, lunch. . . . **Elk Cove Inn** (see "Where to Stay"). Prix-fixe dinner with wine $:intermediate. No cards. Call ahead to see if they have space for nonguests to sample the German or French dishes that issue forth from the kitchen at this homey place. Cl. Mon.-Wed.

Delis/picnic spots: Get your provisions at The Pelican, Main St. or the Cheese Shop, 45050 Little Lake Rd., both in Mendocino, or the Earthly Delights Delicatessen, 18500 N. Hwy. 1, Fort Bragg. Put the provisions together in the sea breeze at the Mendocino Headlands (which is one side of Main St., Mendocino), Russian Gulch, Van Damme, or MacKerricher state parks.

Mill Valley/Mt. Tamalpais

Mill Valley's and Mt. Tam's accommodations are few but slightly varied, with choices between camping or hosteling on the mountain and staying in a highway motel near the bay. Dining likewise ranges from snacks and meals on Mt. Tam and in Muir Woods to seafood, international cuisine, and locally popular restaurants in Mill Valley. Also see Sausalito/Bayside Marin and San Rafael/Northern Marin.

Area code: 415. All have a Mill Valley 94941 address.

WHERE TO STAY

Highway motels: **Howard Johnson's,** 160 Shoreline Hwy., 332-5700, 800/654-2000. $:intermediate. All cards. Standard 100 rooms, color TV, pool, bar. . . . **Motel Alto,** 817 Redwood Hwy., 388-9979. $:intermediate. Major cards. Small 18 rooms, 7 with kitchens. . . . Also **TraveLodge** and local motels.

Tamalpais inn: **West Point Inn,** 1000 Panoramic Hwy., 388-9955. $:budget. Woodsy and tucked into Tam's hillside, the inn offers inexpensive hostel-like rooms.

Camping: Mt. Tamalpais State Park, 6 miles W of Mill Valley on Panoramic Highway. About 18 primitive walk-in camping sites, with picnic tables, bathrooms, fishing, hiking, nature trail, and horseback-riding trail nearby. The park may later open a hostel on the ocean at Steep Ravine and establish more back-country camping, after the master plan is completed.

WHERE TO EAT

Middle Eastern, locally popular: **Davood's,** 22 Miller Ave., 388-2000. $:intermediate. MC, VI. Owned by an Iranian, this very Mill Valley spot is "downtown," features stained glass, natural wood, roll-back (laid-back?) roof, live jazz. Persian specialties with California touches, including curries, kabobs, casseroles, dolmas, seafood, tempting desserts.

French: **Le Camembert,** 200 Shoreline Hwy., 383-8000. $:intermediate. AE, MC, VI. Three Norman dining rooms with countryside touches, and French specialties. . . . **El Paseo,** 7 El Paseo, 388-0741. $:intermediate. Popular, downtown.

Italian: **Giramonti,** 655 Redwood Hwy., 383-3000. $:intermediate-expensive. MC, VI. Facing Shelter Bay's marshy waterline, Giramonti features fresh seafood (calamari, scampi), veal (piccata, saltimbocca), pasta (tortellini Adriana, spaghetti carbonara). Cl. Mon.

German: **The Buckeye,** Hwy. 101 (at Mill Valley/Stinson Beach exit), 332-1292. $:intermediate. Major cards. Full bar. Gemutlichkeit und Wiener

Schnitzel have been served since 1937 in this German chalet. Other entrees: roast goose, prawns, prime rib, sauerbraten.

Mexican: **El Pescador,** 707 Redwood Hwy., 381-0411. $:budget-intermediate. MC, VI. Palms and wood in a motel restaurant that has different Mexican seafood dishes, such as robalo tapado (sea bass), hauchinango Yacateco (red snapper), and camarones Veracruzana (prawns) plus the usuals.

Chinese: **Yet Wah,** 50 Strawberry Town & Country shopping center, 388-2412. $:budget-intermediate. AE, MC, VI. Part of a Bay Area Mandarin chain, Yet Wah has stuffed chicken wings, Tsing Tao beef, butterfly shrimp, lemon chicken, and other delectables.

Outdoors and/or in the parks: **Muir Woods Snack Bar,** next to the gift shop, 388-7059. . . . **Mountain Home,** 810 Panoramic Hwy., on Mt. Tamalpais, 381-0103. Popular for Sunday brunch. . . . **Tourist Club** (*Die Naturfreunde*), off Panoramic Hwy. (turnoff is 2.2 miles NW of Muir Woods turnoff). Snacks, beer, wine, on deck and balconies within the forest. . . . **West Point Inn,** 1000 Panoramic Hwy., 388-9955. Porches for alfresco lemonade, tea, coffee.

Napa

Despite being the seat of a winegrowing county, Napa is really your all-American small city. Accommodations are predictable; and the American and Continental-menued restaurants don't have the big wine cellars you might expect. But everything is pleasant, the ambiance wholesome. All listed places have a Napa city address: area code 707, zip code 94558.

WHERE TO STAY

The ritzy place. **Silverado Country Club and Resort,** 1600 Atlas Peak Rd. (off Hwy. 121 N of Napa), 255-2970. $:expensive-luxury. All cards. The air of the Silverado is best described by this quote from their brochure: "Since Amanda's learned to pilot the 310, we find ourselves at Silverado almost every weekend. There's no parking problem at the Napa Airport, and it's only 7 miles from the courts." 2 Robert Trent Jones–designed links; golfer Johnny Miller lives along one fairway. 5 pools, balconied cottages, condo units with fireplaces, 2 dining rooms, etc. Amfac developed the 1870 mansion–ranch house and 1,200 acres as a resort in 1966.

Condos for rent: **Silverado** (see above). . . . **The Fairways at Silverado,** 100 Fairway Dr., 255-6644. $:expensive. "Spanish casitas" with all amenities, overlooking one of the golf courses.

Can't go wrong: **Wine Valley Lodge,** 200 S. Coombs, 224-7911. $:intermediate. MC, VI. . . . **Holiday Inn–Napa Valley,** 3425 Solano Ave., 253-7433. $:intermediate. Major cards. . . . **Best Western Downtown Motel,** 2nd & Coombs, 226-1871. $:budget.

Pretty basic: **Motel 6,** 33800 Solano Ave., 226-1811. $:budget.

RV camping: Napa Valley Camping Resort, 1962 Capell Valley Rd., 226-9133.

WHERE TO EAT

Carriage trade: **Oliver's,** Security Pacific Bank Bldg., 1700 2nd St./Washington, 252-4555. $:expensive. AE, MC, VI. Full bar. The better Continental entrées in elegant surrounds. . . . **Silverado main dining room** (see "Where to Stay"). $:expensive. Major cards. Full bar. Coat and tie Fri.-Sat. Don't get the Bernaise on your tie, though.

Old Victorian house: **Carriage House,** 1775 Clay/Jefferson, 255-4744. $:intermediate. AE, MC, VI. Full bar. 6-item menu plus daily special, in typical little-restaurant style.

Country French: **Bon Appetit,** 4120 St. Helena Hwy., 252-7311. $:intermediate. MC, VI. The chef-owner used to make wine, now whips up quiche, pâté, soups, and other dishes for noontime (especially) wine tourists. Modest corkage fee if you have brought your own wine.

Old standbys: **Jonesy's Famous Steak House,** Napa County Airport, 224-2945. $:intermediate. AE, MC, VI. It is famous. Amanda might pilot the 310 to have a big salad and steak here. . . . **The Red Hen,** 5091 St. Helena Hwy. (Hwy. 29 N of town), 255-9801. $:budget. MC, VI. Families will like this good old American country restaurant—in an antique-filled barn—for its standard, hearty servings of chicken, turkey, ham, roast beef, and fish.

Unchecked new French: **La Boucane,** 1778 Second St., 253-1177. . . . **Bernard et Suzette Restaurant Français et Oyster Bar,** 902 Main St., 252-8700. Both cl. Mon.

Italian plus: **Ruffino's,** 645 1st St., 255-4455. $:intermediate-expensive. AE, MC, VI. Also seafood, steak. Cl. mid-June—mid-July. . . . **Depot Hotel,** 806 4th St., 255-9944. $:budget-intermediate. Pasta and lots of it, family-style.

A little French: **La Gamelle,** 1010 Lincoln, 226-2633. $:budget-intermediate. MC, VI. The owner is in the kitchen.

Mexican: **Jalisco Restaurant,** 4050 Byway E., 224-8717. $:budget. MC, VI. Full bar. No surprises on the menu but imaginative drinks like a Tequila Sunrise.

If you can stomach it: **The Cedars,** Nabors shopping center, 2762 Old Sonoma Rd., 255-0524. Lebanese, American, and vegetarian—plus belly-dancers Fri.-Sun. evenings.

Lunch: **Carriage House** and **La Gamelle** have lunch weekdays, **Oliver's** Mon.-Sat. and **Jonesy's** Tues.-Sat. . . . **Sandwiches Unlimited,** 304 Lincoln/Silverado Trail, 253-0432. Extensive grill and sandwich list. Open 7 days. . . . **Napa Bakery,** 1517 3rd St., 255-4557. Makes extra-sour French bread daily.

Delis/picnic spots: You can get lunch ingredients at several places: Paolino's, 1091 Parkway Mall, 255-4177; Perry's, 810 Randolph, 252-7044; Fickle Pickle, 1222 Trancas, 252-0233 (next door is a wineshop, Chick's); Nunn's Cheese Barn, 1427 Main, 255-0262. (We can't bring ourselves to consider the Ptomaine Deli; no kidding.) These delis are open 7 days. The urban picnic spot is Fuller Park, Jefferson & Oak, or you can journey NE on Atlas Peak Rd. (past Silverado) to the city's Milliken Reservoir Recreation Area. Alternatively, keep the fixings and wait till you come to a winery with picnic tables and wine fresh from the salesroom.

Petaluma/Cotati Valley

Petaluma, midway between here and there, is a stop, not a destination. Area code: 707. Zip codes: Cotati/Rohnert Park 94928, Petaluma 94952.

WHERE TO STAY

Standard accommodations: **Best Western Petaluma Inn,** 200 S. McDowell Ave. (Hwy. 101 & E. Washington), Petaluma, 763-0994. $:budget. Major cards. Restaurant, pool. . . . **Regal 8 Inn,** 6288 S. Santa Rosa Ave., Rohnert Park, 544-1420. $:budget. Major cards.

RV camping: Sonoma Grove, 7450 Cristobal Rd., Rohnert Park, 795-9333. . . . San Francisco North/Petaluma KOA, 20 Rainsville Rd., Petaluma, 763-1492. Some tent sites, but it's open land.

WHERE TO EAT

MBA restaurant: **Steamer Gold Landing,** 1 Water St., Petaluma, 763-6876. $:intermediate-expensive. MC, VI. Trendy, hip-flashy—just right for restored shopping gallery, the Great Petaluma Mill. Sit outside for nice Sunday brunch on way to Alexander Valley.

Lunch sunnyside up: **The Eggery,** 4480 Bodega Ave., Petaluma, 762-7228. MC, VI. Wine, beer. Omelettes made at your table in one of Petaluma's former chicken houses. Dinners, Sunday brunch. Cl. Mon.

Freeway specials: **Sonoma Joe's (Casa Montero),** 5151 Redwood Hwy. N., Petaluma, 795-5800. $:intermediate. AE, MC, VI. Full bar. American menu with some specialties; children's menu. No unpleasant surprises, except perhaps the gift shop. . . . **Cattlemen's,** 5012 Petaluma Blvd. N., Petaluma, 763-4114. $:intermediate. Major cards. Full bar. Good red meat.

Century-old roadhouse: **Washoe House,** Stony Point Rd. & Roblar Rd. (SW of Cotati), Petaluma 795-4544. $:budget-intermediate. MC, VI. Steak, chicken (in a basket), and the like in 1859 stage stop with much historical memorabilia.

The great picnic place: **Marin French Cheese Co.,** 7500 Red Hill Rd., Petaluma, 762-6001. Farm and cheese factory on road wandering south of Petaluma. Very popular. See Chapter 5 for details.

St. Helena/Central Napa Valley

St. Helena and the two tiny crossroads settlements to the south, Oakville and Rutherford, comprise the urban heart of Napa Wine Country. Strangely, there's a surplus of good places for lunch, a relative scarcity of good dinner restaurants and interesting accommodations. But one can always go north to Calistoga or south to Yountville if the choices don't appeal.

Area code: 707. Zip codes: Oakville 94562, Rutherford 94573, St. Helena 94574.

WHERE TO STAY

Country inns: **Wine Country Inn,** 1152 Lodi Lane (turn off Hwy. 29 at Freemark Abbey), 963-7077. $:expensive (breakfast included). MC, VI. Of the two St. Helena and two Yountville inns, this is the only one specifically built to accommodate guests—and very good accommodations they are. Constructed, finished, decorated, and operated by one remarkable family, the 1975 inn is modern in an old-fashioned way; for instance, the bedsteads look antique but were handcrafted not long ago by one of the sons, and the framed stitchery on the walls and quilts were handmade by the lady of the house. 25 rooms, most with balconies or patios. Cheerful, quiet, and our choice. . . . **Chalet Bernensis Inn,** 225 South St., Helena Hwy. (next to Sutter Home Winery), 963-4423. $:intermediate (breakfast included). A most charming building, an 1884 gray-and-white Victorian, the inn has five bathless, antique-filled rooms upstairs for guests and three antique-filled rooms.

Good motel: **Harvest Inn,** Box 65 (1 Main St.), 963-9463. $:expensive. AE, MC, VI. Half-timbered 19-unit motel, vintage 1979, with efficiency units, fireplaces, antiques.

WHERE TO EAT

Best new reputation: **Miramonte,** 1327 Railroad Ave., St. Helena, 963-3970. $:expensive-luxury. MC, VI. Wine, beer. Overnight success. Brief but serious menu; good California wines only. In restored stone Miramonte Hotel.

A little French: **La Belle Helene,** 1345 Railroad Ave., St. Helena, 963-9984. $:expensive. No cards. Always on a short list of the Napa Valley's best restaurants. Do reserve.

Popular with wine-tour packages: **Abbey Restaurant,** at Freemark Abbey, 3020 N. St. Helena Hwy., St. Helena, 963-2706. $:intermediate. MC, VI. Heavily patronized at lunch by Gray Liners; ordinary folk can find a place to sit at dinner. French, Italian, and American entrées of acceptable quality.

A little different: **Oakville Public House,** Hwy. 29, Oakville, 944-9997. $:budget-intermediate. No cards. In the British pub tradition, which means there's food available for drinkers.

Nouvelle Chinese: **Maggie Gin's,** 1234 Main St., St. Helena, 963-9764.

$:budget. MC, VI. Wine, beer. Tiny list of dishes cooked cleanly, served cafeteria style.

Nice lunch places: **Lord Bruce,** 1304 Main St., St. Helena, 963-3889. $:budget-intermediate. No cards. Has weekday dinner but best for soups, salads, sandwiches. . . . **Rutherford Square Garden Restaurant,** Rutherford, 963-2617. $:budget. No cards. Full bar. Homemade specialties you can eat outside. . . . Most delis listed below have tables inside or out.

Delis/wine shops/picnic spots: The Napa Valley is one of the best areas to get a selection of cheeses, salami, pickles, olives, artichoke hearts, pickled pig's feet, wurst, chorizo, pepperoncini, lox, sardines, smoked herring, crackers, chips—not to mention dark-baked sourdough French bread and those long, skinny baguettes (for tiny open-face sandwiches). St. Helena's bakery is the Sugarhouse Bakery, 1357 Main St., but delis also have at least the well-known San Francisco sourdough brands. Delis (open every day) in roughly south-north order: at Oakville—Oakville Grocery, Hwy. 29, 944-8802 (well-known place), and Pometta's, Hwy. 29, 944-2365; at Rutherford—The Cottage, Rutherford Sq., 963-2317; S of St. Helena—St. Helena Cheese Factory, at V. Sattui Winery, White Lane & Hwy. 29, 963-7774; in St. Helena—Napa Valley Olive Oil Manufactory, 835 McCorkle Ave., 963-4173 (century-old factory is also well-stocked deli) and W. F. Giugni & Son, 1227 Main, 963-3421; N of St. Helena—Freemark Abbey Gift & Gourmet, Hwy. 29/Lodi Lane, 963-3033. Besides the salesrooms at most wineries, there are some independent wineshops with excellent stocks: Ernie's Wine Warehouse, 699 St. Helena Hwy., St. Helena, 963-7888, is one of the biggest you'll see anywhere, but The Bottle Shop, 1321 Main St., St. Helena, 963-3092, run by a Beringer heir, is good-size. And where are you going to eat and drink all this? Many picnic tables are not advertised, for owners' fear of becoming too popular, but we know of picnic tables at the St. Helena Cheese Factory (V. Sattui Winery) and Burgess Cellars, 1108 Deer Park Rd., plus the town's Crane Park, end of Grayson Avenue. See also the Calistoga, Lake Berryessa, and Yountville sections for more picnic spots. Otherwise, just wine-tour until you see a likely spot, perhaps by the side of Silverado Trail (parallels Hwy. 29 to the east).

San Rafael/Northern Marin

The choices narrow farther north in Marin, compared with the Sausalito-Tiburon and Mill Valley areas. Places to stay tend to be motels and RV parks. Restaurants are much better, with excellent French and other international cuisines.

All listings are in San Rafael. Area code: 415. Zip code: 94901.

WHERE TO STAY

Standard motels: **Villa Rafael Motel,** 1600 Lincoln Ave., 456-4975. $:intermediate. Major cards. Near downtown. 52 rooms, 10 with kitchens, all with color TV, plus pool, sauna, coffee shop, and restaurant, Golden Gate Transit bus service to San Francisco. . . . **Holiday Inn,** 1010 Northgate Dr., 479-8800. $:expensive. Major cards. In northern San Rafael's Terra Linda area on a rise off Hwy. 101. 229 rooms, color TV, pool, other services.

Camping: Marin Mobile Home and RV Park, 2130 Redwood Hwy., 461-5199. Has 171 sites for RVs, plus tent area (though tenters would probably prefer Mt. Tam), pool, 2 saunas, etc. . . . Golden Gate Trailer Park, 2000 Redwood Hwy., 924-0683. Some 35 RV sites.

WHERE TO EAT

French: **Maurice et Charles Bistrot,** 901 Lincoln Ave., 456-2010. $:expensive-luxury. AE, MC. Full bar. Cl. Sun. Considered by most to be Marin's and one of the Bay Area's finest French restaurants, Maurice et Charles' eponymic founders have since gone on to other gastronomic ventures, but the quality remains. Specialties: quenelle truffe du Bistrot, medaillon de veau Alsacienne, sole d'agneau farcie. . . . **La Petite Auberge,** 704 4th St., 456-5808. $:intermediate-expensive. AE, MC, VI. Full bar. Cl. Mon. Also in downtown San Rafael, La Petite Auberge has a French countryside environment, though it's more crowded and less intimate, with features including broiled or poached salmon, calf's brains beurre noir, medaillon of veal with chanterelles. . . . **La Marmite,** 909 Lincoln Ave., 456-4020. $:intermediate-expensive. MC, VI. Wine, beer. Cl. Mon. In the same block as Maurice et Charles and a competitor for the French dinner dollar; Le Marmite's specialties include coq au vin vieux, veau Dijonnais, filet en croûte.

Supper: **The Ivory Coast,** 3rd/A, 453-3354. $:budget. MC, VI. Wine, beer. A former gas station was transformed with fans, palms, and a stuffed lion. Explore the Savanna and discover the black-backed jackal and chimpanzee sandwiches, soups, quiches.

Mexican: **Ramona's,** 1025 C St., 454-0761. $:intermediate. Wine, beer. Cl. Mon. Ramona opened her first restaurant at the ripe old age of 14 in 1937 and has been going strong since, serving chicken mole, arroz con pollo, panuchos, as well as the usuals.

Indonesian: **Rice Table,** 1617 4th St., 456-1808. $:intermediate. AE, MC, VI. Wine and beer. Cl. Mon. Feast on an exotic 12-dish rijstaffel.

Seafood: **Dominic's Harbor Restaurant,** 507 Francisco Blvd., 456-1383. $:intermediate-expensive. Major cards. Full bar. A large, enthusiastic establishment with its own docks for Sunday boat brunchers, plus decks and indoors for seafood and Italian lunches and dinners.

Basque: **Le Chalet Basque,** 405 N. San Pedro Road, 479-1070. $:intermediate. MC, VI. Cl. Mon. One mile from the Marin Civic Center, Le Chalet serves hardy, filling dinners, emphasizing lamb and other meat entrées such as Azouria Basque.

Japanese: **Yoshida,** 810 3rd St., 456-3844. $:intermediate. Downtown, informal, quick with tempura, yakitori, kushi yaki, nabemono and other dishes. . . . **Fujiyama,** 2130 4th St., 456-8774. $:intermediate-expensive. AE, MC, VI. Cl. Mon. Steaks, plus Japanese specialties.

California: **Andalou,** 3rd/E St., 454-4900. $:intermediate-expensive. MC, VI. Cl. Mon. In a renovated downtown Victorian; Andalou's California specialties may include barbecued oyster brochette, roast leg of lamb, veal Floriovo, and other fresh seafood, lamb, and chicken dishes.

Bakeries: F'oodles, 3140 Kerner Blvd., 457-5000. Custom cakes and pastries. . . . California Bakery, 919 4th St., 453-3513. Danish pastries. . . . Viking Pastry, 1007 C St., 453-1328. Swedish bread and pastries.

Deli: Belli-Deli, 1304 2nd St., 456-2626. . . . El Siboney, 1335 4th St., 454-2868. . . . F'oodles, 3140 Kerner Blvd., 457-5000. . . . Ivory Coast, 3rd/A St., 453-3354.

Santa Rosa

Santa Rosa is an All-American freeway city, so the range of choice among accommodations and restaurants is fairly limited. Area code: 707, zip codes as listed.

WHERE TO STAY

Big meeting places: **El Rancho Tropicana,** 2200 Santa Rosa Ave., 95401, 542-3655. $:intermediate. Major cards. 300 rooms: this is a convention hotel (formerly a Sheraton). 3 pools, playground, etc. . . . **Los Robles Lodge,** 925 Edwards Ave., 95401, 545-6330. $:intermediate. Major cards. 90 rooms; most facilities.

Many other motels including. **Best Western Hillside Inn,** 2901 4th St, 95405, 546-9353. $:budget. Major cards. . . . Also **Holiday Inn, 2 Trave-Lodges,** another **Best Western, Regal 8, Motel 6,** and local establishments.

Camping: Spring Lake County Park, off Hwy. 12 adjacent to Annadel State Park, has 31 tent and RV sites available first come, first served. North Star Mobile Park, 3200 Santa Rosa Ave., 545-0982, has some spaces for RVs. See also Sonoma/Sonoma Valley section below.

WHERE TO EAT

Best for Santa Rosa and visiting gourmets: **La Province,** 521–525 College/Mendocino, 526-6233. $:expensive. AE, MC, VI. Wine. Two bungalows connected by breezeway disguise the 1978-new restaurant begun by chef and maître d' formerly of two of Marin's finest French restaurants. Fine French lunch and dinner menus plus long California wine list. Survival is predicted. Cl. Sun., holidays.

Lunching in old Victorian: **Marshall House,** 835 2nd St., 542-5305. No cards. Wine only. The owner prepares the various casseroles, oversees the gift shop, flower garden. Cl. Sun., major holidays.

Dining in old Victorian: **The Belvedere,** 727 Mendocino Ave., 542-1890. $:intermediate-expensive. MC, VI. Full bar. A charmer of a house. Lunch, weekend brunch, dinner every day, served on garden patio if the weather's nice. No surprises on regular menu but examine the specials. Entertainment Tues.-Sun. Art and gifts too.

Two Italians: **Fiori Grace & Company Pub Café,** 2755 Mendocino Ave., 527-7460. $:intermediate-expensive. AE, MC, VI. Full bar. American and Italian inevitables—prime rib, seafood, veal, pasta—in stained-glass modern surroundings. . . . **La Fontana,** 19 Old Courthouse Sq., 545-4797. $:intermediate. MC, VI. Full bar. Big Italian-and-steak "Venetian showplace" with a big white marble Florentine fountain.

Two Germans: **Black Forest Inn,** 138 Calistoga Rd., 539-4334. $:intermediate. AE, MC, VI. Full bar. Teutonic atmosphere and specialties, also other fare. . . . **Kleist's Heidelberg,** 6422 Old Redwood Hwy., 838-9986. $:budget-intermediate. MC, VI. German menu and smorgasbord too.

Two Mexicans: **Old Mexico,** 4501 Montgomery Dr., 539-2599. $:intermediate. Major cards. Full bar. The chef-owner uses family recipes. Lots of decor. Guitar music Fri.-Sun. . . . **Rosie's Cantina,** 570 E. Cotati Ave., Cotati, 795-9211. $:budget. Wine, beer. Less elaborate. Entertainment.

Countercultural: **Mandala Café,** 650 5th St., 527-9797. $:budget. No cards. International natural foods—which is to say, vegetarian. Entertainment at dinner.

Eggzactly: **Omelette Express,** 112 4th St. (Railroad Sq.), 525-1690. MC, VI. Wine, beer. In 300 consecutive breakfasts, lunches, or dinners you could try every omelette they make. Also sandwiches, chili, etc.

Delis/picnic spot: Traverso's, 3rd & B, 542-2530. (cl. Sun.); Perry's Deli, 1220 Mendocino Ave., 528-2704, or 1117 Sebastopol Rd., 545-4272; Canevari's, 695 Lewis Rd./Humboldt, 546-4269. Wine Cave, 2255 Cleveland Ave., 525-9463, claims to carry 95 percent of North Coast wines, also has deli items. The picnic spot is shady Juillard Park, across Santa Rosa Ave. from the Luther Burbank Gardens.

Sausalito/Bayside Marin

Sausalito, Belvedere, Tiburon, Corte Madera, Larkspur, San Anselmo, and other bayside southern Marin towns feature a variety of restaurants catering to residents and visitors alike, ranging from coffee house–bookstores to waterfront hangouts and establishments to international and seafood specialty spots. Places to stay are either inns/downtown hotels or highway motels. For more accommodations and information, see San Rafael/Northern Marin and Mill Valley/Mt. Tamalpais.

Area code: 415. Zip codes: Sausalito 94965, Belvedere/Tiburon 94920, Corte Madera 94925, Larkspur 94939, Kentfield/Greenbrae 94904, Ross 94957, San Anselmo 94960.

WHERE TO STAY

Downtown hotels/inns: **Alta Mira Hotel,** Box 706 (Bulkley Ave./Princess), Sausalito, 332-1350. $:budget-expensive. AE, DC, MC, VI. A romantic, hillside getaway, good for a mini or second honeymoon with 14 Moderne rooms and 14 cottages. Known for its view-full Sunday brunch (see "Where to Eat"). . . . **Casa Madrona,** 156 Bulkley Ave./Princess, Sausalito, 332-0502. $:intermediate-expensive. AE, MC, VI. An intimate old (1885) lumber baron's mansion is now an inn with a French air. Some rooms without bath but most with a bay view. Just up the hill from the Village Fair shopping gallery. Shares premises with Le Vivoir restaurant (see "Where to Eat"). . . . **Sausalito Hotel,** 16 El Portal/Bridgeway, Sausalito, 332-4155. $:intermediate-expensive. AE, MC, VI. In the heart of the hubbub, the Sausalito Hotel has watched the action since the early 1900s. Each of the 15 rooms is individually furnished with antiques, and 5 share baths.

Modern motels: **Tiburon Lodge Motor Hotel,** 1651 Tiburon Blvd., Tiburon, 435-3133. $:intermediate-expensive. Major cards. Standard motel with 91 rooms, pool, patios, restaurant. . . . **Best Western Corte Madera Inn,** 1815 Redwood Hwy./Madera Blvd., Corte Madera, 924-1502. $:expensive. 90 rooms, patios, garden, big pool and wading pool, whirlpool, playground, laundry, restaurant.

WHERE TO EAT

Waterfront-casual: **Zack's,** Bridgeway/Turney, Sausalito, 332-9779. $:budget-intermediate. Full bar. Zack's swings, and has since 1958, especially for under-30s, with live music, dancing, turtle races Wed. night, grilled burgers, sandwiches, steaks, brunch on the deck. . . . **Sausalito Food Co.,** 305 Harbor Dr./Bridgeway, Sausalito, 332-0535. $:intermediate. MC, VI. Wine, beer. Join the crowd indoors or out for brunch, lunch, dinner. . . . **The Trident,** 558 Bridgeway, Sausalito, 332-1334. $:budget-expensive. Full bar. Between downtown and the water, under Ondine (see below) with superlative views, hanging plants, and wood, weekend throngs eating brunch, sandwiches, organic roast chicken, teriyaki steak. . . . **Flynn's Landing,** 303 Johnson/Bridgeway, 332-1031. $:budget-intermediate. Full bar. Local, laid-back, and less touristy, with a seafood emphasis, including bouillabaisse, rex sole, sand dabs. . . . **Sam's Anchor Café,** 27 Main, Tiburon, 435-4527. $:intermediate. MC, VI. Full bar. Pull up your boat and join the semiclothed bodies on the outdoor decks or indoor rooms for Sunday brunch, Ramos gin fizz, burgers and Champagne, seafood. . . . **The Dock,** 25 Main, Tiburon, 435-4559. $:intermediate-expensive.

AE, MC, VI. Full bar. Dock your boat, etc. Views and slightly fancier with an older clientele. Specialties: coquilles St. Jacques, other seafood, chicken sautée, beef stroganoff, roast duckling.

Waterfront-dressier: **Ondine,** 558 Bridgeway, Sausalito, 332-0791. $:expensive. Major cards. Full bar. Upstairs over the Trident, Ondine is well established, formal (for Sausalito), and commands superb bay views. Specialties: crab legs Ondine, pheasant Vladimir, boneless squab Montmorency, poulet sauté Patricia, Grand Marnier soufflé. . . . **Spinnaker,** 100 Spinnaker Dr., Sausalito, 332-1500. $:intermediate-expensive. AE, MC, VI. On the yacht harbor, the Spinnaker's specialty appropriately is seafood, such as rex sole meuniere, fried prawns, swordfish, crab Louis. . . . **Sally Stanford's Valhalla Inn,** 201 Bridgeway/Richardson, Sausalito, 332-1792. $:expensive. Major cards. Full bar. Ms. Stanford, a former madame turned respectable restaurateur and Sausalito mayor, runs her bayside Victorian (1870) with period decor, superb view, cackling parrot, Continental cuisine including seafood.

Seafood: Many of the places listed above, plus: **Seven Seas,** 682 Bridgeway, Sausalito, 332-1304. $:intermediate. AE, DC, MC, VI. Wine, beer. In downtown Sausalito since 1959, with a sign indoors that reads KEEP CLAM, the Seven Seas has a friendly atmosphere and fresh seafood. Specialties: cherrystone clams, bluepoint oysters, cracked crab, bouillabaisse, cioppino, prawns Provençale, scallops au beurre, baked stuffed turbot, poached salmon. . . . **Yankee Lobsterman,** 1809 Larkspur Landing Circle, Larkspur, 461-9191. $:budget-intermediate. MC, VI. Wine, beer. Fresh lobster is the raison d'être here. Owner John Polando is from Marblehead, Mass.; his sister, who is in Marblehead, air-freights live fish. Twelve hours from Atlantic to Pacific, take your pick from the tank and then put on your bib at picnic tables. Also Ipswich clams, baked stuffed quahogs, baked Boston scrod. . . . **Sabella's of Marin,** 9 Main St., Tiburon, 435-2636. $:intermediate-expensive. MC, VI. Full bar. On the waterfront, Sabella's is one of an empire of seafood establishments, with a wait inevitable for dinner. Indoor and outdoor dining on broiled swordfish, sand dabs meuniere, stuffed turbot, Maine lobster.

Hillside Continental: **Alta Mira Hotel Dining Room** (see "Where to Stay"). $:intermediate-expensive. Full bar. On a sunny Sunday hundreds brunch at the Alta Mira, sipping fizzes while they wait (avoid Mother's Day, the crowds are horrendous). Lunches and dinners served also with the view. Specialties: eggs Benedict, eggs Alta Mira, million-dollar crab Louis, abalone steak supreme amandine, prime rib.

French: **Le Vivoir,** 156 Bulkley Ave./Princess, Sausalito, 332-1850. $:intermediate-expensive. Major cards. Full bar. Cl. Tues. Downstairs in the charming Casa Madrona (see "Where to Stay"), though separately run, with a terrace and bay view. Le Vivoir's dinner specialties include chateaubriand, les pigeons de Berville, and canard de l'Esterel; they make their own pastry and

bread. . . . **Guernica,** 2009 Bridgeway, Sausalito, 332-1512. $:intermediate.
AE, MC, VI. French-Basque environs and entrees, including rack of lamb,
duck with olives, and bouillabaisse.

Indian: **Moti Mahal,** 2650 Bridgeway, Sausalito, 332-6444. $:intermediate.
MC, VI. Wine, beer. Formerly in Berkeley, Moti Mahal spruced itself up for
its new upscale Sausalito location and has live Indian music with dinner which
might include pakora, samosa, curries, papadum.

Spanish: **El Greco,** 85 Red Hill Ave., San Anselmo, 456-3696. $:intermedi-
ate. Full bar. A well-designed, black-and-white and beamed Spanish interior
sets the mood for tapas, paellas, marinated lamb, veal with mushrooms and
raisins.

Victoriana: **Lark Creek Inn,** 234 Magnolia, Larkspur, 924-7766. $:inter-
mediate. AE, MC, VI. Full bar. Cl. Mon. Built in 1898 as the Murphy home
under the redwoods; Lark Creek Inn's Victorian charm and spaciousness are
pleasant for brunch, lunch, and dinner, such as soup, lobster tails, veal dijon-
nais, eggs Hussarde, shrimp Victorian crepe.

Variable: **464 Magnolia,** Larkspur, 924-6831. $:intermediate. MC, VI.
Wine and beer. Cl. Mon. Variety is the spice and way of life at 464, with hundreds of different entrée dishes offered each year, changing daily, including sal-
timbocca, trout with crab and oysters, sole Cardinal, lemon mousse.

Coffee houses/bakeries: Upstart Crow & Co., 749 Bridgeway, Sausalito,
332-0390. Browse with books, sip coffee and nibble pastries. . . . Peter Pan
Donuts, 2829 Bridgeway, Sausalito, 332-6767. Donuts and cappuccino with
the locals. . . . François Coffee House, 777 Bridgeway, Sausalito, 332-3350.
Pastries and coffee in the Village Fair. . . . Sweden House Bakery, 35 Main,
Tiburon, 435-9767. European pastries and sandwiches on the waterfront. . . .
Cat's Cradle, 1125 Magnolia, Larkspur, 461-0744. Special breads, pastries,
pies, lunches. Two Beans & a Pod, 1509 San Anselmo Ave., San Anselmo,
457-8477. Bookcases, coffees, pastries, other snacks. . . . The Cottage, 727 Sir
Francis Drake Blvd., San Anselmo, 453-4837. Real English teas with sand-
wiches, homemade scones, crumpets, tea, plus breakfast, lunch.

Delicatessens/picnics to go: Sausalito Gourmet Delicatessen, 209 Caledo-
nia, Sausalito, 332-4880. Tiburon Cheese Co., 110 Main, Tiburon, 435-4888.
Maison Gourmet/Petrini's, 270 Bon Air Shopping Center, Greenbrae, 461-
1711. Town Hall Delicatessen and Gourmet Shop, 520 San Anselmo Ave.,
San Anselmo, 456-8656. Picnics are pleasant along Bridgeway in Sausalito, as
well as in local parks. Or take one to Mt. Tam.

Sebastopol/Apple Country

The country roads in this good farming area cross at Sebastopol. A good reason
to stop there or in Occidental is a big country dinner for the whole family. Area
code: 707. Zip codes: Occidental 95465, Sebastopol 95472.

WHERE TO STAY

Motels: **Occidental Lodge,** Box 306 (3700 Bohemian Hwy.), Occidental, 874-3623. $:budget. Major cards. Associated with Negri's (see "Where to Eat"). 20 units plus pool. . . . Otherwise Union Hotel (see "Where to Eat") runs **Union Motel.** Hmm?

Funky-dory: **Blackberry Inn,** 3657 Church St., Occidental, 874-3023. $:budget. B&B&antiques. New & old.

WHERE TO EAT

What's cooking in Sebastopol? Country French, mostly: **Le Pommier,** 1015 Gravenstein Hwy. S., 823-9865. $:intermediate. AE, MC, VI. Wine. Standard saucy-French menu but the plates are Occidentally full. Minimal decor. Cl. Mon. . . . **Chez Peyo,** 2295 Gravenstein Hwy. S., 823-9802. $:budget-intermediate. MC, VI. Wine. Short menu (e.g., roast duckling, rack of lamb Provençale, filet mignon) plus daily special. French-Basque in style, with large portions. . . . **Vast's Garden Dining** (formerly Gobblers Restaurant), 5186 Gravenstein Hwy. S., 795-4747. $:intermediate. No cards. Wine, beer. Home-cooked American specialties—turkey, smoked ham, spareribs, biscuits, pies—served up in restored turkey barn on the Vast farm.

What's cooking in Occidental? Italian and more Italian: Occidental is practically nothing but restaurants—three of them, all big, all Italian, with nearly identical menus, all packed with people (10,000 on a Mother's Day) waiting to get a table for a big family-style five-course meal. The three are **Fiori's,** 823-8188, the flashiest; **Union Hotel,** 874-3662, oldest and funkiest; and **Negri's,** 823-5301, perhaps most acceptable to nonlocals. Most give you a very filling but not particularly good meal for $:budget, or you can spend a bit more for fancier fare. All take AE, MC, VI, and have full bars, sometimes very full and noisy.

Lunch stops: **Giovanni's Delicatessen & Wine Shop,** 171 Pleasant Hill Ave. N., Sebastopol, 823-1331. Sit down inside or outside, or take deli sandwich out to a winery on the Russian River Wine Rd. or friendly farm on the Sonoma Farm Trails (see Chapter 5). Open 7 days. . . . Another popular deli-restaurant is **Town's,** 6970 McKinley/Main, Sebastopol, 823-1822. Cl. Sun.

Sonoma/Sonoma Valley

The town for which so much is named is small but, being a charming place to visit, has a wide variety of decent-to-gourmet restaurants. There are comparatively few places to stay, as is usual with areas so close to San Francisco.

Area code: 707. Zip codes: Boyes Hot Springs 95416, Glen Ellen 95442, Kenwood 95452, Sonoma 95476.

WHERE TO STAY

Comfortable motels: **London Lodge Motel,** 13740 Arnold Dr., Glen Ellen, 938-8510. $:budget. AE, DC, MC, VI. 22 units next to rustic London Lodge restaurant (see "Where to Eat"). Pool. . . . **El Pueblo Motel,** 896 W. Napa St., Sonoma, 996-3651. $:budget. MC, VI. 41 rooms; pool.

Old-new inn: **Sonoma Hotel,** 110 W. Spain St./1st St. Sonoma, 996-2996. $:intermediate-expensive (incl. breakfast). AE, MC, VI. Erstwhile commercial building of 1880s has been Plaza Hotel (1920s–74) and Waywith Inn (1974–76). 16 rooms (5 with bath) furnished with matched late-Victorian bedroom sets, 1 room with Vallejo family antiques, and downstairs has been refurbished. Faces corner of Sonoma Plaza. . . . **Swiss Hotel** (see "Where to Eat"), an old-time bar and restaurant, may have a few rooms in the ca. 1850 adobe; inquire.

Grand but old resort: **Sonoma Mission Inn,** Box 1 (18140 Sonoma Hwy.), Boyes Hot Springs, 996-1041. $:expensive-luxury. MC, VI. One of the last' old-fashioned resorts in this hot-springs area, a Spanish mission-style resort with lawns and trees, swimming pool, shuffleboard, ping-pong, and pool, even a library. Reopened in 1980 after a necessary restoration to appeal to the carriage-trade wine-tripper, but the neighborhood is still funky.

Camping: Sugarloaf Ridge State Park, Adobe Canyon Rd. off Hwy. 12 in the northern Sonoma Valley, has 50 campsites but—listen up, good buddy—the sites are not only primitive and available only first come, first served, but also may be difficult to get to in an RV or with a trailer. The RV alternative is a commercial campground, General Hooker Park, 16820 Sonoma Hwy., Sonoma, 996-0966. Backpackers have an alternative, too: there are 5 tent sites a 2-mile walk in at Hood Mountain Regional Park, Los Alamos Rd. off Hwy. 12; reservations required (527-2041).

WHERE TO EAT

Country French: **Au Relais,** 691 Broadway (Hwy. 121), Sonoma, 996-1031. $:expensive. AE, MC, VI. Full bar. A reservations-necessary Wine Country destination for years. An interesting Victorian cottage with Art Nouveau touches inside and outside. There's a landscaped patio for drinking or dining alfresco when it's not too fresco. Varied French menu includes—in portions that may be too filling—canard Normande (roast duckling cooked with apples), poulet sauté Berrichone (chicken with mushrooms, bacon, onions, sherry), cassoulet, poached salmon, petite escalope de veau Charcutière (veal in cream and Dijon mustard), plus a daily special; also pastries, long California and French wine list. The bar is busy. Cl. late Jan.–early Feb.

Mexican food of note: **La Casa,** 121 E. Spain St., Sonoma, 996-3406. $:budget-intermediate. AE, MC, VI. Full bar. A Mexican lunch or dinner is appropriate for a Sonoma stopover. Located across from the mission in El Paseo. The menu has some nonstandard dishes from different regions of Mexico: chimichangas (thin, deep-fried tortillas stuffed with spiced meat, vegetables), halibut à la Veracruzana (prepared in tomato and olive sauce), tortilla soup, enchiladas suiza, fresh tamales. Cl. Mon.

What the menu is depends on this and that: **Depot Hotel 1870,** 241 1st St. W., Sonoma, 938-2980. $:intermediate-expensive. AE, MC, VI. Wine. The chef decides on the three or four entrées, serves them with four courses. Reservations requested—it is popular with visitors and locals. Cl. Mon.-Wed.

French country: **Capri,** 101 E. Napa St., Sonoma, 996-3866. $:expensive. MC, VI. Wine, beer. Former Italian restaurant has two chefs who turn out good, fresh, unpretentious provincial French dishes: rabbit in red wine and mushroom sauce, chicken with artichoke and mushroom cream sauce, quail stuffed with pâté.

Italian and Chinese, no kidding: **Swiss Hotel,** 18 W. Spain St., Sonoma, 996-9822. Chinese $:budget, Italian $:budget-intermediate. MC, VI. Full bar. Hotel of 1850 has been locally famous and popular for several decades as a restaurant and bar. Not fancy. The chef is Chinese. Cl. Mon.-Tues.

Finally, Italian-American: **El Dorado on the Plaza,** 405 1st St. W., Sonoma, 996-3030. $:intermediate. MC, VI. Full bar. Popular restaurant all day long (cl. Wed.-Thurs. for private parties). In historic adobe (ca. 1836-46) on NW side of the plaza.

Steaks, seafood, and specialties: **London Lodge** (see under "Where to Stay"). $:intermediate. Major cards. Full bar. Among the specialties are beef stroganoff, sautéed sweetbread, stuffed filet of sole. Also steak or fried chicken with Champagne at a special price for two, and a Monday family dinner ($:budget). Rustic lodge is on Sonoma Creek.

Steak-and-potatoes American: **Bunny's Kountry Kitchen,** 9900 Sonoma Hwy., Kenwood, 833-4001. $:budget-intermediate. MC, VI. Full bar. Highway food of good quality, including biscuits with honey butter.

What do you make of this?: **Mother Flugger's Old Same Place,** 13875 Sonoma Hwy., Glen Ellen, 996-0177. Best for lunch, with exotic sandwiches, soups, etc.

Hidden: **Golden Bear Lodge,** 1717 Adobe Canyon Rd., Kenwood. $:intermediate. MC, VI. Full bar. Rustic lodge on Sonoma Creek, with drinks on the patio or by the fireplace, depending on the weather. Popular for its smorgasbord.

Good for lunch: **Eastside Grocery and Oven Room,** 133 E. Napa St., Sonoma, 938-4909. Also a Friday-night BBQ. . . . **Peter Yerry's Espresso Café,** 139 E. Napa St., Sonoma, 996-5559. Snacks, too.

Sunday brunch: **The Grapes Café,** 9575 Sonoma Hwy., Kenwood, 833-4100. Breakfast, lunch, Sunday brunch in this little place. Cl. Mon. . . . **Glen**

Ellen Inn, 13670 Arnold Dr., Glen Ellen, 938-3478. No cards. Make reservations now for the 10:30–3 brunchtime. Many omelettes. . . . Also **Au Relais, Eastside Grocery, Depot Hotel 1870** (call first), **El Dorado on the Plaza.**

Delis, bakery, and picnic spots: As everyone who comes back from Sonoma knows, the deli to tell everyone about is the Sonoma Cheese Factory, 2 W. Spain St., 996-5225. The firm, also called Sonoma Jack on the Plaza, has been making Jack cheese since 1931, providing wine and gourmet deli items to visitors since 1945. Indoor and garden seating. Open daily 9–6. AE, MC, VI. . . . If you're putting together a picnic, get your sourdough French bread fresh from the Sonoma French Bakery, 468 1st St. E., 996-2691. Open Wed.-Sat. 8–6, Sun. 8–12. . . . Another deli is the Old Sonoma Creamery, 400 1st St. E. (across from the bakery), 938-2938, and another cheese factory with sales room is Vella Cheese Co., 315 2nd St. E., 938-3232 (cl. Sun.). Near the bakery is a Chinese deli serving dim sum and piroshki, among other things: Brundage-Sonoma, 492 1st St. E., 938-4388. . . . N of Sonoma, in Boyes Hot Springs, is Vine-Yard Liquor & Deli, 18915 Sonoma Hwy., 996-8722. . . . The shady Sonoma Plaza makes a good picnic spot; so also the grounds of Vallejo's Lachryma Montis half a mile away, off W. Spain St. At last report, wineries with picnic facilities included Sebastiani, Buena Vista, and Hacienda, all in Sonoma, and Kenwood Winery and Chateau St. Jean, up Sonoma Valley; it's polite to buy a bottle of wine at the winery.

Sonoma Coast

The rolling-coast and roller-coaster of a highway along the Sonoma shore are a trip you might want to take only if there's a friendly bed or table to stop at. Here are the choices, more satisfactory in accommodations than in restaurants. (See also Gualala, Mendocino, and Fort Bragg sections above.)

Area Code: 707. Bodega 94922, Bodega Bay 94923, Jenner 95450 (includes Fort Ross, Timber Cove, Stillwater Cove, Ocean Cove), Sea Ranch 95497.

WHERE TO STAY

Weekend escape for BMW and Mercedes owners: **Sea Ranch Lodge,** Box 44 (60 Sea Walk Dr. on Hwy. 1), Sea Ranch, 785-2371. $:intermediate-expensive. MC, VI. Not an intimate little place but certainly an interesting destination. 20 rooms are condo-modern, most with fireplaces, views of coastal meadow and, yes, coastal ocean. Guests can use the development's heated pool, sauna, tennis courts, and 9-hole golf course as well as the public's shoreline. Restaurant, bar, modern general store in same building.

Weekend escapes for VW and Toyota owners: **Chanslor Ranch,** Box 327, Bodega Bay, 875-3386. 2 miles north of town. $:intermediate (incl. breakfast). 700-acre working ranch has 3 rooms and bunkhouse (for 8) for guests. The proprietors encourage horseback riding in the hills and along shore. . . . **Still-**

water Cove Ranch, 22555 Hwy. 1, Jenner, 847-3227. $:budget-intermediate. At Stillwater Cove, 12 miles N of Jenner. Only 6 rooms in the small buildings of the old Stillwater Cove School for boys. Some fireplaces, kitchens, but no common or dining rooms. A rural retreat: deer graze on the grounds.

Rustic, scenic modernity: **Timber Cove Inn,** 21780 Hwy. 1, Jenner, 847-3231. 3 miles N of Fort Ross. $:intermediate-expensive. MC, VI. Original owner rescued this inn and made it a destination again. Not cozy but wonderful rugged location. Some more expensive rooms have fireplaces, sunken tubs, waterbeds. Restaurant, gift shop.

Motels at good locations, which is a definite improvement over most motels: **Best Western Bodega Bay Lodge,** Box 357 (Hwy. 1), Bodega Bay, 875-3525. $:intermediate. Major cards. Patios or balconies, bay views. . . . **The Tides Motel,** Box 186 (Hwy. 1), Bodega Bay, 875-3553. $:budget-intermediate. MC, VI. Somewhat busier location near popular restaurant (see "Where to Eat"), photogenic fishing wharfs. . . . **Salt Point Lodge** (formerly Ocean Cove Motel), 23255 Hwy. 1, Jenner, 847-3234. At Ocean Cove, 17 miles N of Jenner. $:budget-intermediate. MC, VI. Your basic motel, nice for fishermen and divers.

House rentals: It's not cheap but for $300 (or a lot more) per week you can rent a Sea Ranch house from some doctor or architect through Rams Head Rentals, Box 123 (1000 Annapolis Rd.), Sea Ranch, 785-2427.

Public camping: Salt Point State Park has 31 primitive tent and RV sites; first come, first served. Two units of Sonoma Coast State Beach have camping: Wright's Beach has 30 sites, flush toilets; Bodega Dunes has 98 sites, flush toilets, and showers; Ticketron reservations. . . . Westside County Park, 47 spaces, and Doran County Park, 138 spaces—both parks are at Bodega Bay—and Gualala Point County Park, 29 sites, are available first come, first served.

Commercial camping: Gualala River Redwood Park, Box 101 (County Road 501, E of town), Gualala, 884-3533, has 140 tent and RV spaces, full facilities; reservations accepted.

WHERE TO EAT

Fresh seafood is unloaded outside on the wharf: **The Tides Restaurant,** Hwy. 1, Bodega Bay, 875-3553. $:intermediate. MC, VI. Full bar. Salmon, crab, sole, shrimp, rock cod, oysters—whatever's in season can be caught and be on your plate in hours. Get a window seat. Fisherman's Wharf without the crowds.

Should be better: **Sea Ranch Restaurant,** 60 Sea Walk Dr. (in building with lodge and store), Sea Ranch, 785-2371. $:intermediate-expensive. MC, VI. The development being a class operation, the cuisine—steak, lamb, seafood—should be more imaginative. But it's the only place to eat in miles, the views are delicious, the trend-setting architecture is worth talking about.

New ownership: **Murphy's Jenner-by-the-Sea,** Hwy. 1, Jenner, 865-2377.

$:intermediate. AE, MC, VI. Full bar. No longer a Formica coffee shop handy as a clam-chowder stopover in midafternoon; now you have to sit down and have a meal at proper hours. American-Continental menu. Sunday brunch.

More casual places: **River's End,** Hwy. 1, Jenner, 865-2484. Short orders for passers-by.... **Bernardo's Seafarer Inn,** Hwy. 1, Bodega Bay, 875-2383. Also a deli.... **Bodega Harbour** golf course has a restaurant; 21301 Heron Blvd., Bodega Bay, 875-3503.

Homecooked Italian: **Dinucci's,** Valley Ford (almost on the Marin County line), 876-3260. $:budget-intermediate. MC, VI. Full bar. Big family-style meals with something filling—steak, seafood, Italian—in the middle.

Ukiah/Inland Mendocino County

Ukiah and Willits are mainly stopping-over places between the Bay Area and the Mendocino coast or Redwood Country. Area code: 707. Zip codes: Redwood Valley 95470, Ukiah 95482, Willits 95490.

WHERE TO STAY

A few motels for weary travelers: All of the following are $:budget, take major credit cards, and have pools and the usual. In Ukiah: **Lu-Ann Motel,** 1340 N. State St., 462-8873; **Best Western Satellite Lodge,** 406 S. State St., 462-8611; and **Manor Inn,** 950 N. State St., 462-7584.... In Willits (inland terminus of the Skunk): **Best Western Ridgewood Park,** S. Redwood Hwy. (5 miles S of town), 459-5373; and **Pepperwood Motel,** 452 S. Main St., 459-2231.

Resort: **Brooktrails Lodge,** Box 297 (Sherwood Rd.), Willits, 459-5311. $:budget-intermediate. AE, MC, VI. Motel units or cottages under the redwoods, with pools, tennis, golf, fishing.

Commercial camping: Le Trianon Resort, 11 miles E of Calpella on Hwy. 20. No reservations taken. Full facilities, including cabins.... KOA Kamp Ground, Box 946 (1600 W. Hwy. 20), Willits, 459-6179. One-third of the 75 sites are for tents.... Hidden Valley Campground, 29801 N. Hwy. 101, Willits, 459-2521. Smaller, less developed.

Public camping: Corps of Engineers has two fee campgrounds on north shore of Lake Mendocino, available first come, first served. Tenters can try the primitive, no-fee Bureau of Land Management sites in the Cow Mountain area between Ukiah and Clear Lake; take Talmage Hwy. to Mill Creek Rd. to New Cow Mtn. Rd. (call 462-3873 in Ukiah for information). For closest State Park camping, see Fort Bragg, Garberville, and Mendocino sections above.

WHERE TO EAT

Wine visitor's choice: **The Lido,** 228 E. Perkins St., Ukiah, 462-2212. $:intermediate-expensive. Major cards. Accompanied by a Mendocino wine, there's red meat (including prime rib), white meat (including quail with grape dressing), seafood and Italian.

Skunk Train passenger's choice: **Hunter's Inn,** 280 E. Commercial St., Willits, 459-4681. $:intermediate. MC, VI. Salad bar and Continental-American entrees. Patio or inside dining. Across from the depot.

Oak-barbecued steaks: **Broiler Steak House,** 8400 Uva Dr., Redwood Valley (7 miles N of Ukiah), 485-7301. $:intermediate. MC, VI. Full bar. Big and popular. Dinner only.

The old place: **Palace Bar & Grill,** 272 N. State St., Ukiah, 468-9291. $:intermediate. AE, MC, VI. 1891 hotel has oyster bar, charcoal broiler.

All you can eat: **Fjord's Smorg-Ette & Gift Shoppe,** 1351 N. State St., Ukiah, 462-7606. $:budget. No cards. Filling food including teriyaki chicken wings, garlic spaghetti, vegetarian dishes, stock-pot soup, homemade pie.

Vegetables for lunch, pie for dessert: **The Lunch Box,** 114 S. School St., Ukiah, 462-6868. Jack salad is an original. Cl. Sat.-Sun.

Delis: In Ukiah, Pear Tree Deli, 506 E. Perkins St., 462-4352, and KC Deli, 2200 N. State St., 468-5535, are both open daily; Chick's House of Spirits has local wines plus deli counter. . . . In Willits, Bilbo's Deli, 236B E. Commercial St., 459-2920, where you can sit down.

Yountville/Southern Napa Valley

Of the five sections of the Napa Valley, Yountville has the best selection of restaurants, ranging from the dining room at the California branch of a French Champagne house to an all-American diner. Accommodations, more limited, include two of the region's most congenial tiny inns. The best lodging and meals are obtained by reserving well ahead of your visit.

Most everything listed is in or near the hub of Yountville, Vintage 1870, the old winery-turned-shopping gallery you can see from Hwy. 29. Yountville area code is 707, zip code 94599.

WHERE TO STAY

Cozy inns: **Magnolia Hotel,** Drawer M (6529 Yount St.), 944-2056. $:expensive (breakfast included). No cards. We mean cozy: 4 rooms with bath on 2nd floor, 2-bedroom suite on 3rd floor, all charmingly furnished but chairless, which discourages one from doing other than sleeping; and no garden. Brick-and-stone building dates to 1873, became a restaurant-inn in 1966. . . . **Burgundy House Country Inn,** 6711 Washington St., 944-2711. $:expensive (breakfast and unlimited house wine included). No cards. A bit more elbow room here: 6 rooms in main 1870s stone building (least desirable is the downstairs room)—no private baths but two shared baths are super—also 3 cottages, one a small Italianate house. Eclectic decor, furnishings (some happen to be for sale). Our choice in Yountville. . . . **Webber Place,** 6610 Webber Ave., 944-8304. $:expensive. 3 rooms in restored in-town farmhouse.

No surprises: **Best Western Napa Valley Lodge,** Box L (Madison & Hwy. 29), 944-2468. $:intermediate-expensive. All cards. Attractive. You can see vineyards from balconied rooms (others have patios).

WHERE TO EAT

Fine dining and wining among the vines: **Domaine Chandon,** at the winery, California Dr. (Veterans Home exit off Hwy. 29), 944-2467. $:luxury. AE, MC, VI. Reservations a must. Classic and nouvelle cuisine of the Champagne and other regions, served in a modern dining room or outside on the terrace overlooking the vineyards. There's considerable class here, and it's the place to be seen if there's anyone around who might recognize you. Cl. Mon.-Tues.

Small and quality: **French Laundry,** 6640 Washington St., 944-2380. $:expensive. No cards. Reservations required. Wine. Prix-fixe dinner or selections from list of Continental and country-French entrées, served in 3 little rooms. One of the Wine Country's choicest morsels. Cl. Mon. . . . **Magnolia Hotel** (see "Where to Stay"). $:expensive. No cards. Wine. Prix-fixe five-course meals, mainly French but only one per night Thurs.-Sun., so call ahead for information and a seat in the intimate below-stairs dining room.

Northern Italian: **Mama Nina's,** 6772 Washington St., 944-2112. $:intermediate. AE, MC, VI. Full bar. The pasta is homemade and popular. There's another Mama Nina's in Cloverdale, in northern Sonoma. Cl. Wed.

An American classic: **The Diner,** 6476 Washington St., 944-2626. From dawn to midafternoon Tues.-Sun. this re-created 1930s soda-fountain/diner serves breakfast (specialty omelettes and distinctive french fries) and lunch. In the evening Thurs.-Sat., it undergoes a transformation into **El Diner,** serving Latino specialties and Dos Equis and other Mexican beers.

The old standby. **Grape Vine Inn Restaurant,** 7331 St. Helena Hwy , 944-2488. $:intermediate. AE, MC, VI. Full bar. American-Italian restaurant popular at lunch and dinner with both wine people and bus-tourists. Prime rib and veal Parmigiana are the specialties.

Buffalo stew and entertainment too: **Yountville Restaurant & Coffee Saloon,** 6480 Washington St., 944-2761. $:budget-intermediate. No cards. Wine, beer. Connoisseurs can compare the gaminess of the buffalo stew here vs. that at Tommy's Joynt, S.F. Anyway, down it or the fish or steak before the place gets too noisy with C&W. No dinners. Mon.-Tues.

Lunch places: **Chutney Kitchen,** Vintage 1870, 944-2788. MC, VI. Likably decorated soup-salad-sandwich restaurant in a semiopen space in the gallery's main floor and small patio. Specialty: chutney pound cake and cheesecake. Cl. Mon. . . . **Vintage Café,** under the same management, outside in the old railway depot; 944-2614. Esteemed charcoal-grilled burgers. Becomes a bar Fri.-Sat. evenings. . . . **Juiced for You,** in one of the old railway cars next to Vintage 1870; 944-2177. Specialties: many kinds of fresh juice, natural-food sandwiches. . . . Also serving lunch are **Domaine Chandon** (see "Where to Stay"), with reasonably priced luncheons on the terrace, and **Napa Valley Cheese Co.** (see below). . . . Serving Sunday Champagne brunch are the **French Laundry** and **Yountville Restaurant** (see above).

Delis/picnic spots: Yountville is where a lot of wine tasters put together picnic lunches for the drive north through the valley. At Vintage 1870 (cl. Mon.) are the Wurst Place, 944-2224, and The Kitchen Store, 944-8100, and for wine, Groezinger Wine Co., 944-2331. The local picnic place is the city park, next to the cemetery at Jackson and Washington, or you can drive until you see a winery with picnic facilities.

INDEX

accommodations, 277–322
  locating of, 283–284
  price categories for, 280–282
  reservations for, 282
  see also camping; specific cities and regions
Adams, Leon D., 42
air travel:
  in Eureka area, 259–260
  in Marin County, 205
  on Mendocino Coast, 229
  in Northern Redwoods, 274
  on Sonoma Coast, 215
  in Sonoma County (interior), 163
  in Southern Redwoods, 241, 242–243, 246
Albion, Calif., 220, 228
Almadén (winery), 6, 10, 53, 58, 63, 71
Alton, Calif., 249
American Automobile Association, ix, 133, 164
Amerine, M. A., 46, 93, 95
Anchor Bay, Calif., 218–219
Angelica, 27, 74
antiques, xi, 114, 122, 125–126, 227
aperitifs, 11, 14, 28, 74
Appellation d'Origine Contrôlée (AOC), 48, 53–54
appellation system, 85
  BATF on, 48–53
Apple Country, 131, 155
  accommodations and restaurants in, 313–314
aquariums, in Eureka area, 251
Arcata, Calif., 256–258
architecture:
  in Eureka area, 248–249, 251, 254–255, 257–258
  information sources for, x, 214, 249
  in Marin County, 181–182, 183, 184–186
  on Mendocino Coast, 221–223
  in Napa Valley, 107, 117–118, 119, 121, 123

architecture: (cont'd)
  on Sonoma Coast, 213–214
  in Sonoma County (interior), 133, 146–147, 152–154, 162
  in Southern Redwoods, 245
"aroma," meaning of, 92
art:
  in Eureka area, 249, 254, 257
  fairs and festivals, xi, 181
  on Mendocino Coast, 218, 219, 221, 223, 227
  on Sonoma Coast, 209, 213
Asti, Calif., 141, 162, 163

ballooning, hot-air, 107, 109–110, 122
Barbera, 46, 47, 95
beaches:
  in Eureka area, 249, 258, 259
  in Marin County, 178, 180, 189, 192, 193, 194, 202–203, 204
  on Mendocino Coast, 219, 221, 224, 227–228
  in Northern Redwoods, 265–266, 273
  on Sonoma Coast, 210–211
  in Southern Redwoods, 243
Beatrice Foods, 10
Beaujolais, 35, 40–41
Beaulieu Vineyards, 5, 10, 18, 60, 115
  wines of, 9, 36, 45, 63, 69
Belvedere, Calif., 183, 184
Beringer Wines, 5, 10, 60, 116–117
bicycling:
  in Marin County, 179, 182, 184, 207
  on Mendocino Coast, 221, 224, 228, 229
  in Napa Valley, 127–128
  on Sonoma Coast, 210, 215
  in Sonoma County (interior), 151, 163–164
  in Southern Redwoods, 246
bird-watching, 180, 184, 192, 193
"blanc de," 72, 85
boating:
  in Eureka area, 248, 259

boating: *(cont'd)*
on Mendocino Coast, 228
in Mendocino County (interior), 162
in Northern Redwoods, 273
in Sonoma County, 151
in Southern Redwoods, 241, 243
see also canoeing; kayaking
boat tours, 253–254, 260, 269
Bodega, Calif., 209
Bodega Bay, Calif., 209–210
Bohemian Grove, 159–160
Bolinas, Calif., 192–193, 205, 206
Boonville, Calif., 219, 220, 228
Bordeaux, 35, 43, 53
Bordeaux bottle, 75–76
"bottled by," meaning of, 54
"bouquet," meaning of, 92
boutiques, 5, 52, 110
second labels used by, 62–63
brandy, 3, 7, 14, 22, 27
breweries, 10, 148
Brookside Vineyards, 10, 60, 71
Buena Vista Winery, 8, 60, 132, 134–135
Bureau of Alcohol, Tobacco and Fire-arms (BATF), 32, 71, 74, 78
on appellation system, 48–53
on bottom line of label, 54–56, 63–64
on varietal labeling regulations, 42–44
on vintage labeling regulations, 65–68
Burgundy, 6, 13, 34, 58
blending of, 35–36, 96
Burgundy bottle, 76
buses:
in Eureka area, 260
in Marin County, 183, 184, 185, 191, 205–206
on Mendocino Coast, 228–229
in Napa Valley, 127, 128
in Northern Redwoods, 274–275
in Sonoma and Mendocino counties, 163
in Southern Redwoods, 241, 246

Cabernet Sauvignon, 9, 13, 15, 30, 38, 52, 75
blending of, 24, 25, 43–44
description of, 95–96
price of, 11, 43, 69, 78–79
regions for, 46, 47
calendar of events, x–xi
for North Coast Wine Country, 104–105
California, University of, viticulture studies at, 8, 10, 43, 46, 94
California Growers (winery), 6, 59
California Wine Growers' Association, 8

Calistoga, Calif., 112, 125–126, 156, 163, 169
accommodations and restaurants in, 125, 284–286
wineries near, 119–121
camping:
in Eureka area, 259
fees for, 282
in Marin County, 191, 202
on Mendocino Coast, 218–219, 220, 221, 224, 228
in Mendocino County (interior), 162
in Napa Valley, 124–125
in Northern Redwoods, 267, 270, 273, 274
on Sonoma Coast, 210, 214
in Sonoma County (interior), 150, 151, 156, 157, 185, 164
in Southern Redwoods, 240, 242, 243, 244
canoeing, 156–157, 160, 221, 241, 269
Caspar, Calif., 224, 228
"cellared and bottled by," meaning of, 55
Central Valley, as wine-producing re-gion, 6, 17, 20, 47
Chablis, 6, 12, 13, 34, 36, 58, 76
Champagne, 8, 10, 14, 56–57
dryness scale for, 73
as generic name, 14, 34, 35
making of, 16, 23, 28–29
Chardonnay, 11, 13, 15, 26, 30, 38, 40, 52, 76, 96
regions for growing of, 46, 47
Chateau Montelena (winery), 62–63, 120–121
Chateau St. Jean (winery), 52, 62, 136
Chenin Blanc, 38, 46, 47, 76
description of, 96–97
Chianti, 13, 34
China Camp, 187
Christian Brothers, 5, 25, 26, 59
Mont La Salle Vineyards and Winery of, 113
Wine and Champagne Cellars of, 117–118
Chroman, Nat, 25
Claret, 13, 34, 76
Clear Lake, 162
coastal areas, 171–229
information sources for, x, 229
introduction to, 173–175
of Marin County, 177–207
of Mendocino County, 216–229
of Sonoma County, 208–215
Coca-Cola Bottling Company, 10, 55
cocktail wines, 11, 13, 14
Cognac, 10

Crane, George B., 112
Cream Sherry, 14
credit cards, 282
Crescent City, Calif., 270–273, 274
    accommodations and restaurants in,
    286–287
Cresta Blanca Winery, 71, 142–143
Cribari (winery), 37, 58
Cuvaison (winery), 120

degree-days, 46–47
Delicato (winery), 59
dessert wines, 11, 14, 27–28, 74
    see also specific wines
Domaine Chandon (champagnery), 27*n*,
    60, 114
Drake, Sir Francis, 178, 185, 194–201
    brass plate scandal and, 195, 198–201
Dry Creek Vineyard, 51, 139
Dry Sherry, 14

Edmeades Vineyards, 68
Elk, Calif., 219
Emerald Riesling, 8, 47, 73, 97
"Estate Bottled," 51–52
Eureka, Calif., 250–255
    accommodations and restaurants in,
    253, 260, 287–289
    harbor cruises in, 253–254
    history of, 250–251
    Old Town in, 254–255
Eureka area, 238, 247–260
    accommodations and restaurants in,
    253, 259, 260, 287–289
    festivals in, 249, 259
    highlights of, 247
    practical information for, 259–260

fairs, xi, 188, 249
farms, 155, 169, 225
fermentation, 9, 10, 14, 21–23
Ferndale, Calif., sightseeing in, 248–249
ferries, in Marin County, 183, 184, 185,
    191, 204–205
Fetal Alcohol Syndrome (FAS), 75
fishing:
    in Eureka area, 248, 249, 251–252,
    259
    events related to, x, xi, 210, 269
    information sources for, x, 269
    in Marin County, 182
    on Mendocino Coast, 219, 220, 225,
    228
    in Mendocino County (interior), 162
    in Napa Valley, 122
    in Northern Redwoods, 267, 268–269,
    270, 273, 274

fishing: *(cont'd)*
    on Sonoma Coast, 210, 213, 214
    in Sonoma County (interior), 151, 157
    in Southern Redwoods, 240, 242, 243,
    244
flowers, 213, 225, 274
flower shows, xi, 184
Food and Drug Administration (FDA),
    74, 75
Foppiano Vineyards, 139
Fort Bragg, Calif., 223, 228, 229, 264
    accommodations and restaurants in,
    289–290
    sightseeing in, 225–227
Fort Ross, 211–212
Franzia (winery), 6, 10, 55, 59
Freemark Abbey Winery, 118–119
French Colombard, 41, 46, 47, 97
Fumé Blanc, 38, 40, 76, 101–102

Gallo (winery), 6, 37, 47, 56, 57–58
Gamay Beaujolais, 40–41, 46, 76, 97
Gamay Noir, 25
Garberville, Calif., 241, 242, 243
    accommodations and restaurants in,
    241, 290–292
gardens, 154, 225, 272
Garolla (crusher-stemmer), 20–21
gay population, 133
geology, x
Gewürztraminer, 38, 46, 72, 76, 97
Geyser Peak Winery, 10, 51, 60, 141,
    162
geysers:
    in Napa Valley, 107, 125
    in Sonoma County, 131, 161–162
Geyserville, Calif., 134, 163, 169, 213
    wineries near, 140–142, 162
Giumarra (winery), 6, 59
Glen Ellen, Calif., 134, 163
gliding, 126
Golden Gate Bridge, x, xiii–xiv
Golden Gate National Recreation Area,
    178, 189, 192
golf, xi, 157, 241, 243
Gomberg, Louis R., 59*n*
Grand Noir, 25
grapes, 3, 15–21, 95–103
    alternate varietal names for, 40–42
    crushing of, 20–21
    hazards to, 17–18, 67
    in 1973–74 recession, 11
    raisin, 6, 9, 15–16
    ripeness of, 10–11, 18–20
    table, 6, 9, 16
    time for harvest of, 66–68
    wine, 5, 6, 15

grapes: *(cont'd)*
 wine price related to variety of, 81–82
 see also wines; *specific varieties*
Gray Riesling, 40, 97
Green Hungarian, 41, 97
Grenache Rosé, 13, 38, 46, 97–98
Grignolino, 98
"grown, produced and bottled by,"
 meaning of, 54
Gualala, Calif., 213, 214, 218, 229
 accommodations and restaurants in,
 218, 292–293
Guerneville, Calif., 134, 158–159, 163,
 169
 accommodations and restaurants in,
 293–295
 wineries near, 131, 136–137
Guglielmo, Emilio (winery), 37, 60
Guild (winery), 6, 58
Gundlach-Bundschu Winery, 71

Hanns Kornell Champagne Cellars, 61,
 62, 110, 119
Hanzell Vineyards, 62, 135–136
Healdsburg, Calif., 134, 160–161, 163,
 169
 accommodations and restaurants in,
 295–297
 wineries near, 138–140, 161
Heintz, William F., 70, 71
Heitz Cellars, 6, 52, 56, 62, 116
Hennessy Cognac, 10
Heublein, 10, 43
hiking and walking, x
 in Eureka area, 259
 in Marin County, 179, 180, 184, 189,
 191, 193, 194, 201–202
 on Mendocino Coast, 219, 220, 221,
 224–225, 228
 in Mendocino County (interior), 162
 Napa Valley tours and, 121
 in Northern Redwoods, 265, 266–267,
 270, 273
 in Sonoma County, 150–151, 157, 158,
 162
 in Southern Redwoods, 240–241, 242,
 244
Hilgard, Eugene W., 8
historical societies:
 in Marin County, 185
 on Mendocino Coast, 222, 223
 in Mendocino County (interior), 163
 in Napa Valley, 121
 in Northern Redwoods, 271
 in Sonoma County, 147
history, local, information source for, x
Hop Kiln Winery, 26, 62, 138, 161
horseback riding:
 in Marin County, 202

horseback riding: *(cont'd)*
 on Mendocino Coast, 220
 in Sonoma County, 150–151, 157, 158
horse races, xi
hunting, in Northern Redwoods, 274

Inglenook Vineyards, 5, 9, 10, 58, 63, 110
 information for visits to, 115
Inverness, Calif., 203–204, 205
Italian Swiss Colony, 5, 10, 43, 45, 56
 Sonoma winery of, 141–142, 162

jazz, xi, 115, 141, 159
Jenner, Calif., 211
jogging, 184, 189
Johnson, Hugh, 25, 36, 38, 45, 64, 66,
 99
 on Napa Valley wine districts, 108–
 109
Johnson's Alexander Valley Wines, 140

kayaking:
 on Mendocino Coast, 221
 in Northern Redwoods, 269
Kenwood, Calif., 134, 136
Klamath, Calif., 269, 274
Korbel Champagne Cellars, 5, 60, 131,
 156
 information for visits to, 136–137
Krug, Charles, Winery, 5, 9, 37, 60, 63,
 118
 history of, 111–112

label-reading test, 87–90
Lake Berryessa, 122, 297
Lake County, 162, 169, 286
Landmark Vineyards, 137
Larkspur, Calif., 184–185, 191
Leggett, Calif., 239, 240, 245
libraries:
 on Mendocino Coast, 222
 wine, 123
Lichine, Alexis, 15
Liebfraumilch, 35
lighthouses, 203, 219, 224, 271
literary landmarks:
 in Napa Valley, 107, 123, 126–127
 in Sonoma County, 131, 146, 148–150
Little River, Calif., 221, 228, 229
livestock shows, xi
Lohr, J. (winery), 35, 60
London, Jack, 131, 146, 148–150
lumber mills, 227, 245, 263–264

McKinleyville, Calif., 258
"made and bottled by," meaning of, 54–
 55
Madeira, 74
Malvasia Bianca, 98

Manchester, Calif., 219
maps, ix, 122, 214, 228
    Farm Trails, 155, 169
    Sonoma County (interior), 155, 164, 169
    marijuana, 241
Marin City, Calif., 188, 205, 206
Marin County, 5, 177–207
    accommodations and restaurants in, 190, 204, 207, 297–299, 302–303, 307–309, 310–313
    conducted tours in, 207
    festivals in, 181, 188
    highlights of, 177–178
    information source for, 229
    practical information for, 180, 191, 204–207
    what to see and do in, 178–204
marine life refuges:
    in Marin County, 180
    on Sonoma Coast, 210
Marin Headlands, 179–181, 205
    trails on, 180
Marshall, Calif., 204
Martini, Louis M., Winery, 5, 9, 37, 60
    information for visits to, 110–111, 116
Masson, Paul (winery), *see* Paul Masson
Médoc, 35, 43
Mendocino, Calif., 228, 229
    sightseeing in, 221–223
Mendocino Coast, 216–229
    accommodations and restaurants of, 218, 219, 220, 221, 222, 224, 225, 289–290, 292–293, 299–302
    festivals on, 227
    highlights of, 216–218
    information source for, 229
    Navarro River Valley on, 219–220
    practical information for, 228–229
    what to see and do on, 218–228
Mendocino County (interior):
    accommodations and restaurants in, 286, 319–320
    area and zip codes for, 134
    other attractions in, 162–163
    travel information for, 169
    wineries in, 132, 142–143
Mendocino Headlands, 223
Merlot, 24, 38, 98
Mill Valley, Calif., 188–191, 205
    accommodations and restaurants in, 190, 302–303
    parks in, 189–191
Mirassou (winery), 6
Mission, 7, 42, 98–99
missions, 130, 144–145, 185
Möet and Chandon, 10, 35, 113–114
Mondavi, Robert, Winery, 5, 10, 37, 40, 60

Mondavi, Robert, Winery: *(cont'd)*
    information for visits to, 114–115
Monterey Cabernet, 63
Monterey Vineyard (winery), 6, 10, 55
Moselle, 13, 34, 76
Mt. St. Helena, 126, 156
Mt. Tamalpais, 189–190, 191, 205
    accommodations and restaurants in, 190, 302–303
Muscat (or Moscato) Canelli, 99
Muscatel, 9, 14, 74
Muscat of Alexandria, 99
museums:
    in Eureka area, 251, 254, 256
    Indian, 135, 162, 163
    in Marin County, 184
    on Mendocino Coast, 222, 227
    in Mendocino County (interior), 162, 163
    in Napa Valley, 107, 113, 123, 125
    in Northern Redwoods, 271
    on Sonoma Coast, 209
    in Sonoma County (interior), 131, 135, 150, 153, 154, 159, 160
    in Southern Redwoods, 240
    wine, 113
musical events:
    jazz, xi, 115, 141, 159
    in Marin County, 188, 204
    on Mendocino Coast, 225
    in Napa Valley, 115, 118, 121
    in Sonoma County, 138, 140, 141, 159

Napa, Calif., 109, 112, 163, 169
    accommodations and restaurants in, 303–305
    sightseeing in, 121
    wineries near, 113–114
Napa Gamay, 40–41, 46, 99
Napa Highlands, 122–123
    accommodations and restaurants in, 297
Napa Valley, 17, 46, 106–128
    accommodations and restaurants in, 118, 122, 124–125, 284–286, 303–305, 306–307, 320–322
    area and zip codes for, 112
    five vineyard districts of, 108–109
    geography of, 107–109
    highlights of, 106–112
    history of wine industry in, 111–112
    practical information for, 127–128, 169
    transportation information for, 127–128
    what to see and do in, 112–127
    wineries in, 9, 10, 106, 110–121
National Distillers, 10
Native Americans, 270

Native Americans: *(cont'd)*
museums and, 135, 162, 163
re-created village of, 202
reservations of, 253, 265
natural history, information source for, x
Navarro, Calif., 219, 228
Navarro River Valley, 219–220
Nervo Winery, 10, 140–141
Nestlé, 10, 11
Nichelini Vineyard, 115
North Coast:
calendar of events for, 104–105
as wine-producing region, 4, 5, 17
see also Mendocino County; Napa
Valley; Sonoma County
Northern Redwoods, 238, 261–276
accommodations and restaurants in,
269, 272, 275
festivals in, 269, 274
highlights of, 261
Klamath River area in, 267–270
practical information for, 274–275
what to see and do in, 261–274
Northspur, Calif., 227
Novato, Calif., 187–188, 205
Noyo Flat, Calif., 225, 228

Oakville, Calif., 112, 122
wineries near, 114–115
Occidental, Calif., 155
"old vines," meaning of, 70
Olema, Calif., 203, 204, 205
Olmo, Harold P., 40–41
Orange County Fair (1979), 80
oxidation, 23, 65
Paicines Vineyard, 53
parachuting, in Napa Valley, 107, 124
Parducci Wine Cellars, 60, 143
parks:
in Eureka area, 252–253, 258, 259
in Marin County, 182, 184, 187, 189–
191, 194, 201–203, 204
on Mendocino Coast, 219–221, 223–
225
in Mendocino County (interior), 162
in Napa Valley, 122–123, 124–125,
126–127
in Northern Redwoods, 261–267, 270,
272–274
on Sonoma Coast, 210, 213, 214
in Sonoma County (interior), 131,
145–146, 147, 149–152, 157–158,
160
in Southern Redwoods, 239, 240–241,
242, 243–245
pasteurization, 23
Paul Masson (winery), 13, 37, 73
size of, 6, 10, 53, 59

Paul Masson (winery): *(cont'd)*
varietals of, 40, 53, 72
Pedroncelli Winery, J., 60, 141
Perelli-Minetti (winery), 59
Petaluma, Calif., 133, 134, 163
accommodations and restaurants in,
305
sightseeing in, 152–153
Petite Sirah, 38, 40, 46, 99–100
petrified forests, 107, 126, 131, 163
Philo, Calif., 219, 228
phylloxera, 8–9
Pillsbury, 10, 11
Pink Champagne, 14
Pinot Blanc, 46, 47, 100
Pinot Noir, 15, 16, 25, 38, 46, 76, 97
description of, 100
Pinot St. George, 100–101
Pocket Encyclopedia (Johnson), 66
Point Arena, Calif., 218, 219
Point Reyes National Seashore, 178, 194,
201–204, 205, 206
Point Reyes Station, Calif., 203, 205
Pope Valley Winery, 62, 118
Port, 9, 14, 21, 23, 27, 34, 61, 74
prices:
of accommodations and restaurants,
280–282
general information on, ix
of wine, 41–42, 78–87
"private reserve," meaning of, 69
"produced and bottled by," meaning of,
54
Prohibition, 6, 9, 42, 112, 132

quilt shows, on Mendocino Coast, 227

railroads:
antique: in Napa Valley, 107, 125–126
in Eureka area, 249
on Mendocino Coast, 226–227, 228
miniature, in Sonoma County, 147
Rainier beer, 10
Ralston, William C., 8
red wines, 12, 27
fermentation process for, 21–22
see also specific wines
Redwood Country, 231–276
accommodations and restaurants in,
241, 243, 246, 253, 260, 269, 272,
275, 286–289, 290–292
Eureka area in, 238, 247–260
information sources for, 275–276
introduction to, 233–238
Northern, 238, 261–276
Southern, 238, 239–246
Redwood Empire Association, ix, 169,
229, 275

redwoods:
  coastal vs. Sierra, 233–234
  discovery of, 237–238
  harvesting of, 263
  in Marin County, 190–191
  on Mendocino Coast, 219–220
  roots, bark, trunk, and crown of, 236–237
  in Sonoma County, 157–158
  survival of, 234–236
Reich, Philip, 52–53
Requa, Calif., 269
restaurants, 277–322
  locating of, 283–284
  price categories of, 280–282
  reservations for, 282
  see also specific cities and regions
retirees, in Sonoma Valley, 133
Rhine bottle (Hock bottle), 76
Rhine Wine, 13, 34, 36
Riesling, 41, 76, 112
Rio Dell, Calif., 248, 260
Ripley, Robert L. "Believe It or Not," 131, 154
Rockport, Calif., 228
rodeos, xi
rosé wines, 34, 85
  fermentation process for, 21–22
  see also specific wines
Rubin, Hank, 70
Ruby Cabernet, 8, 46, 47, 101
Ruby Port, 27
Russian River Valley, 133, 155–157, 158–159, 169
  accommodations and restaurants in, 293–297
  coastal access from, 160, 210–211
  geysers in, 161–162
  wineries in, 131–132, 136–142
Russian River Vineyards, 62, 136
Russians, 7, 126
  Fort Ross and, 211–212
  in Sonoma and Mendocino, 130, 144
Rutherford, Calif., 112, 122
  wineries near, 115

St. Helena, Calif., 112, 169
  accommodations and restaurants in, 124, 306–307
  sightseeing in, 123–124
  wineries near, 115–119
Salinas Valley (winery), 55
Samoa, Calif., 255–256
San Andreas Fault, 193, 219
San Francisco, x, xiii, xiv
  driving to Redwood Country from, 239–240
  giant wineries in, 58

San Francisco: *(cont'd)*
  transportation to Marin County from, 183, 184, 185, 205–206
  views of, 179, 184
  Wine Institute in, 35, 66, 164
  Wine Museum in, 113
San Joaquin Valley, 4
San Martín (winery), 6, 45, 60
San Rafael, Calif., 185
  accommodations and restaurants in, 307–309
  sightseeing near, 185–187
Santa Rosa, Calif., 131, 133, 163, 169
  accommodations and restaurants in, 309–310
  sightseeing and events in, 153–155
Sattui Winery, 62, 115–116
Sausalito, Calif., 177, 205
  accommodations and restaurants in, 310–313
  sightseeing and events in, 181–183
Sauterne, 13, 34, 53, 67
Sauvignon Blanc, 38, 46, 76, 101
Schieffelin liquor importers, 10, 71
Schlitz beer, 10
Schramsberg Vineyard, 61, 62, 119
Scotia, Calif., 239, 245
Scottish festival, in Santa Rosa, 154–155
Sea Drift, Calif., 192
Seagram's, 10
sea lions, 219
Sea Ranch, 213–214, 215
Sebastiani Vineyards, 5, 35, 60, 131–132, 135
Sebastopol, Calif., 155, 163
  accommodations and restaurants in, 313–314
  wineries near, 132
Sémillon, 46, 47, 101, 102
Shakers, furniture workshops of, 204
Shelter Cove, Calif., 242–243
Sherry, 9, 14, 23, 28, 34, 74
shopping:
  on Mendocino Coast, 219, 223, 227
  in Mendocino County (interior), 143
  in Napa Valley, 107, 118, 121, 122, 123–124
  in Sausalito, 181
  in Sonoma County, 146, 148, 150, 155, 159
  in Southern Redwoods, 240, 241
Sierra (winery), 6, 57
sightseeing rating system, viii–ix
Simi Winery, 5, 10, 60, 70–71, 72, 139–140
Singleton, V. S., 46, 93, 95
skin diving, 213, 228, 243
Sonoma, Calif., 133, 134, 144–148, 169

Sonoma, Calif.: *(cont'd)*
  accommodations and restaurants in, 146, 314–317
  history of, 144–146
  sightseeing in, 145–148
  wineries near, 134–136, 147
Sonoma Coast, 208–215
  accommodations and restaurants on, 214, 215, 317–319
  festivals on, 210
  highlights of, 208
  information source for, 229
  practical information for, 215
  what to see and do on, 208–214
Sonoma County (interior), 5, 129–142
  accommodations and restaurants in, 140, 146, 150, 155, 164, 293–297, 305, 309–310, 313–317
  area and zip codes for, 134
  festivals in, 147–148, 152, 154–155, 158–159, 160
  geography of, 130–131
  history of, 130
  history of winegrowing in, 132
  social diversity in, 132–133
  travel information for, 169
  wineries in, 5, 52, 134–142, 147, 160, 161
  wine valleys in, 131–133
Sonoma Vineyards, 5, 25, 26, 60, 137–138
Southern Redwoods, 238, 239–246
  accommodations and restaurants in, 241, 243, 246, 290–292
  highlights of, 239–240
  King Range mountains in, 241–243
  practical information for, 245–246
  what to see and do in, 240–245
Souverain Cellars, 5, 10, 49, 60, 140
Sparkling Burgundy, 14
Sparkling Muscat, 14
sparkling wines, 10, 12, 14, 61
  see also specific wines
spas, in Napa Valley, 107, 125
Steiman, Harvey, 72
Sterling Vineyards, 5, 10, 60, 110, 120, 125
Stevenson, Robert Louis, 6, 107, 123, 126–127
Stinson Beach, Calif., 192, 205, 206
Strong, Rod, 25
swimming:
  in Eureka area, 248, 259
  in Marin County, 175, 192
  on Mendocino Coast, 220
  in Mendocino County (interior), 162
  in Northern Redwoods, 270, 273
  in Sonoma County, 157, 160

swimming: *(cont'd)*
  in Southern Redwoods, 240, 241, 244
Sylvaner, 102

table wines, 9, 11, 20
  clarifying and aging of, 23
  making of, 21–27
  types of, 13
  see also specific wines
Tawny Port, 27
Taylor California Cellars (winery), 6, 55, 58
Taylor Wine Company, 10, 55, 58
tennis, in Sonoma County, 157
theaters:
  in Marin County, 189–190
  on Mendocino Coast, 223
  in Napa Valley, 122
  in Sonoma County, 140, 141, 147–148, 158
Thompson, Bob, 25, 36, 64, 108–109
Tiburon, Calif., 183–184
Tokay, 9
transportation:
  in Marin County, 183, 184, 185, 191, 204–207
  on Mendocino Coast, 228–229
  in Napa Valley, 127–128
  in Northern Redwoods, 274–275
  in Sonoma and Mendocino counties (interior), 163–164
  on Sonoma Coast, 215
  in Southern Redwoods, 241, 242–243, 245–246
travel information, viii–xi
  calendar of events and, x–xi
  for coastal areas, 229
  maps, ix, 122, 155, 164, 169, 191, 214, 228
  in other books, ix–x
  primary source of, ix
  for Redwood Country, 275–276
  for Wine Country, 169
trees:
  identification of, x
  on Mendocino Coast, 219–221
  in Sonoma County, 150, 157–158
  see also Redwood Country; redwoods
Trefethen Vineyards, 113–114
Trinidad, Calif., 258–259, 260

Ukiah, Calif., 134, 163, 169, 229
  accommodations and restaurants in, 319–320
  routes to, 219, 245
  wineries near, 132, 142–143, 162–163
United Farm Workers, 57
United Vintners (co-op), 10, 43, 56–57

United Vintners (co-op): *(cont'd)*
    brand names of, 58

varietal wines, 9, 13, 24–26, 38–45, 72
    alternate names for, 40–42
    labeling regulations for, 42–44
Vermouth, 14
Vino Rosso, 34
vintage:
    defined, 65
    labeling regulations for, 65–66
    in selection of wines, 85–86
"vintage selection," meaning of, 69
"vinted and bottled by," meaning of, 56

Warm Springs Dam, 133, 162
water-skiing, 122, 162
    in Southern Redwoods, 241
Weibel Champagne Cellars, 60, 143
Wente Brothers (winery), 6, 60, 76, 97
Westport, Calif., 228, 229
whale watching, x, 202
White Port, 27
White Riesling, 15, 38, 40, 41, 46, 47,
    52, 97
    description of, 102–103
white wines, 11, 12
    fermentation process for, 21, 22
    see also specific wines
wildlife sanctuaries, 183–184, 194, 254,
    256
Willits, Calif., 227, 228, 245
Windsor, Calif., 134, 163
    wineries near, 137–138, 160
Wine Country, 1–169
    climate in, 107–108
    five regions in, 46–48
    information sources for, 164–169
    Napa Valley in, 17, 106–128
    Sonoma and Mendocino in, 129–169
    touring in, 103–105
"Winegate" (1974), 33
Wine Institute, 35, 66, 164
wineries:
    founding date of, 70–71
    giant, and brand names, 57–59
    medium-size, and brand names, 59–60
    price related to size of, 80–81
    small, and brand names, 60
    touring of, 112–121, 134–143
wines, 3–105
    additives to, 26

wines: *(cont'd)*
    advertising of, 32, 57–58, 59, 63
    aging of, 11, 23–24, 28
    alcohol content of, 13, 14, 34, 74–75
    appellation system for, 48–53, 85
    basic types of, 12–14
    blending of, 24–26, 42–45, 49
    bottling of, 27, 75–76, 86
    brand names of, 57–63
    California, books on, 168
    California vs. French, 3, 32, 53–54
    clarifying of, 23, 24
    criteria for selection of, 84–87
    defined, 12
    educational opportunities and, 169
    festivals, xi, 147–148, 160
    general books on, 166–168
    generic, 13, 14, 33–36, 85
    history of making of, 6–12
    introduction to, 5–30
    periodicals on, 164–166
    prestigious designations of, 68–72, 86
    price of, 41–42, 78–87
    principal areas for production of, 5–6
    producers of, 54–64
    proprietary, 13, 37–38, 85
    reading bottle of, 31–90
    second labels used on, 62–63
    source of, 45–54
    uniformity in, 25
    U.S. regulation of, 26, 31–32, 34–35,
        42–45, 48–53, 54–56, 63–64, 65–66,
        74–75, 78
    varietal, 9, 13, 24–26, 38–45, 95–103
    vintage of, 65–66, 85–86
Wines and Vines, 14–15, 38–39, 56, 70,
    76
wine tasting, 91–105
    basic criteria and qualities in, 92–95
    UC-Davis standards for, 94
Winkler, A. J., 46
wrestling, xi, 153

Yountville, Calif., 112, 121–122
    accommodations and restaurants in,
        122, 320–322

Zen retreat, in Marin County, 192
Zinfandel, 29–30, 38, 40, 46, 70, 76
    description of, 103
zoos, in Eureka area, 253